Author: HARTNETT

Title: The social sciences in
studies

Classmark: LC 7~

UN
S.

12/3/82

The Social Sciences in Educational Studies

A selective guide to the literature

The Social Sciences in Educational Studies

A selective guide to the literature

Edited by Anthony Hartnett
School of Education, University of Liverpool

 HEINEMANN EDUCATIONAL BOOKS

For Elizabeth, Stephen and Marion

Heinemann Educational Books Ltd
22 Bedford Square, London WC1B 3HH

LONDON EDINBURGH MELBOURNE AUCKLAND HONG KONG
SINGAPORE KUALA LUMPAR NEW DELHI IBADAN NAIROBI
JOHANNESBURG EXETER (NH) KINGSTON PORT OF SPAIN

First published 1982

British Library Cataloguing in Publication Data
The Social sciences in educational studies.
  1. Educational sociology
  I. Hartnett, Anthony
  370.19   LC191

ISBN 0-435-80409-X

Filmset by Inforum Ltd, Portsmouth
and printed by Biddles Ltd, Guildford, Surrey.

Contents

Foreword

Over the past ten years we have seen a number of books which attempt to establish, re-shape or focus a field of study; readers in this or that. This book is somewhat unusual in that it neither attempts to establish, nor to re-shape or focus; on the contrary it attempts to inform. It attempts to give its readers a general account of the range of work available in any one division of the social sciences' application to education. Of course, there has been selection, emphasis and focus, but placed at the service of no one paradigm. While this may mean that the collection will be criticised for omission, emphasis, focus and for unevenness in the format of individual papers, I suspect that many lecturers and students will be pleasantly surprised at the range of work covered by this book and to find that the field is less restricting and restricted than they may have thought.

Basil Bernstein
Professor in the sociology of education
and head of the Sociological Research Unit
University of London Institute of Education

Acknowledgements

I am indebted to John Vaughan, tutor-librarian of the School of Education Library, University of Liverpool, who, in increasingly difficult circumstances, provided a very efficient and delightful library in which to work. Over the years, he and the library staff (Wendy Spalton, Helena Cross, Martin Kay, Hazel Crebbin and Ann Battisby) have built up one of the best education libraries in the country where courteous and unfailing help seems unlimited.

Mrs Helena Cross, who also acted as an indefatigable research assistant, played a major role in obtaining books and articles, in checking references, in photocopying, and in helping with the general preparation of the book.

Mrs Kath Moore typed and retyped, usually from poor manuscripts, all the joint work that I undertook in this book with Michael Naish. Mrs Moore also typed all the references to all the sections, turning them into an immaculate typescript which was ready for press. In addition, she spotted errors and inconsistencies, improved our English, proof-read as she went along, and undertook complex revisions of the manuscript.

John White and Gordon Reddiford made valuable comments on an earlier draft of the section that I wrote with Michael Naish.

Caroline Dawnay (my literary agent) helped with the difficult period when the book was just an idea and kept a watchful eye on the interests of the contributors.

I am also indebted to the Research Committee of the University of Liverpool (and in particular to Dr John Padley, the Academic Secretary), for a series of grants from the University's Research Fund. These made it possible to process the references contained in this book and to explore the literature for the section that I have written with Michael Naish.

I owe a debt to the students whom we have taught during recent years, particularly those on our Master of Education option 'Knowledge, ideology and educational practice', and on the Diploma in Special Education. Their questions and interest have been a constant source of intellectual encouragement.

Finally, I would like to thank the contributors who made the book possible.

Anthony Hartnett:, March 1981

Notes about the contributors

Anthony Hartnett
(editor) – Lecturer in the sociology of education, School of Education, University of Liverpool
Sandra Acker Lecturer in education, Faculty of Education, University of Bristol
Michael W. Apple Professor of curriculum and instruction, School of Education, Department of Curriculum and Instruction and Elementary Education, University of Wisconsin–Madison, USA
Basil Bernstein Professor in the sociology of education and head of the Sociological Research Unit, University of London, Institute of Education
Christopher Boehm Associate professor of anthropology, Department of Sociology, Anthropology and Philosophy, Northern Kentucky University, USA
Brian Davies Professor of education, Centre for Science Education, Chelsea College, University of London
Ray Derricott Senior lecturer in education, School of Education, University of Liverpool
A. D. Edwards Professor of education, School of Education, University of Newcastle
Martyn Hammersley Lecturer in the sociology of education, Faculty of Educational Studies, Open University
Eric Hoyle Professor of education, School of Education, University of Bristol
Fred Inglis Reader in education, School of Education, University of Bristol
Charles Jenkins Lecturer in physical education, Department of Physical Education, University of Birmingham
W. E. Marsden Senior lecturer in education, School of Education, University of Liverpool
David Marsland Senior lecturer, Department of Sociology, Brunel University, and Director of the Regional Training Consultative Unit (Youth Services)
Michael Naish Lecturer in the philosophy of education, School of Education, University of Liverpool
Sharlotte Neely Associate professor, Department of Sociology, Anthropology and Philosophy, Northern Kentucky University, USA
Michael Parkinson Lecturer in politics, Department of Political Theory and Institutions, University of Liverpool
Geoffrey Pearson Lecturer in sociology, Postgraduate and Undergraduate Schools of Applied Social Studies, University of Bradford
Ken Richardson Lecturer in the psychology of education, Faculty of Educational Studies, Open University

Joel Taxel Assistant professor of education, Department of Language Education, University of Georgia, USA

Patsy Taylor Graduate student, School of Education, University of Liverpool

David Thomas Senior lecturer in special education and head of the subdepartment of Special Education, School of Education, University of Liverpool

Barry Troyna Research associate, SSRC Research Unit on Ethnic Relations, University of Aston in Birmingham

John Vaughan Tutor–librarian, School of Education, University of Liverpool

Andrea Vierra Assistant professor of educational anthropology, University of New Mexico, USA

Rob Walker Lecturer in sociology, Centre for Applied Research in Education, University of East Anglia

Introduction
Anthony Hartnett and Michael Naish

It cannot be repeated sufficiently often that the so-called 'disciplines' on which our academic organization is founded are no more than techniques; they are means to an end but no more than that. . . . it will be a sad day when we allow the techniques we have learned or which we teach to dictate the questions which can be asked.

C.H. Gombrich

. . . a specialist does not generally confront a situation where he is required to examine the assumptions on which his discipline rests. He applies the tools and methods of his craft . . . and his faith in which is constantly reinforced by the imposing consensus professionals tend to build up through inertia, timidity and the common habit of citing each other's work.

B. Parekh

. . . Individuals discuss and engage in debate only with others who already share much of their basic orientation. They never have to take seriously alternative conceptions of their activity because this professional activity is not open to challenge by others of a different persuasion . . . Unfortunately, curriculum discourse and a good deal of educational thought in general have been more concerned with both conceptual and social stability than with change, more interested in a search for prior consensus than in the critical give and take that supports genuine advances.

M. Apple

Professors of Education are appointed presumably to profess the subject of Education . . . If they cannot discover this subject (perhaps because there is none) they might properly declare themselves out of business. This rarely if ever happens.

N. Nilsson[1]

This book is intended to have three main purposes. The first is to be a source book for students and others interested in education and social sciences; the second is to act as a case study in the creation, transmission, and utilisation of educational belief; and the third is to give rise to a number of issues about the nature of educational studies and about their relationship to social science.

1. A source book for students

The book provides bibliographical maps of the literature in 21 subject or topic areas that are important in educational studies. Although the maps offer a necessarily incomplete picture of the state of art, they are sufficiently comprehensive and structured both to provide useful material for those looking for perspectives, ideas and research findings for essays, projects and dissertations, and also to point the way to further literature in the various areas. Many of the authors note gaps in the literature that they cite and suggest where further reading can be found.

In addition, the book is theoretically eclectic. This is because it contains the work of authors who have different views and because we agree with Brian Davies (p. 33) that social life is too complex and too interesting to be explained from a single viewpoint. In particular, an attempt has been made to include relevant literature from the USA and to contrast it with British material. The differences between these two traditions often raise interesting theoretical and practical questions. Moreover, the contributors to the book have been encouraged to tackle their chosen areas in the ways that they think best. Some have written essays with a small number of references, while others have provided more references and less discussion. In either case, different readers can take different things from the book. It should offer what might be called 'academic help' to students on initial, in-service, and advanced courses in education and, at the same time, provide material of general interest to teachers in the classroom, to parents, and to others interested in education.

2. A case study in educational belief

The book also provides a means of looking at the generation, transmission, modification, utilisation and forms of educational belief, knowledge, and ideology, and at the relationship of these to the theoretical and institutional frameworks within which the study of education is undertaken (Hartnett and Naish 1980, pp. 258–9). This can best be seen if the material in the sections is considered in four groups.

(i)

There is that material which is from what might be called the 'basic disciplines', that is, areas like anthropology and sociology *tout court*. Material of this kind can be seen in the contributions of Andrea Vierra, Christopher Boehm, and Sharlotte Neely on anthropology; Brian Davies on sociology; Bill Marsden on historical studies; and Fred Inglis on literary studies.

Each of these areas can and should make a contribution to educational studies, and the essays give what, in their authors' views, is the main literature. Some are general surveys and others deal with more specific issues. Taken together, they all raise questions about the criteria by which literature has been selected and about the role of such selections in defining the area of educational studies.

Ideally, we would have liked contributions from social psychology, cultural studies, Marxism, and comparative studies. Shortage of space, however, and the limitations of the editor's persuasive skills, made this impossible.

(ii)

Other material is specifically related to educational belief, knowledge, and ideology. The section by Anthony Hartnett and Michael Naish attempts to provide a general framework, derived from the sociology of knowledge and from epistemology, for the study of educational beliefs and ideologies. It looks at the sources and at kinds of educational beliefs, at some issues about how and by whom such beliefs are adjudicated, and at their functions both within the educational system and within the wider society.

Michael Parkinson examines the general area of educational policy-making and politics, and Barry Troyna is concerned with the response of the educational system to black pupils in British schools. The processes whereby educational policy-makers (especially the DES) generate educational beliefs, and incorporate selections from social science to justify policy decisions, and non-decisions, are under-explored and worth more attention. Michael Parkinson and Barry Troyna both have something to say about them.

Sandra Acker looks at women and education and shows how sociologists of education have 'mostly failed to analyse ways schooling might support women's subordinate social and economic position' (p. 144). Literature is discussed which suggests that education may be important in the reproduction of 'gender relations'; that we need to develop the concept of 'gender chances'; and that 'gender seems to pervade school life' (p. 146). David Marsland argues for the indispensability of the notion of youth in sociology and formulates an alternative to those popular sociological theories that assume that the notion of class can explain (nearly) everything. He suggests that 'the sub-culture of youth, in its singularity and its many and changing varieties, is a major cultural phenomenon of modern society' (p. 162) and that sociology has suffered from approaches (especially Marxist) which fail to take account of its importance.

Mike Apple and Joel Taxel raise a number of issues about

ideology and the curriculum and, in particular, about those involved in the relationships between 'the form and content of the curriculum, the hidden curriculum', ideological reproduction, and 'the perspectives educators employ to order, guide and give meaning to their own and students' activity' (p. 173). The section also examines 'the interconnections between ideology and the internal characteristics of schools' (p. 168). Ken Richardson looks at the role of the biological sciences in the development of psychology in education, and in its origins and maintenance of beliefs about the nature of human beings. Psychology is an important source of belief for teachers and policy-makers and the section provides a number of useful approaches to this topic. Rob Walker makes some suggestions about the use of case studies in applied research and raises general questions about the nature and status of research knowledge in education. Such knowledge, or what is taken to be knowledge, has been a source of educational belief.

Each of the sections in this group suggests that there are gaps and limitations in many accounts of the sociology of education, and, taken together, they suggest that what an area of study (such as the sociology of education) does *not* emphasise, generate and transmit to students, is as interesting as its orthodoxies and conventions. We need to understand why (and how) some views are adopted and how this relates to wider questions of power and ideology. The selections, content, form and evaluation of teacher education are likely to be central areas for research if these kinds of questions are to be adequately answered.

(iii)

The third type of material is concerned with areas that are usually believed to have a fairly direct bearing on practice and policy in education. This material is about language, the teaching profession, classrooms, and organisations. Tony Edwards examines the contributions of the sociology of language to the work of classroom teachers. Eric Hoyle considers how the professions have been studied, and raises issues about the role of knowledge in legitimating teaching as a profession. Martyn Hammersley discusses some of the literature on classrooms, and suggests (p. 227) that they are a 'key site in which to explore the nature of schooling and the impact on it of changing social conditions'. Finally, Brian Davies looks at work on educational organisations and suggests (p. 243) that research in that area has been 'among the more conservative and moribund reaches of the social sciences'. Some of the research covered in these sections (e.g. that of Bernstein on language) has been an important source of belief for those concerned with educational practice and policy.

(*iv*)

The final type of material is from areas where social exigencies have required courses, teaching and research, but where the development of a specifically sociological view has been uneven, limited or non-existent. In special education, David Thomas and Patsy Taylor argue (p. 257) that the 'clinical ideology', which is central to special schooling, has 'muted search for a wider theoretical perspective' and that 'such an ideology is hostile to sociological viewpoints'. They provide some ideas as to why this may be the case. Geoff Pearson offers a detailed selection from the considerable literature on deviance in sociology. This enables the discussion by David Thomas and Patsy Taylor to be placed in a particular sociological context and to make explicit that although there is a lot of literature on deviance, very little of it seems to have penetrated (or influenced) special education. Geoff Pearson's section suggests what might be missing in the way of research, perspectives and approaches. Charles Jenkins looks at the growing literature on physical education, and Ray Derricott surveys the literature on curricular innovation where the emphasis is on change, invention, development, diffusion and adoption (p. 284).

Each of the four types of material can be read in such a way as to provide evidence on the generation, transmission, and utilisation of social scientific data (concepts, perspectives, theories and research) in the theory and practice of education. The material in (ii) above makes detailed suggestions as to how this can be done. Readers will find it useful to compare sections with each other. They will find conflicts, agreements, gaps and areas that need more research and thought. These can be seen in Andrea Vierra *et al.*, Sandra Acker and Ken Richardson (on biological factors in the explanation of social factors); Barry Troyna, David Marsland and Sandra Acker (on the explanatory power of race, youth and gender); Rob Walker and David Marsland (on what constitutes good research); David Thomas and Patsy Taylor, and Geoff Pearson (on deviance); and Mike Apple and Joel Taxel, and Ray Derricott (on the curriculum).

The concluding section of this bibliography is by John Vaughan who indicates some of the ways in which students can search the literature and follow up ideas for further reading.

3. Educational studies and social science

One thing that this book might do is to give rise to some disquiet about the current state of educational studies, and to suggest that in spite of the considerable literature in many areas, there is still at the centre of educational studies a series of complex political, moral, theoretical, and other problems which await exploration. Many of these have their origins in the contentious and uncertain relationships between educational theory, social scientific research, educational research, and educational practice and policy.

Nilsson (1972) suggests that there are two exigencies in educational studies which pull them in different directions. There is, firstly, the tendency to place emphasis on such disciplines as philosophy, psychology, and sociology, and to insist that educational studies have the same academic rigour and intellectual status as these. Secondly, there is the tendency towards classroom teaching. This usually involves an emphasis on practical training for what is regarded as the real world of schools.

When attempts are made to reconcile these two exigencies, what is taken to be practical relevance is often achieved at the expense of intellectual respectability; and with claimed relevance, goes a playing down of the political and moral complexities of education. This gives rise to what might be called 'survival conservatism' – that is, a set of attitudes and skills which are thought to enable new teachers to adapt themselves to however the educational world is constituted at any particular time. Here, theoretical work is likely to be incorporated into educational studies simply to lend them respectability or is likely to be used selectively to back favoured practices and policies. This approach attempts to limit theoretical studies to a subsidiary, reassuring and legitimating role.

A more radical approach to theoretical studies is to see them making 'survival conservatism' impossible or, at the very least, as identifying it for what it is. Seen in this way theoretical studies should 'narrow the area of what is unquestioned in education' and 'make teachers, policy-makers, and others more aware of their own values, more critical of what might be called "official views", more aware of the values of those they teach, and more aware of what is not known, and so of what they do not know' (Hartnett and Naish 1976, pp. xv–xvi).

If educational studies are to attempt to match up to the complexity of the issues raised by educational practice and policy, they will have to take on the unexplored political, moral, theoretical and other problems mentioned earlier. Many of these problems can be considered under seven 'dimensions', each of which should have a central place in any fully developed view of educational studies. These dimensions are discussed below.

(i) Moral dimension

As Fred Inglis (p. 79) suggests, quoting Leavis, a 'marked moral intensity' should characterise the practice of education and its theoretical study. This is because moral issues are central to education. They arise most obviously, though not exclusively, about the identification of children's and students' educational and other interests; about the justification for believing that professionals are the best judges of these interests; about the roles of non-professionals (e.g. parents) in their identification; about the compatibilities, and the balance between children's students', professionals' and parents' interests.

Relevant work on this dimension can be found in the discussions by Mike Apple and Joel Taxel who argue (p. 174) that there are pressures in education to convert moral issues into technical ones and that these pressures should be resisted; by David Thomas and Patsy Taylor who show that one possible consequence of special schooling may be to convert institutional and political failures into failures of individual children; by Rob Walker who (p. 195) looks at moral issues in research and evaluation; and by Eric Hoyle who distinguishes professionalism and professionality, and shows how they have different implications for the interests of clients.

(ii) Political dimension

Education is inescapably a political area. It raises, for example, justificatory issues about power and its distribution; about the formal and informal processes whereby educational resources are distributed; about how some social groups benefit from education and schooling while others do not; and about how these issues relate to the distribution of power, wealth and status in the wider society. As Hollis (1971, p. 153) argues, educational practices and policies imply a political theory and 'every political theory itself makes educational demands . . . every educational policy is a political policy'. This means that political and social theory must play a large part in any adequately developed view of educational studies.

Moreover, the study of education and, more specifically, education research, inevitably involve political issues. Firstly, issues arise about the definition of the situation and the problem to which the research is ostensibly addressed. There is always the danger of educational researchers taking over problems as defined by powerful groups – taking as opposed to making problems, in Seeley's (1966) terms. Some evidence for this is provided by the existence of research entrepreneurs and managers in educational research who often obtain large budgets for research (on the most sensitive issues) because they are prepared to ask the right questions in the right way. Secondly, decisions about access both to research funds and to organisations must involve political issues. Thirdly, issues about the publication and the use of research findings are also largely political (Bennett 1978). Each of these three issues (three of many) involves important questions about the relationships between educational research and power, and gives rise to issues in political theory (Shipman 1976).

Particularly interesting in this context is the fact that much educational research is focused on children and teachers and very little on powerful organisations such as the DES, policy-making groups within governments, HMIs and LEAs. When accounts are available of such organisations or groups, they tend to be 'insider' views, written by people who have, for example, been members of the inspectorate or who have worked in government. Michael Parkinson, for example (p. 115) argues that despite its 'growing significance the precise role of the DES in policy-making remains unexplored' and he points out (p. 116) that Kogan (1975) 'pays little attention to the changing role and growth in power of the DES'.

Barry Troyna's essay provides a detailed case study of how the DES has responded to black pupils in British schools. His thesis is that the Department has the power to develop a national policy in this area but that it does not wish to do so because of wider assumptions within government about 'assimilation and a conception of society as indivisible' (p. 139). He characterises the reaction of the DES as passive – 'doing good by stealth', heedful of local autonomy and variety, concentrating on rhetoric rather than precise policies, and tolerant of 'benign neglect' by LEAs on the issue (p. 134). (Further perspectives and literature on this area can be found in Tomlinson (1977 and 1980) and Little (1978).)

The accounts given by Michael Parkinson and Barry Troyna of the DES can be usefully compared with that presented by Dennis Lawton (1980) in *The Politics of the School Curriculum* where he argues that the DES wants more power over both the curriculum and assessment (based on a 'dangerously obsolete model of evaluation' – p. 131). He characterises the Department's approach in this area of policy as active, resolute, determined to assert central power against local autonomy, secret and concentrating on precise programmes of assessment and evaluation.

The contradiction between these two different approaches taken by the Department needs explanation. In the area of assessment, it would appear that the DES has taken an active role in policy-making. For black pupils, however, its approach has been that of non-decision-making (Bachrach and Baratz 1962 and 1963). The Department's response to specific policy issues may

well depend largely on how it thinks they will affect its own power
and influence (Hartnett 1981), and on what assumptions are made
by its personnel. Lawton, for example, suggests that HMIs and civil
servants, who share similar social and educational backgrounds,
'tend to make the same kind of assumptions, and tend to possess
similar beliefs, ideologies and obsolete theories' (pp. 28–9). Barry
Troyna concludes that 'In refusing to formulate a policy based on
the principle of "multiculturalism", the DES acknowledges its
reluctance, which is shared with central government, to concede
any institutional or political power to the black communities'
(p. 139). What is required is more research on the personnel
in the DES; on its modes of policy-making and non-decision-
making; and on the consequences of its activities for the practice of
education.

Education is not alone in concentrating its research on those who
have the least power. Geoff Pearson (p. 266) notes a similar tendency in research into crime, where there appears to be a fair
amount on unsuccessful crime but very little on successful crime by
the powerful. Yet, as Brown (1969, p. 166) says, working 'from the
top down' in organisations may be more difficult but may 'in the
end be more revealing'. The sections by Michael Parkinson and
Barry Troyna, and the literature cited above, should be useful in
provoking discussion on these issues.

(iii) Epistemological dimension
Any adequate view of educational studies should make explicit the
kinds of knowledge on which it relies, their sources, and their
reliability. Brian Davies (p. 33) draws attention to some of the
disputes and contradictions in sociology, and this bibliography as a
whole should indicate how little educational studies possess in the
way of securely established knowledge. Part of the section by
Anthony Hartnett and Michael Naish (pp. 88–113) cites material
relevant to this dimension. (See also Bell and Newby 1977 and
Dockrell and Hamilton 1980.)

(iv) Interdisciplinary dimension
The development of academic disciplines takes place within a process of historical change, in which chance and accident often play
some part, and there is no guarantee that the institutional and
theoretical frameworks within which educational studies are pursued make for the most fruitful investigation of educational problems.

In England, for example, educational studies are often organised along single subject lines (e.g. history, philosophy, psychology,

and sociology of education), while some single subjects (e.g. social anthropology) which might be thought to have a place in educational studies are ignored. Yet many educational problems cut across these conventional subject boundaries.

To take an example, teachers and others involved in the educational system have to deal with interactions between (a) conscious, complex, and unique individuals who are to some extent free agents (Lacey 1979; Greene 1978; Hartnett and Naish 1981); (b) social groups; (c) organisations which may also have unique characteristics (David Marsland, p. 157); (d) local educational and social contexts; (e) political and economic changes; and (f) social systems in the widest sense. Many educational problems are concerned with the interactions, incompatibilities, and other relationships *between* these levels of analyses rather than with issues that arise solely within them (cf. Martyn Hammersley's discussion of the micro-macro problem on p. 234). Any adequate treatment of these cross-level problems requires that educational studies be, in part at least, interdisciplinary.

Some of the ways in which interdisciplinary studies might develop can be seen in this bibliography. The section 'Towards a sociology of educational belief' calls on both philosophy and sociology; links can be seen between the sections on historical and sociological studies and between anthropology, psychology, and classrooms. Fred Inglis' remarks on fictions, sociologies, and gossip (p. 74) should suggest how areas of social life might be productively discussed in an interdisciplinary fashion by the joint use of aspects of social science, literature, the visual arts, and political philosophy.

(v) Theory and practice dimension
In education, problems about theory and practice are raised in acute forms. Many people engaged in education are involved in practical activities which raise difficult issues about the relationship of theory to practice and about the purpose of educational studies. As Rob Walker suggests (p. 196) it is widely felt that educational research has a 'poor record' in contributing to professional practice, and that the cleavage between 'theory' and 'practice' has been institutionalised within schools of education and in the training of teachers. Martyn Hammersley, too, comments on the split in classroom studies, between pure and applied research (p. 233). Further issues about this dimension are raised in Hartnett and Naish (1976, 1977 and 1980).

(vi) Historical dimension
Educational studies need to be undertaken with overt reference to

their own intellectual and social history. The acute epistemological issues about the status of claims made by educational theorists can be examined fruitfully only if today's fashions and fads are seen (and worn) in the light of those of yesterday. An historical critique of experts' advice to teachers is needed, and one that is as good as that by Ehrenreich and English (1979) of experts' advice to women. Historically uninformed educational studies may make the world safe for today's experts but at too great a cost elsewhere.

(vii) Evaluative dimension
Along with questions about *how* the view of educational studies outlined in the dimensions is to be taught, comes the closely related question of how educational studies are to be evaluated. Such evaluation raises problems about the purpose of educational studies and about the kinds of groups who are meant to constitute their audiences. Who should evaluate initial, in-service, and advanced courses for teachers? What kind of criteria should be used? How should they be applied? Should such institutions such as the DES and LEAs, whose interests may not be compatible with any fully developed view of educational studies, have any say in how they are to be judged? And if so, how much?

Any adequate educational studies must be explicit about, and fully conscious of, issues related to their evaluation.

Conclusion
This introduction has offered a view of what, in part, any adequate educational studies should look like and has indicated how this bibliography might help to promote it. One implication of the discussion here is that educational studies are not sources of simple solutions to simple problems – solutions which, as it were, can be instantly and successfully implemented on Monday morning. The problems raised by educational practice and policy (and so by educational studies properly conceived) are as difficult and intractable as those raised in other areas of social life; and there is no reason why educational studies should settle for poor questions, poor arguments and even poorer answers.

Notes
[1] Introductory quotes as follows:
C. H. Gombrich (1969) *In Search of Cultural History* (Clarendon Press) p. 46.
B. Parekh (1970) 'Scholarship and ideology', *Cross Currents*, Fall, p. 465.
M. Apple (1974) 'The process and ideology of valuing in educational settings' in M. Apple *et al.* (eds.) *Educational Evaluation: analysis and*

responsibility (McCutchan Publishing) pp. 3–4.

N. Nilsson (1972) ' "Professor of Education": an indefinite description', *Proceedings of the Philosophy of Education Society of Austrialia*, **1**, 1, June, pp. 42–61.

References

Bachrach, P. and Baratz, M. S. (1962) 'The two faces of power', *American Political Science Review*, **56**, pp. 947–52 and (1963) 'Decisions and non-decisions: an analytical framework', *American Political Science Review*, **57**, pp. 641–51.

Bell, C. and Newby, H. (eds.) (1977) *Doing Sociological Research* (Allen & Unwin).

Bennett, N. (1978) 'Educational research and the media', *Westminster Studies in Education*, **1**, pp. 23–30.

Bernstein, B. (1970) 'Education cannot compensate for society', *New Society*, 26 Feb., pp. 344–7.

Brown, R. (1969) 'Some aspects of mass media ideologies' in P. Halmos (ed.) *Sociological Review Monograph no. 13* (University of Keele) pp. 155–67.

Dockrell, W. B. and Hamilton, D. (1980) *Rethinking Educational Research* (Hodder & Stoughton).

Ehrenreich, B. and English, D. (1979) *For Her Own Good: 150 Years of the Experts' Advice to Women* (Pluto Press).

Greene, M. (1978) 'Teaching: the question of personal reality', *Teachers College Record*, **80**, 1, Sept., pp. 23–35.

Hartnett, A. (1981) 'The secret garden and the vegetable patch: towards a sociology of the D.E.S.' Review essay, *Journal of Curriculum Studies*, **13**, 2, pp. 170–72.

Hartnett, A. and Naish, M. (1976) *Theory and the Practice of Education* (2 vols.) (Heinemann Educational Books).

Hartnett, A. and Naish, M. (1977) 'Educational theory: bromide and barmecide', *Journal of Further and Higher Education*, **1**, 3, pp. 63–75.

Hartnett, A. and Naish, M. (1980) 'Technicians or social bandits? Some moral and political issues in the education of teachers' in P. Woods (ed.) *Teacher Strategies: exploration in the sociology of the school* (Croom Helm).

Hartnett, A. and Naish, M. (1981) 'The P.G.C.E. as an educational priority area', *Journal of Further and Higher Education*, forthcoming.

Hartnett, A. and Naish, M. (in preparation) *Scepticism, Ideology and Educational Practice*.

Hollis, T. (1971) 'The pen and the purse', *Proceedings of the Philosophy of Education Society of Great Britain*, **5**, 2, pp. 153–69.

Kogan, M. (1975) *Educational Policy-making* (Allen & Unwin).

Lacey, C. (1979) 'Choice and constraint and the possibility of autonomous behaviour' in L. Barton and R. Meighan (eds.) *Schools, Pupils and Deviance* (Nafferton Books) pp. 167–79.

Lawton, D. (1980) *The Politics of the School Curriculum* (Routledge & Kegan Paul).

Little, A. N. (1978) *Educational Policies for Multi-Racial Areas* (Inaugural

Lecture, Goldsmiths' College, University of London).
Nilsson, N. (1972) ' "Professor of Education": an indefinite description', *Proceedings of the Philosophy of Education Society of Australia*, **1**, June, pp. 42–61.
Seeley, J. R. (1966) 'The making and taking of problems: towards an ethical stance', *Social Problems*, **14**, pp. 382–9.
Shipman, M. D. (1976) (ed.) *The Organisation and Impact of Social Research* (Routledge & Kegan Paul).
Tomlinson, S. (1977) 'Race and education in Britain 1960–1977, an overview of the literature' *Sage Race Relations Abstracts*, **2**, 4, Nov., pp. 3–33.
Tomlinson, S. (1980) 'The educational performance of ethnic minority children', *New Community*, **8**, 3, pp. 213–35.

1 Anthropology and educational studies
Andrea Vierra
Christopher Boehm
Sharlotte Neely

Anthropology is the study of humans – of human biology and of the behaviour and thought of humans in cultural groups. Anthropologists are interested in the relations between biology and culture and in understanding cultural similarities and differences. One of the discipline's basic tenets is that culture is learned. Anthropological contributions therefore include studies of the process and content of informal learning, for example cross-cultural research on socialization – and studies of the institution of education, for example research on the relationship between schools and society.

Educators, too, are interested in the relations between biology, behavior, and thought and in understanding people's similarities and differences. There is therefore a real potential for all of anthropology to be of interest to educators. But all of anthropology is, of course, well beyond the scope of this review. The anthropological contributions we will discuss will be those that focus either on informal learning or on the institution of education. Readers with broader interests should consult an introductory anthropology text (e.g. Harris 1975).

Primate socialization
The study of non-human primates makes a unique contribution to understanding human behavior: they are our species' closest living relatives, and, in some cases, experiments can be performed on non-humans which would be ethically or practically precluded with human subjects. Reviews of primate socialization studies can be found in Poirier's introductions to his volumes on primate development and socialization (1972, 1977). Caution must be exercized, however, in extending findings for any species to another.

The mother–infant bond is the first social relationship of non-human primates, and conditions the infant's subsequent social behavior. Relations between adult males and infants vary, from intimate to almost non-existent. This and other aspects of socialization are influenced by the group's social structure. In some groups, for example, mothers interact freely with most or all group members, exposing their infants to a wide range of potential models and social interactions. In other groups, mothers interact almost exclusively with a small group of female kin, which restricts their infants' social horizons as well. The infant's ultimate status in the group is often conditioned by its mother's status, probably because it learns status-related behavior from its mother.

Peer relations can be at least as important for social development as is the mother–infant bond. Juvenile males often spend their time in large, rowdy, all-male play groups, while juvenile females tend to interact more with adult females and to engage in quieter play, including play-mothering. When research findings, such as these, are similar for human and non-human primates, it is tempting to infer a biological basis for the behaviors in question – in this case, for sex differences in behavior. But such inferences are not always sound (Liebowitz 1978).

In a discussion of the relevance of primate findings to the social sciences, Washburn suggests that 'the school system is based on a series of traditional mistakes': for example the 'separation of education from life' and the substitution of discipline for internal motivation. 'Through a profound misunderstanding of the nature of primate biology, the schools reduce the most intelligent primate to a bored and alienated creature' (1973, p. 131).

Ethological studies of children

Ethological approaches to child behavior and child-rearing are characterized by their method – careful, extended observation of behavior in natural settings – and by their biological approach to behavior. Ethological work has begun to establish that human infants, like the newborn in many other species, undergo a biologically controlled process of attachment, typically to mother (e.g. Bowlby 1969).

Attachment not only functions for protection but also provides the infant with an early model of subsistence and reproductive behavior – its mother (Konner 1972). Among Africa's !Kung Bushmen, whose traditional hunting-and-gathering way of life is in many respects representative of most of our species' evolutionary history, high mother–infant contact and high maternal indulgence of infants are followed by independence later in childhood (Konner 1976). This finding questions the Western 'spoiling' theory of infant care. However, high contact and indulgence may be easier for !Kung mothers than for Western mothers: among the !Kung, motherhood increases an already high level of social interaction, and there is plenty of help with child care; in the West, mothers and their small children tend to be socially isolated (DeVore and Konner 1974).

In many societies, children have multiple caretakers, including non-maternal adults and other children (Weisner and Gallimore 1977). This does not seem to impede their development; and children benefit from the parenting practice that accrues when they caretake other children (Konner 1975).

Freedman and Omark (1973) present an interesting overview of ethological contributions to education, in which they specify educational implications.

Sex differences in behavior
It can be difficult to distinguish between biologically determined and learned differences in male and female behavior. While it appears that there are at least some biologically determined behavioral differences between males and females, it is also clear that these differences are subject to learned modification (Maccoby and Jacklin 1974).

Typically, cultural learning intensifies biological sex differences (D'Andrade 1966); but sometimes it does not (Martin and Voorhies 1975). Among hunter-gatherer !Kung, cultural pressures for sex-differentiated behavior are absent (Draper 1975); in other cultures, assigning domestic work to boys lessens the difference between boys' and girls' behavior (Whiting and Edwards 1973); and among the Tchambuli, Western sex-role stereotypes seem to be completely reversed (Mead 1935).

Western cultures have traditionally promoted sex-differentiated behavior which is linked to lower status and lesser opportunity for females. Changing social conditions are beginning to permit wider ranges of behavior for both males and females. Goetz (1978) discusses sex-role culture in schools. Volume 6 of the *Council on Anthropology and Education Quarterly* (1975) contains an issue devoted to women in schools.

Race and intelligence
In 1969, an educational psychologist published an argument that racial variation in IQ-test scores is largely due to genetics and that compensatory education to boost IQ is therefore doomed to fail (Jensen 1969). Understandably, this touched off a flurry of responses, some of them more polemical than substantive.

In the early 1970s, the Social Science Research Council in the

United States decided to sponsor an objective survey of existing evidence on racial differences in intelligence. An anthropologist specializing in human genetics was among the three scientists who undertook the task. They concluded that 'average differences in the scores of members of different US racial–ethnic groups on intellectual–ability tests probably reflect . . . in part genetic differences among the groups.' However, 'the differences among individuals *within* racial–ethnic (and socio-economic) groups greatly exceed in magnitude the average differences between such groups' (Loehlin, Lindzey, and Spuhler 1975, pp. 238–9).

Group membership thus has relatively little value in predicting any individual's IQ; individual conditions, including genetic ones, are much better predictors. Additional research is likely to demonstrate differences between groups in patterning of intellectual abilities, rather than overall intellectual inferiority or superiority of any particular group (p. 241).

The acquisition of culture

Culture is the focus of much anthropological work, but the emphasis is on describing and explaining cultural patterns, not on the process by which culture is learned. In a recent review, Tindall notes that 'there are no theories of the process of cultural transmission' – only 'theory work' (1976, p. 195). Some of this theory work (Gearing 1973b, 1975) focuses on the inter-psychic aspects of culture transmission. Other theory work is more holistic in scope (Dobbert 1975; Kimball 1974).

Beatrice and John Whiting, after many years of work with a number of associates, have generated the following model of learning in culture (J. Whiting 1973). The environment and history of a culture condition its maintenance systems – for example its economy, settlement pattern, and division of labor. These in turn condition a child's learning environment – for example the settings in which the child spends his or her time, the status of the child's caretakers, and the tasks assigned to the child. The child becomes an adult, whose behavior and psyche are in part a product of culturally conditioned experience. The adult's behavioral and psychic patterns are similar to those of the other adult members of his or her culture, since most of them had similar childhood experiences. These shared psychic patterns are manifest in the projective–expressive systems of the culture – for example its ritual, ceremony, games and art.

In a six-culture test of the Whiting model, child behavior was found to be related to household composition: in cultures with independent nuclear-family households, children are 'sociable–intimate'; in cultures with patrilineal extended families, children are 'authoritarian–aggressive'. Child behavior is also related to socio–economic complexity: in complex cultures, children are more egoistic and less nurturant; in cultures at the middle level of complexity, children are more nurturant and less dependent and dominant (Whiting and Whiting 1975). Maternal warmth and stability and the permissiveness with which mothers socialize their children depend on the mother's work load and the household composition (Minturn and Lambert 1964).

The Whitings draw on a number of psychological theories to predict the nature of links between categories in their model. Freudian theory predicts projective–expressive systems of culture from childhood experiences. In a large cross-cultural study, Whiting and Child (1953) were able to confirm some of their Freudian hypotheses – for example in cultures typified by negative sanctions on children's aggression, repressed aggression is often projected in cultural beliefs that illness is caused by sorcery or witchcraft.

Social learning theory is also employed. Children imitate the behavior of individuals perceived to control and withhold resources. In cultures where father's appearance in mother–child households is infrequent, boys have little opportunity to imitate males. If, as often happens, these cultures are highly patrifocal, traumatic initiation rites at puberty, often involving abrupt and prolonged separation of boys from females and/or physically painful ceremonies, help assure that boys adopt male behavior (Burton and Whiting 1961; Whiting, Kluckholn, and Anthony 1958).

The Whitings have significantly advanced the cause of the cross-cultural comparative method, especially of quantitative analysis of a large sample of cultures (for a review, see LeVine 1970). Following their lead, a number of studies have appeared showing statistical associations between aspects of culture, child life, and personality. Some of this work, like the Whitings', is deductive or at least linked to theory-building; some of it represents the inductive, atheoretical search for associations which the computer has made possible in so many disciplines.

A large number of studies are available on socialization in particular cultures. Bibliographies of such studies can be found in T. Williams' useful text on socialization (1972) and in Roberts and Akinsanya (1976a). Draper (1974) reviews some aspects of the comparative socialization literature, and LeVine (1969) presents an anthropological approach to culture, personality, and socialization. In a detailed outline, Henry (1960) identifies categories of information relevant to the study of culture acquisition; the outline has considerable heuristic value. Hilger (1960) and Whiting, Child, and Lambert (1966) have published methodological guides to the study of child life in cultural settings.

For those who wish to do quantitative cross-cultural work on socialization, the journal *Ethnology* is involved in the ongoing publication of the values of cultural variables for a large sample of the world's cultures, coded for quantitative analysis. These data are also available on pre-punched computer cards. Recent issues have included child-life variables for some societies (Barry *et al.* 1976, 1977; Barry and Paxson 1971; Barry and Schlegel 1979). The *Human Relations Area Files* index cultural variables, including child variables, for a large number of societies.

Conscious tuition is not a necessary ingredient of culture transmission (Gearing 1973a). In smaller societies, culture is transmitted by kin and neighbors, largely as a by-product of daily life. Adult roles are essentially undifferentiated, except by sex and age, and all or almost all adult behavior in all spheres of social life is visible to children; thus learning can proceed primarily by imitation. Life's rewards come from being an accepted member of the group; a child has little opportunity or motivation to become anything else. The advent of larger societies and particularly of schools has brought about a number of changes in the modes of culture transmission.

Schooling and society

A large amount of anthropologists' time is devoted to explaining particular aspects of culture – that is, to identifying the social functions of particular customs and the conditions under which particular customs emerge. Schooling is a conspicuous institution in many societies, yet surprisingly few anthropologists have concerned themselves with the functions of schooling and the condition under which formal schooling occurs.

Yehudi Cohen's (1970) work represents the major contribution here. He argues that schools emerged in response to pressures during the evolution of civilizational states. Such states required an elite class of individuals who could operate between smaller, constituent societies in the service of the larger civilization. Schools provided a national locale, often distant from students' homes, in which to inculcate in these elite individuals a national ideology.

Only recently has schooling been extended to the masses. This gives them certain technical competence so that they can carry out more technical roles. As with the elite, it also functions to subvert local allegiances, replacing more overtly coercive controls of the past. Universal schooling, however, does not imply social equality. Social-class distinctions are maintained by having different curricula or different schools for commoners and the elite. Schooling does not serve egalitarian aims or the quest for truth. It provides a universal experience, teaching the same dogma to all students in the same way.

Others tend to similar views on particular points. The emphases of schooling depend on political conditions, and the development of intellect is never of primary concern (Wallace 1961). In the United States, universities can be considered religious institutions because they are responsible for the perpetuation of a world view – that of science (Dobbert 1974).

In its emphasis on change, contemporary schooling does a sort of 'deliberate violence' to 'people's developed personalities' – their habits, ideas, language, beliefs and emotional allegiances (Mead 1970, p. 9). The function of education is not to free the mind but to confine it (Henry 1963): the individual must learn to view the world as the culture specifies, even in the face of contradictory evidence.

> If all through school the young were provoked to question the Ten Commandments, the sanctity of revealed religion, the foundations of patriotism, the profit motive, the two-party system, monogamy, the laws of incest, and so on, we would have more creativity than we could handle.
>
> *Henry 1963, p. 288.*

Anthropologists have come to view schools as a social problem, not as a solution (Singleton 1973).

Hostetler and Huntington (1971) document the struggle of the Old Order Amish to maintain control of their schools in the presence of considerable opposition from government officials. Warren (1967) focuses on the role of the school in bringing a traditional German village into the mainstream of industrial society.

The ethnographic study of schools
Social anthropology is built on ethnography – on essentially qualitative and descriptive, holistic accounts of particular societies by anthropologists who immerse themselves in the cultures being studied for extended periods of time. Anthropologists tend to view general, descriptive ethnographies as useful in themselves. Anthropologists with problem orientations also do ethnographic research, to generate and occasionally to test hypotheses, and cross-cultural studies rely heavily on existing ethnographies. Comprehensive discussions of ethnographic methods and of the role of ethnography in anthropology can be found in Naroll and Cohen (1970) and in Pelto and Pelto (1978).

Educational researchers have recently 'discovered' ethnography and are employing ethnographic methods in studying schools (Wilson 1977). Ethnographic work in schools can yield fine-grained, sensitive, in-depth analysis of the processes of schooling. But ethnography is not always the best choice for applied research, since it is a 'low-yield venture' in terms of time required (Wolcott 1976, p. 26) and since ethnographers require autonomy in their field work. Those hiring ethnographers should pay careful attention to the ethnographer's qualifications, because the individual is 'the main instrument of research' (p. 30).

Anthropologists working outside their own cultures can arrive at understandings that are not apparent to natives. This advantage tends to be lost when school ethnographies are done by members of the societies in which the schools are located (Khlief 1974). However, some anthropologists feel that the ethnographer must ultimately 'go native' in order to understand the perspective of a cultural insider. This can be difficult unless the ethnographer can find a cultural role. Teacher is the insider role most often employed by school ethnographers (e.g. King 1974). Burnett (1976), Singleton (1976), and Warren (1974) describe the conduct of their ethnographic work in schools. Volume 34 of *Human Organization* (1975) contains a special issue on the ethnography of schools.

A number of school ethnographies have been published. The examples that follow do not include those on minority schooling or on schools in developing nations. Henry (1957), in his study of a suburban fourth-grade classroom, labels the teacher's promotion of intra-group aggression the 'witch-hunt syndrome'. Lacey (1970) concludes that the achievement motivation of many students in a British boys' school is eroded by their relative failure in the intensely competitive environment engendered by the school. Based on their study of an innovative elementary school, Smith and Keith (1971) suggest that gradual, incremental change is more likely to succeed than is immediate, pervasive change. Taba (1955) notes that school reinforces children's pre-existing social biases rather than compensates for them. Wolcott (1973), in a study of a suburban elementary school, finds that the principal's function is to maintain continuity, not to facilitate change.

These and other ethnographies of schools are in print; some have a problem orientation, and some at least implicitly result in hypothesis generation. But at present each study seems to stand alone, like an isolated piece of some enormous puzzle. Perhaps in the near future the pieces will begin to be put together and 'grounded theory' will begin to emerge from the ethnographic study of schools (cf. Smith and Pohland 1976).

Cognitive and linguistic anthropology

To study education cross-culturally, it is necessary to understand the human mind as a phenomenon which varies significantly with socio–cultural conditions. Segall, Campbell and Herskovits (1966) studied the influence of culture on visual perception, with findings which suggest that certain cultural milieus profoundly affect basic perception of forms. Implications for validity of 'universal' intelligence tests are obvious. Redfield (1943) and Wallace (1970) deal with relations between world view or personality and cultural learning.

The work of Cole and Scribner (1974) presents a general approach to cultural differences in cognition and problem-solving. More specifically, cultural differences emerge in logico-meaning systems (Kaplan 1966), cognitive styles (R. Cohen 1969; Drucker 1971; Feldman *et al*. 1974; Goodman 1962), and memory functions (Cole and Gay 1972). Cross-cultural research using Piagetian approaches to cognitive development of children has been conducted in more than a dozen cultures (Dasen 1977; DeAvila and Havassy 1976; Otaala 1972; Tremaine 1975). There appear to be broad similarities in cognitive development everywhere, but such basic findings must be tempered with the insight that specific cultural differences in cognitive styles may still present serious problems when education systems are 'exported'.

Since education depends so heavily on communication, cross-cultural linguistic differences are also very important to educators. A basic work on the relation of language and culture is Whorf's (1956). He believes that each language shapes perception and thought in a different way. Interested readers should also consult the more moderate versions of the 'Whorfian hypothesis' (Hoijer 1954). The linguist Firth (1950), following Malinowski, deals with the relation of language and personality, while Hall (1959) stresses the importance of non-verbal communication.

Hymes (1971, 1972) has written excellent overviews treating the various approaches to linguistic theory in the context of educational problems and relating styles of learning to linguistic differences. The relation of language to the 'culture of childhood' (Opie and Opie 1960) and to learning processes (Bernstein 1964) are also of general interest as a background for understanding more specific educational problems which are language-related.

Minority education

Anthropologists' focus on such issues as culture change, cultural pluralism, and ethnic persistence has led to the study of cultural minorities; particularly where anthropologists turn their attention to Western cultures, they tend to concentrate on minority groups. Much of this work focuses on educational issues. Aarons, Gordon, and Stewart (1969) present a good overview of minority education.

Formal education can be a powerful tool in operationalizing 'melting-pot' theories. The classic anthropological examination of this use is Mead's (1959) *The School in American Culture*, with its section on the role of the urban school in acculturating the children of European immigrants. In order to foster national loyalties and a uniform world view, family and ethnic loyalties are undermined. Certainly, this has largely been the goal for American Indian education as well.

With American anthropology's emphasis on Native Americans, some of the best examples of problems in minority education have come from studies of American Indians. Fuchs and Havighurst (1972), drawing from the National Study of American Indian Education, focus on the use of formal education as an acculturative tool. Polgar's (1960) article on the Fox (or Mesquakie) Indians is one of the earliest considerations of biculturation.

Conceptually, biculturation offers an alternative to acculturation. As with the notion of bilingualism, the implication is that one can learn two sets of knowledge equally well – that it is not necessary to eliminate one set and replace it with another. Whichever view is taken can have a profound effect on education in determining whether minority students are perceived as deprived or merely different. Wax (1971) points out the different world view many American Indian children bring to the classroom; their perspective often values, among other things, group needs over individual achievements. Different world views must be taken into account if workable educational techniques are to be developed for minority students, especially if biculturation, rather than acculturation, is the goal.

Numerous books and articles exist on the educational problems of minorities other than American Indians (e.g. Carter and Segura 1979; McDermott 1974; Ogbu 1974; Rosenfeld 1971; Ward 1971).

Language has a longer history of recognition as a problem in minority education than has culture. Regarding dialect differences, there exists controversial research which suggests that nonstandard English is deficient in vocabulary as well as in total grammatical patterns. This view has had an effect on educational goals. Even those who suggest that non-standard dialects are as rich as standard ones often point out the economic and social advantages that accrue to the person who can converse in the standard dialect of his or her language. Cazden (1966) presents one of the best reviews of the issue of sub-cultural differences in language and their effects on education.

Class and ethnicity seem to affect dialect and speech patterns differently. Lesser, Fifer and Clark (1965) suggest that the pattern of mental abilities is determined by ethnicity, while how well the full range of the pattern is learned is determined by class. Because standard-language deficiency is so often associated with poverty, F. Williams' (1970) and Leacock's (1971) studies of poverty have relevant chapters on bilingualism and bidialectism.

General sources
Articles reviewing work in anthropology and education include those by Brameld and Sullivan (1961), Burnett (1979), Gearing (1973a), Gearing and Tindall (1973), Shunk and Goldstein (1964), Sindell (1969) and Wolcott (1967). Burnett (1974) and Rosenstiel (1977) have published annotated bibliographies.

Kimball edits the *Anthropology and Education* series and George and Louise Spindler edit the *Case Studies in Education and Culture* series, which includes books on culture transmission in traditional societies as well as books on schools and their communities throughout the world. *The Anthropology and Education Quarterly* (initially entitled the *Council on Anthropology and Education Newsletter* and then the *Council on Anthropology and Education Quarterly*) has been published since 1970.

Edited volumes in anthropology and education include those by Gruber (1961), Ianni and Storey (1973), Lindquist (1970), Mayer (1970), Middleton (1970), Roberts and Akinsanya (1976a, 1976b), Spindler (1955, 1963, 1974), and Wax, Diamond and Gearing (1971). Authored volumes include those by Brameld (1957), Eisenstadt (1956), Kneller (1965), and Stenhouse (1967). Volume 9 of the *Journal of Research and Development in Education* (1976) contains an entire issue devoted to anthropology and education.

Two sub-fields of anthropology with relevance to education have been omitted from our discussion. One of them, the anthropological study of play, has been recently and comprehensively reviewed by Schwartzman (1976). The other, international development education, is too large a field to be encompassed within this review. Interested readers are referred to Adams and Bjork (1968).

Acknowledgments
We wish to thank Marion Lundy Dobbert, Ann Nihlen, and Harry F. Wolcott for their helpful comments on an earlier version of this section.

References

Aarons, A., Gordon, B. and Stewart, W. (eds.) (1969) 'Linguistic–cultural differences and American education', *Florida Foreign Language Reporter*, **7**, 1.

Adams, D. and Bjork, R. (1968) *Education in Developing Areas* (David McKay).

Barry, H., Josephson, L., Lauer, E. and Marshall, C. (1976) 'Traits inculcated in childhood: cross-cultural codes 5', *Ethnology*, **15**, pp. 83–106.

Barry, H., Josephson, L., Lauer, E. and Marshall, C. (1977) 'Agents and techniques for child training: cross-cultural codes 6', *Ethnology*, **16**, pp. 191–230.

Barry, H. and Paxson, L. (1971) 'Infancy and early childhood: cross-cultural codes 2', *Ethnology*, **10**, pp. 466–508.

Barry, H. and Schlegel, A. (1979) 'Adolescent initiation ceremonies: a cross-cultural code', *Ethnology*, **18**, pp. 199–210.

Bernstein, B. (1964) 'Elaborated and restricted codes: their social origins and some consequences', *American Anthropologist*, **66**, pp. 55–69.

Bowlby, J. (1969) *Attachment and Loss Vol. 1: Attachment* (Basic Books).

Brameld, T. (1957) *Cultural Foundations of Education: An Interdisciplinary Exploration* (Harper & Brothers).

Brameld, T. and Sullivan, E. (1961) 'Anthropology and education', *Review of Educational Research*, **31**, pp. 70–79.

Burnett, J. (1974) *Anthropology and Education: An Annotated Bibliographic Guide* (Human Relations Area Files Press).

Burnett, J. (1976) 'Event description and analysis in the microethnography of urban classrooms', in J. Roberts and S. Akinsanya (eds.) (1976a) op. cit., pp. 288–98.

Burnett, J. (1979) 'Anthropology in relation to education', *American Behavioral Scientist*, **23**, pp. 237–74.

Burton, R. and Whiting, J. (1961) 'The absent father and cross-sex identity', *Merrill-Palmer Quarterly of Behavior and Development*, **7**, pp. 85–95.

Carter, T. and Segura, R. (1979) *Mexican-Americans in School: A Decade of Change* (College Entrance Examination Board).

Cazden, C. (1966) 'Subcultural differences in child language: an interdisciplinary review', *Merrill-Palmer Quarterly of Behavior and Development*, **12**, pp. 185–219.

Cohen, R. (1969) 'Conceptual styles, culture conflict, and nonverbal tests of intelligence', *American Anthropologist*, **71**, pp. 828–56.

Cohen, Y. (1970) 'Schools and civilizational states', in J. Fischer (ed.) *The Social Sciences and the Comparative Study of Educational Systems* (International Textbook) pp. 55–147.

Cole, M. and Gay, J. (1972) 'Culture and memory', *American Anthropologist*, **74**, pp. 1066–84.

Cole, M. and Scribner, S. (1974) *Culture and Thought: A Psychological Introduction* (John Wiley).

D'Andrade, R. (1966) 'Sex differences and cultural institutions', in E. Maccoby (ed.) *The Development of Sex Differences* (Stanford University Press) pp. 174–204.

Dasen, P. (1977) *Piagetian Psychology: Cross-Cultural Contributions* (Gardner Press).

DeAvila, E. and Havassy, B. (1976) *Mexican American Schoolchildren: A Neo-Piagetian Analysis* (Georgetown University Press).

DeVore, I. and Konner, M. (1974) 'Infancy in hunter-gatherer life: an ethological perspective', in N. White (ed.) *Ethology and Psychiatry* (University of Toronto Press) pp. 113–41.

Dobbert, M. (1974) 'Education, schools, and cultural mapping', in G. Spindler (ed.) (1974) op. cit., pp. 205–18.

Dobbert, M. (1975) 'Another route to a general theory of cultural transmission: a systems model', *Council on Anthropology and Education Quarterly*, **6**, pp. 22–6. Reprinted in J. Roberts and S. Akinsanya (eds.) (1976a) op. cit., pp. 205–12.

Draper, P. (1974) 'Comparative studies of socialization', in B. Siegel *et al.* (eds.) *Annual Review of Anthropology* (Annual Reviews) pp. 263–77.

Draper, P. (1975) 'Cultural pressure on sex differences', *American Ethnologist*, **2**, pp. 602–16.

Drucker, E. (1971) 'Cognitive styles and class stereotypes', in E. Leacock (ed.) *The Culture of Poverty: A Critique* (Simon and Schuster) pp. 41–62.

Eisenstadt, S. (1956) *From Generation to Generation: Age Groups and Social Structure* (Free Press).

Feldman, C. *et al.* (1974) *The Development of Adaptive Intelligence: A Cross-Cultural Study* (Jossey-Bass).

Firth, J. (1950) 'Personality and language in society', *Sociological Review*, **42**, pp. 37–52.

Freedman, D. and Omark, D. (1973) 'Ethology, genetics, and education', in F. Ianni and E. Storey (eds.) *Cultural Relevance and Educational Issues: Readings in Anthropology and Education* (Little, Brown) pp. 250–83.

Fuchs, E. and Havighurst, R. (1972) *To Live on This Earth: American Indian Education* (Anchor).

Gearing, F. (1973a) 'Anthropology and education', in J. Honigmann (ed.) *Handbook of Social and Cultural Anthropology* (Rand McNally) pp. 1223–49.

Gearing, F. (1973b) 'Where we are and where we might go: steps toward a general theory of cultural transmission', *Council on Anthropology and Education Newsletter*, **4**, pp. 1–10. Reprinted in J. Roberts and S. Akinsanya (eds.) (1976a) op. cit., pp. 183–94.

Gearing, F. (1975) 'Structures of censorship, usually inadvertent: studies in a cultural theory of education', *Council on Anthropology and Education Quarterly*, **6**, pp. 1–9. Reprinted in J. Roberts and S. Akinsanya (eds.) (1976a) op. cit., pp. 194–205.

Gearing, F. and Tindall, B. (1973) 'Anthropological studies of the educational process', in B. Siegel *et al.* (eds.) *Annual Review of Anthropology* (Annual Reviews) pp. 95–105.

Goetz, J. (1978) 'Theoretical approaches to the study of sex-role culture in schools', *Anthropology and Education Quarterly*, **9**, pp. 3–21.

Goodman, M. (1962) 'Culture and conceptualization: a study of Japanese and American children', *Ethnology*, **1**, pp. 374–86.

Gruber, F. (ed.) (1961) *Anthropology and Education* (University of Pennsylvania Press).

Hall, E. (1959) *The Silent Language* (Doubleday).

Harris, M. (1975) *Culture, People, and Nature* (Crowell).

Henry, J. (1957) 'Attitude organization in elementary school classrooms', *American Journal of Orthopsychiatry*, **27**, pp. 117–33. Reprinted in J. Roberts and R. Akinsanya (eds.) (1976b) op. cit., pp. 169–82.

Henry, J. (1960) 'A cross-cultural outline of education', *Current Anthropology*, **1**, pp. 267–305. Reprinted in J. Roberts and S. Akinsanya (eds.) (1976a) op. cit., pp. 100–70.

Henry, J. (1963) *Culture Against Man* (Random House).

Hilger, M. (1960) *Field Guide to the Ethnological Study of Child Life* (Human Relations Area Files Press).

Hoijer, H. (ed.) (1954) *Language in Culture: Proceedings of a Conference on the Interrelations of Language and Other Aspects of Culture* (American Anthropological Association).

Hostetler, J. and Huntington, G. (1971) *Children in Amish Society: Socialization and Community Education* (Holt, Rinehart & Winston).

Hymes, D. (1971) 'On linguistic theory, communicative competence, and the education of disadvantaged children', in M. Wax, S. Diamond and F. Gearing (eds.) *Anthropological Perspectives on Education* (Basic Books) pp. 51–66.

Hymes, D. (1972) 'Introduction', in C. Cazden, V. John and D. Hymes (eds.) *Functions of Language in the Classroom* (Teachers College Press) pp. xi–lvii.

Ianni, F. and Storey, E. (eds.) (1973) *Cultural Relevance and Educational Issues: A Reader in Anthropology and Education* (Little, Brown).

Jensen, A. (1969) 'How much can we boost IQ and scholastic achievement?', *Harvard Educational Review*, **39**, pp. 1–123.

Kaplan, R. (1966) 'Cultural thought patterns in intercultural education', *Language Learning*, **16**, pp. 1–20.

Khlief, B. (1974) 'Issues in anthropological fieldwork in the schools', in G. Spindler (ed.) (1974) op. cit., pp. 389–98.

Kimball, S. (1974) *Culture and the Educative Process: An Anthropological Perspective* (Teachers College Press).

King, A. (1974) 'The teacher as a participant–observer: a case study', in G. Spindler (ed.) (1974) op. cit., pp. 399–410.

Kneller, G. (1965) *Educational Anthropology: An Introduction* (John Wiley).

Konner, M. (1972) 'Aspects of the developmental ethology of a foraging people', in N. Blurton Jones (ed.) *Ethological Studies of Child Behaviour* (Cambridge University Press) pp. 285–304.

Konner, M. (1975) 'Relations among infants and juveniles in comparative perspective', in M. Lewis and L. Rosenblum (eds.) *Friendship and Peer Relations* (John Wiley) pp. 99–129.

Konner, M. (1976) 'Maternal care, infant behavior and development among the !Kung', in R. Lee and I. DeVore (eds.) *Kalahari Hunter-Gatherers: Studies of the !Kung San and their Neighbors* (Harvard University Press) pp. 218–45.

Lacey, C. (1970) *Hightown Grammar: The School as a Social System* (Manchester University Press).

Leacock, E. (ed.) (1971) *The Culture of Poverty: A Critique* (Simon & Schuster).

Lesser, G., Fifer, G. and Clark, D. (1965) *Mental Abilities of Children from Different Social-Class and Cultural Groups* (University of Chicago Press).

LeVine, R. (1969) 'Culture, personality and socialization: an evolutionary view', in D. Goslin (ed.) *Handbook of Socialization Theory and Research* (Rand McNally) pp. 503–41.

LeVine, R. (1970) 'Cross-cultural study in child psychology', in P. Mussen (ed.) *Carmichael's Manual of Child Psychology* (John Wiley) pp. 559–612.

Liebowitz, L. (1978) *Females, Males, Families: A Biosocial Approach* (Duxbury Press).

Lindquist, H. (ed.) (1970) *Education: Readings in the Process of Cultural Transmission* (Houghton Mifflin).

Loehlin, J., Lindzey, G. and Spuhler, J. (1975) *Race Differences in Intelligence* (W. H. Freeman).

Maccoby, E. and Jacklin, C. (1974) *The Psychology of Sex Differences* (Stanford University Press).

McDermott, R. (1974) 'Achieving school failure: an anthropological approach to illiteracy and social stratification', in G. Spindler (ed.) (1974) op. cit., pp. 82–118.

Martin, M. and Voorhies, B. (1975) *Females of the Species* (Columbia University Press).

Mayer, P. (ed.) (1970) *Socialization: The Approach from Social Anthropology* (Tavistock).

Mead, M. (1935) *Sex and Temperament in Three Primitive Societies* (William Morrow).

Mead, M. (1959) *The School in American Culture* (Harvard University Press).

Mead, M. (1970) 'Our educational emphases in primitive perspective', in J. Middleton (ed.) *From Child to Adult: Studies in the Anthropology of Education* (Natural History Press) pp. 1–13.

Middleton, J. (ed.) (1970) *From Child to Adult: Studies in the Anthropology of Education* (Natural History Press).

Minturn, L. and Lambert, W. (1964) *Mothers of Six Cultures: Antecedents of Child Rearing* (John Wiley).

Naroll, R. and Cohen, R. (eds.) (1970) *A Handbook of Method in Cultural Anthropology* (Natural History Press).

Ogbu, J. (1974) *The Next Generation: An Ethnography of Education in an Urban Neighborhood* (Academic Press).

Opie, I. and Opie, P. (1960) *The Lore and Language of School Children* (Oxford University Press).

Otaala, B. (1972) *The Development of Operational Thinking in Primary School Children: An examination of some aspects of Piaget's theory among the Iteso children of Uganda* (Teachers College Press).

Pelto, P. and Pelto, G. (1978) *Anthropological Research: The Structure of Inquiry* (Cambridge University Press).

Poirier, F. (1972) 'Introduction', in F. Poirier (ed.) *Primate Socialization* (Random House) pp. 3–28.

Poirier, F. (1977) 'Introduction', in S. Chevalier-Skolnikoff and F. Poirier (eds.) *Primate Bio-Social Development: Biological, Social and Ecological Determinants* (Garland) pp. 1–39.

Polgar, S. (1960) 'Biculturation of Mesquakie teenage boys', *American Anthropologist*, **62**, pp. 217–35.

Redfield, R. (1943) 'The primitive world view', *Proceedings of the American Philosophical Society*, **96**, pp. 30–36.

Roberts, J. and Akinsanya, S. (eds.) (1976a) *Educational Patterns and Cultural Configurations: The Anthropology of Education* (David McKay).

Roberts, J. and Akinsanya, S. (eds.) (1976b) *Schooling in the Cultural Context: Anthropological Studies of Education* (David McKay).

Rosenfeld, G. (1971) *Shut Those Thick Lips: A Study of Slum School Failure* (Holt, Rinehart & Winston).

Rosenstiel, A. (1977) *Education and Anthropology: An Annotated Bibliography* (Garland).

Schwartzman, H. (1976) 'The anthropological study of children's play', in B. Siegel, A. Beals and S. Tyler (eds.) *Annual Review of Anthropology* (Annual Reviews) pp. 289–328.

Segall, M., Campbell, D. and Herskovits, M. (1966) *The Influence of Culture on Visual Perception* (Bobbs-Merrill).

Shunk, W. and Goldstein, B. (1964) 'Anthropology and education', *Review of Educational Research*, **34**, pp. 71–84.

Sindell, P. (1969) 'Anthropological approaches to the study of education', *Review of Educational Research*, **39**, pp. 593–605.

Singleton, J. (1973) 'Schooling: coping with education in a modern society', in T. Weaver (ed.) *To See Ourselves: Anthropology and Modern Social Issues* (Scott, Foresman) pp. 278–80.

Singleton, J. (1976) 'The ethnography of a Japanese school: anthropological field technique and models in the study of a complex organization', in J. Roberts and S. Akinsanya (eds.) (1976a) op. cit., pp. 279–88.

Smith, L. and Keith, P. (1971) *Anatomy of Educational Innovation: An Organizational Analysis of an Elementary School* (John Wiley).

Smith, L. and Pohland, P. (1976) 'Grounded theory and educational ethnography: a methodological analysis and critique', in J. Roberts and S. Akinsanya (1976a) op. cit., pp. 264–79.

Spindler, G. (ed.) (1955) *Education and Anthropology* (Stanford University Press).

Spindler, G. (ed.) (1963) *Education and Culture: Anthropological Approaches* (Holt, Rinehart & Winston).

Spindler, G. (ed.) (1974) *Education and Cultural Process: Toward an Anthropology of Education* (Holt, Rinehart & Winston).

Stenhouse, L. (1967) *Culture and Education* (Thomas Nelson).

Taba, H. (1955) *School Culture: Studies of Participation and Leadership* (American Council on Education).

Tindall, B. (1976) 'Theory in the study of cultural transmission', in B. Siegel, A. Beals and S. Tyler (eds.) *Annual Review of Anthropology* (Annual Reviews) pp. 195–208.

Tremaine, R. (1975) *Syntax and Piagetian Operational Thought: A Developmental Study of Bilingual Children* (Georgetown University Press).

Wallace, A. (1961) 'Schools in revolutionary and conservative societies', in F. Gruber (ed.) *Anthropology and Education* (University of Pennsylvania Press) pp. 25–54.

Wallace, A. (1970) *Culture and Personality* (Random House).

Ward, M. (1971) *Them Children: A Study in Language Learning* (Holt, Rinehart & Winston).

Warren, R. (1967) *Education in Rebhausen: A German Village* (Holt, Rinehart & Winston).

Warren, R. (1974) 'The school and its community context: the methodology of field study', in G. Spindler (eds.) (1974) op. cit., pp.426–41.

Washburn, S. (1973) 'Primate field studies and social science', in L. Nader and T. Maretzki (eds.) *Cultural Illness and Health* (American Anthropological Association) pp. 128–34.

Wax, M. (1971) *Indian Americans: Unity and Diversity* (Prentice-Hall).

Wax, M., Diamond, S. and Gearing F. (eds.) (1971) *Anthropological Perspectives on Education* (Basic Books).

Weisner, T. and Gallimore, R. (1977) 'My brother's keeper: child and sibling caretaking', *Current Anthropology*, **18**, pp. 169–90.

Whiting, B. and Edwards, C. (1973) 'A cross-cultural analysis of sex differences in the behavior of children aged three through eleven', *Journal of Social Psychology*, **91**, pp. 171–88.

Whiting, B. and Whiting, J. (1975) *Children of Six Cultures: A Psycho-Cultural Analysis* (Harvard University Press).

Whiting, J. (1973) 'A Model for Psycho-Cultural Research' *Annual Report 1973* (American Anthropological Association) pp. 1–14.

Whiting, J. and Child, I. (1953) *Child Training and Personality: A Cross-Cultural Study* (Yale University Press).

Whiting, J., Child, I. and Lambert, W. (1966) *Field Guide for a Study of Socialization* (John Wiley).

Whiting, J., Kluckhohn, R. and Anthony, A. (1958) 'The function of male initiation ceremonies at puberty', in E. Maccoby, T. Newcomb and E. Hartley (eds.) *Readings in Social Psychology* (Henry Holt) pp. 359–70.

Whorf, B. (1956) *Language, Thought, and Reality: Selected Writings* (Technology Press of Massachusetts Institute of Technology).

Williams, F. (ed.) (1970) *Language and Poverty: Perspectives on a Theme* (Markham).

Williams, T. (1972) *Introduction to Socialization: Human Culture Transmitted* (C. V. Mosby).

Wilson, S. (1977) 'The use of ethnographic techniques in educational research', *Review of Educational Research*, **47**, pp. 245–65.

Wolcott, H. (1967) 'Anthropology and education', *Review of Educational Research*, **37**, pp. 82–95.

Wolcott, H. (1973) *The Man in the Principal's Office: An Ethnography* (Holt, Rinehart & Winston).

Wolcott, H. (1976) 'Criteria for an ethnographic approach to research in schools', in J. Roberts and S. Akinsanya (eds.) (1976b) op. cit., pp. 23–44.

2 Sociology and the sociology of education
Brian Davies

This section is concerned with introductory literature to sociology and to the sociology of education, and argues that the sociology of education means sociology *applied* to education. The only useful way to approach the sociology of education is through sociology proper. Well applied, it opens up a whole range of understandings about who goes to which schools and colleges, what processes they undergo there, and to what ends or purposes.

The educational process itself is set in an overlapping series of experiences which also occur in the family, the peer group, the club, church, workplace, and so on. In all of these locations, men and women learn their culture, including the means, if any, of changing it. 'Man' undergoes a lifelong process of initiation into a world of facts, values and practices, which include the rules of their own alteration and transmission between persons and generations. In a very important sense, the main thing which sociology has to explain about society is how its rules and procedures get 'built into' people in the form of their social selves and identities, and how in turn these people through their actions create the regular patterns of life at all levels and make them work. The 'past' of this process is called history and the present makes up sociology. Men and women are 'made' by society and in turn make it. Society is composed of vast patterns of activity in families, schools, government, and so on, which are perfectly real – they have a 'structure'. Men and women experience them as real 'things'. At the same time they also experience them in a personal and potentially unique way within their individual consciousness. This duality, the contrast between social structure (with its markers in the law, class inequalities, gender differences, the ordinary rules of behaviour governing an encounter, and so on) and subjective meaning, and even more their action upon one another, is the exciting stuff out of which sociology is made.

It should already be possible to see why there is no easy way of grasping sociology and applying it directly to our understanding of schools, classrooms and so on. There simply is no such thing as 'sociology' if by that we mean one, neat, commonly agreed-to set of ideas that make up the 'subject'. No single set of ideas is complex enough to account for the whole variety of things that make up social life. Many sociologists acknowledge this and are happy to combine a number of views (also called approaches and perspectives) according to the particular problem or issue upon which they wish to focus, whether it be mother–child relationships, divorce, industrial unrest or the teaching of mathematics. Traditionally, however, sociology has grown up in its modern form over the past 130 years or so as a number of different, sometimes not only competing but highly antagonistic 'schools of thought'. In this sense, it is no different from any of the other social sciences, for example psychology or economics, except that its 'problem' is greater as it wants to include the *whole* range of social events, including those described by its neighbours.

This does give it a further 'bite': its ambitions have led it to want to account for social change and stability themselves. This takes any version of it deep into the problems of power and legitimacy (questions about existing patterns of rights and obligations). No society has yet existed without hierarchy – social differences in terms of who gets what wealth, other resources including prestige, and the right to run other people's existences. In our sort of capitalist society (private ownership of productive resources), our main form of hierarchy is class. Like any other it not only ensures that people are rewarded differently but also that they are valued differently. Moreover, this invidious valuation is deeply ingrained in the belief system which not only regulates people's behavior, but *constitutes* their identities. Deliberate social change, therefore, has always promised to upset existing patterns of who has and who has not, at both the ownership and the belief levels. Achieving it means mobilising force to change either or both levels. The first step in such mobilisation seems to be the necessity of simplifying the possibility of change itself by 'abolishing' opposing beliefs. Competition among belief systems in the everyday world is a usual accompaniment to competition for dominance among groups. Some sociologies, especially within Marxism, have come to argue that this state of affairs requires us to drop one of our most cherished, science-rational beliefs, that is to say, that *is* and *ought* do not entail one another. On the contrary, Marxists argue that their analysis of *is* points to how it *ought* to be. This means that as a form of belief it tends to 'consume' others; as a form of understanding it requires the abandonment of other views. In short, like any absolute belief it requires converts.

The implications for anyone starting to study sociology and

wanting to apply it to education are serious. One has to aim to get to know a variety of approaches with their distinctive concepts, theoretical positions and methods. At the same time one has to be aware that some of them are likely to attempt to 'convert', as well as inform, the student (Magee 1974). An initial survival kit is therefore important and this includes an historical perspective on the various schools of thought – Marxist, functionalist, interactionist and so on: how they arose in particular social contexts.

There are passionate differences between these and other approaches. The Marxist will argue that society is inherently full of conflict under capitalism – that differences in people's interests are fundamentally rooted in their position in the economic base or production part of society. Some own, some are owned. The former, capitalists, industrialists, landlords and so on, by one means or another, control the State and its politicians and 'fix up' special means whereby families, schools, the mass media and so on induce the mass of people to accept the correctness of their position and its necessity (legitimacy). In this, schools play a vital part not so much in transmitting the curriculum in terms of maths, science, history, etc., but in putting children through forms of behaviour which prepare them for the relations of production in factories, offices, and so on.

Structural functional theory (with its roots also going back, like Marxism, to the 19th century, particularly to Durkheim) argues that society is essentially consensual. It works because it is firmly cemented by shared values which are very effectively built into us by the process that we now call socialisation. It recognises that social differences exist but tends to see them as inevitable and necessary in some form. Schooling is viewed in a curiously similar way as it is by conflict theorists. It is a set of procedures not so much to do with gaining subject knowledge (though Durkheim certainly thought this important at the secondary stage) as for making children more similar, before they are inevitably made more different to suit the jobs and the wider social positions they will fill outside.

A third broad approach originated with Weber (and through him Schutz) on the one hand, and on the other, Americans like G. H. Mead, who come to focus upon man as having subjective experience, as a meaning-giver and -maker. It does not abandon the idea of being able to make general statements about social behaviour, but rather insists that if they are to be adequate, they must take the subjective side of his/her experience into account. Some recent followers of this perspective, for example ethnomethodologists, would argue that we really need to throw away a great deal of our traditional theorising about society and go back to square one in concentrating on the painstaking build-up of information on how the everyday world is created. The implications of this view for the understanding of school life are vital, for school is above all a place where a long-term attempt is made to deliberately form and change the views and identities of pupils. Schools are places full of meanings and their effects upon individuals.

Introductory literature on the above approaches can be found in a number of categories:

1. 'Introductions to sociology

Textbooks have changed quite a lot over the last 20 years in sociology. Nowadays they tend to focus either on social theories or on more descriptive accounts of social structure, with chapters on the family, social stratification, education, the economy and so on. With the theory emphasis, going back to the 1950s, Mills (1959) still presents a very important argument as to whether sociology can ever be more than a humanistic 'craft'. Berger (1966) is especially forceful in posing the problem of how far man is a social product or a producer of social life. Berger and Berger (1976) is especially useful for beginners. Cohen (1968) is more difficult, but is a very clear account of many key issues in the debates between theories. Coulson and Riddell (1980) provide the clearest introduction to a Marxist or conflict view. Fletcher (1980) argues clearly but unconvincingly that sociology is a single subject.

Books which pay some regard to different theories, but which are mainly concerned with presenting information about society, include Cotgrove (1978) and Haralambos and Heald (1980). Worsley *et al.* (1977, 1978a, 1978b) offer a package that spans theory and description. Westergaard *et al.* (1977) is a good guide to the literature on the sociology of modern Britain. Useful Open University material is to be found in Thompson and Tunstall (1971) and Bocock *et al.* (1980). Rex (1974) is difficult but has some marvellous articles on the recent state of British sociology as to theory, research and description.

In the last decade or so there has been a tremendous battle going on between the different schools in sociology. Collins (1975), Hansen (1976), Wells (1978), Skidmore (1979) and Harris (1980) will all help in suggesting some of the causes of the war. Collins is very clear and Jarvie (1972) makes a useful distinction between understanding and explanation in sociology, which if it had been better grasped and accepted over the last decade or so, would have prevented a lot of conceptual mess.

2. Historical development

Bottomore and Nisbet (1979) represents a complete coverage,

through a range of specialist essays, of the most important areas of sociology's development, and it deals with every school of thought. Raison (1979) consists of short, but highly authoritative, articles on individual social thinkers reprinted from *New Society*. Among the attempts by single people to write broad histories, Aron (1969, 1970) and Fletcher (1972) are powerful, with very clear accounts of great thinkers. Nisbet (1967) takes a different approach, focusing on 'unit' or basic ideas running through sociology.

More difficult books which have been very influential in shaping both how sociologists look back at theory development and define its present shape, include Berger and Luckman (1971), Gouldner (1971, 1976) and Giddens (1976, 1979). The first had a huge impact in pushing sociology toward a view of man as maker of the social; the second emphasised the reflexive nature of social life and sociology itself; while Giddens argues increasingly cogently that we need the key idea of 'structuration' to show how the individual and the social structure are linked. The thread running through all three, concerns this fundamental issue of how social structure acts upon people and how they act as agents upon it. As good a criterion as any for the adequacy of any social theory is how it manages to frame and answer this question.

A developing sense of what sociology is about also depends on knowing how it does, or might link up with other social sciences such as economics, politics, history, etc. For a consideration of these issues, see Yinger (1965), Runciman (1963) and Blackburn (1972).

3. Key sociologists and sociological perspectives

Reading many of the great thinkers in the original is often very difficult, because of their style, sometimes the difficulty of their translation into English, and because they are dealing with difficult ideas, for a specialist audience, in a past age. Some acquaintanceship with their special ways of arguing is part of getting a real feel for sociology and so too is a sense of their lives and times which can be grasped best through biography.

(i) On Durkheim: Lukes (1973) offers a biography, and Giddens (1972) a selection of the originals with a good introductory essay. Douglas (1971) is an example of how a modern Durkheimian works, outside education. Bernstein (1977) is the best known Durkheimian in the sociology of education. His language work (1973, 1974) is founded on a deep appreciation of its role as the symbolic linkage between social structure and the person. His work on education is much more concerned with Durkheim's chief concern

– how social and cultural transmission and the reproduction of society are intertwined.

(ii) On Marx: McLellan (1973) offers a biography, McLellan (1971) the originals, with commentary. Many sub-schools of Marxism, associated with different interpretations of his work and/or the writings of subsequent scholars, have grown up, making it an enormous task to claim to 'know' all his ideas. Walker and Gamble (1972), Walker (1978) and Nichols (1980) all try to stick with the master. Taylor (1979) applies the ideas to the area of development, itself very important in the modern worlds one to three, and particularly appropriate in the light of Marx's own emphasis on historical social change.

The main branches of Marxism important for modern social theory in the West are best traced as follows. Lenin's conversion of Marxism into active revolutionary doctrine is described by Conquest (1973). The Marxist view that regards itself as necessarily political even in academic discourse is clearly laid out by Althusser (1971). His ideas have made a lot of impact on the sociology of education, where schooling is assigned a key role in achieving 'correspondence' between the attributes of individual educands and the needs of the system of productive relations, that is, education fits people out with the attitudes and abilities which the world of work and its owners require. In this, it repeats what earlier sociologists with Durkheimian and functionalist views have said. 'Critical' Marxism, going back to the Frankfurt school of the 1920's is clearly traced in its development by Jay (1973), which can be compared with the account given by Slater (1977) from an 'insider' standpoint. Habermas (1979) is the leading present-day thinker in this area. His very difficult way of writing makes something like Scott (1978) valuable as an introduction. Critical theory has continued the tradition of wishing to treat Marxism as something more than creed or dogma. Its followers have cross-fertilised it with other disciplines such as Freudian psychology, aesthetics and economics in attempting to make it a developing approach to society and to clarify the meaning of 'praxis', the is–ought, theory–practice fusion. Habermas is most important for his application of philosophic and historical ideas to types of knowledge and communication. In a period where in education we are looking for deeper ways to understand the curriculum, this may be an important way forward. The approach has more to offer than a 'critical' approach like that exemplified by Fay (1975). Other approaches directly applicable to curriculum process include Lukac (1971) and Gramsci (1971), the latter particularly enjoying popularity on account of his notion of hegemony – the dominance of the ruling class in cultural matters – both in relation to ideology (Larrain 1979).

In a sense we are all Durkheimians and Marxists now, because we all recognise the existence of the social in its own right, and because we know how powerfully the material, productive world shapes and penetrates it (Hirst 1975).

(iii) On Weber: Macrae (1974) offers biography and Gerth and Mills (1970) a selection of originals with a commentary. Like Durkheim and Marx, Weber's contributions to present-day thinking are numerous. He acknowledges his own 'debate' with Marx in arguing that ideas had an autonomous force in social life and that class divisions need to be refined by considering prestige via status and party position. Equally important, he wished to allow space in his analysis for the ideas he had gained from German historians who argued about the hermeneutic – meaningfully patterned – character of the social. This led them both to his famous arguments about value freedom (we always choose to study things because of their value relevance to us, but having done so, we should strive for objectivity in the actual process of their study), and the need to consider both the objective and subjective dimensions of human action by combining methods of analysis so as both to build 'ideal type' models for comparing with the real world and employing *verstehen* (empathetic understanding) in 'grasping' the meaning of events to others. His idea of types of social action also concerns the connection between the varying 'objective' or value- or affectively-laden grounds for behaviour in relation to other persons or institutions. The social class concerns which have dominated sociology and the sociology of education for 40 years and more are Weberian rather than Marxist in conception. His emphasis on the 'dual' nature of the social has become one of the central beliefs of most sociologists, though it has come down to us filtered largely through the views of others like Parsons and Schutz, often visibly distorted.

(iv) On structural functionalism: as an approach, this has more or less completely dominated sociology for three decades from the 1940s. Its towering figure was Parsons, who in 1936 produced his famous synthesis of the ideas of Durkheim, Weber and Pareto which provided the starting point for a vast outpouring of conceptualisation and research. These can be traced in Isajiw (1968) and Turner and Maryanski (1979). Parsons' own role is well covered by Bershady (1973) and Rocher (1974). His distinctive view of society's organic, equilibriating nature was drawn partly from a reading of Durkheim but also from tendencies in the social psychology

of his day. His ideas that all societies and parts of societies have the same basic sets of tasks or functional prerequisites – of adaptation, goal attainment, integration and latency (also called pattern main-tainence or tension-management) comes from these roots. Roughly, this means that resources must be harnessed and the output thus produced applied to selected ends or goals in terms of distribution rules which people must be brought to accept. Dis-putes arising out of the application of these rules will have to be settled or lead to changed rules, or else to activities that take people's minds off the disputes. All practices and institutions, more or less, 'do' or are 'for' one or more things in this sense. Societies are structured rather like Chinese boxes, with cultural systems (the realm of knowledge and values) and social systems (made up of institutions like governments, churches, families, schools, etc.), within which people play roles, the players being individuals inhabiting personality systems (where they have ingested their norms which guide the role behaviour, having gone through a Freud-like early childhood experience which laid down the identity-basis). Socialisation is a key concept and deviance is viewed as the result of its imperfections. This is a sociology that believes in its objectivity.

If all this comes transmitted from Durkheim, then it is from Weber that Parsons gets his ideas of action (his whole approach becomes characterised as 'instrumental activism') and power. Many would say he gets this latter, of all his borrowings, most seriously wrong, analogising it to money and its circulation and arguing that it tended to have a zero sum (more for you, less for me) character. Bashing up Parsons' ideas has become a great sport, but there is no question that one of the ways in which he should be regarded as an outstandingly interesting thinker is as a case of the relationship between his thought and his 'times'. There is a white Anglo-Saxon Protestant tenor to his schema, a difficulty with explaining conflict and change, which is there right through to the end. How far is this the man and how far the conceptual structure which he chooses to inhabit? See Buckley (1967) for the best avail-able argument about the nature of system concepts in social analysis.

Structural functional analysis *was* almost the whole of the sociol-ogy of education until the mid 1960s and is still a dominant influ-ence. To ask what are schools, classrooms, teaching, curricula and so on *for* is to ask functional questions; to ask how it is that humans have purposes, accomplish them or not, monitor and refurbish their social arrangements, is again to ask how systems behave.

(v) Symbolic interactionism. The only real 'competition' to functionalism in American sociology in the 1950s and 1960s came from
symbolic interactionists, particularly in relation to issues of socialisation and deviance; see Meltzer *et al.* (1975) and Manis and
Meltzer (1978). They draw their inspiration largely from the works
of G. H. Mead, whose ideas and biography are well covered in
Miller (1973). Mead's work lay in a tradition of pragmatist philosophy along with William James and John Dewey. His own main
concern was to show the relationships between mind, self and
society, and to explain how the human organism, knowledge,
knowing and action were tied together in complex, interacting
knots. He is now best known for his ideas on the development of
the social self and an emphasis on the lifelong continuity of personal socialisation and change. A good deal of recent work on
classrooms in sociology of education has been symbolic interactionist in character, looking at the meaning that teachers and
pupils assign to one another, how classroom interaction is sustained, the nature of language, the generation of deviance and so
on.

(vi) Phenomenology and ethnomethodology. Partly out of dissatisfaction with more established sociologies like functionalism and their
complex 'system building', a number of American sociologists in
the early 1960s mounted a real push for a return to basics in the
subject. This took the form of emphasising how little we know
about the 'everyday' properties of social life, about the minute-
by-minute fashion in which we construct and sustain, mainly
through speech, our social world. Garfinkel (1967) is best known in
this respect as the originator of ethnomethodology. Cicourel
(1964, 1973), who had earlier developed a powerful critique of
traditional sociological methods, now combines ideas from
linguistics, especially Chomsky, and phenomenological philosophy
which emphasised the importance of perception and consciousness in the determination of the everyday social world. Pivcevic
(1970) shows how the phenomenology of Husserl is joined up with
Weber by Schutz and provides one historical back-up for this work,
alongside the existentialism of Sartre and Merleau-Ponty. Douglas
(1971) and Turner (1974) present good selections of work in this
new 'man as agent' view. Phillips (1977) shows how it links up with
the analysis of language as such. Roche (1973) argues that there is a
'humanistic' affinity between a whole range of approaches that
treat man as social creator, including symbolic interactionism and
even Wittgensteinian philosophy. Indeed, in the last-named area,
Winch (1958) has argued that traditional social science, looking for

causes and predictions of a traditional 'objective' kind, is impossible. Human action is essentially rule-following – to explain it is to
know the rule under which it was produced. This type of analysis
has also been of great interest in the study of schools, not least
because it forces us to drop our preconceptions in an area, when
our heads tend to be stuffed full of them. To go into schools and
classrooms with the eyes of a 'judgemental dope' (which was what
Garfinkel suggested sociologists should do), aware of the preconceptions of our natural attitude (*à la* Schutz) is to see the everyday
world of children and teachers clearly and even shockingly. Alas,
what this approach, like symbolic interactionism, fails to do for us is
to help locate the scenes we see in wider institutions or structures
which we know help to determine them. For this reason, a good
deal of phenomenology swung across to Marxist explanations in
the 1970s, as Smart (1976) shows, so as to provide a basis for
explaining what was all too easily 'rendered problematic' by micro-
investigation. The marriage has proven somewhat uneasy.

(vii) Structuralism: few sociologists can actually get by without the
concept of structure in their explanations. They differ more in
terms of how they explain it and investigate it than as to whether it
is there or not. Mainly from the contribution of Saussure to modern linguistics (see Culler 1976), various versions of structuralism
have become popular in social exploration. Their common root lies
in their view of knowledge which in all cases comes down to the idea
that it is simply structure or relation, beneath which there lies
merely an arbitrary basis. Robey (1973) is a good survey of its
various forms. It was most powerful until recently in anthropology,
mainly through the work of Levi-Strauss (see Leach 1970). Piaget
(1971) in cognitive psychology and Foucault (1970), interested in
the socio-historical growth of 'knowledges' represent other
strands. In recent years, Marxists have taken it in as a promising
'dissolver' of any potential knowledge status quo arguing that its
traditionally arbitrary basis can always be viewed as actual practices
in a cultural system. Just as the world of production is 'possessed' so
too is there ownership of the means of enunciation (see Coward
and Ellis 1977). The potential of this approach for education must
be very real, though it is as yet largely undeveloped. The whole
rationale of formal schooling is its aim of message transmission.
Who transmits what to whom, why and to what effect, are issues as
yet only barely penetrated by research, some of which must surely
take a structuralist stance.

(viii) Sociological methods. All these 'approaches' contain people
who are not only spinning concepts and theories but some of whom

are actually collecting data as the basis of these activities. There are only a small number of data collection methods available to social scientists – one can ask, look, or read something already there. Asking means questionnaires or interviews; looking means either standardly or 'naturally' recording the interaction before you, reading means going into existing documents, statistics etc. Some sociologists are not interested (i.e. don't think it's worth doing or is do-able) in research at all in the usual sense. Many Marxists would regard most of it as wasted motion as they know the story already. They are keener on changing the system, in definite ways. Sharp (1980), for instance, is a dreadfully clear account of this view. At the edge of phenomenology, research is also regarded as in-existent as argued by McHugh (1974). Poetry is all. Most sociologists most of the time, however, have believed in Durkheim's injunction that the social is real, that it can be objectively categorised and then attacked methodologically to produce news about its causes and function.

A good deal of the material on sociological methods is not about how to do it but whether to. A deep distrust has grown up of sociology's understandable past urge to 'be like science' – to use empirical methods, that is those depending upon the idea that there is a world 'out there' that can be described, measured, generalised about and even predicted. This view is often now called 'positivism', but the term has a pretty slippery usage. Some of the distinctions made are worse than useless – for example the well-known ones between sociologies of 'order' and 'control' (Dawe 1970) and the 'normative' and the 'interpretive' (Wilson 1971). Both suggest that sociologies and their methods can be sorted roughly into those emphasising man as made (and measurable) and man as maker (and only 'appreciable').

With hindsight, these distinctions can be seen to be shot through with the value preferences and short-sightedness of their makers. All sociologies, including those varieties which concentrate on the meaningful nature of the social, are empirical and positivist if they collect and generalise about data. There are no simple parallels between quantitative and qualitative data, objective and subjective analysis. There are more differences in how far researchers think they can generalise, how far they can produce covering (as opposed to local and limited) explanations than there are non-empirical (or non-positivist) methods. The alternative is poetry, whether of the 'analyst', beyond phenomenology or Marxist his-toricist kind. The 'standard' traditional moves in these complex debates can be traced compactly in Ryan (1970) and Giddens (1974), and in more narrative form in Keat and Urry (1975) and

Hamilton (1974). The modern form of the 'is sociology a science?' argument centres most around Popper's debate (see Magee, 1973) with Kuhn (1970) which is taken up in Lakatos and Musgrave (1970) and discussed by Feyerabend (1975). The best recent 'resolutions' of the issues are found in Gouldner (1976) and Giddens (1976, 1979).

At the mundane level of how to actually do it, if one decides that there is something to do, Ford (1975) provides a gentle if over-whimsical review of how to collect and conceptualise data. Bulmer (1977) is a lot narrower but readable. Galtung (1969) is still the best statement of measurement methods. Zetterburg (1966) is best on the traditional and now largely suspect view that research can aim at verifying theory. Cicourel (1964) is the classic first cloud across this measurement horizon. Becker (1971), Denzin (1970), and Glaser and Strauss (1968) provide the rationale and advice for symbolic interactionist techniques. Garfinkel (1967) describes ethnomethodology. Phillips (1973) shows what scepticism about methods follows when one adopts a moralistic 'man makes meaning' posture. The social context of research is well brought out by Shipman (1972), Bell and Newby (1977) and Brenner *et al*. (1978).

4. *Introduction to sociology of education*

Introductions take the form either of overviews, outlining the field but not aiming at being exhaustive in terms of content; textbooks; and readers (collections of articles). Education is not one of the richer areas of sociological studies; it has always been mixed up with teacher training, itself not notoriously intellectual. Education itself, a practical activity with more urgency than wit, tends to exert a clammy hand on disciplines that lend themselves to it. The dampness tends to come from the normative, practical bent of the field. Certainly, as sociology has gone through its prolonged warfare of the 1960s and 1970s, its applications to educational analysis have often redoubled rather than clarified confusion. These issues are all raised in 'overviews' by Bernbaum (1977), Bernstein (1977) and Wexler (1976). There is an interesting range of 'national' views of education in Kloskowska and Martinotti (1977). Banks (1978) provides only a minimally annotated bibliography. Davies (1981) provides up-to-date commentary on a range of key areas.

Among textbooks, the best known in Britain is Banks (1976) which has been accused of being functionalist, positivist and conservative. These accusations normally do not come from those who want a proper textbook (i.e. one representing all views) but rather from those who would simply prefer their own bias to be dominant. One of the book's benefits is that it shifts only when the literature merits it – behind the avant-garde. Bernstein (1977) is not strictly a textbook, but his Durkheimian vision, increasingly aimed to take account of Marx, constitutes the most influential single presence in post-war thinking. Swift (1969) is short and pungent, but has never been revised. Levitas (1974) is readable, Marxist, and not tempted to silly relativism. Sarup (1978) represents the more recent type of Marxism that tries to combine phenomenological sympathies with very deterministic views of structure and gets into a hopeless muddle. Reid (1978) is uneven, with an inadequate introduction about types of approaches, but with several excellent later chapters, especially on educational opportunity and educability and the classroom literature, all as full as Banks' but more brightly written. Robinson (1981) is the most interesting attempt to date to combine a really 'open' look at theoretical approaches with full coverage of major topics (including knowledge and the curriculum) and research – where available. Davies (1976) presupposes familiarity with sociological theory and claims to show how different approaches can be applied to the understanding of schooling.

It is difficult to recommend American textbooks, which traditionally avoid controversy. Sexton (1976b) has always been the exception to which Hurn (1978), Brembeck (1971) and Havighurst and Neugarten (1975) may be added.

Collections of readings are particularly important in recent sociology of education. As much as anything, this reflects the consciousness of diversity and change in the area. It also reflects the extent to which the major academic change – the rise of 'new directions' in the sociology of education in the early 1970s (groups claiming to draw upon phenomenological insights to question existing theories and practices, many of whom later found Marxism more satisfactory) – involved people who believed in collective outlooks rather than shared ones. The major institutional factor in this period was the rise of the Open University and, in particular, its faculty of Educational Studies. This has resulted in a lot of publications of course units and readers which have become of importance in 'defining' the field as taught in the impressionable world of teacher training.

These influences have each produced distinctive collections. Among the first, in America, we have Sexton (1976a), Hansen and Gerstl (1967), Stub (1975) and Cave and Chessler (1974). Henry (1971) must also be mentioned, for although not strictly a reader, it contains lovely examples of the traditional ethnographic approach imported from anthropology which some later, lesser lights have wanted to turn into an exclusive approach. Among the British, we have a traditional 'inclusive' strand from Halsey, Floud and Anderson (1965), through Hopper (1971), Brown (1973), Eggleston (1974) to Karabel and Halsey (1977), the latter rather too anxious to score easy points off the shifting target of 'new directions'. A parallel type of 'covering' reader with an eye rather more keenly fixed on change, trends and critique is represented by Flude and Ahier (1974), Gleeson (1977), Barton and Meighan (1978) and Barton *et al*. (1980), the last two reporting the proceedings of an annual conference on the field based at Westhill College.

The second strand, representing the changing emphasis of 'new directions' is found in Young (1971), Beck *et al*. (1976), Jenks (1977) and Whitty and Young (1976). Though not neatly depictable, one can say that these have in common an antagonism to traditional Durkheimian, Weberian or functionalist approaches, which are all branded as 'positivist'. They favour mixes of interactionism, phenomenology and Marxism. Their most important net contribution has been to highlight the traditional neglect of major aspects of knowledge processes at the curricular level. A lot of their early work was very naïve in its relativism. This appeared to sanction the beliefs both that change in education was just a question of teachers thinking it possible and that 'destroying' knowledge was a prerequisite to ending inequality of educational treatment. These tendencies are definitively and savagely put down by Flew (1976). These emphases gave way to those which viewed knowledge and cultural transmission in more Marxist ways. That is to say, they tended to be seen largely as issues of ideological imposition on the part of hegemonic groups (Apple 1980). The most pungent puncturing of this solemn solipsising is found in Musgrove (1980).

The third source of readers (and very important course unit material) has been the Open University. Course E282, *School and Society*, whose reader was Cosin *et al*. (1971), celebrated and disseminated much of the early 'new directions' and a whole lot more. E352, *Education, Economy and Society*, whose reader was Bell *et al*, (1973) was its more orthodox relation, never inspiring as much devotion, standing as it did as an eclectic depiction of structural and system approaches to education and its problems. Course E282 became E202, *Schooling and Society*, with two readers, Dale *et al*. (1976) and Hammersley and Woods (1976). These perfectly represent the unreconciled 'battle' in the field. The first contains a 'radical', mainly Marxist approach (which got the lion's share of attention and publicity), while the second ploughs a mainly symbolic interactionist furrow about school processes. Nowhere in the course are they reconciled, though their co-presence is acknowledged. Hopes for *rapprochement* are naturally felt more keenly by the less absolutist partner (see Woods 1980a and b). E352 has been superseded by E353 *Society, Education and the State*, whose readers are the two volumes edited by Dale *et al.* (1981). This course represents a strong swing toward the Marxist element only partly present in E352 and now cut adrift from its Durkheimian and Weberian moorings. This will prove to be a loss, but at least some of the course material is clearer than E202 in divorcing itself from simplistic ideas of education–production correspondence as argued by Bowles and Gintis (1976). See O'Keeffe (forthcoming) for a clear critique of this approach.

The area of the sociology of education, then, is quite well served for introductions. It would be good to think that there was an accompanying wealth of research in progress, but this is not the case. Indeed, the most powerful recent tendencies on the theoretical front have had a bad influence on the flow of discovery. Many Marxists will say frankly that it is unnecessary – action is more important and enough is known to accomplish this. Education itself, anyway, is not earmarked as a crucial site for the class struggle (Sharp 1980). When they do carry out research (Sharp and Green 1975; Willis 1977), a quick interactionist dip is turned into an orgy of criticism of capitalism and its dupes. Never have so few stood for so many with so much methodological unclarity as in studies such as these (see Hargreaves, 1978). The 'interpretive', mainly symbolic interactionist, researchers whose preserve has been mainly classrooms, focusing on pupils, are usually more honest (if not always clearer) about their ethnographic techniques. However, they tend to be equally 'stuck' in their capacity to show how the local relates to the wider framework. While they produce interesting descriptions, their efforts tend to cumulate only slowly and painfully. Given the dramatic fall from fashion in system measurement, the choice facing the young researcher often seems to be an untidy one between the overblown or the infinitesimally little. We are all in danger of becoming prey to the unchecked conceptual speculator.

The common pursuit continues to be in locating the nature, causes and consequences of inequality in the social hierarchy, as education and wider cultural transmission play a part in them. Measurement-oriented description and analysis is not dead in America (see the journal *Sociology of Education* for proof). Not all the historical work which has become popular of late is cavalier as to its historical base; see for example Smith (1980). The first two volumes of the *British Journal of the Sociology of Education* testify to an empirically renewed and sophisticated emphasis on transmission within school settings. We must be realistic about the source of the our feelings about the 'shortcomings' of education. It *is* an 'adjustable container' and it is therefore a constant prey to urges to either abolish or transform it or to denigrate its purpose. The leakage of this pressure into sociology of education gives it much of its recent unlovely, proselytising air, and gives to many of its arguments their unsatisfying, solipsistic nature. Complex, plural societies are hard to explain and the part education plays in them (as in any other) is far too easy to oversimplify and the urge to do so, if one wants change, is real.

References

Althusser, L. (1971) *Lenin and Philosophy and Other Essays* (New Left Books).

Apple, M. (1980) 'Curricular form and the logic of technical control' in Barton, L. *et al.* (1980) op., cit.

Aron, R. (1969, 1970) *Main Currents in Sociological Thought* (2 vols.) (Penguin).

Banks, O. (1976) *The Sociology of Education* (Batsford).

Banks, O. (1978) *The Sociology of Education: a bibliography* (Frances Pinter).

Barton, L. and Meighan, R. (eds.) (1978) *Sociological Interpretations of Schooling and Classrooms: a reappraisal* (Nafferton).

Barton, L., Meighan, R. and Walker, S. A. (eds.) (1980) *Schooling, Ideology and the Curriculum* (Falmer Press).

Beck, J. *et al.* (eds.) (1976) *Worlds Apart* (Collier Macmillan).

Becker, H. S. (1971) *Sociological Work* (Allen Lane).

Bell, C. and Newby, H. (eds.) (1977) *Doing Sociological Research* (Allen & Unwin).

Bell, R., Fowler, G. and Little, R. (eds.) (1973) *Education in Great Britain and Ireland* (Routledge & Kegan Paul).

Berger, P. L. (1966) *Invitation to Sociology* (Penguin).

Berger, P. L. and Berger, B. (1976) *Sociology: a biographical approach* (Penguin).

Berger, P. L. and Luckmann, T. (1971) *The Social Construction of Reality* (Penguin).

Bernbaum, G. (1977) *Knowledge and Ideology in the Sociology of Education* (Macmillan).

Bernstein, B. (ed.) (1973) *Class, Codes and Control* vol. 2 *Applied Studies toward a Sociology of Language* (Routledge & Kegan Paul).

Bernstein, B. (1974) *Class, Codes and Control* vol. 1 *Theoretical Studies toward a Sociology of Language* 2nd rev. edn. (Routledge & Kegan Paul).

Bernstein, B. (1977) *Class, Codes and Control* vol. 3 (Routledge & Kegan Paul).

Bershady, H. (1973) *Ideology and Social Knowledge* (Blackwell).

Blackburn, R. (ed.) (1972) *Ideology in Social Science* (Fontana).

Bocock, R., Hamilton, P., Thompson, K. and Waton, A. (eds.) (1980) *An Introduction to Sociology* (Fontana and Open University Press).

Bottomore, T. and Nisbet, R. (eds.) (1979) *A History of Sociological Analysis* (Heinemann Educational Books).

Bowles, S. and Gintis, H. (1976) *Schooling in Capitalist America* (Routledge & Kegan Paul).

Brembeck, C. S. (1971) *Social Foundations of Education* (John Wiley).

Brenner, M. *et al.* (eds.) (1978) *The Social Contexts of Methods* (Croom Helm).

Brown, R. (ed.) (1973) *Knowledge, Education and Cultural Change* (Tavistock).

Buckley, W. (1967) *Sociology and Modern Systems Theory* (Prentice Hall).

Bulmer, M. (ed.) (1977) *Sociological Research Methods: an introduction* (Macmillan).

Carnoy, M. (ed.) (1972) *Schooling in a Corporate Society: the political economy of education in America* (Wiley).

Cave, W. M. and Chessler, M. A. (eds.) (1974) *Sociology of Education: an anthology of issues and problems* (Macmillan).

Cicourel, A. V. (1964) *Method and Measurement in Sociology* (Free Press).

Cicourel, A. V. (1973) *Cognitive Sociology* (Penguin).

Cohen, P. S. (1968) *Modern Social Theory* (Heinemann Educational Books).

Collins, R. (1975) *Conflict Sociology* (Academic Press).

Conquest, R. (1973) *Lenin* (Fontana).

Cosin, B. R. *et al.* (eds.) (1971) *School and Society* (Routledge & Kegan Paul and Open University).

Cotgrove, S. S. (1978) *The Science of Society* (Allen and Unwin).

Coward, R. and Ellis, J. (1977) *Language and Materialism: developments in sociology and the theory of the subject* (Routledge & Kegan Paul).

Coulson, M. A. and Riddell, D. S. (1980) *Approaching Sociology* (Routledge & Kegan Paul).

Culler, J. (1976) *Saussure* (Fontana).

Dale, I. R. *et al.* (eds.) (1976) *Schooling and Capitalism* (Routledge & Kegan Paul and Open University).

Dale, R., Esland, G., Fergusson, R. and MacDonald, M. (eds.) (1981a) *Education and the State: Schooling and the national interest* (Falmer Press/Open University Press).

Dale, R., Esland, G., Fergusson, R. and MacDonald, M. (eds.) (1981b) *Education and the State: politics, patriarchy and practice* (Falmer Press/Open University Books).

Davies, B. (1976) *Social Control and Education* (Methuen).

Davies, B. (ed.) (1981) 'The state of schooling', *Educational Analysis*, **3**, 1.

Dawe, A. (1970) 'The two sociologies', *British Journal of Sociology*, **21**, 2, 208–18.

Denzin, N. K. (1970) *The Research Act in Sociology* (Butterworths).

Douglas, J. D. (ed.) (1971) *Understanding Everyday Life* (Routledge & Kegan Paul).

Eggleston, J. (ed.) (1974) *Contemporary Research in the Sociology of Education* (Methuen).

Fay, B. (1975) *Social Theory and Political Practice* (Allen & Unwin).

Feyerabend, P. (1975) *Against Method* (New Left Books).

Fletcher, R. (1972) *The Making of Sociology* (3 vols.) (Nelson).

Fletcher, R. (1980) *Sociology: its nature, scope and elements* (Batsford).

Flew, A. (1976) *Sociology, Equality and Education* (Macmillan).

Flude, M. and Ahier, J. (eds.) (1974) *Educability, Schools and Ideology* (Croom Helm).

Ford, J. (1975) *Paradigms and Fairy Tales* (2 vols) (Routledge & Kegan Paul).

Foucault, M. (1970) *The Order of Things* (Tavistock).

Galtung, J. (1969) *Theory and Methods of Social Research* (Allen & Unwin).

Garfinkel, H. (1967) *Studies in Ethnomethodology* (Prentice Hall).

Gerth, H. H. and Mills, C. W. (eds.) (1970) *From Max Weber* (Routledge & Kegan Paul).

Giddens, A. (ed.) (1972) *Emile Durkheim: selected writings* (Cambridge University Press).

Giddens, A. (ed.) (1974) *Positivism and Sociology* (Heinemann Educational Books).

Giddens, A. (1976) *New Rules of Sociological Method* (Hutchinson).

Giddens, A. (1979) *Central Problems in Social Theory: action, structure and contradiction in social analysis* (Macmillan).

Glaser, B. G. and Strauss, A. L. (1968) *The Discovery of Grounded Theory* (Weidenfeld & Nicolson).

Gleeson, D. (ed.) (1977) *Identity and Structure: issues in the sociology of education* (Nafferton).

Gouldner, A. W. (1971) *The Coming Crisis of Western Sociology* (Heinemann Educational Books).

Gouldner, A. W. (1976) *The Dialectic of Ideology and Technology* (Macmillan).

Gramsci, A. (1971) *Selections from the Prison Notebooks*, edited and translated by Quintin Hoare and Geoffrey Nowell-Smith (Lawrence & Wishart).

Habermas, J. (1979) *Communication and the Evolution of Society* (Heinemann Educational Books).

Halsey, A. H., Floud, J. and Anderson, C. A. (eds.) (1965) *Education, Economy and Society* (Free Press).

Hamilton, P. (1974) *Knowledge and Social Structure* (Routledge & Kegan Paul).

Hammersley, M. and Woods, P. (eds.) (1976) *The Process of Schooling* (Routledge & Kegan Paul and Open University).

Hansen, D. A. (1976) *An Invitation to Critical Sociology* (Free Press).

Hansen, D. A. and Gerstl, J. E. (eds.) (1967) *On Education: Sociological Perspectives* (Wiley).

Haralambos, M. and Heald, R. M. (1980) *Sociology: Themes and Perspectives* (University Tutorial Press).

Hargreaves, D. (1978) 'Whatever happened to symbolic interactionism', in L. Barton and R. Meighan (eds.) *Sociological Interpretations of Schooling and Classrooms: a reappraisal* (Nafferton).

Harris, C. C. (1980) *Fundamental Concepts and the Sociological Enterprise* (Croom Helm).

Havighurst, R. J. and Neugarten, B. L. (1975) *Society and Education* (Allyn & Bacon).

Henry, J. (1971) *Essays on Education* (Penguin).

Hirst, P. Q. (1975) *Durkheim, Bernard and Epistemology* (Routledge & Kegan Paul).

Hopper, E. (ed.) (1971) *Readings in the Theory of Educational Systems* (Hutchinson).

Hurn, C. J. (1978) *The Limits and Possibilities of Schooling: an introduction to the sociology of education* (Allyn & Bacon).

Isajiw, A. (1968) *Causation and Functionalism in Sociology* (Routledge & Kegan Paul).

Jarvie, I. C. (1972) *Concepts and Society* (Routledge & Kegan Paul).

Jay, M. (1973) *The Dialectical Imagination* (Heinemann Educational Books).

Jenks, C. (ed.) (1977) *Rationality, Education and the Social Organisation of Knowledge* (Routledge & Kegan Paul).

Karabel, J. and Halsey, A. H. (eds.) (1977) *Power and Ideology in Education* (Oxford University Press).

Keat, R. and Urry, J. (1975) *Social Theory as Science* (Routledge & Kegan Paul).

Kloskowska, A. and Martinotti, G. (eds.) (1977) *Education in a Changing Society* (Sage).

Kuhn, T. S. (1970) *The Structure of Scientific Revolutions* (University of Chicago Press).

Lakatos, I. and Musgrave, A. (eds.) (1970) *Criticism and the Growth of Knowledge* (Cambridge University Press).

Larrain, J. (1979) *The Concept of Ideology* (Hutchinson).

Leach, E. (1970) *Levi Strauss* (Fontana).

Levitas, M. (1974) *Marxist Perspectives in the Sociology of Education* (Routledge & Kegan Paul).

Lukac, G. (1971) *History and Class Consciousness* (Merlin).

Lukes, S. (1973) *Emile Durkheim, His Life and Work* (Allen Lane).

McHugh, P., Raffel, S., Foss, D. C. and Blum, A. F. (1974) *On the Beginning of Social Enquiry* (Routledge & Kegan Paul).

McLellan, D. (1971) *The Thought of Karl Marx* (Macmillan).

McLellan, D. (1973) *Karl Marx, His Life and Thought* (Harper & Row).

Macrae, D. (1974) *Weber* (Fontana).

Magee, B. (1973) *Popper* (Fontana).

Manis, J. and Meltzer, B. (eds.) (1978) *Symbolic Interactionism* (Allyn & Bacon).

Meltzer, B. N., Petras, J. W. and Reynolds, L. T. (1975) *Symbolic Interactionism: genesis, varieties and criticism* (Routledge & Kegan Paul).

Miller, D. L. (1973) *George Herbert Mead: self, language and the world* (University of Texas Press).

Mills, C. W. (1959) *The Sociological Imagination* (Oxford University Press).

Musgrove, F. (1980) *School and the Social Order* (John Wiley).

Nichols, T. (ed.) (1980) *Capital and Labour. A Marxist Primer* (Fontana).

Nisbet, R. A. (1967) *The Sociological Tradition* (Heinemann Educational Books).

O'Keeffe, D. (forthcoming) *The Sociology of Human Capital* (Routledge & Kegan Paul).

Phillips, D. L. (1973) *Abandoning Method* (Jossey-Bass).

Phillips, D. L. (1977) *Wittgenstein and Scientific Knowledge* (Macmillan).

Piaget, J. (1971) *Structuralism* (Routledge & Kegan Paul).

Pivcevic, E. (1970) *Husserl and Phenomenology* (Hutchinson).

Psathas, G. (ed.) (1973) *Phenomenological Sociology: issues and applications* (John Wiley).

Raison, T. (ed.) (1979) *The Founding Fathers of Social Science* (Scolar Press).

Reid, I. (1978) *Sociological Perspectives on School and Education* (Open Books).

Rex, J. (ed.) (1974) *Approaches to Sociology* (Routledge & Kegan Paul).

Robey, D. (ed.) (1973) *Structuralism: an introduction* (Clarendon Press).

Robinson, P. (1981) *Sociological Perspectives on Education* (Routledge & Kegan Paul).

Roche, M. (1973) *Phenomenology, Language and the Social Sciences* (Routledge & Kegan Paul).

Rocher, G. (1974) *Talcott Parsons and American Sociology* (Nelson).

Runciman, W. G. (1963) *Social Science and Political Theory* (Cambridge University Press).

Ryan, A. (1970) *The Philosophy of the Social Sciences* (Macmillan).

Sarup, M. (1978) *Marxism and Education* (Routledge & Kegan Paul).

Scott, J. P. (1978) 'Critical social theory: an introduction and critique', *British Journal of Sociology*, **29**, 1, pp. 1–21.

Sexton, P. C. (ed.) (1967a) *Readings on the School in Society* (Prentice-Hall).

Sexton, P. C. (1967b) *The American School: a sociological analysis* (Prentice-Hall).

Sharp, R. (1980) *Knowledge, Ideology and the Politics of Schooling: towards a Marxist analysis of education* (Routledge & Kegan Paul).

Sharp, R. and Green, A.G. (1975) *Social Control and Education* (Routledge & Kegan Paul).

Shipman, M. D. (1972) *The Limitations of Social Research* (Longman).

Skidmore, W. (1979) *Theoretical Thinking in Sociology* (Cambridge University Press).

Slater, P. (1977) *Origin and Significance of the Frankfurt School* (Routledge & Kegan Paul).

Smart, B. (1976) *Sociology, Phenomenology and Marxist Analysis* (Routledge & Kegan Paul).

Smith, M. (1980) 'The evaluation of curricular priorities in secondary schools: regulations, opinions and school practices in England, 1903–4', *British Journal of the Sociology of Education*, **1**, 2, pp. 153–72.

Stub, H. R. (ed.) (1975) *The Sociology of Education: a source book* (Dorsey).

Swift, D. F. (1969) *The Sociology of Education* (Routledge & Kegan Paul).

Taylor, J. G. (1979) *From Modernization to Modes of Production* (Macmillan).

Thompson, K. and Tunstall, J. (eds.) (1971) *Sociological Perspectives* (Penguin).

Turner, J. H. and Maryanski, A. (1979) *Functionalism* (Benjamin/Cummings).

Turner, R. (ed.) (1974) *Ethnomethodology* (Penguin).

Walker, A. (1978) *Marx: his theory and its context* (Longman).

Walton, P. and Gamble, A. (1972) *From Alienation to Surplus Value* (Sheed & Ward).

Wells, A. (ed.) (1978) *Contemporary Sociological Theories* (Goodyear).

Westergaard, J., Weyman, A. and Wiles, P. (1977) *Modern British Society — a bibliography* (Frances Pinter).

Wexler, P. (1976) *The Sociology of Education: Beyond Equality* (Bobbs Merrill).

Whitty, G. and Young, M. (eds.) (1976) *Explorations in the Politics of School Knowledge* (Nafferton).

Willis, P. (1977) *Learning to Labour: How Working Class Kids Get Working Class Jobs* (Saxon House).

Wilson, T. P. (1971) 'Normative and interpretive paradigms in sociology', in J. D. Douglas (ed.) (1971) op. cit.

Winch, P. (1958) *The Idea of a Social Science* (Routledge & Kegan Paul).

Woods, P. (ed.) (1980a) *Pupil Strategies: Explorations in the Sociology of the School* (Croom Helm).

Woods, P. (ed.) (1980b) *Teacher Strategies: Exploration in the Sociology of the School* (Croom Helm).

Worsley, P. *et al.* (eds.) (1977) *Introducing Sociology* (Penguin).

Worsley, P. *et al*. (eds.) (1978a) *Modern Sociology* (Penguin).
Worsley, P. *et al*. (eds.) (1978b) *Problems of Modern Society* (Penguin).
Yinger, J. M. (1965) *Toward a Field Theory of Behaviour* (McGraw Hill).
Young, M. F. D. (ed.) (1971) *Knowledge and Control: new directions for the sociology of education* (Collier-Macmillan).
Zetterberg, H. L. (1966) *On Theory and Verification in Sociology* (Bedminster Press).

3   Historical studies and the sociology of education
W. E. Marsden

There are at least three respects in which links have been established between the history and the sociology of education:

1. where sociologists have used the past as a kind of resource base or laboratory from which to draw lessons or conclusions, or support (or even refute) theories, seen as of relevance to current educational debates;
2. where sociologists have applied their theories and concepts to the educational past as a means of more scientific explanation of that past;
3. where historians have applied sociological theories and concepts as a means of refining their own understanding of the educational past.

The first part of this survey relates to (1), discussing briefly the contributions historical understandings and materials pertaining to education might make to current study. The second part relates to (2) and (3), though no consistent attempt is made to determine whether the contributions cited are those of historians or sociologists. The third part identifies 'centres of interest' which have increasingly attracted the attention of historians and sociologists of education.

Three further introductory points need to be made. The first is that each area of sociological study represented in this text, such as the sociology of language, has a historical context. But few of these areas can be covered in this highly selective survey. Any such survey must reflect a personal, and possibly unbalanced, view of the field. Others would, for example, lay less stress than here on notions of 'grassroots' study, striving to recreate the experience of people living and being schooled in the past. This would, however, seem to be the sort of area in which links between history and social science are especially close. Secondly, the survey is confined to literature pertaining to the 19th and 20th centuries, during which period 'universal, compulsory and free' elementary and then secondary education evolved, in response to the demands of an increasingly industrialised and urbanised economy. The accompanying social revolution also promoted the development of sociology as a discipline, attempting to make sense of the new social interactions and dislocations that were engendered. Thirdly, reference here to 'historians' and 'sociologists' is usually an attenuation of convenience for 'historians of education' and 'sociologists of education'.

The contributions of history

Each field of educational study carries with it a historical perspective. It would seem essential to a rounded understanding of our particular 'culture' that we place education and its social and political linkages in this temporal perspective, and not as occurrences which have recently and suddenly sprung into being. In a general sense, there is little in the spheres of human institutions and interactions that is new. In education today, as in past periods, forces of progress and reaction, conflicting political ideologies and social values, and economic and administrative constraints, impinge. Present issues are often paralleled, though not exactly, in the past, which provides a body of knowledge which potentially can contribute towards a more critical awareness of the present. It may also be argued that involvement in happenings at several stages removed in time can lead to a helpful detachment from thorny issues. The fact that contemporary educational problems can be personally charged (by our own children coming up to school age, for example) can readily result in something more than academic role-conflicts, and in polarised and emotive responses. A historical understanding might help to encourage 'spectrum thinking': an awareness of different colourings, or of various 'shades of grey'. Additionally, and perhaps provocatively, it might be suggested that historical understanding can promote a more humble and constructively sceptical counterpoint to the over-enthusiastic espousal of new trends, and an ability to accommodate the notion that progress, where it exists, is normally slow progress. It can also, of course, induce conservative, reactionary, and even cynical attitudes to change.

Historical methodology is also important. Primacy is given to the meticulous and comprehensive collection and verification of evidence, as part of an inductive approach to generalisation. The historian is in a sense a conservationist, concerned for comprehensive, idiomatic and empathetic resource use, protective of his 'environment' from the depredations of temporally and possibly structurally alien academic constructs. The capacity to sort out and enjoy the detail of events is an appropriate counter to the erstwhile propensity of incautious social scientists to pack these events into predetermined pigeon-holes, and impose an insulting determinism on historical actors. At the same time, it can occasion an excessive devotion to chronology and empirical detail, which in turn can be compensated by the infusion of ideas and skills from the social sciences.

Not least, the data which makes up educational history can be of compelling interest in its own right. Many new to the subject have become fascinated by contact with family or school records of linkages between education and the local community, as well as by consultation of second hand sources covering broader educational issues. These are vital components of personal cultural heritages.

In historical study, the use of *primary source materials* is a *sine qua non*. For the beginning student, Maclure's (1965) selection of educational documents is useful. For a more in-depth approach, Vaughan and Argles (1969) and Argles (1971) cover British government publications concerning education. The publication of British Parliamentary Papers on education by Irish Universities Press has been of crucial importance. The reports of the great 19th century commissions, and of the unique 1851 Education Census, are also published in this series. Their reliability as sources, and nature as ideological statements, are appraised by Johnson (1977) and Sutherland (1977). The equally valuable Minutes and Reports of the Committee of Council on Education are available in, among other places, some department of education libraries (see Higson, 1967 and 1976).

Secondary sources are important, however, especially where the priority lies in acquiring an overview of the development of English education. Here the most lively accounts remain those of Armytage (1964) and Lawson and Silver (1973). Standard introductions to popular education include those of Lowndes (1937), Sturt (1967), Eaglesham (1967), Wardle (1971), Selleck (1968 and 1972) and Hurt (1971 and 1979a). The public school sector has been well served by Bamford (1967), Simon and Bradley (1975) and Honey (1977). The emergence of different types of secondary system in this century has been traced by Banks (1955) and Rubinstein and Simon (1973), and a selection for such education by Gordon (1980). A grasp of the relations between church and state is prerequisite to an understanding of 19th century provision, and here the authorities are Cruickshank (1963), Murphy (1971) and, for the Sunday School movement, Laqueur (1976).

The growth of educational administration under increasing state involvement is covered by Gosden (1966) and Bishop (1971), while West (1975) has offered a thought-provoking but doubtfully valid case against such intervention. Simon's trilogy (1960/1974a; 1965 and 1974b), tracing the relationship between education and the labour movement, spans the years 1780–1940, while Bernbaum (1967) ties education to its social context in the latter part of that period. Detailed studies of educational politics and policy-making, at local and national levels, have been made by Murphy (1959), Fraser (1977) and Sutherland (1973). Parkinson (1970) and Barker (1972) document the Labour Party's involvement in education in this century, Gosden (1976) educational policy and administration in the World War II period, and Fenwick (1976) post-war secondary school reorganisation. For more detailed study, an under-used secondary source is the higher degree thesis. Gilbert and Holmes's (1979) guide to this source is indispensable.

Sociology and the history of education

Educational history in the late 1960s and 1970s has, particularly in the United States, been characterised by a lively methodological debate, largely though not entirely wrapped round the infusion of sociological methodology. In Britain, Musgrave's (1968) text, applying what he termed 'theories of the middle range' to 19th century education, was seminal, though Banks's earlier (1955) approach to the growth of secondary education had been overtly sociological. Musgrave again (1970), Turner (1969) and Bernbaum (1971) fuelled the 1970s discussions, renewed in a recent review essay (Warwick and Williams 1980). The initial response of historians of education was not always enthusiastic (see Charlton 1971). One historical reviewer conditionally thanked Musgrave for his reader, *Sociology, History and Education* (1970), for attempting 'to save students from the major disease by inoculating them with a dose of live virus' (Elton 1971).

The methodological debate in Britain had been anticipated by a decade of 'revisionism' in the United States, spear-headed by Bailyn's (1960) demand for an educational history more in tune with general social and cultural history. A larger culture shock, however, was induced by Katz's (1968b and 1970) overturning of 'reformist' interpretations of American educational history. He portrayed mass education as an alienating rather than a reforming process, a view given wider publicity by the appearance of Bowles and Gintis's (1976) influential study. Such 'radical revisionism' was quickly attacked on the grounds that current social concerns rather than historical actuality were dictating the selection of content (see, for example, Ravitch 1977). The emergence of a synthesis, combining the *brio* and conviction of the radical revisionists, with an appreciation of the nuances and ambiguities of educational development, has been documented by Cohen (1973, 1976 and 1977), and in Kaestle (1978) and Warren (1978).

In this country, Bailyn-type pleas surfaced in articles by Simon (1966), Sutherland (1969) and Briggs (1972). The extremes of the American debate have perhaps been avoided though there has been an increase in methodological discussion, as articles by Webster (1976), Silver (1977a and b), Joan Simon (1977), and Marsden (1977c) testify.

An academic growth industry in recent years has been the application by sociologists and historians of social science theories and concepts in the historical context. Some of these can be tabulated:

1. *social conflict* theory, applied by Vaughan and Archer (1971) and Smith (1977) in comparative studies of Britain with France and North America respectively;
2. *social control*, a broad concept pioneered in this context by Johnson (1970 and 1976) in relation to the development of mass education in the early 19th century; also used by Shapin and Barnes (1977) with reference to the scientific education of artisans; by Laqueur (1976) in relation to Sunday schools; by Shapin and Barnes (1976) and Vallance (1973–4) *vis-à-vis* 19th century elementary education; and discussed by Musgrove(1979) and Silver (1980) in critical appraisals of the current educational condition;
3. *socialisation*, as applied to popular education is the theme of a set of readings edited by McCann (1977), and is also found, at least implicitly, in a number of studies of the elite sector, by Mangan (1975) on the cult of games, Hearl (1976) on military education, Ong (1959) and Campbell (1968) on the function of the classics and by Wilkinson (1963) and Bishop and Wilkinson (1967) on the development and maintenance of a political elite;
4. *bureaucratisation*, found in studies by Musgrove (1971) of the British case, and notably by Katz (1968a, 1971 and 1976a) in the American, and in another trans-Atlantic comparison by Smith (1976);
5. *ideology*, as conceptualised in Raynor and Grant's (1972) historical perspective on 'patterns of curriculum';
6. additionally, Tyack (1976) has taken a more eclectic and pluralist approach in applying a complementary range of social science concepts to the development of compulsory schooling in the United States. This, though used for a different purpose, can also be found in Musgrove (1979).

There are clearly omissions here, including social classification, reproduction and deficit theories; and concepts such as hegemony, sponsored and contest mobility, and educational inequality and opportunity. It is important that such terms, prior to historical application, should be more carefully defined than they have often been hitherto.

Specific centres of interest

1. The history of the curriculum

An increasingly popular study, the history of the curriculum is a topic perhaps best pursued in an inter-disciplinary framework. It may be significant that the pivotal general text in this area, by Gordon and Lawton (1978), is the combined effort of an historian and sociologist. Apart from this, Gordon (1977) and Bramwell (1961 and 1964) have explored the forces impinging on curriculum change in the elementary school. Though there is not space here to deal with specific subject areas (for a bibliography see Marsden (1979b)), Layton's (1973) study of the origins of the contemporary school science curriculum sets a standard for others to follow.

The essentially competitive ethos of higher level elementary and of secondary education is highlighted in Morris's (1961), Roach's (1970) and Hoskin's (1979) varied studies of the emergence of the modern examinations system, while Simon (1970) has surveyed the evolution of classification and streaming in English schools over a 100-year span: all testimony to the change from a 'sponsored' to a 'contest mobility' situation which it was hoped the system would promote.

The studies of Dyhouse (1976 and 1977), Burstyn (1977), Pederson (1979), and essays in Delamont and Duffin (1978) illustrate the breadth of interest which has emerged in the development of distinctive curricula for girls in the 19th century.

For the post-war period, Gordon (1979) and the Helburns (1979) have surveyed the major forces affecting curriculum change in this country and the United States respectively. Here again, lack of space makes it impossible to document the material available on specific areas of recent curriculum development.

2. Urban education

Previous neglect of the study of the history of urban education has increasingly been redressed in the 1970s. This has particularly been the case in the United States, where important accounts of education in urban society have been written by Lazerson (1971), Kaestle (1973), Schultz (1973), Ravitch (1974), Tyack (1974), and Troen (1975), while Kaestle and Vinovskis's account of Massachusetts (1980) has a strong urban component. In this country we are well behind, though new ground has been broken in Reeder's (1977) collection of readings on 19th century urban education.

3. 'Grassroots' studies

Much attention has been paid to urban schooling, however, in the attempt to recreate the experience of scholars and their parents and teachers in the 19th century context. This elusive field depends on the continuing existence of relevant records, such as census enumerators' returns and school admission registers, giving the possibility of detailed linkages between school and community.

North America is fortunate in the greater richness of the resource base which has survived, on which have been built sophisticated quantitative studies, such as Katz's work (1976b) on Hamilton, Ontario. Effective use of attendance data has been made by Bamman (1972), Katz (1972) and Katz and Davey (1978). Clifford (1978) has eschewed quantification in her exploration of 'personal history' reports, but with the same object of establishing detailed home–school linkages, and while Kaestle and Vinovskis's study (1980) is largely based on statistical processing, it accepts the need to complement this by a qualitative approach.

The more limited availability of detailed aggregate records in Britain has hampered though not prevented similar studies. Bamford (1965), Coleman (1972), Marsden (1977a and 1979a), Goldstrom (1978), Dixon (1979) and Crompton (1979) have explored in various ways the potential for educational research in the 1851 Education Census, and in the census enumerators' books of 1851, 1861 and 1871.

These and other studies, have, perhaps hazardously, used level of attendance as a surrogate for parental attitudes towards schooling. An early example of such work is Rubinstein's (1969) monograph on London attendance during the School Board era. At the institutional level, the Silvers (1974), Madoc-Jones (1977) and Scudamore (1979) have successfully explored some unusually well-preserved 19th century school records. Fascinating accounts of schooling and community in slum environments have been provided by Parsons (1978), pioneering the use of oral evidence, and Roberts (1976), making the most of his personal experience.

4. Regional variations

As today, regional variations in educational provision were potent causes of disparities in educational opportunity. Stephens's monograph (1973) on regional variations in provision was a timely reminder of the previous neglect of this factor. An important focus of study has been the regional variation of literacy levels, in papers by Stone (1969), Sanderson (1972) and Stephens (1977), among others.

Though the intent behind the 1870 Education Act was to fill in gaps in provision through the establishment of rate-aided school boards, the potential for local manoeuvre in a decentralised system is apparent in studies by Nelson (1977), Spence (1978), Marsden (1977b and 1978), Hurt (1979b) and Rimmington (1977) of the idiosyncrasies of local decision-making in differing geographical settings.

5. *Teachers, managers and inspectors*

It must be said that there is precious little documentation of the interaction among these 'providing' parties in educational development, or between them and the recipients. It must be sufficient here to allude to more general studies, such as Tropp's well-known surveys of the status of the school-teacher (1953 and 1957); Gosden's (1972) and the Horns' (1979) work on the growth of the teaching associations; Bamford's (1973) and Pederson's (1975) respectively on public schoolmasters and private schoolmistresses; Gordon's (1974) on Victorian school managers; and Ball's (1965) on the formative years of the inspectorate.

6. *Childhood and youth*

The rigid boundary definitions once maintained between the study of children and young people in school, and of childhood and youth in general, are now breaking down. More interest is being taken in the informal agencies of education (see Dent, 1979). Horn (1974) has described the experience of the Victorian country child, but fuller attention has been concentrated on the discontents of urban youth, as part of the increased interest in the impact of social Darwinism on educational thinking, broadly defined, and society in the late 19th century. This has been manifest in work by Armytage (1970), Sutherland (1972), Dyhouse (1976), Reeder (1977), Lowe (1979), and in Springhall's (1977) ground-breaking study of the emergence of certain British youth movements.

In North America, Kett (1971–2) has investigated aspects of adolescence and youth; Gaffield and Levine (1978) and Cremin (1978) links between family, schooling and community, the former in a specific locale, the latter more generally; while May (1973), Gillis (1975), Houston (1972) and Schlossman (1978) have devoted their attention to studies of juvenile delinquency, in England, Canada and the United States respectively. Street-corner youth has been not the least of the centres of interest of sociologists of education and sociologists in general as this century has progressed, and now the historian is bringing his skills to bear on the discussion.

Conclusion

At this stage the impact of the convergence of interest of sociologists and historians of education is hard to assess. While many historians of education remain likely to react negatively to any hint of colonisation by social scientists, it is significant that in the foregoing sections the names of writers belonging to both groups appear. The guardians of academic identity are prone to conduct their disputes in theoretical discourse, while in practice many are opportunistic and eclectic. The consecration of compartmentalised intellectual 'views' can be diversionary, savouring of defensive academic ritual, or even of attitudinal rigidity. There has been a healthy shift from both 'desert empiricism' and 'grandiose generalisation', by which labels historical and social scientific thought have respectively been stereotyped. Whether or not the changes have resulted in higher levels of scholarship than hitherto is an open question. They have certainly led to different types of scholarship, and made for some the history of education a livelier arena in which to work, opening up broader approaches to the study of the linkages between education and society in the past.

References

Argles, M. (1971) *British Government Publications in Education during the Nineteenth Century* (History of Education Society: Guides to Sources in the History of Education, no. 1).

Armytage, W. H. G. (1964) *Four Hundred Years of English Education* (Cambridge University Press).

Armytage, W. H. G. (1970) 'Battles for the best: some educational aspects of the welfare-warfare state in England', in P. Nash (ed.) *History and Education: the educational uses of the past* (Random House) pp. 283–307.

Bailyn, B. (1960) *Education in the Forming of American Society* (University of North Carolina Press).

Ball, N. (1965) *Her Majesty's Inspectorate, 1839–49* (Oliver and Boyd /University of Birmingham Institute of Education).

Bamford, T. W. (1965) *The Evolution of Rural Education, 1850—1964* (University of Hull).

Bamford, T. W. (1967) *The Rise of the Public Schools* (Nelson).

Bamford, T. W. (1973) 'Public school masters: a nineteenth century profession', in T. G. Cook (ed.) *Education and the Professions* (Methuen for History of Education Society) pp. 29–47.

Bamman, H. P. (1972) 'Patterns of school attendance in Toronto,

1844–1878: some spatial considerations', *History of Education Quarterly*, **12**, 3, pp. 381–410.

Banks, O. (1955) *Parity and Prestige in English Secondary Education* (Routledge & Kegan Paul).

Barker, R. (1972) *Education and Politics 1900–1951. A study of the Labour Party* (Oxford University Press).

Bernbaum, G. (1967) *Social Change and the Schools, 1918–1944* (Routledge & Kegan Paul).

Bernbaum, G. (1971) 'Sociological techniques and historical study', in History of Education Society (ed.) *History, Sociology and Education* (Methuen) pp. 1–22.

Bishop, A. S. (1971) *The Rise of a Central Authority for English Education* (Cambridge University Press).

Bishop, T. J. H. and Wilkinson, R. (1967) *Winchester and the Public School Elite* (Faber).

Bowles, S. and Gintis, H. (1976) *Schooling in Capitalist America: educational reform and the contradictions of economic life* (Routledge & Kegan Paul).

Bramwell, R. D. (1961) *Elementary School Work 1900–25* (University of Durham Institute of Education).

Bramwell, R. D. (1964) 'Forces of curricular change with special reference to English education', *Paedagogica Historica*, **4**, pp. 312–25.

Briggs, A. (1972) 'The study of the history of education', *History of Education*, **1**, 1, pp. 5–22.

Burstyn, J. (1977) 'Women's education in England during the nineteenth century: a review of the literature 1970–1976', *History of Education*, **6**, 1, pp. 11–20.

Campbell, F. (1968) 'Latin and the elite tradition in education', *British Journal of Sociology*, **19**, 3, pp. 308–25. Reprinted in P. W. Musgrave (ed.) (1970) *Sociology, History and Education: a reader* (Methuen) pp. 249–64.

Charlton, K. (1971) 'History and sociology: afterthoughts and prior questions', in History of Education Society (ed.) (1971) *History, Sociology and Education* (Methuen) pp. 49–59.

Clifford, C. J. (1978) 'History as experience: the uses of personal history documents in the history of education', *History of Education*, **7**, 3, pp. 183–96.

Cohen, S. (1973) 'New perspectives in the history of American education 1960–1970', *History of Education*, **2**, 1, pp. 79–96.

Cohen, S. (1976) 'The history of the history of American education 1900–1976: the uses of the past', *Harvard Educational Review*, **46**, 3, pp. 303–8.

Cohen, S. (1977) 'The history of urban education in the United States: historians of education and their discontents', in D. A. Reeder (ed.) *Urban Education in the Nineteenth Century* (Taylor & Francis), pp. 115–32.

Coleman, B. I. (1972) 'The incidence of education in mid-century', in E. A. Wrigley (ed.) *Nineteenth-Century Society: essays in the use of quantitative methods for the study of social data* (Cambridge University Press) pp. 397–410.

Cremin, L. A. (1978) 'Family-community linkages in American education: some comments on the recent historiography', *Teachers College*

Record, **79**, 4, pp. 683–704.

Crompton, F. G. (1979) 'Occupational mobility and elementary education in nineteenth century Northamptonshire', in R. Lowe (ed.) *New Approaches to the Study of Popular Education, 1851–1902* (History of Education Society Occasional Publication no. 4) pp. 59–67.

Cruickshank, M. (1963) *Church and State in English Education* (Macmillan).

Delamont, S. and Duffin, L. (eds.) (1978) *The Nineteenth-Century Woman: her cultural and physical world* (Croom Helm).

Dent, K. S. (ed.) (1979) *Informal Agencies of Education* (History of Education Society).

Dixon, P. J. (1979) 'School attendance in Preston: some socio-economic influences', in R. Lowe (ed.) *New Approaches to the Study of Popular Education, 1851–1902* (History of Education Society Occasional Publication no. 4) pp. 43–58.

Dyhouse, C. (1976) 'Social Darwinistic ideas and the development of women's education in England', *History of Education*, **5**, 1, pp. 41–58.

Dyhouse, C. (1977) 'Good wives and little mothers: social anxieties and the schoolgirls' curriculum, 1890–1920', *Oxford Review of Education*, **3**, 1, pp. 21–35.

Eaglesham, E. J. R. (1967) *The Foundations of Twentieth Century Education in England* (Routledge & Kegan Paul).

Elton, G. R. (1971) 'Review of Musgrave, P. W. (ed.) *Sociology, History and Education: a reader*', *Journal of Educational Administration and History*, **3**, 2, pp. 62–3.

Fenwick, I. G. K. (1976) *The Comprehensive School, 1944–1970: the politics of secondary school re-organization* (Methuen).

Fraser, D. (1977) 'Education and urban politics c. 1832–1885', in D. A. Reeder (ed.) *Urban Education in the Nineteenth Century* (Taylor & Francis) pp. 11–26.

Gaffield, C. and Levine, D. (1978) 'Dependency and adolescence on the Canadian Frontier: Orilla, Ontario in the mid-nineteenth century', *History of Education Quarterly*, **18**, 1, pp. 35–47.

Gilbert, V. F. and Holmes, C. (1979) *Theses and Dissertations on the History of Education presented at British and Irish Universities between 1900 and 1976* (History of Education Society Guide to Sources in the History of Education, no. 6).

Gillis, J. (1975) 'The evolution of juvenile delinquency in England, 1880–1914', *Past and Present*, **67**, pp. 96–126.

Goldstrom, J. M. (1978) 'Education in England and Wales in 1851: the Education Census of Great Britain, 1851', in R. Lawton (ed.) *The Census of Social Structure: an interpretative guide to nineteenth century censuses for England and Wales* (Frank Cass) pp. 224–40.

Gordon, P. (1974) *The Victorian School Manager: a study in the management of education 1800–1902* (Woburn Press).

Gordon, P. (1977) 'Commitments and developments in the elementary school curriculum 1870–1907', *History of Education*, **6**, 1, pp. 43–52.

Gordon, P. (1979) ' "A unity of purpose": some reflections on the school curriculum, 1945–70', in W. E. Marsden (ed.) *Post-war Curriculum Development: an historical appraisal* (History of Education Society) pp. 1–8.

Gordon, P. (1980) *Selection for Secondary Education* (Woburn Press).

Gordon, P. and Lawton, D. (1978) *Curriculum Change in the Nineteenth and Twentieth Centuries* (Hodder and Stoughton).

Gosden, P. H. J. H. (1966) *The Development of Educational Administration in England and Wales* (Blackwell).

Gosden, P. H. J. H. (1972) *The Evolution of a Profession: a study of the contribution of teachers' associations to the development of school teaching as a professional occupation* (Blackwell).

Gosden, P. H. J. H. (1976) *Education in the Second World War: a study in policy and administration* (Methuen).

Hearl, T. W. (1976) 'Military education and the school curriculum 1800–1870', *History of Education*, **5**, 3, pp. 251–64.

Helburn, N. and Helburn, S. (1979) 'Stability and reform in recent American curriculum', in W. E. Marsden (ed.) *Post-war Curriculum Development: an historical appraisal* (History of Education Society) pp. 29–48.

Higson, C. W. J. (1967 and 1976) *Sources for the History of Education (+ Supplement)* (The Library Association).

Honey, J. R. de S. (1977) *Tom Brown's Universe: the development of the public school in the nineteenth century* (Millington Books).

Horn, C. A. and Horn, P. L. R. (1979) 'Aspects of the development of teacher trade unionism in Britain: 1860–1914', *Journal of Further and Higher Education*, **3**, 2, pp. 3–10.

Horn, P. (1974) *The Victorian Country Child* (Roundwood Press).

Hoskin, K. (1979) 'The examination, disciplinary power and rational schooling', *History of Education*, **8**, 2, pp. 135–46.

Houston, S. E. (1972) 'Victorian origins of juvenile delinquency: a Canadian experience', *History of Education Quarterly*, **12**, 3, pp. 254–80.

Hurt, J. (1971) *Education in Evolution: church, state, society and popular education 1800–1870* (Rupert Hart-Davis).

Hurt, J. (1979a) *Elementary Schooling and the Working Classes 1860–1918* (Routledge & Kegan Paul).

Hurt, J. S. (1979b) 'Board school or voluntary school: some determinants', in R. Lowe (ed.) *New Approaches to the Study of Popular Education, 1851–1902* (History of Education Society Occasional Publication no. 4) pp. 2–15.

Johnson, R. (1970) 'Educational policy and social control in early Victorian England', *Past and Present*, **49**, pp. 96–119.

Johnson, R. (1976) 'Notes on the schooling of the English working class 1780–1850', in R. Dale, G. Esland and M. MacDonald (eds.) *Schooling and Capitalism: a sociological reader* (Routledge & Kegan Paul and Open University Press) pp. 44–54.

Johnson, R. (1977) 'Elementary education: the education of the poorer classes', in P. Ford and G. Ford (eds.) *Government and Society in Nineteenth Century Britain: commentaries on British parliamentary papers: education* (Irish University Press) pp. 5–67.

Kaestle, C. F. (1973) *The Evolution of an Urban School System: New York city, 1750–1850* (Harvard University Press).

Kaestle, C. F. (guest ed.) (1978) 'Education and American society: new historical interpretations', *History of Education*, **7**, 3, pp. 167–244 (whole issue).

Kaestle, C. F. and Vinovskis, M. A. (1980) *Education and Social Change in*

Nineteenth-Century Massachusetts (Cambridge University Press).

Katz, M. B. (1968a) 'The emergence of bureaucracy in urban education: the Boston case, 1850–1884', *History of Education Quarterly*, **8**, pp. 155–88; 319–57.

Katz, M. B. (1968b) *The Irony of Early School Reform: educational innovation in mid-nineteenth century Massachusetts* (Harvard University Press).

Katz, M. B. (1970) 'Education and social development in the nineteenth century: new directions for inquiry', in P. Nash (ed.) *History and Education: the educational uses of the past* (Random House) pp. 83–114.

Katz, M. B. (1971) *Class, Bureaucracy and Schools: the illusion of educational change in America* (F.A. Praeger).

Katz, M. B. (1972) 'Who went to school?', *History of Education Quarterly*, **12**, 3, pp. 432–54.

Katz, M. B. (1976a) 'The origins of public education: a reassessment', *History of Education Quarterly*, **16**, 4, pp. 381–407.

Katz, M. B. (1976b) *The People of Hamilton Canada West: family and class in a mid-nineteenth century city* (Harvard University Press).

Katz, M. B. and Davey, I. E. (1978) 'School attendance and early industrialization in a Canadian city: a multivariate analysis', *History of Education Quarterly*, **18**, 3, pp. 271–93.

Kett, J. H. (1971–2) 'Adolescence and youth in nineteenth century America', *Journal of Interdisciplinary History*, **2**, 2, pp. 283–98.

Laqueur, T. W. (1976) *Religion and Respectability: Sunday schools and working class culture 1780—1850* (Yale University Press).

Lawson, J. and Silver, H. (1973) *A Social History of Education in England* (Methuen).

Layton, D. (1973) *Science for the People: the origins of the school science curriculum in England* (Allen & Unwin).

Lazerson, M. (1971) *Origins of the Urban School: public education in Massachusetts, 1870–1915* (Harvard University Press).

Lowe, R. (1979) 'Eugenicists, doctors and the quest for national efficiency: an educational crusade, 1900–1939', *History of Education*, **8**, 4, pp. 293–306.

Lowndes, G. A. N. (1937) *The Silent Social Revolution: the expansion of public education in England and Wales 1895–1935* (Oxford University Press).

McCann, P. (1977) 'Popular education, socialization and social control: Spitalfields 1812–1824', in P. McCann (ed.) *Popular Education and Socialization in the Nineteenth Century* (Methuen) pp. 1–40.

Maclure, J. S. (ed.) (1965) *Educational Documents: England and Wales, 1816–1963* (Methuen).

Madoc-Jones, B. (1977) 'Patterns of attendance and their social significance: Mitcham National School 1830–1839', in P. McCann (ed.) *Popular Education and Socialization in the Nineteenth Century* (Methuen) pp. 41–66.

Mangan, J. A. (1975) 'Play up and play the game: Victorian and Edwardian public school vocabularies of motive', *British Journal of Educational Studies*, **23**, pp. 243–35.

Marsden, W. E. (1977a) 'Social environment, school attendance and educational achievement in a Merseyside town, 1870–1900', in P. McCann (ed.) *Popular Education and Socialization in the Nineteenth Century* (Methuen) pp. 193–230.

Marsden, W. E. (1977b) 'Education and the social geography of nineteenth century towns and cities', in D. A. Reeder (ed.) *Urban Education in the Nineteenth Century* (Taylor & Francis) pp. 49–73.

Marsden, W. E. (1977c) 'Historical geography and the history of education', *History of Education*, **6**, 1, pp. 21–42.

Marsden, W. E. (1978) 'Variations in educational provision in Lancashire during the school board period', *Journal of Educational Administration and History*, **10**, 2, pp. 15–30.

Marsden, W. E. (1979a) 'Census enumerators' returns, schooling and social areas of the late Victorian town: a case study of Bootle', in R. Lowe (ed.) *New Approaches to the Study of Popular Education, 1851–1902* (History of Education Society Occasional Publication no. 4) pp. 16–33.

Marsden, W. E. (1979b) 'Historical approaches to curriculum study', in W. E. Marsden (ed.) *Post-war Curriculum Development: an historical appraisal* (History of Education Society) pp. 77–102.

May, M. (1973) 'Innocence and experience: the evolution of the concept of juvenile delinquency in the mid-nineteenth century', *Victorian Studies*, **17**, pp. 7–29.

Morris, N. (1961) 'An historian's view of examinations', in S. Wiseman (ed.) *Examinations and English Education* (Manchester University Press) pp. 1–43.

Murphy, J. (1959) *The Religious Problem in English Education: the crucial experiment* (Liverpool University Press).

Murphy, J. (1971) *Church, State and Schools in Britain, 1800–1970* (Routledge & Kegan Paul).

Musgrave, P. W. (1968) *Society and Education in England since 1800* (Methuen).

Musgrave, P. W. (1970) 'A model for the analysis of the development of the English educational system from 1860', *Transactions 6th World Congress of Sociology*, **4**, pp. 65–82. Reprinted in P. W. Musgrave (ed.) *Sociology, History and Education: a reader* (1970) (Methuen) pp. 15–29.

Musgrove, F. (1971) 'Historical materials for the study of the bureaucratization of education', in History of Education Society (1971) *History, Sociology and Education* (Methuen) pp. 33–48.

Musgrove, F. (1979) *School and the Social Order* (Wiley).

Nelson, P. (1977) 'Leicester suburban school boards', *History of Education*, **6**, 1, pp. 53–63.

Ong, W. J. (1959) 'Latin language study as a renaissance puberty rite', *Studies in Philology*, **56**, 2, pp. 103–24. Reprinted in P. W. Musgrave (ed.) *Sociology, History and Education: a reader* (1970) (Methuen) pp. 232–48.

Parkinson, M. (1970) *The Labour Party and the Organisation of Secondary Education, 1918–1965* (Routledge & Kegan Paul).

Parsons, C. (1978) *Schools in an Urban Community: a study of Carbrook, 1870–1965* (Routledge & Kegan Paul).

Pederson, J. S. (1975) 'Schoolmistresses and headmistresses: elites and education in the nineteenth century', *The Journal of British Studies*, **15**, 1, pp. 135–62.

Pederson, J. S. (1979) 'The reform of women's secondary and higher education: institutional change and social values in mid and late Victorian England', *History of Education Quarterly*, **19**, 1, pp. 61–91.

Ravitch, D. (1974) *The Great School Wars: New York City 1805–1973: a history of the public schools as battlefields of social change* (Basic Books).

Ravitch, D. (1977) 'The revisionists revised: studies in the historiography of American education', *Proceedings of the National Academy of Education*, **4**, pp. 1–84.

Raynor, J. and Grant, N. (1972) 'Patterns of curriculum' units 2 and 3 *The Curriculum: Context, Design and Development* E.283 (Open University Press).

Reeder, D. A. (1977) 'Predicaments of city children: late-Victorian and Edwardian perspectives on education and urban society', in D. A. Reeder (ed.) *Urban Education in the Nineteenth Century* (Taylor & Francis) pp. 75–94.

Rimmington, G. T. (1977) 'English rural school boards 1870–1903', in History of Education Society (eds.) *Studies in the Local History of Education* (Occasional Publication no. 3) pp. 34–45.

Roach, J. (1970) *Public Examinations in England, 1850–1900* (Cambridge University Press).

Roberts, R. (1976) *A Ragged Schooling: growing up in the classic slum* (Manchester University Press).

Rubinstein, D. (1969) *School Attendance in London, 1870–1904: a social history* (University of Hull).

Rubinstein, D. and Simon, B. (1973) *The Evolution of the Comprehensive School, 1926–1966* (Routledge & Kegan Paul).

Sanderson, M. (1972) 'Literacy and social mobility in the industrial revolution in England', *Past and Present*, **56**, pp. 75–104.

Schlossman, S. (1978) 'End of innocence: science and the transformation of progressive juvenile justice, 1899–1917', *History of Education*, **7**, 3, pp. 207–18.

Schultz, K. (1973) *The Culture Factory: Boston public schools 1789–1860* (Oxford University Press).

Scudamore, C. N. J. (1979) 'The pupils of the Bridge Street school, Birmingham, 1892–3', in R. Lowe (ed.) *New Approaches to the Study of Popular Education, 1851–1902* (History of Education Society Occasional Publication no. 4) pp. 34–42.

Selleck, R. J. W. (1968) *The New Education: the English background 1870–1914* (Pitman).

Selleck, R. J. W. (1972) *English Primary Education and the Progressives 1914–39* (Routledge & Kegan Paul).

Shapin, S. and Barnes, B. (1976) 'Head and hand: rhetorical resources in British pedagogical writing', *Oxford Review of Education*, **2**, 3, pp. 231–54.

Shapin, S. and Barnes, B. (1977) 'Science, nature and control: interpreting Mechanics' Institutes'. Reprinted in R. Dale, G. Esland and M. MacDonald (eds.) *Schooling and Capitalism: a sociological reader* (Routledge & Kegan Paul and Open University Press) pp. 55–65.

Silver, H. (1977a) 'Aspects of neglect: the strange case of Victorian popular education', *Oxford Review of Education*, **3**, 1, pp. 57–69.

Silver, H. (1977b) 'Nothing but the present, or nothing but the past?', Inaugural Lecture, Chelsea College (University of London). Reprinted in *Educational Research*, **20**, 3, pp. 181–91.

Silver, H. (1980) *Education and the Social Condition* (Methuen).

Silver, P. and Silver H. (1974) *The Education of the Poor: the history of a national school 1824–1974* (Routledge & Kegan Paul).

Simon, B. (1965) *Education and the Labour Movement 1870–1920* (Lawrence & Wishart).

Simon, B. (1966) 'The history of education', in J. W. Tibble (ed.) *The Study of Education* (Routledge & Kegan Paul) pp. 91–132.

Simon, B. (1970) 'Classification and streaming: a study of grouping in English schools, 1860–1960', in P. Nash (ed.) *History and Education: the educational uses of the past* (Random House) pp. 115–59.

Simon, B. (1974a) *The Two Nations and the Educational Structure 1780–1870* (Lawrence and Wishart). First edn. (1960) entitled *Studies in the History of Education, 1780–1870*.

Simon, B. (1974b) *The Politics of Educational Reform, 1920–1940* (Lawrence & Wishart).

Simon, B. and Bradley, I. (eds.) (1975) *The Victorian Public School* (Gill & Macmillan).

Simon, J. (1977) 'The history of education in past and present', *Oxford Review of Education*, **3**, 1, pp. 71–86.

Smith, D. (1976) 'The urban genesis of school bureaucracy: a transatlantic comparison', in R. Dale, G. Esland and M. MacDonald (eds.) *Schooling and Capitalism: a sociological reader* (Routledge & Kegan Paul and Open University Press) pp. 66–77.

Smith, D. (1977) 'Social conflict and urban education in the nineteenth century: a sociological approach to comparative analysis', in D. A. Reeder (ed.) *Urban Education in the Nineteenth Century* (Taylor & Francis) pp. 95–114.

Spence, M. (1978) 'The pattern of school boards in Hampshire (1870–1902)', *History of Education Society Bulletin*, **21**, pp. 25–39.

Springhall, J. (1977) *Youth, Empire and Society: British Youth Movements, 1883–1940* (Croom Helm).

Stephens, W. B. (1973) *Regional Variations in Education during the Industrial Revolution 1780–1870: the task of the local historian* (University of Leeds Educational Administration and History Monograph no. 1).

Stephens, W. B. (1977) 'Illiteracy and schooling in the provincial towns, 1640–1870: a comparative approach', in D. A. Reeder (ed.) *Urban Education in the Nineteenth Century* (Taylor & Francis) pp. 27–48.

Stone, L. (1969) 'Literacy and education in England, 1640–1900', *Past and Present*, **42**, pp. 69–139.

Sturt, M. (1967) *The Education of the People: a history of primary education in England and Wales in the nineteenth century* (Routledge & Kegan Paul).

Sutherland, G. (1969) 'The study of the history of education', *History*, **54**, pp. 49–59.

Sutherland, G. (1973) *Policy-making in Elementary Education 1870–1895* (Oxford University Press).

Sutherland, G. (1977) 'Secondary education: the education of the middle classes', in P. Ford and G. Ford (eds.) *Government and Society in Nineteenth Century Britain: commentaries on British parliamentary papers: education* (Irish University Press) pp. 137–95.

Sutherland, N. (1972) ' "To create a strong and healthy race": school children in the public health movement 1880–1914', *History of Education Quarterly*, **12**, 3, pp. 304–33.

Troen, S. K. (1975) *The Public and the Schools: shaping the St. Louis system 1838–1920* (Missouri University Press).

Tropp, A. (1953) 'The changing status of the teacher in England and Wales', *The Yearbook of Education 1953* (Evans) pp. 147–70. Reprinted in P. W. Musgrave (ed.) *Sociology, History and Education: a reader* (1970) (Methuen) pp. 193–214.

Tropp, A. (1957) *The School Teachers: the growth of the teaching profession in England and Wales from 1800 to the present day* (Heinemann Educational Books).

Turner, C. M. (1969) 'Sociological approaches to the history of education', *British Journal of Educational Studies*, **17**, 2, pp. 146–55.

Tyack, D. B. (1974) *The One Best System: a history of American urban education* (Harvard University Press).

Tyack, D. B. (1976) 'Ways of seeing: an essay on the history of compulsory schooling', *Harvard Educational Review*, **46**, pp. 355–89. Reprinted in D. R. Warren (ed.) (1978) *History, Education and Public Policy* (McCutchan Publishing Corporation) pp. 56–89.

Vallance, E. (1973–4) 'Hiding the hidden curriculum: an interpretation of the language of justification in nineteenth century educational reform', *Curriculum Theory Network*, **4**, 1, pp. 5–21.

Vaughan, J. E. and Argles, M. (1969) *British Government Publications concerning Education: an introductory guide* (School of Education, University of Liverpool).

Vaughan, M. and Archer, M. S. (1971) *Social Conflict and Educational Change in England and France, 1789–1848* (Cambridge University Press).

Wardle, D. (1971) *English Popular Education 1780–1970* (Cambridge University Press).

Warren, D. R. (1978) 'A past for the present', in D. R. Warren (ed.) *History, Education and Public Policy* (McCutchan Publishing Company) pp. 1–20.

Warwick, D. and Williams, J. (1980) 'History and the sociology of education', *British Journal of Sociology of Education*, **1**, 3, pp. 333–46.

Webster, C. (1976) 'Changing perspectives in the history of education', *Oxford Review of Education*, **2**, 3, pp. 201–13.

West, E. G. (1975) *Education and the Industrial Revolution* (Batsford).

Wilkinson, R. H. (1963) 'The gentlemanly ideal and the maintenance of a political elite', *Sociology of Education*, **37**, 1, pp. 9–26. Reprinted in P. W. Musgrave (ed.) (1970) *Sociology, History and Education: a reader* (Methuen) pp. 126–42.

4 Literary studies and the sociology of education
Fred Inglis

This paper affirms a high degree of identity, both of method and interest, between the sociologist of education and the critic of literature. This identity is in part structural, in part progressive. Sociologist and critic alike tense themselves against the profound puzzle that men and women maintain a human community at all, maintain it so completely, so continuously, and with such variety. The sociologist of education, more precisely, attends to those universal processes of culture whereby an older generation seeks to reproduce the forms of continuity in a younger. What shall the parents tell the children about how to live well in the future? The answer to that question, if it is conservable, is to be found, among other places, in the capacious category 'literature' on the library shelves, and the critic is its official custodian. To ask what stories conserve or subvert a culture is to ask for a society's literature. The connections between criticism, education, and sociology could not be more direct – at once, as I put it, structural *and* progressive. And yet, at first sight, and in the divisions of intellectual labour, the association of modern sociology with the academic study of literature may have a merely licentious look. Within sociology itself, the numerically powerful remain, understandably enough, the hunters and gatherers of numbers. The strong tradition of that sociology which sees its business as the mapping of the inchoate enormousness of industrial society onto manageable matrices has been apt, along with historians, to use literature as so much qualitative evidence intended to help the tables of figures get up and walk. It will not of course do to suppose, as a fashion left over from the campus bazaars of 1968 has it, that a positivist social science is by definition deadly – Richard Bernstein's classic manual (1978) summarises Ernest Nagel's still unrefuted case for hard-line empiricism with great tidiness. But Richard Bernstein is more to our purposes in this terse review in his emphasis upon a form of social theory which, in seeking for valid procedures of interpretation in relation to social understanding, pushes its inquiries into the cloudy, thick substantiality of the intersubjective world we all live in. In speaking up for an interpretative human science, he joins a scattered chorus of contemporary voices, among whom the best known are probably Charles Taylor (1978), Jurgen Habermas (1975), Pierre Bourdieu (1977) and most recent and impressive, Richard Rorty (1980). These men are some of the most powerful theorists now abroad for a philosophical hermeneutics, that is to say, for a thoroughly grounded epistemology of interpretation.

This review begins from the present widespread dissatisfaction with a limitedly positivist version of sociology in order to insist from the start upon the straightforward and long-standing connections between sociology, literary theory, and literature itself. Furthermore, since British sociology (and, latterly, French and American sociology as well) has so vigorously concerned itself with education and, as this volume testifies, has produced the results of its inquiries in such profusion, it is as well to point out these connections from the start, and to see them as partly identities of interest and of forms of thought, partly as contingent though illuminating likenesses, partly as a local though historical response to particular, often political circumstances.

I shall seek to contextualise this last remark in greater detail further on in the essay. Here it is perhaps enough to recall that dissatisfaction amongst certain sociologists and political scientists with the reductive implications of head-counting empiricism led them to look specifically for an interpretative theory capable of returning to the figures on the tables the intentions, purposes, and lived practices which were remorselessly excluded by the books of numbers. They found such a theory in literary criticism and found also, in a particular school of its application, an account of how to turn such modalities of interpretation to non-literary aspects of language, and the life which is lived in that language. And this has proved opportune for human scientists at large, uniting them in a strife conventionally enforced by the divisions into different disciplines marked out between intellectual labours.

It is important not to misunderstand nor to undervalue the significance of the statistical and nomothetic inquiry which, following the parent subject, dominated the sociology of education at its inception, and gave irrefutable force to arguments about, for instance, distribution and opportunity which are central to the legitimations of a mass society. But it quickly became clear that such procedures failed entirely to gain purchase upon the nature, process, and meaning of experience itself. Literary studies were not the only available model for gaining such purchase, but they seemed a natural source of help, especially in an English intellectual landscape deeply influenced since 1920 or so by the prominence and eminence of the cultural reinterpretation initiated by teachers of literature at Cambridge. Such help was forthcoming, especially from novelists and their expositors, in restoring experience itself as a central category in the conceptual frameworks of sociology in general, and its focus on education in particular. This restoration was after a time glossed as the advent of a phenomenological version of sociology; that is to say, a version which, picking up Husserl's great meditations (1961), concentrated on redescribing as minutely as possible the conditions and movements of consciousness and experience.

At once, however, Husserl's new epigoni collided with the difficulty the master himself never resolved: how to select from the unstoppable flow of consciousness what was significant. At heart, the difficulty is aesthetic, and when the phenomenologist grapples with the aesthetic organisation of his material he glimpses the new philosophical hermeneutician moving steadily towards him until they meet in the 'third realm', or upon the ground of literary criticism.

Hermeneutics as a term originates in Aristotle (in the *Organon*) but its present chic is derived from the interpreters of scripture in the disputes of the 17th century. Its relevance here is that it offers a name to a newly revived and potentially broad church of social theorists who have commonly repudiated the doctrinaire forms of positivism in the name of a social inquiry intent upon the understanding of human action in terms of its rationality. The immediate problematic, from whichever direction the social theorists advanced, was and remains the status and validity of their particular interpretations, a problematic banally aligned along the entirely misleading subjective–objective axis. Put like this, however, the difficulty of interpretation is foolishly misconceptualised. Instead – and borrowing from Rorty (1980) – we may say that the hermeneuticians, amongst whom English literary critics since Richards (1924), Empson (1935) and Leavis (*passim*) are far and away the most theoretically developed, are seeking not for forms of a realist epistemology, but for richer, more creative and life-driving interpretations of the home-made narrative within which every man and woman must live. To determine the structure of rationality in the ensemble of texts which *is* a society in action (Geertz's (1975) way of putting it) is to recover the values and meanings which, in true *or* false consciousness, give shape to what men and women do.

To speak thus is to ask what stories may be capable of throwing an encompassing structure around given events to contain and lend them significance. Such a formulation gives literature, and indeed its preliterate versions, a very long sociological shadow indeed. It can hardly be a shadow to measure in this essay. What we can take, however, is a cue from the cognitive psychologists, amongst whom Bruner (1972) is the most famous and Richard Gregory (1974) the most vigorously hypothetical and idiosyncratic, and say that myths and their cognate but more individual sibling, fictions, are first of all the characterising creation of man's most distinctive faculty, his imagination, and secondly, that they are his essential instruments for the mapping and probing of the world. On this argument, fiction stands to experience as model to reality, and each is endlessly adjusted in the busy traffic between concept and percept in order to make sense of the inchoate surges of substance and accident, and to hold them down under the name of experience.

'Experience' is itself a curiously uncontested notion in the thought of sociologists, as it often is in the thought of literary critics. For the latter, however, although experience poses no problems of *recognition* – people are supposed to know perfectly well when they have had an experience, and even what it is they ponder over when they seek to learn from it – there is a strength in the concept for them which is drastically absent in sociology. In literary criticism, experience is typically preceded by such adjectives as 'immediate', 'personal', 'felt', 'lived'. These adjectives point, no doubt, to the rather innocent attitude to life held by some critics: a straightforward force which the individual sees approaching and then possesses in a quite uncomplicated way. Well, there are of course ignored difficulties there, concerning the unseen structures of social life, of ideology, power, and kinship, which shape our ways of seeing the world, and serve to turn raw events into whatever it is we call experience. But the adjectives 'felt', 'lived' and so forth are important for our purposes because they require the critic to theorise the way in which life, immediacy, and feeling are rendered in rhetorical language. So long as the same critic does not fall into the trap of supposing that this life can be directly decoded from the words on the page, and acknowledges what Skinner (below) teaches us of the relations between text and context, then it is clear that analysis of the rhetoric of fictions approaches the central mystery of the human sciences: how language means, and particularly how the very odd-looking linguistic devices of metaphor and metonymy enable us to interpret and organise the world.

Taking the psychologists' cue is a way of emphasising the analogy between model and narrative, and of saying that both are the products of insistently human processes. If we follow literary students onto the cultural ground of myths and fictions, we shall understand those fictions only if we see theory, however obliquely, as a number of modes of mapping the world according to the conventions available to the author's peculiar intentions (Skinner 1970, 1972a, 1972b, 1975). And once we have set those students to work on the social action making up a written text, it is easy to see that by stretching the term 'sociology' to the more generous limits implied by the phrase 'social theory', all literature may be seen as sociology.

That is to say, with Collingwood (1924) as well as Rorty, that art is the first of the sciences; or, less epigrammatically, that the literary form is the earliest and the most fundamental form of self-reflexive and self-critical thought. The old literature and the new sociology alike seek the patterns of personal and social history which are faithful to the corrugations of real life *and* make an aesthetics of that life believable and visible. The new sociology of the 19th century represents a claim to do the work of the old more rigorously, of course, and according to the deliberately critical and reforming temper which it took from Kant and, let us say, Bentham. The old social theories, politics on one hand (*Leviathan* perhaps, or *Areopagitica*) and fictions on the other (*Paradise Lost* or *King Lear*), may be presented in structurally the same form as the new: they prefigure in the clotted, dense mannerism of the early baroque the cultural meanings of the great clash of the political and religious order. So too Marx, Mill, Weber, de Tocqueville, and Durkheim, giant cliffs of the new sociology in whose shadow any present-day social theorist must write, sought to prefigure the cultural meanings of the vast economic drive towards the industrial city.

This way of putting things seeks to align all models of man along a uniform intentionality; that is, it claims that *any* organised thought takes, in essence and structure, a narrative form, and constitutes a conceptual matrix to be laid over the chaos of experience, tightened or loosened to make a more or less satisfactory fit, and switched on in order to print out a rational account of how men order and make sense of their lives in both nature and culture. Thus fictions, sociologies, and everyday gossip are all alike as potential metaphors for analogising and therefore understanding experience.

To collapse very diverse discourses into one in this way is momentarily to join a recent minority rush amongst the intellectuals towards a casual and promiscuous relativism. I will deal with the dangers of this tendency in a moment; but my brief sketch of the monolithic and monistic form of *all* disquisition upon the social life of men – *humanitas* and the humanities as we may say – has three purposes. The first is to emphasise the *meanings* (as opposed to the functions) of literature as rational accounts of experience which attempt the always difficult feat of understanding other minds and behaviours by, on the one hand, recreating them as faithfully as possible so that we know what it is like to *be* a Hamlet or an Othello, and on the other representing subjective experience just as accurately in the name of the writer's impersonal representativeness and in the hope of winning the recognition from his audience, in Dr Johnson's moving words (1781) about Gray's *Elegy in a Country Churchyard*, that although the reader has 'never seen the notions in any other place; yet he that reads them here, persuades himself that he has always felt them'.

The act of *recognising* oneself as described in terms which are at once original, familiar, and enlightening is at the heart of human narrative, and is the point of poetry. The good poet has a larger purpose, however, and one which insofar as he is a good man marks him from the poor poet and the gossip; Sir Philip Sidney (1583) in apologising for poetry and defending it against the queen of Renaissance science, history, reminded his audience at the time of a rather earlier crisis in western philosophy (Husserl 1937) and in the Humanities (Plumb 1964) than our own, that the poet

> commeth unto you with a tale which holdeth children from play and olde men from the chimney corner; and pretending no more, doth intende the winning of the mind from wickednesse to vertue . . . indeed in poetrie, which has a grate power to imitate and to render the image of things, if any man seems to produce only that which pleases, that man wanders far from the proper science.

Sidney's is only one, well-known voice from the anthologies reminding students of literature that the point of their studies is moral, and that merely to please an audience is not enough; it is his business 'to instruct' it; that is, to present his image of things in the light (Abrams 1957) of the finest life he can imagine for men and women. To do this he will need all the intelligence and sensibility and imaginative capaciousness at his command. It follows that the student of literature will want to distinguish the greatest writers in their chosen languages, and this will only sound elitist (or ideological) to sociologists committed to an epistemology which is capable of disregarding the epistemic facts of intelligence and imaginative power. It does *not* follow, as we shall see, that the student will not read lesser writers; only that judgement and discrimination are inseparable from the human sciences, behind whatever disciplinary brass plate they are practised.

This marks the second purpose of this polemic: to insist that literary studies serve to remind students that the classical aim of the politics which is a synonym for sociology is to enable human beings to live good and just lives in a political community. For a long time, such a teleological inspiration has seemed a sentimental irrelevance to the practice of a serious sociology. Assorted criticisms, most honourably from the left of politics, have joined Chomsky (1969) in the striking recrudescence of Marxism in Western thought over the past 20 years, and have pointed out that a purportedly value-free sociology[1] did its considerable bit towards keeping the liberal intellectual and his colleagues in the giant bureaucracies squarely in the seats of consultative power.

The third purpose of my long historical gesture is to recollect for readers that any social narrative is political (and therefore, no doubt, ideological), and that the efforts of literary critics to codify techniques for the interpretation of texts bring together the twin aims of the best in the new hermeneutics: to combine scientific understanding of society with a believable picture of the good and just life. The politicising of experience in the academies since 1968 should have found literary studies readier and less apathetic or abstruse than they presently are.

II

It was strictly necessary to mark the ground for that brief and passing handclasp between story-telling and social theories at the level of the common-sense culture, and between literary studies and sociology at the academic level. But in Britain at least there has been a much closer connection between the two ever since, as we may say, philosophy was displaced at Oxford and Cambridge as the centre of the human sciences.

It is always a tricky business explaining, or alleging to explain, intellectual change in terms of social ideas. There is a strong expatriate front of anti-historicists in a number of the disciplines of British human science: Namier, Gombrich, Popper, Berlin, all knights of a broken table. In a now celebrated, occasionally notorious paper, Perry Anderson (1968), editor of *New Left Review* and the most catholic and active syncretist of the neo-Marxism his journal seeks to write into British frames of mind, arraigned all such men and their henchpersons for having signally failed to provide the structure of English academic study with its organising centre. In the unutterable name of anti-Marxism, Anderson claimed, the ideologues of piecemeal social theory fought the very notion of totality, since a total social theory would call into question the comfortable privileges underpinning their genteel quietism and the cultivated fluency with which they expounded empirical techniques calculated to keep radical noses away from the larger patterns of class history. In the private lives of these intellectual suburbs, the metropolitan centre remained absent. Under the combined pressure of a man of genius, the always centripetal pull of intellectual history, and its contingently innovative and parochial status at the two most powerful universities which in the 1920s wrote everybody else's syllabus, English literature as schematised by F. R. Leavis improbably took on the crown of the human sciences, usurping 'the absent centre'. Leavis then became the focus of this discussion: the cultural meta-history he constructed from his revaluation of the map of English literature provides the most ambitious and convincing sociology to emerge from Britain in the past half-century.

Anderson's is a florid and compelling picture. It is of a piece with the rise to prominence of more or less *Marxisant* versions of cultural sociology, and it should figure directly on the reading list of anyone following through the arguments of this chapter. We may contest it as explanation: Marxists have their own reasons for placing the theory of ideology at the centre of their political problematic; the proletariat in the rich West having so signally failed to come up to historical scratch, they need a new explanation for the power of a bourgeois hegemony. Where Anderson is brilliantly accurate, however, is in identifying Leavis's version of English as the paramount discipline of a social theory in the years for which Leavis's own journal *Scrutiny* (1932–53) lasted.

The grounds of his great enterprise must have looked very different from Leavis's own desk, and look different also to those now who accept as legitimate Leavis's justifications of his work. The intellectual tradition which he wrote for himself and his collaborators was there to hand, to be reshaped as any really original thinker must reshape what he reads into the new argument capable of answering the insistent interrogation of contemporary experience. He was at work in a Cambridge which had kept up strong links with the dissenting tradition, in which the liberal utilitarian temper of Leslie Stephen and Henry Sidgwick was strong, and into which he came from stretcher-bearing as a pacifist right through the 1914–18 war to read history and English. When he arrived[2], he found Owen Chadwick anthropologising medieval literature, Mansfield Forbes as advocate of a zestful, intelligent eclecticism across many of the human sciences, A. C. Haddon conducting the business of the new school of social anthropology, and I. A. Richards teaching the moral sciences tripos. More than that, Leavis came from a war in which the dreadful incompetence of those who

started it and their most senior officers had destroyed half a generation, and in so doing had shown themselves unfit to wield authority at all. The experience focused the swirling, multiform years of
pre-war opposition to the power and possessions of a ruling class
no longer able to contain and express the headlong drives of the
new technology, nor to direct to their ends with anything like
sufficient degrees of freedom and tolerance the uneven pulsations
of capital.

For a man of Leavis's education and social formation the critical
break in authority was cultural. Given his powerful idealism (in
both the colloquial and the philosophic senses), his major intuition
was to sense (as sociologists have recently had to relearn from
Durkheim and Mauss) that culture cannot be understood as simply
material, but must also be understood as spiritual and metaphysi-
cal. Accordingly, he set himself the task of identifying life and
death in his own culture, and of providing himself with a historiography to match.

The tradition of thought was, as I emphasised, already there in
both ethos and example. Raymond Williams has picked out (1958)
for *his* special purposes one version of the line of thinkers available
for an intellectual to whom the formative examples of the best
intellectual journals were A. R. Orage's *The New Review*
(1885–1911), Ford Madox Hueffer's *The English Review* (which
published D. H. Lawrence for the first time, and lasted from
1891–1929) and, shortlived because post-war, but decisive in
Leavis's thinking, *The Calendar of Modern Letters* (1925–7). These
first two journals spoke up for an attentive, critical public for whom
– as Annan (1955) notes – intellectual practice of both a dissenting
and an accommodating kind and the exercise of political power lay
not too far apart; the last, edited by a cosmopolitan and highly
cultivated Marxist, C. H. Rickword, spoke with dignity and dedica-
tion from a position necessarily in the margins of society against the
deadly gentilities of a ruling class culture which had so completely
failed its people and *their* people. Leavis saw that he could only
capture a more defensible social position by speaking within the
walls of a major university but in terms fiercely hostile to its dead
academicism and its world-weary disregard for the vital human
resource of meaning. The task in hand was to resituate the noblest,
most energising tenets of English Romantic individualism in a
polity and a way of life over which many groups contended list-
lessly for dominance, in which, as the best new poets told him, men
were crying in the wilderness, and the great begetting image of his
civilisation was become, in Pound's words from his majestic poem,
Hugh Selwyn Mauberly (1919):

... an old bitch gone in the teeth,
... a botched civilization ...
... two gross of broken statues,
... a few thousand battered books.

To tackle such a task, Leavis took two main instruments: I. A. Richards's and William Empson's practical criticism, that is the exacting, close, responsive redescription of the most local effects of poetic and dramatic language; and the construction of a broad historiodicy into which the liturgy of a gone Christianity was rewritten as the loss of a pre-industrial paradise and the emergence into an industrial present of the best of distinctively post-Blakean men and women – independent, unafraid, apart, and – in Leavis's great phrases – 'distinguished by a vital capacity for experience, a kind of reverent openness before life, and a marked moral intensity' (Leavis 1948). These people were the novelists of the 19th century: Jane Austen, Charlotte Brontë, George Eliot, Henry James, Joseph Conrad, and supremely D. H. Lawrence and (though a later qualifier) Dickens (Leavis and Leavis 1970).

With his twin, mighty engine Leavis turned to identify the deep decline of spirit brought about by industrial culture, and to mark the greatest writers as points of resistance to that onward, headlong destructiveness. Within this at once delicate and sweeping procedure, the greatest writers provide, explicitly and implicitly, images of the best life a given history may imagine for itself, at the same time as, in negation, they provide a language for the active criticism of that life as really lived. Thus, Dickens names for what it was (and is) the coarseness and inhumanity of the utilitarianism which shaped the doctrines of production and capital – Bounderby and Merdle – in the Victorian political economy. When Leavis comes to the 20th century, he deploys Lawrence and T. S. Eliot as a double heuristic with which to interpret the dissolution of community and the godless and hapless self-assertiveness of the times. It is simply false to say that he ignores the material conditions of culture: he saw them with the responsiveness and penetration of the great artist in himself. He saw them most typically in his great study of Lawrence (1955) where he points to Lawrence's luck as a novelist in starting from the material conditions he did: the social relations of the mining community, the inextricability of rural and industrial work, the close-packed houses, the gang and butty system in the mines, the garden produce and flowers, the old and new landowners, the church and chapel. The idealising note *is* there, no doubt; but so also is the rare insistence that a man both makes *and* is made by culture, that genius *and* ordinary soul need luck to take their chances, and that sociology (and especially the sociology of education), like all the human sciences, is empty or brutal if it cannot both understand and judge, faithfully recreate the grain of the life it studies and see clearly when that life dwindles or coarsens.

Leavis, it may be said, is England's Hegel; it is only odd to sociologists that English and not sociology provided 'the absent centre', because there has always been so much written in the English mode of letters which led directly to social theory, and we may say from our own deep and justified sense of standing at the hinge of an epoch, that those writings which follow the line so brilliantly picked out by Raymond Williams in *Culture and Society* are best characterised as speaking the voice of dissent, resistance, and in the accents of a radical earnestness (see Inglis 1982).

This brief biographical sketch of Leavis's social formation is set out here with the plain intention of confuting a Western sociology which has reductively misread his work. Particularly in the sociology of education the casual research student may pick up a dozen slovenly references to Leavis's 'elitism', 'reactionary view of education', 'anti-democratic stance', to say nothing of his membership of 'a happy peasantry'. But these criticisms fall into a vulgar political Manicheism which crudely consigns all social argument either to the dark or the light, and decides upon such designation by merely referring to a list of approved and despised attitudes, and filing the adherents accordingly. They are of a piece with that dismal poverty in British sociology which leaves its practitioners helpless before the movement of politics and history; its most regular practice was born of the tranquil (and admirable) reconstruction of town and country by the Allied Nations after 1945; creating a Welfare State, they devised a functionalist sociology with which to justify and administer it (Gouldner 1972). Well, functionalism has its uses, though fewer than it supposes, but it is conceptually unable either to explain the diachronic structures of society or to understand the dialectical forms of culture; in short, it cannot write a sociology of meaning.

But education *is* the re-creation of meaning, even at its most instrumental (work is the central meaning of the labour culture). I have insisted on the context, the formation, and the telos of Leavis's work in order to offer a substantive, rather than a reviewer's or surveyor's argument. The sociology he provides gives us a way of valuing life in everyday circumstances, an ideal reality against which to test it (Blake and Dickens were solid, actual men), and a believable, congenial political trajectory against which to measure the scale of everyday language.

III

Leavis, however, was the last great liberal – the last voice, for all their differences, of the kind of class intelligence, daring, integrity and swashbuckle which spoke through R. G. Collingwood, Keynes, and Russell. Leavis's critical theory (*sic*) was tensed at a point between the individual and the community of values – the great theme of T. S. Eliot and D. H. Lawrence. As the great surges of change in the world economic and political order begin to come through, that position which it was the business of his intricate, sinewy, but strained prose to hold has become untenable. Leavis's bequest has been divided equally on Left and Right hands: the crude political categories will do, if only at first, to code the uses made of his ideas in cultural analysis as it crosses into the sociology of education. To put it simply, the Left has sought to revise his picture of the remorseless decline in cultural life by studying the small details of that life and finding a surprising resistance to the onslaughts of mass culture.

So Richard Hoggart (1957) went to the texts of Hunslet life in the 1930s and 1940s and found in its clichés and workaday saws, its close kitchens and garrulous working men's clubs, its tasty foods and dogged endurance, a decency and strength which boded well for the human heart, even as oppressed by late capitalism. He took from Leavis a language with which to honour and, above all, to *recognise* the industrial working class. His contribution to our subject is that he enabled formal educationists to cherish the felt experience – of Saturday movies and Al Read, of street games and courting patterns – with which most children come to school, and to include it as theirs, and treasure it accordingly.

Brian Jackson, working at about the same time (1961) taught the same lesson but, so to speak, in a reverse order. Following the speech and cultural sensibility of working-class boys at Huddersfield grammar school, he drew a new model of pupils' resistance to and estrangement from the patterns of an institution to which they were only expected to show gratitude; he followed this up in Hoggart's idiom by showing memorably, if partially, what it was in the community life which those boys really lived from and by (Jackson 1966).

David Holbrook (1961, 1964) coincided with Jackson and Hoggart, and similarly took his characteristic and intoxicating lead from Leavis's magazine *Scrutiny's* map of cultural decline, although bracing himself against its darkest prophecies.[3] Holbrook of all these men affected the classroom most directly; it has latterly become trivially fashionable to deride him for his undoubtedly hectic commination against contemporary culture. But Holbrook, in his best work at any rate, turned the delicacy and responsiveness of practical criticism not only upon the fatuities of popular culture, but more tellingly upon the written and spoken language of 'the rejected'. He found there a convincing and moving expression of innocence, creativeness, and *hope* working itself out in symbol and cadence which lay far outside respectable forms. Holbrook did his very considerable bit towards *recognising* all speech as human and customary, and towards re-establishing that continuity and traditionality in a language which must be continually renamed in each generation if those essences of community are to be maintained. Deny a child its speech, and you break that child's link with custom and ceremony. Holbrook's polemical assertion of this truth has done more for educational freedoms, and those freedoms as shaped by the sociological imagination, than all the busy tape recordings of the language developers. He has been in a broad sense followed, though with greater care and a less prodigal output, by the Rosens (1973), by Andrew Wilkinson (1975), by Barnes *et al.* (1971), and by James Britton (1970). Each of these authors would, I guess, vigorously disclaim kinship with Holbrook, but each takes his place in the broad mainstream of the socially conscientious progressivism which marks these neo-Leavisites. What they share is the original premise that life lives in language; what they insist on, in other words, is taking Leavis's great phrase 'the inevitable creativeness of ordinary everyday life' with absolute seriousness, and on finding the educational conditions in which that creativeness may make its expression in, as the rather dull Bullock report (1975) had it, a language for life.

All writers named began from English studies. At the very broadest, they may be allied to the large movement of thought which characterises the human sciences of the past 50 years and which identifies the problematic – that is, the structure of infinitely regressive particular problems – of understanding and interpreting human behaviour as focused by language, its many acts and texts. Language and its composition marks the elusive boundary between the idealist and materialist universes, and it cannot be surprising that in the English-speaking countries, written language, rich and diverse as those cultures provided it, was the obvious first subject-matter.

By far the most important theorist of the post-war literary critics-turned-sociologists has been and remains Raymond Williams. As this potted history recounts, he began by offering a bibliography as a tradition; as such *Culture and Society* is extremely convincing. But he went much further, via *The Long Revolution* and *Modern Tragedy* to *The Country and the City* and beyond in an effort to offer a drastic, dedicatedly anti-capitalist and still humanly valid revaluation of everything a still blandly and cruelly dominant system of elites had made of the writings they hired and sold onto the syllabuses of their juniors. Williams has said that Leavis and Marx were the two greatest influences on his intellectual life, but he has made a very different geometry out of those two planes of inquiry.

Williams has followed a rather serpentine and circuitous line of advance, not so much because, as in Anderson's imperious view, he had to 'take a detour' through the only social theory available, as that no system was at all adequate to his purposes. Certainly English Marxism in the form in which he found it – the form whose crudeness and rigidity had been so clearly arraigned by Leavis – would not do. So he set himself to the construction of his own hermeneutic for the plotting of the relations between imagination and power, letters and politics (Williams 1979).

Enough has perhaps been said of Leavis's social formation to suggest the difficulty and solitude of such an enterprise. Williams took from the books and from Cambridge what he wanted, but in bringing his own history as a border Welshman (son of a railway signalman), pre-war Welsh communist and wartime tank commander in the Guards at the age of 22, he insisted, in a way new to English studies and social theory, on the significance and presence of personal experience. His subject matter was not so much his own life, as the questions to which that life drove and drives him, representative of all he is, to seek answers of a kind absolutely unprovided for by the conventional ways of doing social theory. This is of course the usual process of revaluation, but in Williams' case it took on the striking, memorable colour and form of his special gifts and rhetoric. He interrogated the process whereby intellectual systems of production invisibly and pervasively shape the values, pieties, and sanctions which speak through the class appointed to maintain them. It was natural that an inquiry directed at the link between the shaping spirit of imagination and the intermittently brutal or discreet forces which seek to do the shaping for it in the name of the political order, should lead Williams to consider the wider network of the mass media he prefers to call 'public communications' (Williams 1974). But in all his work, whether novels or criticism, he has been moved by the great imperatives of a humanist socialism – freedom, equality, justice, brotherhood, reason, happiness.

It is however disappointingly difficult to speak of further work in the sociology of culture and education which derives from Williams's own. One may certainly speak of a few, rather solitary, disjoined books which stand visible for miles around in the flat, infertile plains of present-day English studies: Robinson (1973) and Mulhern (1979) have, from exceedingly counterposed political embrasures, restated a scrutineering view of criticism which, as in most of the tradition I have described, gives a theory of critical judgement a point of purchase on present-day education without itself claiming to be timelessly located amongst the 'free-floating intelligentsia'. Both men situate themselves on the shoulders of their predecessors and dispraise the present in the name of the imaginable best future that present may lead onto.

Such an attempt is, at its largest, the best contribution English studies can make to social theory. It can ask, in the famous phrase of its master's voice, 'what do men really live by? In what does the significance of life reside?'

> What are days for?
> Days are where we live.
> They come, they wake us
> Time and time over.
> They are to be happy in:
> Where can we live but days?
>
> Ah, solving that question
> Brings the priest and the doctor
> In their long coats
> Running over the fields.

It is now, surely, a question which also brings the critical theorist running. It is hoped that his language has deepened and learned resonance from the sane, affirmative speech which is the best literary criticism. Poole (1972, 1975) has written a magnificent and polemical primer out of his experience and his reading of Kierkegaard which will serve as a general admonition to all social methodists; in advertising 'deep subjectivity', he is the cue for our ending upon the combination of hermeneutics and critical theory which is the implicit foundation of this essay. Hermeneutic method, as Brown, Bauman, Giddens, and many others insist, returns meaning to the agent and interpretation to the participant–observer. 'The only answer is to be very intelligent' said T. S. Eliot in his aged eagle's voice. We may instead repeat the remark as though it were a levelled revolver.

If we do so with the Marxists, we become critical theorists in the wake of Stuart Hall (Centre for Contemporary Cultural Studies, Birmingham 1971–79). They have yielded up much in the name of an educational present whose dismal purpose is to reproduce a docile labour force comfortably held down by the mystifying privileges of property-owners and power-holding managers. They have pointed to a future in which a free, open Marxism may create a different classroom. Either programme has come to pretend, from the solitude of powerlessness, too much in the way of both explanation and prediction. There is no theory, hard as Habermas (1975) tries, presently capable of totalising industrial society as once Marx and Durkheim claimed to do. It is nonetheless important to identify the theory of ideology as crucial to the understanding of social continuity; and ideologies, whether a fix or a help, are merely what men and women live by. But far better study them, insofar as education makes ideologies and values explicit, as an ensemble of texts (Ricoeur 1971, Geertz 1975) each as various as an individual poem, than to credulously suppose that one of the big functionalisms will smoothly gather in all that a people have sowed and reaped.

Accordingly, there is no theory which can situate as giant an institution as education in a totality. Yet we continue to try to speak of the unity of being and culture, and of the numinous. The contribution of English studies to social theory at large, and the sociology of education in particular, is to make such a language speakable.

Notes

[1] Most compactly and famously rebutted by Taylor (1969). See also Inglis (1979).
[2] Placed with exquisite accuracy on the line Marx drew between economic base and cultural superstructure: Leavis's father made pianos.
[3] *Scrutiny*, Leavis's magazine, was reissued in 1963 by Cambridge University Press in 20 volumes.

References

Abrams, M. H. (1957) *The Mirror and the Lamp* (Harvard University Press).
Anderson, P. (1968) 'Components of the national culture', in R. Blackburn and A. Cockburn (eds.) (1969) *Student Power* (Penguin) pp. 214–83.
Annan, N. (1955) 'The intellectual aristocracy', in J. H. Plumb (ed.) *Studies in Social History: a tribute to G. M. Trevelyan* (Oxford University Press) pp. 112–46.
Austin, J. L. and Urmson, J. O. (1965) *How to do Things with Words* (Oxford University Press).
Barnes, D., Britton, J. and Rosen, H. (1971) *Language, the Learner and the School* (Penguin).
Bauman, Z. (1978) *Hermeneutics and Social Science* (Hutchinson).
Berlin, I. (1976) *Vico and Herder* (Hogarth Press).
Bernstein, R. J. (1978) *The Restructuring of Social and Political Theory* (University of Pennsylvania Press and Hutchinson).
Bourdieu, P. and Passeron, J-C. (1977) *Reproduction in Education, Society*

and Culture (Sage Publications).

Britton, J. (1970) *Language and Learning* (Allen Lane, the Penguin Press).

Brown, R. H. (1978) *A Poetic for Sociology* (Cambridge University Press).

Bruner, J. S. (1962) *On Knowing: essays for the left hand* (Harvard University Press).

Bruner, J. S. (1972) *The Relevance of Education* (Allen & Unwin).

Chomsky, N. (1969) *American Power and the New Mandarins* (Chatto & Windus).

Collingwood, R. G. (1924) *Speculum Mentis* (The Clarendon Press).

Collingwood, R. G. (1970) *The Idea of History* (Oxford University Press).

Douglas, M. (1970) *Purity and Danger* (Routledge & Kegan Paul).

Empson, W. (1935) *The Structure of Complex Words* (Chatto & Windus).

Fay, B. (1975) *Social Theory and Political Practice* (Allen & Unwin).

Gadamer, H. G. (1977) (translated and edited by Linge, D. E.) *Philosophical Hermeneutics* (University of California Press).

Geertz, C. (1975) *The Interpretation of Cultures* (Hutchinson and Basic Books).

Geertz, C. (1980) *Negara: the theatre state in nineteenth century Bali* (University of Princeton Press).

Giddens, A. (1976) *New Rules of Sociological Method* (Hutchinson).

Gouldner, A. W. (1972) *The Coming Crisis of Western Sociology* (Heinemann Educational Books).

Gouldner, A. (1976) *The Dialectic of Ideology and Technology* (Macmillan).

Gregory, R. (1974) 'Psychology: towards a science of fiction', *New Society*, 23 May.

Habermas, J. (1975) *Legitimation Crisis* (Heinemann Educational Books).

Hoggart, R. (1957) *The Uses of Literacy* (Penguin).

Hoggart, R. (1967) *The Literary Imagination and the Study of Society* (University of Birmingham).

Hoggart, R. (1969) *Contemporary Cultural Studies* (University of Birmingham).

Holbrook, D. (1961) *English for Maturity* (Cambridge University Press).

Holbrook, D. (1964) *The Secret Places* (Methuen).

Husserl, E. (1937) (translated by Carr, D. 1970) *Crisis of European Sciences and Transcendental Phenomenology* (Northwestern University Press).

Husserl, E. (1961) *Cartesian Meditations* (Martinus Nijhoff, The Hague).

Inglis, F. (1975) *Ideology and the Imagination* (Cambridge University Press).

Inglis, F. (1979) 'Bourdieu, Habermas, and the condition of England', *Sociological Review*, **27**, 2, pp. 353–69.

Inglis, F. (1982) *Radical Earnestness: English social theory 1880–1980* (Martin Robertson).

Jackson, B. (1966) *Working Class Community* (Routledge & Kegan Paul).

Jackson, B. and Marsden, D. (1962) *Education and the Working Class* (Routledge & Kegan Paul).

Johnson, S. (1956) *Lives of the Poets, vol. II* (Oxford University Press).

Leavis, F. R. (1948) *The Great Tradition* (Chatto & Windus).

Leavis, F. R. (1955) *D. H. Lawrence Novelist* (Chatto & Windus).

Leavis, F. R. (1968) *A Selection from Scrutiny* (2 vols) (Cambridge University Press).

Leavis, F. R. (1975) *The Living Principle* (Chatto & Windus).

Leavis, F. R. and Leavis, Q. D. (1970) *Dickens the Novelist* (Chatto & Windus).

Mulhern, F. (1979) *The Moment of 'Scrutiny'* (New Left Books).

O'Neill, J. (1972) *Sociology as a Skin Trade* (Heinemann Educational Books).

Plumb, J. H. (ed.) (1964) *Crisis in the Humanities* (Penguin).

Poole, R. (1972) *Towards Deep Subjectivity* (Allen Lane, The Penguin Press).

Poole, R. (1975) 'From phenomenology to subjective method', *New Universities Quarterly*, **29**, 4, pp. 412–41.

Richards, I. A. (1924) *The Principles of Literary Criticism* (Routledge & Kegan Paul).

Ricoeur, P. (1971) 'The model of the text: meaningful action considered as a text', *Social Research*, **38**, pp. 529–62.

Robinson, I. (1973) *The Survival of English* (Cambridge University Press).

Rorty, R. (1980) *Philosophy and the Mirror of Nature* (Basil Blackwell).

Rosen, H. and Rosen, C. (1973) *The Language of Primary School Children* (Penguin).

Sidney, Sir. P. (1951, ed. E. S. Shuckburgh), *An Apologie for Poetrie* (Cambridge University Press).

Skinner, Q. (1970) 'Conventions and the understanding of speech acts', *Philosophical Quarterly*, **20**, pp. 118–38.

Skinner, Q. (1972a) 'Social meaning and the explanation of social action', in P. Laslett, W. G. Runciman and Q. Skinner (eds.) *Philosophy, Politics, Society, Series IV* (Basil Blackwell) pp. 136–57.

Skinner, Q. (1972b) 'Motives, intentions, and the interpretation of texts', *New Literary History*, **3**, pp. 398–408.

Skinner, Q. (1975) 'Hermeneutics and the role of history', *New Literary History*, **7**, pp. 209–32.

Taylor, C. (1969) 'Neutrality in political science', in P. Laslett and W. G. Runciman (eds.) *Philosophy, Politics, and Society, 3rd Series* (Basil Blackwell) pp. 25–58.

Taylor, C. (1978) 'Interpretation and the sciences of man', in R. Beehler and A. Drengson *Philosophy of Society* (Methuen) pp. 156–203.

Wilkinson, A. (1975) *Language and Education* (Oxford University Press).

Williams, R. (1958) *Culture and Society 1780–1950* (Chatto & Windus; Penguin 1961).

Williams, R. (1961) *The Long Revolution* (Penguin).

Williams, R. (1966) *Modern Tragedy* (Stanford University Press).

Williams, R. (1973) *The Country and the City* (Chatto & Windus).

Williams, R. (1974) *Television: technology and cultural form* (Fontana/Collins).

Williams, R. (1976) *Communications* (Penguin).

Williams, R. (1979) *Politics and Letters: interviews with New Left Review* (New Left Books).

5 Towards a sociology of educational belief
Anthony Hartnett
Michael Naish

Introduction

There would seem to be nothing distinctive about educational beliefs that would exclude them from the same kind of sociological analysis as that to which political, religious, and other beliefs have been subjected. The sociological study of educational beliefs is worth undertaking because it should further an understanding of the reasons for what would seem to be their frequent deficiencies.

This section of the bibliography is concerned with those aspects of the sociology of knowledge which can be used both to explain the origins, acceptance, maintenance, and rejection of beliefs about educational practices and policies, and to explain how these beliefs might be both the causes and consequences of certain social structures. It begins with a short discussion of the sociology of knowledge in general. Issues are first raised about the definition of the area. There are then brief comments on four classic sociologists of knowledge (Marx, Weber, Mannheim and Durkheim) and on some of the relationships between the sociology of knowledge and epistemology. The rest of the section is concerned specifically with the sociology of educational beliefs, and is divided into six main sections with the following titles: Some sources of educational beliefs, Kinds of educational beliefs, The adjudication of educational beliefs, Functions of educational beliefs, Further issues, and Postscript. The term 'the sociology of belief' rather than 'the sociology of knowledge' is used in the title of the section, and sometimes in the text, on the grounds that it gives a more accurate account of the area. Much of what sociologists study is not knowledge, nor even what passes for it, but is, at best, belief.

The sociology of knowledge: general issues

Definitions of the area

At a very general level the sociology of knowledge can be described as the study of the relationships between (1) the 'artefacts of consciousness' or what Stark (1967, p. 476) calls 'knowledge, thought and culture' and (2) 'social structure, that is . . . social groups . . . institutions and societies' (Bottomore 1956, p. 56). Such an account permits a number of different orientations, and Berger and Luckman (1967, p. 16) argue that the sociology of knowledge has 'thus far been the history of its various definitions'.

One question concerns what the term 'artefacts' is used to cover. On a narrow account, it might be used of, say, science and theoretical ideas only or, more widely, like Berger and Luckman (1967, p. 15), of 'whatever passes for "knowledge" in a society' or, more widely still, like Crane (1972, p. 129) of 'the whole array of cultural products' – that is to say, knowledge of all types (practical, common-sense, scientific, political etc.) as well as art, music, and so on. This widest account would seem to be the most useful in that restricting the scope of the term 'artefacts of consciousness' to one or other type of knowledge seems arbitrary, or at least to owe less to theoretical considerations than it should. Another question concerns the scope of the term 'social structure'. Is the sociologist, in the case of science, for example, to be concerned with the relationships between science and society as a whole or between specific scientific theories and specific social structures in science? Or between ideology and society as a whole or between particular ideologies and particular social groups (e.g. professions) or with both? A further question concerns the nature of the relationships between artefacts and the social structure. Are the relationships to be looked at as going one way only or as reciprocal? And exactly what kind of explanation can be given of them? Are they to be explained deterministically? Or still causally but in a weaker sense? Or not causally at all?

Differences in orientation, however, do not preclude different sociologists from sharing common ground, and examples of questions that they ask are:

1. How exactly do specific social structures affect the kinds of knowledge available in a society at a given time?
2. Exactly what social structures (and what related social processes) promote the conservation, extension, transmission, reception, or suppression of different kinds of knowledge in different societies, and in different social groups, in different times? (cf. Bottomore 1956, p. 57).
3. What particular features of social structures can be related to what particular features of the knowledge available at a given time?
4. How best are different kinds of knowledge distinguished and

what sociological accounts can be given of the origins and relationships of these kinds of knowledge?

5. What are the social functions of these different kinds of knowledge? How are they related to differences in social structure? What social structures do they help to maintain or to undermine or to inhibit?
6. To what extent do various kinds of knowledge owe their existence to their social functions as opposed to other factors?
7. What is the role of the concept of ideology in explaining the relationships between knowledge and social structure?
8. What are the relationships between knowledge and interests (e.g. political, class, and professional interests)?
9. What are the relationships between knowledge and power? How does the exercise of power affect the production or suppression of various kinds of knowledge and their transmission? How do various kinds of knowledge legitimate the distribution and exercise of power in society and in various social groups? How does the need for legitimation affect the nature of the knowledge that various social groups possess? (Wrong, 1979).

Brief overviews of the area are Stark (1967) and Coser (1968). Other useful short statements are Bottomore (1956), Parsons (1959), Popper (1966, chapter 23), and Mitchell (1979). Selections from the literature can be found in Curtis and Petras (1970), Remmling (1973), and Hamilton (1974). Specific problems are examined in Horton and Finnegan (1973), Horowitz (1961), Bloor (1976), Bailey (1980), Borhek and Curtis (1975) and in Dixon (1980). Relevant literature in the history of ideas, an area very germane to the sociology of knowledge, can be found in Evetts (1973), Lovejoy (1940), Dunn (1968) and Skinner (1969).

Four classic sociologists of knowledge
Some idea of the history and scope of the area can be gained from looking at some of the classic work in it.

Marx undoubtedly holds the central position in the sociology of knowledge. As Berger and Luckman (1967, pp. 17–18) note, the 'root proposition of the area' is derived from Marx's claims that 'man's consciousness is determined by his being' and that ideology consists of 'ideas as weapons for social interests'. Brief introductions to Marx are McLellan (1975) and Berlin (1978). Useful selections from Marx's own work can be found in Bottomore and Rubel (1963, pp. 169–74) and C. W. Mills (1963, pp. 42–80). Additional literature on Marx can be found in Section 2 of this bibliography.

Weber's debate with Marx over the importance of ideas in social change is central to the development of the field. One common view is that Weber, unlike Marx, believed that in 'the unique transformation of traditional Europe to capitalism it is what people thought and believed that was decisive' (Macrae 1974, p. 80). Weber's work on the protestant ethic and capitalism was a 'cautious attempt to correct a deterministic explanation of social change' (Curtis and Petras 1970, p. 37). Introductions to Weber's thought can be found in Macrae (1974), Bendix (1962) and Giddens (1971, especially pp. 119–84). For a useful example of Weber's own work in the sociology of knowledge, see his 'Chinese literati' (reprinted in Cosin 1972, pp. 230–41). See, too, Gerth and Mills (1948) and Weber (1976, 2nd edn.).

Durkheim has had a considerable influence upon Bernstein and, through him, on the sociology of education. For a good introduction to the educational aspects of Durkheim's work see Karabel and Halsey (1977, pp. 71–7) who argue (p. 72) that 'no sociologist of education has yet surpassed – in depth or in breadth – [Durkheim's] investigation of the relationship between social structure and educational transmission', and that Durkheim was the first sociologist to demonstrate 'how larger patterns of power and control penetrate the process of schooling and the structure of educational knowledge'. A general introduction to Durkheim is Giddens (1978) and a detailed and classic biography is Lukes (1975). Issues about Durkheim's epistemology are raised by P. Q. Hirst (1975) and a useful translation of Durkheim's *The Evolution of Educational Thought* is by Collins (Durkheim 1977).

Mannheim was responsible for distinctive developments both in the sociology of knowledge and in the sociology of education. Curtis and Petras (1970, p. 10) suggest that, since 1936 and the publication of his *Ideology and Utopia*, Mannheim has been the individual 'most frequently associated with the sociology of knowledge. Mannheim's theory revolves round the central concepts of ideology, utopia and relationism. Defining the sociology of knowledge as the study of the relationship between knowledge and existence, Mannheim examines the genesis of ideas in terms of social processes characteristic of particular historical periods'. Introductions to his work are in Coser (1971, pp. 429–63), Kecskemeti (in Mannheim 1952, pp. 1–32), and Merton (1968, pp. 543–62). For Mannheim's own work, see Mannheim (1952, 1953, 1960). Heeren (1971) discusses Mannheim's view of intellectuals; see also Hall (1979).

The sociology of knowledge and epistemology
One important factor which gives rise to diverse approaches to the

sociology of knowledge is different and conflicting views about its relationship to epistemology. Issues arise, for example, about whether the sociology of knowledge has made epistemology redundant or whether any fruitful sociology of knowledge can be developed independently of epistemology.

The conventional distinction between epistemology and sociology of knowledge is usually drawn in terms of a distinction between logical and empirical issues. Sociology of knowledge is usually taken to be concerned with empirical (often causal) relationships between knowledge, or what is claimed to be such, and social structure. Epistemology is usually taken to be concerned with a number of interrelated logical issues about the nature, scope, and origins of knowledge and of other conceptually linked notions such as belief and rationality, and about the justification of claims to knowledge and to rational belief. Conceived in this way, epistemology would seem to contain an essentially normative element. See Flew (1961, chapter 4) on the standards of inductive arguments, and MacIntyre (1971).

For the history of epistemology, see Hamlyn (1967a) and for some of the main epistemological traditions see Acton (1967), Hamlyn (1967b), R. J. Hirst (1967), Popkin (1967) and Williams (1967). Epistemological questions arise in a number of different ways but for some recent discussions that give some idea of their origins and nature, see Popper (1963 Introduction), Pollock (1968) and Chisholm (1973). For more comprehensive treatments see Ayer (1956), Quine and Ullian (1970), and Lehrer (1974). Kekes (1976) is a lucid and non-technical defence of the ideal of rationality against sceptical attacks. Bartley's (1964, chapters 4 and 5) proposed solution to one central epistemological issue has been influential. It is criticised by Watkins (1969, 1971) who is in turn criticised by Settle *et al.* (1974).

The inconclusiveness of the epistemological debate has been one reason, among others, why some sociologists of knowledge have adopted what Bloor (1973, 1976) and Law (1975) call 'the strong programme of the sociology of knowledge'. Two main features of it are (1) that sociologists need draw no distinction between true and false or between rational and irrational beliefs and (2) that all beliefs can be causally explained. The adequacy of this view of the sociology of knowledge has been attacked by MacIntyre (1971) on the grounds that rational and irrational belief need different types of explanation and that rational belief cannot be causally explained. MacIntyre's methodological point is exemplified in Smith and Stockman (1972) and is discussed by Keat and Urry (1975, chapter 9). Lukes' (1973) paper suggests that a sociology of knowledge which does not distinguish between rational and irrational beliefs is, on the face of it, unnecessarily restrictive in that it makes it impossible to raise issues about the origins and functions of defective beliefs. This point itself gives rise to an interesting question concerning the extent to which the belief that all beliefs are causally explicable is adopted by sociologists of knowledge more as a result of institutional factors within their discipline (relating to issues of boundary maintenance) than as a result of an adequate understanding of the issues about causal and other explanations. Moreover, sociologists who adopt the strong programme do in fact often distinguish rational from irrational beliefs. They do so when they identify beliefs as ideologies or superstitions. Such judgements about the rationality or irrationality of beliefs are central to the sociological task, since it is the explanation of these beliefs as ideologies and as superstitions that is important.

The epistemological question that arises most immediately here concerns the standards by which rational and irrational beliefs are to be identified. Are such standards culture-bound? Are they cross-cultural? Or are some one and some the other? Much recent literature has been concerned with these questions. General discussion of them can be seen in Trigg (1973), Wilson (1970), and Kekes (1976). All three books contain criticisms of Winch's view as seen in Winch (1958, 1964); see too Winch (1976). Winch is usually understood as defending a form of relativism derived from the work of Wittgenstein. Critiques of Winch are Gellner (1973) and Hollis (1972). Some general issues about relativism are raised by Bambrough (1974), Lukes and Runciman (1974), Williams (1974–5), Flew (1976, chapter 3), Skorupski (1978), and Burke (1979).

The issue of relativism in the natural sciences has been particularly widely discussed since the publication of Kuhn (1962, enlarged edn. 1970). Kuhn's work too can be productively read in the light of the realist/objectivist epistemology of Popper (1959, revised edn. 1968), (1963, revised 3rd edn. 1969) and (1972) and of the anarchic epistemology of Feyerabend (1975) and (1978). For a sociological discussion of Kuhn and Popper, see Bloor (1976). More general issues are raised by Mulkay (1979) and Wallis (1979). A symposium on Kuhn is Lakatos and Musgrave (1970), and some further thoughts are to be found in Kuhn (1974). Scheffler (1967) and Meynell (1975) contain useful discussions of Kuhn. A useful survey of the current debate is Chalmers (1978).

Ethical relativism is discussed in Brandt (1959), Nielsen (1971), Nowell-Smith (1971), Williams (1972), Ladd (1973), Cornman and Lehrer (1974), Harman (1975) and Foot (1978). A valuable discussion of some issues raised by comparisons of ethical and scientific reasoning is Gewirth (1960).

A collection of articles concerned with the role of concepts of rationality in social scientific explanation generally is Benn and Mortimore (1976).

Some sources of educational beliefs

One initial task in the sociology of educational beliefs is to identify their sources and origins. Once these sources have been identified a number of further questions can be asked: How are the sources legitimated? What is the relationship between the social structure of the sources and the nature and the content of the knowledge produced? How do the relationships between the sources and those for whom they are sources affect the nature and content of the knowledge produced? Are the sources producers of genuine knowledge? Other complex questions arise about the level of analysis (social system, institution, group) at which these sources should be studied, about the mode of explanation appropriate to each level, and about the interactions between levels (Durkheim 1977; Feinberg 1975; Bowles and Gintis 1976 and Andreski 1972).

Generally, the knowledge derived from the various sources will have been produced in one of two ways. The first is where social structures and interactions allow room for some degree of disinterested inquiry constituted by such values as objectivity, impartiality, openness to criticism, etc. The second is where social structures and interactions tend to preclude such inquiry. The production of medical knowledge in this latter fashion is discussed by Jewson (1974), and its educational implications are considered by Hartnett and Naish (1977).

We now discuss three specific sources of educational knowledge – academic disciplines, educational research, and educational reports.

Academic disciplines

The most basic way in which academic disciplines can be distinguished is in terms of their logics, that is, in terms of their conceptual schemata and their methods of verification and falsification. This approach can be seen in Hirst (1965, 1966). Hirst's discussions, though nominally about educational theory and liberal education, have implications for academic disciplines since academic disciplines can be distinguished by their relationships to the various forms of knowledge and understanding that Hirst posits. Hirst's work has been influential and widely discussed. See Phillips (1971), Hindess (1972) and the reply to Hindess by Hirst (1973). Brent

(1975) and Warnock (1977) raise a number of further issues. For sociological critiques see White and Young (1975, 1976) and Ahier (in Young and Whitty 1977). Other discussions not specific to Hirst are Schwab (1962), Martin (1969), Harvey (1974) and Walking (1979).

The attempt to distinguish areas of knowledge, or academic disciplines, in Hirst's fashion becomes particularly difficult where the logics are disputed. The existence of different schools of psychology noted by Nagel (1960) illustrate this point. Moreover, definitions of disciplines may depend on normative considerations about what is worth doing, and on other institutional factors. See Hartnett and Naish (1976, vol. 2, pp. 139–57 and 1980, pp. 257–9) for this point. For a sophisticated discussion of some aspects of academic disciplines, see Toulmin (1972).

Some important sociological work that bears on issues about academic disciplines is Apple (1972), Crane (1972) and Sklair (1973). Ben-David and Collins (1966) are concerned with the development of psychology in France, the United States and Britain, and Church (1971) deals with educational psychology between 1905 and 1920 in the United States. Hearnshaw's (1979) biography of Burt is a useful source, as is Johnston and Robbins (1977) on the development of specialities within science. Anderson (1969) discusses the consequences of 'the white emigration' of intellectuals from Europe to Britain on British academic life. Bourdieu (1967) and Hudson (1972) raise issues about academic professionalisation. Karabel and Halsey (1977, especially p. 49), Feinberg (1975) and Gellner (1975) suggest how characteristics of academic disciplines are related to the social structures of the societies in which they arise. For discussions specific to sociology, see Hughes (1967), Gouldner (1971) and Friedrichs (1970). On the role of school text books in defining academic areas, see pp. 169–72 of this bibliography.

On the relationship (or conflict) between ideology and academic disciplines in education see Bernbaum (1977), Apple (1976), and Kaufman (1978). More generally see Runciman in Benewick *et al.* (1973), Ingleby (1970), and Blackburn (1972). For some approaches to the interaction between psychology and society and to critiques of its ideological role, see Watson (1978), Feinberg (1975), Esland (1971, 1977), Bloch and Reddaway (1977), Robinson (1978) and Westland (1978).

Educational research
Educational research is a further source of educational beliefs. Although it is often naively seen as a positivist guide to good

decision-making about practices and policies, political factors and social structures may well affect its creation, content, and dissemination. The effect of the Department of Education and Science on educational research could be a productive area for investigation. General discussions can be found in Husén (1968), W. Taylor (1973), and Bruner (1975). Kitwood (1976) and Karabel and Halsey (1977, pp. 74–7) comment critically on some current research orientations, and Shipman (1976) provides some case study material which can be compared with Bell and Newby (1977).

Educational reports
A third source of educational beliefs is government and other official reports on education. Smith and Stockman (1972) raise issues about the definitions (often socially imposed) of the situation in government reports and about the way that these affect the reports' contents. Literature on defining the situation can be found in McHugh (1968), Stebbins (1967, 1971), and Heeren in Douglas (1971). Government reports are discussed by Burston (1961), Blackstone (1967), McPherson (1968), Grant (1973) and Naish, Hartnett and Finlayson (1976).

Kinds of educational beliefs
Any adequate sociology of educational beliefs will have to distinguish various types of educational knowledge. Four types of knowledge are noted here – common-sense, practical, academic and professional. Sociologists try to explain how such distinctions arise, what are the sources of the various kinds of knowledge, what social purposes are served by distinguishing knowledge in some ways as opposed to others, what the social distribution is of the various kinds of knowledge, and what the relationships are between the various kinds of knowledge. Introductions to some of these issues can be found in Gurvitch (1971, pp. 21–42), Blum (1974), Habermas (1974), Holzner and Marx (1979, pp. 19–25). Two useful collections are Douglas (1971) and Turner (1974). For a discussion specifically on education see Taylor (1978, chapter 7).

Common-sense knowledge
Common-sense knowledge would seem to be best described as that non-specialised knowledge which is acquired for the achievement of practical purposes in what Schütz and Luckman (1974) call 'the everyday life world' (see also Schütz's (1946) discussion of the 'man on the street'). Useful philosophical discussions are Grave (1967), Körner (1970, chapter 4), Popper (1972, chapter 2), and Kekes (1976, pp. 40–59). Nagel (1961, chapter 1) discusses a number of

differences between science and common sense, and Elliot (1974) is a critique of Nagel. See also Schütz (1953), Garfinkel (1962), Douglas (1971, chapter 1) and Thomas (1978). Discussions bearing on education and common-sense knowledge are Perry (1965) and Pring (1976, chapter 5; 1977).

Practical knowledge
Practical knowledge is the knowledge that a person has who knows in fact, as opposed to in theory, how to do things. Important questions about practical knowledge concern its transmission, the role of knowledge expressed in propositions in exercising and acquiring it, and about its judgmental and tacit components. Ryle (1949) is a well-known discussion of practical knowledge. His work and other related literature is discussed, together with some of its educational implications, in Hartnett and Naish (1976, vol. 1, pp. 107–21).

Academic knowledge
Minogue (1973, chapter 4) offers a useful account of academic knowledge which he sharply distinguishes from the kinds of knowledge that are required for action in the world of practice. His discussion can be read usefully with Chomsky (1968, 1969b), Bock (1970), Montefiore (1975), Comroe and Dripps (1976), and Bailey (1980).

Professional knowledge
Professional knowledge may be described as that knowledge which is deemed to be required for the performance of a professional role. Some important questions about it are: Does it in fact enable professionals to provide the services that they claim to offer? To what extent is the knowledge defective and to what extent are its deficiencies acknowledged? To what extent are its deficiencies and the failure to acknowledge them a result of considerations of professional status and boundary maintenance? Professional knowledge is discussed in Freidson (1970a, especially chapter 4, 1970b, chapter 15) and more generally in Holzner and Marx (1979). One interesting question about professional training is how far it can educate for uncertainty without undermining professional status. This is discussed in Scheffler (1977), Lieberman and Miller (1978), Eisner (1977) and Greene (1978). Further issues are raised in Hartnett and Naish (1980).

The adjudication of educational beliefs
A particularly important task for the sociology of educational

beliefs concerns their adjudication – that is, why and how some beliefs are accepted and others rejected by various social groups. This involves both the examination of the relationships between social structures and the acceptance or rejection of beliefs, and also the identification of those structures which promote the adjudication of beliefs solely on their merits and those which do not.

De Grazia (1966) and especially his notion of a 'reception system' provide useful ideas on some of these issues. His rationalistic model of a reception system is meant to explain how knowledge claims and claims to well-grounded belief are assessed on their merits, and the indeterminacy, power, and dogmatic models are meant to explain how they are not.

The rationalistic model is seen in Popper (1966, 5th edn. revised) and conforms to the view of adjudication outlined in Walsh (1971). Walsh is usefully read with Lucas (1958) and Shipman (1972, 1976). Some of the technical difficulties involved in this model can be seen in Feldman (1971) and in Light and Smith (1971). A good example of the way in which conclusions that should be open to revision become taken for granted is Thorpe (1973). Examples where academic work appears to have been judged by professionals other than on its merits can be seen in Medvedev (1969), Polanyi (1969a, 1969b), Koestler (1971), Jensen (1972, Introduction) and Dingle (1972), together with Scriven (1970), Flew (1976, chapter 5), Kamin (1977) and Hearnshaw (1979). The misadjudication of academic work may occur not only within disciplines but also when the work is taken up in the world of practice. Useful discussions of Piaget's work in this context are Sullivan (1967), Kaufman (1978) and Brown and Desforges (1979). Hartnett and Naish (1976, vol. 2) raises some general points about this issue and uses the reception of Bernstein's work as an illustration.

An important group in the adjudication of educational beliefs may be called 'authorities'. Authorities, in this context, can be said to be individuals, or groups or institutions, whose word can reasonably be allowed to carry weight on some matter because they are particularly qualified to offer a well-founded opinion on it. The word of an authority may play an important role in what is taken to be knowledge and reasonable belief, whether within his own professional group or among laymen.

The roles occupied by those who are consulted as authorities are likely to vary. Parekh (1970) draws useful distinctions between intellectuals, professionals, specialists, and experts. These roles are likely to affect the nature and range of the advice that particular authorities give.

Important questions about authorities are: How do individuals come to be taken as authorities? How do relationships between authorities and those who seek their opinion or advice affect the advice given? Is the nature of the opinion sought one that falls within the authorities' competence? Is the area one in which authoritative opinion is possible? Authorities of one sort or another may be consulted and asked to give an opinion which involves a strong moral or political element. Yet there are doubts whether opinions on moral or political issues can be authoritative in the sense at issue. See Bambrough (1956), Ryle (1958), Wilson (1971), Singer (1971–2), Burch (1974) and Eggerman (1979). Further, an opinion might be taken to be authoritative and not be seen in the context of the wider academic debate. See, for example, Sullivan (1967) on Piaget. Piaget's work, as Foss (1969) suggests, seems to have been made to yield advice of a kind which runs beyond what his work would justify. For a valuable general discussion, see Ehrenreich and English (1979) on experts' advice to women.

Issues about authority and knowledge are raised in Quinton (1971) and Pring (1975), and about the intelligentsia and intellectuals in Mannheim (1960), Berlin (1968) and Heeren (1971). See, too, Pincoffs (1972) and Montefiore (1975). Political and moral issues about the relationship of intellectuals to the powers are raised in Seeley (1966), Chomsky (1969a and b), Ross and Staines (1972), Shils (1972) and Brym (1980). Another relevant comprehensive discussion is Benveniste (1973).

Functions of educational beliefs
Some functions (among others) of educational beliefs will be to justify the exercise of power by those who run the educational system, to make practices and policies politically acceptable, and to legitimate the professional status of teachers, teachers of teachers, and educational administrators. These functions may play a major role in the production of educational knowledge, may greatly affect its content, and may create in it the distortions and other epistemological deficiencies that commonly mark ideologies. See, for examples, Naish, Hartnett and Finlayson (1976), Hartnett and Naish (1977); and more generally Freidson (1970a, 1970b, 1971); Pearson (1973, 1975a, 1975b); Edelman (1974); and Ingleby (1974). Larrain (1979, p. 13) notes in his comprehensive review that 'ideology is one of the most equivocal and elusive concepts one can find in social science'. For some definitions of ideology see Minar (1961), Mitchell (1979) Williams (1976, pp. 126–30). A brief overview of the concept is Braybrooke (1967). Specific approaches to ideology can be found in Geertz (1964), Harris (1968), Althusser

(1972), Cosin (1973), Inglis (1975), P. Q. Hirst (1976), Seliger (1977), and Working Papers in Cultural Studies No. 10 (1977). Other useful areas of literature are opened up by Ashford (1972), Benewick *et al.* (1973) and Crespigny and Cronin (1975). Two other interesting papers are Feyerabend (1967) and Wright (1978). Issues about the closed nature of ideologies and their ability to cope with contrary evidence are raised by Festinger (1956) and Cashmore (1979) and, more generally, Janis (1972) and Strauss (1977). Some general methodological issues concerning ideological explanation are raised by Mackie (1975), and other such issues concerning empirical approaches to ideology can be found by detailed comparisons of Geertz (1964), Strauss *et al.* (1964), Rokeach (1968), Borhek and Curtis (1975), Working Papers in Cultural Studies No. 10 (1977), Eysenck and Wilson (1978), and Barrett *et al.* (1979).

The language and rhetoric of ideological discourse in education is discussed by Halpern (1960), Komisar and McClellan (1961), Spencer (1970), Cheverst (1972), Jacoby (1973), Apple (1975) and Inglis (1975). The role of ideology in articulating and protecting professional interests and power is discussed by Wilensky (1964), Lunsford (1968), Dibble (1970), Strauss (1971), and C. W. Mills (1967). Issues about ideology and teachers are raised by Willower (1969), and Ginsburg *et al.* (1980).

A concept closely related to ideology is that of false consciousness, and for a discussion of this relationship see Miller (1972), Plamenatz (1970) and Drucker (1974, chapter 2). The relationship between interests and false consciousness is explored in Runciman (1969) which can be usefully read in conjunction with Armstrong's brief account of rationalisation (1973, chapter 6, section VII). Interests are discussed by Benn (1959–60). Benn defends a normative account of interests as opposed to Barry's naturalistic account (1964, 1965). Connolly (1974) contains a useful discussion of interests in politics, and Peters (1966, chapter 6) discusses interests in the context of educational provision.

One role of the sociology of belief is that of providing a critique of ideological judgement. Such a role raises a number of complex epistemological, empirical and other issues. For useful discussions, particularly of the notion of 'indices of ideological judgement', see Edel (1967, 1968). For a sceptical view of the role of the sociology of belief in this context, see Popper (1966, chapter 23).

Further issues
In general, comparatively little empirical or philosophical work has been undertaken in the sociology of educational beliefs. In particu-

lar, sociologists have not been over-eager to apply the perspectives they use to their own products. There are probably interesting sociological reasons for this.

One intention of this section of the bibliography has been to suggest, in outline, what a sociology of educational belief might look like and how it might be developed. Two areas that could be examined, in addition to this bibliography itself, are 'new directions in the sociology of education' and 'theory and practice in education'. We conclude with a few suggestions about each.

'New directions in the sociology of education' is a particularly interesting area for study both because much of the material is to hand and in current use, and because it was disseminated and taken up quickly and widely. The change that 'new directions' brought about can be partly seen from the fact that the first edition of Banks (1968) contains no references to the sociology of knowledge and that the third edition (1976) contains a chapter on the area. This gives rise to sociological questions about the origins, adjudication and function of the 'new directions' movement. Important questions about it concern its intellectual and political origins and its relationships to wider cultural and political contexts; its academic institutionalisation and its link with various publishing houses; the way its offerings were assessed both by academics and others; the rhetoric and style of its argument and how these relate to its target group (teachers and students teachers); and the effect of all of these things on the nature of the knowledge it offered. Was it a partisan movement more concerned with packaging and selling embryonic ideas than with developing an informed scepticism amongst students? And if it was, why was it?

Some idea of the 'new directions' in the sociology of education can be gained from Young (1971, 1972), Flude and Ahier (1974), Whitty and Young (1976), Young and Whitty (1977). The style and rhetoric of the approach can be seen most readily in Young (1972–3), and White and Young (1975, 1976). Wider questions about the 'new directions' are discussed in Bernbaum (1977) and sociological critiques are Demaine (1977) and Karabel and Halsey (1977, pp. 44–61). The latter also give a useful account of how the new directions were legitimated. Important philosophical issues are raised by Flew (1976, chapters 2 and 3, and 1977). See also Clark and Freeman (1979a and b).

Another useful task for the sociology of educational beliefs would be to look at some of the issues raised by debates about theory and practice in education. Particularly important questions concern the various kinds of knowledge-claim covered by the term 'theory', their sources, their relationships to each other; the adjudication of these claims; their functions not least in legitimating the status of teachers, teachers of teachers and others in the educational system; their role in articulating and protecting interests; the bearing on them of such concepts as false-consciousness and ideology; and the relationships of all of these to the various social structures within the educational system.

Postscript
The issues raised in this section are intended both to be of academic interest and, equally important, to be a means to a more critical approach to educational beliefs, whether they are embodied in current practices and policies or are simply still in the minds of policy-makers, planners and academics. A study of the relationships between (1) the various social structures in the educational system and in the wider society and (2) the form and content of educational beliefs should reveal that these beliefs are not the inviolate and unchanging inhabitants of an empyrean but are the products, and often the debris of social life. Such a study should reveal, too, both the importance of power in the creation, maintenance, evaluation and dissemination of educational beliefs, and also the extent to which current institutional arrangements militate against the production of disinterested, adequately considered, and coherently argued solutions to educational problems. The obstacles to such solutions are many, covert and subtle, and are often to be found where they ought least to be expected.

References
Acton, H. B. (1967) 'Idealism', in P. Edwards (ed.) *Encyclopedia of Philosophy* (Macmillan and Free Press) pp. 110–18, vol. 4.
Althusser, L. (1972) 'Ideology and ideological state apparatuses: notes towards an investigation', in B. R. Cosin (ed.) pp. 242–80.
Anderson, P. (1969) 'Components of the national culture', in A. Cockburn and R. Blackburn (eds.) *Student Power* (Penguin) pp. 214–84.
Andreski, S. (1972) *Social Sciences as Sorcery* (Andre Deutsch).
Apple, M. W. (1972) 'Community, knowledge, and the structure of disciplines', *Educational Forum*, **37**, 1, pp. 75–82.
Apple, M. W. (1975) 'Ivan Illich and deschooling society: the politics of slogan systems', in N. K. Shimahara and A. Scrupski (eds.) *Social Forces and Schooling* (David McKay) pp. 337–60.
Apple, M. W. (1976) 'Rationality as ideology' (review article), *Educational Theory*, **26**, 1, pp. 121–31.
Armstrong, D. M. (1973) *Belief, Truth and Knowledge* (Cambridge University Press).
Ashford, D. E. (1972) *Ideology and Participation* (Sage Publications).
Ayer, A. J. (1956) *The Problem of Knowledge* (Penguin).

Bailey, J. (1980) *Ideas and Intervention: social theory for practice* (Routledge & Kegan Paul).
Bambrough, J.R. (1956) 'Plato's political analogies', in P. Laslett (ed.) *Philosophy, Politics and Society* (First Series) (Blackwell) pp. 98–115.
Bambrough, J. R. (1974) *Conflict and the Scope of Reason*, St. John's College Cambridge lecture March 1973 (University of Hull).
Banks, O. (1968 and 1976) *The Sociology of Education* (1st edn. 1968, 3rd edn. 1976) (Batsford).
Barrett, M. *et al.* (eds.) (1979) *Ideology and Cultural Reproduction* (Croom Helm).
Barry, B. (1964) 'The public interest', *Proceedings of the Aristotelian Society*, Supplementary **38**, pp. 1–18.
Barry, B. (1965) *Political Argument* (Routledge & Kegan Paul).
Bartley, W. W. (1964) *The Retreat to Commitment* (Chatto & Windus).
Bell, C. and Newby, H. (eds.) (1977) *Doing Sociological Research* (Allen & Unwin).
Ben-David, J. and Collins, R. (1966) 'Social factors in the origins of a new science: the case of psychology', *American Sociological Review*, **31**, 4, pp. 451–65.
Bendix, R. (1962) *Max Weber: an intellectual portrait* (Anchor/Doubleday).
Benewick, R. *et al.* (eds.) (1973) *Knowledge and Belief in Politics: the problem of ideology* (Allen & Unwin).
Benn, S. I. (1959–60) ' "Interests" in politics', *Proceedings of the Aristotelian Society*, **60**, pp. 123–40.
Benn, S. I. and Mortimore, S. W. (eds.) (1976) *Rationality and the Social Sciences: contributions to the philosophy and methodology of the social sciences* (Routledge & Kegan Paul).
Benveniste, G. (1973) *The Politics of Expertise* (Croom Helm).
Berger, P. L. and Luckmann, T. (1967) *The Social Construction of Reality* (Allen Lane, The Penguin Press).
Berlin, I. (1968) 'The role of the intelligentsia', *The Listener*, 2 May, pp. 563–5.
Berlin, I. (1978) *Karl Marx: his life and environment* (4th edn.) (Oxford University Press).
Bernbaum, G. (1977) *Knowledge and Ideology in the Sociology of Education* (Macmillan).
Blackburn, R. (ed.) (1972) *Ideology in Social Science* (Fontana/Collins).
Blackstone, T. (1967) 'The Plowden Report', *British Journal of Sociology*, **18**, pp. 291–302.
Bloch, S. and Reddaway, P. (1977) *Russia's Political Hospitals: the abuse of psychiatry in the Soviet Union* (Gollancz).
Bloor, D. (1973) 'Wittgenstein and Mannheim on the sociology of mathematics', *Studies in History and Philosophy of Science*, **4**, pp. 173–91.
Bloor, D. (1976) *Knowledge and Social Imagery* (Routledge & Kegan Paul).
Blum, A. F. (1974) *Theorizing* (Heinemann Educational Books).
Bock, C. V. (1970) *A Tower of Ivory?* Inaugural lecture (Westfield College, University of London).
Borhek, J. T. and Curtis, R. F. (1975) *A Sociology of Belief* (Wiley).
Bottomore, T. B. (1956) 'Some reflections on the sociology of knowledge', *British Journal of Sociology*, **7**, pp. 52–8.

Bottomore, T. B. and Rubel, M. (eds.) (1963) *Karl Marx: selected writings in sociology and social philosophy* (Penguin).

Bourdieu, P. (1967) 'Systems of education and systems of thought', in M. F. D. Young (ed.) (1971) *Knowledge and Control* (Collier-Macmillan) pp. 189–207.

Bowles, S. and Gintis, H. (1976) *Schooling in Capitalist America* (Routledge & Kegan Paul).

Brandt, R. B. (1959) *Ethical Theory: the problems of normative and critical ethics* (Prentice Hall).

Braybrooke, D. (1967) 'Ideology', in P. Edwards (ed.) *Encyclopedia of Philosophy* (Macmillan and Free Press) vol. 4, pp. 124–7.

Brent, A. (1975) 'The sociology of knowledge and epistemology', *British Journal of Educational Studies*, **23**, 2, pp. 209–24.

Brown, G. and Desforges, C. (1979) *Piaget's Theory: a psychological critique* (Routledge & Kegan Paul).

Bruner, J. (1975) 'The role of the researcher as an advisor to the educational policy maker', *Oxford Review of Education*, **1**, 3, pp. 183–210.

Brym, R. (1980) *Intellectuals and Politics* (Allen & Unwin).

Burch, R. W. (1974) 'Are there moral experts?', *The Monist*, **58**, 4, pp. 646–58.

Burke, T. E. (1979) 'The limits of relativism', *Philosophical Quarterly*, **29**, 116, pp. 193–207.

Burston, W. H. (1961) 'The influence of John Dewey in English official reports', *International Review of Education*, **7**, pp. 311–23.

Cashmore, E. (1979) 'More than a version: a study of reality creation', *British Journal of Sociology*, **30**, 3, pp. 307–21.

Chalmers, A. F. (1978) *What Is This Thing Called Science?* (Open University Press).

Cheverst, W. J. (1972) 'The role of metaphor in educational thought: an essay in content analysis', *Journal of Curriculum Studies*, **4**, 1, pp. 71–82.

Chisholm, R. M. (1973) *The Problem of the Criterion*. The Aquinas Lecture (Marquette University Press).

Chomsky, N. (1968) 'Philosophers and public philosophy', *Ethics*, **79**, 1, pp. 1–9.

Chomsky, N. (1969a) *American Power and the New Mandarins* (Penguin).

Chomsky, N. (1969b) 'The responsibility of intellectuals', in T. Roszak (ed.) *The Dissenting Academy* (Penguin) pp. 227–64.

Church, R. L. (1971) 'Educational psychology and social reform in the progressive era', *History of Education Quarterly*, **11**, pp. 390–405.

Clark, J. and Freeman, H. (1979a) 'Michael Young's sociology of knowledge: epistemological sense, or non-sense', *Journal of Further and Higher Education*, **3**, 1, pp. 2–17.

Clark, J. and Freeman, H. (1979b) 'Michael Young's sociology of knowledge: criticisms of philosophers of education reconsidered', *Journal of Further and Higher Education*, **3**, 2, pp. 11–23.

Comroe, J. H. and Dripps, R. D. (1976) 'Scientific basis for the support of biomedical science', *Science*, **92**, 4253, pp. 105–11.

Connolly, W. E. (1974) *The Terms of Political Discourse* (D. C. Heath).

Cornman, J. W. and Lehrer, K. (1974) *Philosophical Problems and Arguments: an introduction* (2nd edn.) (Macmillan).

Coser, L. A. (1968) 'Sociology of knowledge', in D. Sills (ed.) *International Encyclopaedia of the Social Sciences* (Macmillan) pp. 428–33.

Coser, L. A. (1971) *Masters of Sociological Thought* (Harcourt Brace Jovanovich).

Cosin, B. R. (ed.) (1972) *Education: Structure and Society* (Penguin/Open University Press).

Cosin, B. R. (1973) 'Society politics and education' block 3 part 2 Education, Economy and Politics E.352 (Open University Press) pp. 33–61.

Crane, D. (1972) *Invisible Colleges: diffusion of knowledge in scientific communities* (University of Chicago Press).

Crespigny, A. and Cronin, J. (eds.) (1975) *Ideologies of Politics* (Oxford University Press).

Curtis, J. E. and Petras, J. W. (eds.) (1970) *The Sociology of Knowledge: a reader* (Duckworth).

De Grazia, A. (1966) 'The scientific reception system', in A. De Grazia *The Velikovsky Affair* (Sidgwick & Jackson) pp. 171–231.

Demaine, J. (1977) 'On the new sociology of education: a critique of M. F. D. Young and the radical attack on the politics of educational knowledge', *Economy and Society*, **6**, 2, pp. 111–44.

Dibble, V. K. (1970) 'Occupations and ideologies', in J. E. Curtis and J. W. Petras (eds.), op. cit., 1970, pp. 434–51.

Dingle, H. (1972) *Science at the Crossroads* (Martin, Brian, & O'Keefe).

Dixon, K. (1980) *The Sociology of Belief* (Routledge & Kegan Paul).

Douglas, J. D. (ed.) (1971) *Understanding Everyday Life* (Routledge & Kegan Paul).

Drucker, H. M. (1974) *The Political Uses of Ideology* (Macmillan).

Dunn, J. (1968) 'The identity of the history of ideas', *Philosophy*, **XLIII**, 164, pp. 85–104.

Durkheim, E. (1977) *The Evolution of Educational Thought* (translated by P. Collins) (Routledge & Kegan Paul).

Edel, A. (1967) 'Reflections on the concept of ideology', *Praxis*, **4**, pp. 564–77.

Edel, A. (1968) 'Education and the concept of ideology', *Proceedings of the Philosophy of Education Society* (24th Annual Meeting) pp. 70–87.

Edelman, M. (1974) 'The political language of the helping professions', *Politics and Society*, **4**, 3, pp. 295–310.

Eggerman, R. W. (1979) 'Moral philosophy and moral advisers', *Metaphilosophy*, **10**, 2, pp. 161–8.

Ehrenreich, B. and English, D. (1979) *For Her Own Good: 150 years of the experts' advice to women* (Pluto Press).

Eisner, E. W. (1977) 'On the uses of educational connoisseurship and criticism for evaluating classroom life', *Teachers College Record*, **78**, 3, pp. 345–58.

Elliot, H. C. (1974) 'Similarities and differences between science and common sense', in R. Turner (ed.) pp. 21–6.

Esland, G. (1971) 'Teaching and learning as the organisation of knowledge', in M. F. D. Young (ed.) *Knowledge and Control* (Collier-Macmillan) pp. 70–115.

Esland, G. (1977) 'Schooling and pedagogy' (unit 6) and 'Diagnosis and testing' (unit 21) Schooling and Society E.202 (Open University Press).

Evetts, J. (1973) *The Sociology of Educational Ideas* (Routledge & Kegan Paul).

Eysenck, H. J. and Wilson, G. D. (eds.) (1978) *The Psychological Basis of Ideology* (MTP Press).

Feinberg, W. (1975) *Reason and Rhetoric* (Wiley).

Feldman, K. A. (1971) 'Using the work of others: some observations on reviewing and integrating', *Sociology of Education*, **44**, pp. 86–102.

Festinger, L. *et al.* (1956) *When Prophecy Fails* (Harper & Row).

Feyerabend, P. (1967) 'The theatre as an instrument of the criticism of ideologies: notes on Ionesco', *Inquiry*, **10**, pp. 298–312.

Feyerabend, P. (1975) *Against Method: outline of an anarchistic theory of knowledge* (New Left Books).

Feyerabend, P. (1978) *Science in a Free Society* (New Left Books).

Flew, A. G. N. (1961) *Hume's Philosophy of Belief: a study of his first inquiry* (Routledge & Kegan Paul).

Flew, A. G. N. (1976) *Sociology, Equality and Education* (Macmillan).

Flew, A. G. N. (1977) 'Sociologists as surrogates for Berkeley's god', *Open Mind* (The Open University Journal of Philosophy), no. 6, July, pp. 11–15.

Flude, M. and Ahier, J. (eds.) (1974) *Educability, Schools and Ideology* (Croom Helm).

Foot, P. (1978) *Moral Relativism*. The Lindley Lecture (University of Kansas).

Foss, B. (1969) 'Other aspects of child psychology', in R. S. Peters (ed.) *Perspectives on Plowden* (Routledge & Kegan Paul) pp. 42–54.

Freidson, E. (1970a) *Professional Dominance: the social structure of medical care* (Aldine).

Freidson, E. (1970b) *Profession of Medicine: a study of the sociology of applied knowledge* (Dodd Mead).

Freidson, E. (ed.) (1971) *The Professions and their Prospects* (Sage Publications).

Friedrichs, R. W. (1970) *A Sociology of Sociology* (Free Press).

Garfinkel, H. (1962) 'Commonsense knowledge of social structures. The documentary method of interpretation', in J. Scher (ed.) *Theories of the Mind* (Free Press) pp. 689–712.

Geertz, C. (1964) 'Ideology as a cultural system', in D. E. Apter (ed.) *Ideology and Discontent* (Free Press) pp. 47–76.

Gellner, E. (1973) 'The new idealism – cause and meaning in the social sciences', in E. Gellner *Cause and Meaning in the Social Sciences* (Routledge & Kegan Paul) pp. 50–77.

Gellner, E. (1975) 'Ethnomethodology: the re-enchantment industry or the Californian way of subjectivity', *Philosophy of Social Science*, **5**, pp. 431–50.

Gerth, H. H. and Mills, C. W. (eds.) (1948) *From Max Weber: essays in sociology* (Routledge & Kegan Paul).

Gewirth, A. (1960) 'Positive "ethics" and normative "science" ', *Philosophical Review*, **69**, pp. 311–30. Reprinted in J. J. Thomson and G. Dworkin (eds.) (1968) *Ethics* (Harper & Row) pp. 27–47.

Giddens, A. (1971) *Capitalism and Modern Social Theory* (Cambridge University Press).

Giddens, A. (1978) *Durkheim* (Fontana/Collins).

Ginsburg, M. B. *et al.* (1980) 'Teachers' conceptions of professionalism and trades unionism: an ideological analysis', in P. Woods (ed.) *Teacher Strategies* (Croom Helm) pp. 178–212.

Gouldner, A. W. (1971) *The Coming Crisis of Western Sociology* (Heinemann Educational Books).

Grant, G. (1973) 'Shaping social policy: the politics of the Coleman Report', *Teachers College Record*, **75**, 1, pp. 17–54.

Grave, S. A. (1967) 'Common sense', in P. Edwards (ed.) *Encyclopedia of Philosophy* (Macmillan and Free Press) vol. 2, pp. 155–60.

Greene, M. (1978) 'Teaching: the question of personal reality', *Teachers College Record*, **80**, 1, pp. 23–35.

Gurvitch, G. (1971) *The Social Frameworks of Knowledge* (Basil Blackwell).

Habermas, J. (1974) *Theory and Practice* (Heinemann Educational Books).

Hall, J. A. (1979) 'The curious case of the English intelligentsia', *British Journal of Sociology*, **30**, 3, pp. 291–306.

Halpern, B. (1960) ' "Myth" and "ideology" in modern usage', *History and Theory*, **1**, pp. 129–49.

Hamilton, P. (1974) *Knowledge and Social Structure* (Routledge & Kegan Paul).

Hamlyn, D. W. (1967a) 'Epistemology, history of', in P. Edwards (ed.) *Encyclopedia of Philosophy* vol. 3 (Macmillan and Free Press) pp. 8–38.

Hamlyn, D. W. (1967b) 'Empiricism', in P. Edwards (ed.) *Encyclopedia of Philosophy* vol. 2 (Macmillan and Free Press) pp. 499–505.

Harman, G. (1975) 'Ethical relativism defended', *Philosophical Review*, **84**, 1, pp. 3–22.

Harris, N. (1968) *Beliefs in Society* (Penguin).

Hartnett, A. and Naish, M. (eds.) (1976) *Theory and the Practice of Education* vol. 1 *Theory, Values and the Classroom Teacher*; vol. 2 *Academic Disciplines, Educational Policy and the Education of Teachers* (Heinemann Educational Books).

Hartnett, A. and Naish, M. (1977) 'Educational theory: bromide and barmecide', *Journal of Further and Higher Education*, **1**, 3, pp. 63–75.

Hartnett, A. and Naish, M. (1980) 'Technicians or social bandits? Some moral and political issues in the education of teachers', in P. Woods (ed.) *Teacher Strategies: explorations in the sociology of the school* (Croom Helm) pp. 254–74.

Harvey, J. (1974) 'Precising the notion of a discipline', *Educational Philosophy and Theory*, **6**, 1, pp. 13–30.

Hearnshaw, L. S. (1979) *Cyril Burt: Psychologist* (Hodder & Stoughton).

Heeren, J. (1971) 'Karl Mannheim and the intellectual elite', *British Journal of Sociology*, **22**, pp. 1–15.

Hindess, E. (1972) 'Forms of knowledge', *Proceedings of the Philosophy of Education Society of Great Britain*, **6**, 2, pp. 164–75.

Hirst, P. H. (1965) 'Liberal education and the nature of knowledge', in R. D. Archambault (ed.) *Philosophical Analysis and Education* (Routledge & Kegan Paul) pp. 113–38.

Hirst, P. H. (1966) 'Educational theory', in J. W. Tibble (ed.) *The Study of Education* (Routledge & Kegan Paul) pp. 29–58.

Hirst, P. H. (1973) 'Forms of knowledge – a reply to Elizabeth Hindess', *Proceedings of the Philosophy of Education Society of Great Britain*, **7**, 2, pp. 260–71.

Hirst, P. Q. (1975) *Durkheim, Bernard and Epistemology* (Routledge & Kegan Paul).

Hirst, P. Q. (1976) 'Althussér and the theory of ideology', *Economy and Society*, **5**, 4, pp. 385–412.

Hirst, R. J. (1967) 'Realism', in P. Edwards (ed.) *Encyclopedia of Philosophy* vol. 7 (Macmillan and Free Press) pp. 77–83.

Hollis, M. (1972) 'Witchcraft and Winchcraft', *Philosophy of the Social Sciences*, **2**, 2, pp. 89–103.

Holzner, B. and Marx, J. H. (1979) *Knowledge Application: the knowledge system in society* (Allyn & Bacon).

Horowitz, I. L. (1961) *Philosophy, Science and the Sociology of Knowledge* (Charles C. Thomas).

Horton, R. and Finnegan, R. (eds.) (1973) *Modes of Thought* (Faber & Faber).

Hudson, L. (1972) *The Cult of the Fact* (Jonathan Cape).

Hughes, H. S. (1967) *Consciousness and Society* (MacGibbon & Kee).

Husén, T. (1968) 'Educational research and the state', in W. D. Wall and T. Húsen (eds.) *Educational Research and Policy Making* (NFER) pp. 13–22.

Ingleby, D. (1970) 'Ideology and the human sciences: some comments on the role of reification in psychology and psychiatry', *Human Context*, **2**, 2, pp. 159–87.

Ingleby, D. (1974) 'The psychology of child psychology', in M. P. M. Richards (ed.) *The Integration of a Child into a Social World* (Cambridge University Press) pp. 295–308.

Inglis, F. (1975) *Ideology and the Imagination* (Cambridge University Press).

Jacoby, R. (1973) 'The politics of subjectivity: slogans of the American new left', *New Left Review*, **79**, pp. 37–49.

Janis, I. L. (1972) *Victims of Groupthink* (Houghton Mifflin).

Jensen, A. R. (1972) *Genetics and Education* (Methuen).

Jewson, N. D. (1974) 'Medical Knowledge and the patronage system in 18th century England', *Sociology*, **8**, 3, pp. 369–85.

Johnston, R. and Robbins, D. (1977) 'The development of specialities in industrialised science', *Sociological Review*, **25**, 1, pp. 87–108.

Kamin, L. J. (1977) *The Science and Politics of I. Q.* (Penguin).

Karabel, J. and Halsey, A. H. (eds.) (1977) *Power and Ideology in Education* (Oxford University Press).

Kaufman, B. A. (1978) 'Piaget, Marx and the political ideology of schooling', *Journal of Curriculum Studies*, **10**, 1, pp. 19–43.

Keat, R. and Urry, J. (1975) *Social Theory as Science* (Routledge & Kegan Paul).

Kecskemeti, P. (1952) Introduction to Mannheim (1952) *Essays on the Sociology of Knowledge* pp. 1–32.

Kekes, J. (1976) *A Justification of Rationality* (State University of New York Press).

Kitwood, T. (1976) 'Educational research and its standing as science', *Studies in Higher Education*, **1**, 1, pp. 69–82.

Koestler, A. (1971) *The Case of the Midwife Toad* (Hutchinson).

Komisar, B. P. and McClellan, J. E. (1961) 'The logic of slogans', in B. O. Smith and R. H. Ennis (eds.) *Language and Concepts in Education* (Rand McNally) pp. 195–215.

Körner, S. (1970) *Categorial Frameworks* (Blackwell).

Kuhn, T. S. (1962, enlarged edn. 1970) *The Structure of Scientific Revolutions* (Chicago University Press).

Kuhn, T. S. (1974) 'Second thoughts on paradigms', in F. Suppe (ed.) *The Structure of Scientific Theories* (University of Illinois Press) pp. 459–99.

Ladd, J. (ed.) (1973) *Ethical Relativism* (Wadsworth).

Lakatos, I. and Musgrave, A. (eds.) (1970) *Criticism and the Growth of Knowledge* (Cambridge University Press).

Larrain, J. (1979) *The Concept of Ideology* (Hutchinson).

Law, J. (1975) 'Is epistemology redundant? A sociological view', *Philosophy of the Social Sciences*, **5**, 3, pp. 317–37.

Lehrer, K. (1974) *Knowledge* (Oxford University Press).

Lieberman, A. and Miller, L. (1978) 'The social realities of teaching', *Teachers College Record*, **80**, 1, pp. 54–68.

Light, R. J. and Smith, P. V. (1971) 'Accumulating evidence: procedures for resolving contradictions among different research studies', *Harvard Educational Review*, **41**, pp. 429–71.

Lovejoy, A. O. (1940) 'Reflections on the history of ideas', *Journal of History of Ideas*, **1**, 1, pp. 3–23.

Lucas, J. R. (1958) 'On not worshipping facts', *Philosophical Quarterly*, **8**, pp. 144–56.

Lukes, S. (1973) 'On the social determination of truth', in R. Horton and R. Finnegan (eds.) *Modes of Thought: essays on thinking in Western and non-Western societies* (Faber & Faber) pp. 230–48.

Lukes, S. (1975) *Emile Durkheim: his life and work* (Penguin).

Lukes, S. and Runciman, W. G. (1974) 'Relativism: cognitive and moral' (symposium) *Proceedings of the Aristotelian Society*, supplementary **48**, pp. 165–208.

Lunsford, T. F. (1968) 'Authority and ideology in the administered university', *American Behavioral Scientist*, **11**, 5, pp. 5–14.

McHugh, P. (1968) *Defining the Situation: the organisation of meaning in social interaction* (Bobbs-Merrill).

MacIntyre, A. (1971) 'Rationality and the explanation of action', in A. MacIntyre *Against the Self Images of the Age* (Duckworth) pp. 244–59.

Mackie, J. L. (1975) 'Ideological explanation', in S. Körner (ed.) *Explanation* (Blackwell) pp. 183–97.

McLellan, D. (1975) *Marx* (Fontana/Collins).

McPherson, A. (1968) 'The Dainton Report – a Scottish dissent', *Universities Quarterly*, **22**, 3, pp. 254–73.

Macrae, D. G. (1974) *Weber* (Fontana/Collins).

Mannheim, K. (1952) *Essays on the Sociology of Knowledge* (Routledge & Kegan Paul).

Mannheim, K. (1953) *Essays on Sociology and Social Psychology* (Routledge & Kegan Paul).

Mannheim, K. (1960) *Ideology and Utopia: an introduction to the sociology of knowledge* (Routledge & Kegan Paul).

Martin, J. R. (1969) 'The disciplines and the curriculum', *Educational Philosophy and Theory*, **1**, 1, pp. 23–40.

Medvedev, A. Z. (1969) *The Rise and Fall of T. D. Lysenko* (Columbia University Press).

Merton, R. K. (1968) *Social Theory and Social Structure* (enlarged edn.) (Free

Press/Collier Macmillan).

Meynell, H. (1975) 'Science, the truth and Thomas Kuhn', *Mind*, **84**, pp. 79–93.

Miller, D. (1972) 'Ideology and the problem of false consciousness', *Political Studies*, **20**, 4, pp. 432–47.

Mills, C. W. (1963) *The Marxists* (Penguin).

Mills, C. W. (1967) 'The professional ideology of social pathologists', in I. L. Horowitz (ed.) *Power, Politics and People* (Oxford University Press) pp. 525–52.

Minar, D. W. (1961) 'Ideology and political behavior', *Midwest Journal of Political Science*, **5**, 4, pp. 317–31.

Minogue, K. R. (1973) *The Concept of a University* (Weidenfeld & Nicolson).

Mitchell, G. D. (ed.) (1979) *A New Dictionary of Sociology* (Routledge & Kegan Paul).

Montefiore, A. (ed.) (1975) *Neutrality and Impartiality: the university and political commitment* (Cambridge University Press).

Mulkay, M. (1979) *Science and the Sociology of Knowledge* (Allen & Unwin).

Nagel, E. (1960) 'Philosophy in educational research', reprinted in Hartnett, A. and Naish, M. (1976) vol. 2, op. cit., pp. 13–23.

Nagel, E. (1961) *The Structure of Science* (Routledge & Kegan Paul).

Naish, M., Hartnett, A. and Finlayson, D. S. (1976) 'Ideological documents in education: some suggestions towards a definition', in A. Hartnett and M. Naish (eds.) (1976), op. cit., pp. 55–117.

Nielsen, K. (1971) *Reason and Practice: a modern introduction to philosophy* (Harper & Row).

Nowell-Smith, P. H. (1971) 'Cultural relativism', *Philosophy of the Social Sciences*, **1**, 1, pp. 1–17.

Parekh, B. (1970) 'Scholarship and ideology', *Cross Currents*, **Fall**, pp. 455–75.

Parsons, T. (1959) 'An approach to the sociology of knowledge', in *Transactions of the Fourth World Congress of Sociology* vol. IV (International Sociological Association) pp. 25–49.

Pearson, G. (1973) 'Social work as the privatised solution to public ills', *British Journal of Social Work*, **3**, 2, pp. 209–28.

Pearson, G. (1975a) *The Deviant Imagination* (Macmillan).

Pearson, G. (1975b) 'Making social workers: bad promises and good omens', in R. Bailey and M. Brake (eds.) *Radical Social Work* (Edward Arnold) pp. 13–45.

Perry, L. (1965) 'Commonsense thought, knowledge and judgement and their importance for education', *British Journal of Educational Studies*, **13**, pp. 125–38.

Peters, R. S. (1966) *Ethics and Education* (Allen & Unwin).

Phillips, D. C. (1971) 'The distinguishing features of forms of knowledge', *Educational Philosophy and Theory*, **3**, 2, pp. 27–35.

Pincoffs, E. L. (ed.) (1972) *The Concept of Academic Freedom* (University of Texas Press).

Plamenatz, J. (1970) *Ideology* (Pall Mall).

Polanyi, M. (1969a) 'The growth of science in society', in M. Greene (ed.) *Knowing and Being* (Routledge & Kegan Paul) pp. 73–86.

Polanyi, M. (1969b) 'The potential theory of adsorption', in M. Greene (ed.) *Knowing and Being* (Routledge & Kegan Paul) pp. 87–96.

Pollock, J. L. (1968) 'What is an epistemological problem?', *American Philosophical Quarterly*, **5**, 3, pp. 183–90.

Popkin, R. H. (1967) 'Skepticism', in P. Edwards (ed.) *Encyclopedia of Philosophy* (Macmillan and Free Press) vol. 7, pp. 449–61.

Popper, K. R. (1959, 1968) *The Logic of Scientific Discovery* (Hutchinson).

Popper, K. R. (1963; revised 3rd edn. 1969) *Conjectures and Refutations: the growth of scientific knowledge* (Routledge & Kegan Paul).

Popper, K. R. (1966; 5th edn. revised) *The Open Society and Its Enemies: vol. 1 Plato; vol. 2 Hegel and Marx* (Routledge & Kegan Paul).

Popper, K. R. (1972) *Objective Knowledge: an evolutionary approach* (Oxford University Press).

Pring, R. (1975) 'In defence of authority – or how to keep knowledge under control', in D. Bridges and P. Scrimshaw (eds.) *Values and Authority in Schools* (Hodder and Stoughton) pp. 20–37.

Pring, R. (1976) *Knowledge and Schooling* (Open Books).

Pring, R. (1977) 'Common sense and education', *Proceedings of the Philosophy of Education Society of Great Britain*, **11**, pp. 57–77.

Quine, W. V. and Ullian, J. S. (1970) *The Web of Belief* (Random House).

Quinton, A. (1971) 'Authority and autonomy in knowledge', *Proceedings of the Philosophy of Education Society of Great Britain*, **5**, 2, pp. 201–15.

Remmling, G. W. (eds.) (1973) *Towards the Sociology of Knowledge* (Routledge & Kegan Paul).

Robinson, T. (1978) *In Worlds Apart: Professionals and their Clients in the Welfare State* (Bedford Square Press).

Rokeach, M. (1968) *Beliefs Attitudes and Values* (Jossey-Bass).

Ross, R. and Staines, G. L. (1972) 'The politics of analyzing social problems', *Social Problems*, **20**, 1, pp. 18–40.

Ryle, G. (1949) *The Concept of Mind* (Hutchinson).

Ryle, G. (1958) 'On forgetting the difference between right and wrong', in A. I. Melden (ed.) *Essays in Moral Philosophy* (University of Washington Press) pp. 147–59.

Runciman, W. G. (1969) 'False consciousness', *Philosophy*, **44**, pp. 303–13.

Runciman, W. G. (1973) 'Ideology and social science', in R. Benewick *et al.* (eds.) *Knowledge and Belief in Politics* (Allen & Unwin) pp. 13–35.

Scheffler, I. (1967) *Science and Subjectivity* (Bobbs-Merrill).

Scheffler, I. (1977) 'In praise of the cognitive emotions', *Teachers College Record*, **79**, 2, pp. 171–86.

Schütz, A. (1946) 'The well-informed citizen: an essay on the social distribution of knowledge', *Social Research*, **13**, pp. 463–78.

Schütz, A. (1953) 'Common sense and scientific interpretation of human action', *Philosophy and Phenomenological Research*, **16**, 1, pp. 1–37.

Schütz, A. and Luckman, T. (1974) *The Structures of the Life World* (Heinemann Educational Books).

Schwab, J. J. (1962) 'The concept of the structure of a discipline', *Educational Record*, **43**, pp. 197–205.

Scriven, M. (1970) 'The values of the academy (moral issues for American education and educational research arising from the Jensen case)', *Review of Educational Research*, **40**, pp. 541–9.

Seeley, J. R. (1966) 'The making and taking of problems: toward an ethical stance', *Social Problems*, **14**, pp. 382–9.

Seliger, M. (1977) *The Marxist Conception of Ideology* (Cambridge University Press).

Settle, T., Jarvie, I. C. and Agassi, J. (1974) 'Towards a theory of openness to criticism', *Philosophy of the Social Sciences*, **4**, 1, pp. 83–90.

Shils, E. (1972) *The Intellectuals and the Powers and Other Essays* (University of Chicago Press).

Shipman, M. D. (1972) *The Limitations of Social Research* (Longman).

Shipman, M. D. (ed.) (1976) *The Organisation and Impact of Social Research* (Routledge & Kegan Paul).

Singer, P. (1971–2) 'Moral experts', *Analysis*, **32**, pp. 115–17.

Skinner, Q. (1969) 'Meaning and understanding in the history of ideas', *History and Theory*, **8**, pp. 3–53.

Sklair, L. (1973) *Organised Knowledge* (Hart-Davies, MacGibbon/Granada).

Skorupski, J. (1978) 'The Meaning of Another Culture's Beliefs' in C. Hookway and P. Pettit (eds.) *Action and Interpretation: studies in the philosophy of the social sciences* (Cambridge University Press).

Smith, G. and Stockman, N. (1972) 'Some suggestions for a sociological approach to the study of government reports', *Sociological Review*, **20**, 1, pp. 59–77. Reprinted in A. Hartnett and M. Naish (eds.) (1976) *Theory and the Practice of Education* vol. 2 (Heinemann Educational Books) pp. 39–55.

Spencer, M. E. (1970) 'Politics and rhetorics', *Social Research*, **37**, 4, pp. 597–623.

Stark, W. (1967) 'Sociology of knowledge', in P. Edwards (ed.) *Encyclopedia of Philosophy* (Macmillan and Free Press) vol. 7, pp. 475–8.

Stebbins, R. A. (1967) 'Theory of the definition of the situation', *Canadian Review of Sociology and Anthropology*, **4**, pp. 148–64.

Stebbins, R. A. (1971) 'The meaning of disorderly behaviour: teacher definitions of a classroom situation', *Sociology of Education*, **44**, pp. 217–36.

Strauss, A. L. (1971) *Professions Work and Careers* (The Sociology Press).

Strauss, A. L. (1977) *Mirrors and Masks: the search for identity* (Martin Robertson).

Strauss, A. *et al*. (1964) *Psychiatric Ideologies and Institutions* (Free Press).

Sullivan, E. V. (1967) 'Piaget and the school curriculum', *Ontario Institute for Studies in Education – Bulletin*, no. 2, pp. 1–38.

Taylor, W. (ed.) (1973) *Research Perspectives in Education* (Routledge & Kegan Paul).

Taylor, W. (1978) *Research and Reform in Teacher Education* (NFER).

Thomas, D. (1978) 'Sociology and common sense', *Inquiry*, **21**, pp. 1–32.

Thorpe, E. (1973) 'The taken for granted reference: an empirical examination', *Sociology*, **7**, 3, pp. 361–76.

Toulmin, S. (1972) *Human Understanding* (Oxford University Press).

Trigg, R. (1973) *Reason and Commitment* (Cambridge University Press).

Turner, R. (ed.) (1974) *Ethnomethodology* (Penguin).

Walking, P. H. (1979) 'Structure-of-knowledge theory: a refutation', *Educational Studies*, **5**, 1, pp. 61–72.

Wallis, R. (ed.) (1979) *On the Margins of Science: the social construction of rejected knowledge* (Sociological Review Monograph 27, University of Keele).

Walsh, W. H. (1971) 'Knowledge in its social setting', *Mind*, **80**, 319, pp. 321–36.

Warnock, M. (1977) *Schools of Thought* (Faber & Faber).

Watkins, J. W. N. (1969) 'Comprehensively critical rationalism', *Philosophy*, **44**, pp. 57–62.

Watkins, J. W. N. (1971) 'CCR: a refutation', *Philosophy*, **46**, pp. 56–61.

Watson, P. (1978) *War on the Mind: the military uses and abuses of psychology* (Hutchinson).

Weber, M. (1976) *The Protestant Ethic and the Spirit of Capitalism* (2nd edn.) (Allen & Unwin).

Westland, G. (1978) *Current Crises of Psychology* (Heinemann Educational Books).

White, J. and Young, M. (1975) 'The sociology of knowledge' (part 1), *Education for Teaching*, **Autumn**, 98, 4–13.

White, J. and Young, M. F. D. (1976) 'The sociology of knowledge' (part 2), *Education for Teaching*, **Spring**, 99, pp. 50–58.

Whitty, G. and Young, M. F. D. (1976) *Explorations in the Politics of School Knowledge* (Nafferton).

Wilensky, H. L. (1964) 'The professionalization of everyone?', *American Journal of Sociology*, **LXX**, 2, pp. 137–58.

Williams, B. (1967) 'Rationalism', in P. Edwards (ed.) *Encyclopedia of Philosophy* (vol. 7) (Macmillan and Free Press) pp. 69–75.

Williams, B. (1972) *Morality: an introduction to ethics* (Penguin).

Williams, B. (1974–5) 'The truth in relativism', *Proceedings of the Aristotelian Society*, **75**, pp. 215–28.

Williams, R. (1976) *Keywords: a vocabulary of culture and society* (Fontana// Croom Helm).

Willower, D. J. *et al.* (1969) 'Custodialism and the secondary school', *High School Journal*, **52**, 4, pp. 182–91.

Wilson, B. R. (ed.) (1970) *Rationality* (Blackwell).

Wilson, J. (1971) 'Politics and Expertise', *Philosophy*, **46**, pp. 34–7.

Winch, P. (1958) *The Idea of a Social Science and Its Relation to Philosophy* (Routledge & Kegan Paul).

Winch, P. (1964) 'Understanding a primitive society', *American Philosophical Quarterly*, **1**, 4, pp. 307–24. Reprinted in B. R. Wilson (ed.) (1970) *Rationality* (Blackwell) pp. 78–111.

Winch, P. (1976) 'Language, belief, and relativism', in H. D. Lewis (ed.) *Contemporary British Philosophy* (4th series) (Allen & Unwin) pp. 322–37.

Working Papers in Cultural Studies No. 10 (1977) *On Ideology* (Centre for Contemporary Cultural Studies).

Wright, E. (1978) 'Sociology and the irony model', *Sociology*, **12**, 3, pp. 523–43.

Wrong, D. (1979) *Power: its forms bases and uses* (Blackwell).

Young, M. F. D. (ed.) (1971) *Knowledge and Control* (Collier-Macmillan).

Young, M. F. D. (1972) 'On the politics of educational knowledge', *Economy and Society*, **1**, pp. 194–215.

Young, M. F. D. (1972–73) 'Taking sides against the probable', *Educational Review*, **25**, pp. 210–22.

Young, M. and Whitty, G. (eds.) (1977) *Society, State and Schooling* (Falmer Press).

6 Politics and policy-making in education
Michael Parkinson

This review will be concerned with the social science literature on politics and policy-making in education. It will focus upon American as well as British literature, in part because the two countries have faced comparable if different policy dilemmas in recent years; but also because the study of educational decision-making is better developed in the USA and the literature considerably richer, and it does provide some indication of the way in which policy analysis in Britain might develop. The most striking feature of the British literature in this field is how relatively little of it there is. For a variety of reasons discussed below, social scientists in Britain have paid relatively little attention to the process of educational policy-making. As a result the important areas about which we remain ignorant far outweigh those about which we know a little. And the gaps exist at both a theoretical and an empirical level.

Political scientists concerned with policy-making could be expected to focus upon the ways in which public decision-making operates to produce policies which advantage or disadvantage different groups and individuals. Such an approach requires an explicit focus not only upon the formal authority relationships but also upon the distribution of power within the decision-making system and its impact upon the differential distribution of resources. Arguably this can best be realised by an examination of policy-making processes. The contributions of political parties, pressure groups and cultural elites need to be evaluated as carefully as the institutions of government legally responsible for implementing policy. What might be termed the inter-governmental dimension, that is the kind of relationships which have developed between central and local governments and which have become more important during the past decades, require particularly careful analysis. A policy approach would also focus on the issues of policy formulation, implementation and evaluation. But in Britain, with a few exceptions, the discipline has as yet barely developed in these directions.

This situation has been changing during the past decade and

there is now a growing school of policy analysis, but it remains an under-developed field. We know little about the role of political parties or of pressure groups in policy-making and indeed relatively little about how the formal government apparatus of decision-making works. For example, despite its growing significance the precise role of the Department of Education and Science in policy-making remains unexplored. Equally significant, there has been hardly any analysis of the inter-governmental dimension of policy-making. The relationships between central and local government and the shifting balance of power between the two is crucial to any understanding of virtually any policy initiative during the past two decades, and yet little is known about them. This is most visibly true in one of the most controversial policies in the post-war period: the comprehensive reorganisation of secondary education. There have been some studies of national, and rather more of local authority policy-making, but hardly anything which deals at a theoretical level with the interactions of the two levels of government in this policy area. Yet, in the final analysis, this dimension has critically affected the implementation of national policy. The same is true about many other important policies introduced during the post-war period.

There are a number of explanations for these gaps in the literature. One is the dominance in Britain, until recently, of formalistic modes of analysis in much political science which focused attention on the legal and administrative structures of British government rather than upon the dynamics of decision-making. This has changed in recent years but in the field of education, for example, one can still find guides to the decision-making system which are essentially based upon the prescriptions of the 1944 Education Act. The problem is also partly caused by the fact that much of public education is actually provided by local government and study of this field has, until recently, been relatively impoverished. In addition, the conventional wisdom that central government dominates local government and that their relationships need relatively little explanation has also inhibited any exploration of the dynamics of interaction. Recent events and recent analyses have revealed the limitations of that view but our understanding of them has nevertheless been delayed. A further factor inhibiting the growth of policy analysis in education has been the assumption, more strongly held in the USA than in Britain, that education and politics should be kept separate. In the USA this has been virtually an ideology of administrators who have sought to enhance their own autonomy and control over education, but the view can be found in a more diluted version in the country. It rests on the assumption that the only way to provide public services like education is according to rational, administrative criteria and that local or national politics should not be allowed to intrude. Although this has also been eroded of late it has helped inhibit the growth of policy analysis in education.

The British literature: national level politics

The literature on the politics of education in Britain has been developed enormously by Maurice Kogan. During the past decade he has systematically and successfully illuminated many areas of the policy-making process which had previously remained obscure. Kogan (1978) is the best discussion of recent trends in policy debates, but the most complete is Kogan (1975) which explores the changing relationships in educational decision-making from the expansive era of the 1960s to the austerity of the 1970s. It is a comprehensive review of the role of interest groups at the national levels, as well as a useful guide to a number of policy developments. Surprisingly, however, it pays little attention to the changing role and growth in power of the Department of Education and Science (DES). This issue has been developed to some extent by Litt and Parkinson (1979) in their analysis of the growing centralisation of policy-making in education in Britain. The same theme has been elegantly developed for social policy-making in general by Glennerster (1975), which is particularly helpful. The most recent account of the role of the DES is Pile (1979) but this unfortunately suffers from the legalistic approach already mentioned. Fowler (1974) has examined at least cursorily the role of the DES in decision-making but has not developed it very far. Weaver (1979) is helpful. The broadest survey of actors and agencies involved in education is Locke (1974), but his treatment of many issues is rather slight. Kogan's analysis of the role of Ministers of Education (Boyle and Crossland, 1971) is again quite slight but nonetheless interesting. Kogan and Packwood (1974) is revealing about one part of the educational policy-making process which is now almost defunct, the Advisory Committee system, but remains of historical interest. Two good collections of essays are Fowler *et al.* (1973) and Raggart and Evans (1977).

Parties and pressure groups

The literature on the role of political parties in policy-making is surprisingly thin. Parkinson (1970) has traced the development and impact of Labour Party policies for secondary education, and Barker (1972) has done an excellent job on similar issues up to the 1950s. But both are now dated and do not deal with many of the policy changes which have taken place since the mid-1960s. Nor does either of these really fill the need for a study of parties as policy-making machines. Even more surprising, though many works refer to it, there has been no systematic analysis of the contribution of the Conservative Party at all.

The role of pressure groups has been equally neglected. Most general studies touch upon them but there is relatively little detailed analysis. The obvious exceptions are the teacher associations. Manzer's study (1970) of the NUT, despite its age, remains a classic analysis of pressure group activity, which incidentally throws a great deal of light on educational politics in general. This should be complemented by Coates' more recent study (1972) which deals, perhaps less subtly, with a wider range of issues and actors.

Local level studies

The literature on educational decision-making at the local level is rather larger but not necessarily any better grounded theoretically. But again the quality has improved significantly of late. Regan (1979) is the most recent and best guide to the formal relationships. An especially comprehensive review and analysis of decision-making in a single education authority is Saran (1973) which locates the sources of change and reform at the local level, diffused throughout a variety of institutional actors. David's study (1977) of a series of local authorities provides the best study of the role that professional officers play at the local level, and clearly identifies the variety of internal and external constraints, especially resources, which inhibit 'rational' planning of the local authority sector. Jennings (1977) has provided an overview of local policy-making which is helpful for the overtly political dimension, but which remains finally rather superficial. Kogan and van der Eyken (1973) again provide some illuminating material about the role of the Chief Education Officer in an LEA. This should be supplemented by Birley (1970) which is an insider's view of the role of the professional officer in an education authority.

There are a number of studies which deal with local authority policy outputs. Pratt *et al.* (1973) provide an interesting account of the variation in local authority expenditure patterns on education, as do Taylor and Ayres (1969). But neither really analyse their material very fully. An interesting effort to explicate the impact of political and administrative relationships upon local education policies is Boaden (1971) which emphasises the importance of political parties for the policies LEAs pursue. But the most sophisticated and important work in this mode is Byrne and Williamson

(1975). On the basis of careful local studies, they develop a theory about the impact of different LEA policies and expenditure patterns, which goes a long way in reasserting the importance of politics and public policies, as well as social and cultural factors, for individual and class life chances in education.

Relatively little work has been done in this country in a field which is well developed in the USA: the broader community basis of decision-making in education. And most has been concerned with comprehensive reorganisation. Peschek and Brand (1966) remain an interesting if dated approach to community decision-making in two southern LEAs. Batley *et al.* (1970) to some extent replicated their study in two northern communities. There have also been studies by Peterson (1971), Kantor (1974) and Peterson and Kantor (1976) which attempt to develop a theory of the decision-making process at the community level. These are important, but should be treated carefully since their analytic framework is derived from an American context and is occasionally misleading. Some of the recent literature on politics in particular cities goes some way to locate educational policy-making in the context of urban or community decision-making more generally, for example Boaden (1971), Boaden and Alford (1969), Newton (1976) and Saunders (1979). But the dynamics of local education decision-making, and its place in urban or community politics, remains a relatively neglected field.

Policy studies

The policy issue which has received most attention from political scientists is comprehensive school reorganisation. There have been a large number of analyses at both national and local government level, although, as already mentioned, few which deal explicitly with the interaction between the two. Fenwick (1976) is a good analysis of the emergence of the comprehensive idea at the national level, as is Rubinstein and Simon (1973) over a longer time period. Parkinson (1970) also deals with the emergence of the concept from minority to mainstream status. Benn and Simon (1972) have mapped the progress of institutional reform at the grass roots level, but the work is now clearly dated. There are a variety of studies charting the local struggles over school reorganisation, including Peschek and Brand (1966), and Batley *et al.* (1970). Peterson (1971), Kantor (1974) and Peterson and Kantor (1976) are also stimulating analyses of the political processes involved, but once more are problematic in some of their interpretations.

The difficulty of most studies in this area is that they fail to integrate the national and local party processes, particularly at the implementation stage. Little work deals with the interaction between the two levels of government, and we still know little about the capacity of the national government to implement its programmes or the ability of local government to resist. Boaden (1971), Boaden and Alford (1969), Heidenheimer *et al.* (1975), Heidenheimer and Parkinson (1975) and Litt and Parkinson (1979) have all touched on some of the relevant issues but have not fully elaborated them. And none deal in detail with the dynamics of policy implementation, evaluation or control. Griffith (1966) remains the outstanding exception in this area but his work has not been successfully developed or updated. Other policy areas have been touched upon but far less well explored. Burgess and Pratt (1970) is interesting on government policies for the polytechnic sector in higher education. Moodie and Rowland (1974), is good on the internal politics of universities. Halsey and Trow (1970) is also helpful on some aspects of higher education policy as is Litt and Parkinson (1979). Kirp (1979) is an important, if problematic, analysis of the development of education policies for racial minorities in British schools. Halsey (1972) is useful on the development of the policy of positive discrimination in education. Kogan (1978) is a good, if brief, survey of current policy disputes. Killian (1979) is interesting on school busing.

The American literature
The study of educational policy-making in the USA is considerably better developed, and in spite of the institutional differences between the two systems, in many ways suggests guidelines for British students. In stark contrast to Britain, the USA has a pluralistic and decentralised pattern of decision-making where power is widely diffused but generally concentrated at the bottom of the system in the local school districts. It has neither a strong party system nor a strong national bureaucracy to enforce national priorities, and this infinitely more complex model of policy-making and implementation has generated a very rich literature, which addresses a wider range of issues than its British equivalent.

National studies
A classic essay on the philosophy and spirit of educational politics is Eliot (1959). An excellent collection of essays which deals with many of those themes 20 years later is Scribner (1977). There are several good general guides to policy-making in education, including Thompson (1976), Thomas (1975) and Wirt and Kirst (1972). Still a good collection of essays, if dating quickly, is Rosenthal

(1969). There are several good studies analysing the problems of developing and passing legislation at the federal level including Munger and Fenno (1962), Bendiner (1964), Bailey and Mosher (1968), Meranto (1967) and Eidenberg and Morey (1969). There is also a good literature on the inter-governmental dimension which addresses the problems of successfully implementing national policy initiatives in a decentralised system. The best example is the work of Murphy (1971, 1974), which deals specifically with the most important piece of federal legislation for schools, the 1965 Elementary and Secondary Education Act, but which has far broader implications than this single issue.

Studies of state and local politics

There is also a large literature upon the politics of education at state level. Masters *et al.* (1964) is a good if dated exploration of many of the themes. Zeigler and Johnson (1972) have developed an interesting model of educational decision-making using aggregate data. The most comprehensive review of the field which details the increasing politicisation of education at the state level is Wirt (1977). Kirst (1971) is also interesting. The literature on school politics at the local community level is vast and only a small sample can be referred to here. Lutz and Iannaconne (1969) is a good theoretical essay on the subject, as is Peterson (1974). Cistone (1975) and Zeigler *et al.* (1974) are both good studies of the changing patterns of school governance at the local level. Gove and Wirt (1976) is a good collection of essays on the same set of themes. There are a number of excellent studies of educational politics in particular cities. Rogers (1968) is a classic analysis of the capacity of the bureaucracy to frustrate the will of politicians in New York City. Peterson (1976) is an equally important and solid analysis of the relationship between education and city politics in one of the largest cities in the USA, Chicago. Salisbury (1967) is an elegant early exploration of the ideology of the professional bureaucracy in urban school systems and its impact upon the distribution of educational resources. The role of teacher groups has been studied by Rosenthal (1969), and Zeigler (1967).

There is a large literature on the problems and politics of schools at the urban level. Meranto (1970) is a useful brief introduction to this field. But the most interesting recent development in this area is the emergence of a school of urban history which has gone a long way in locating the problems of contemporary school systems, i.e. racism, bureaucratic domination and political isolation, in the growth of urban school systems at the turn of this century. The debate was opened by Katz (1968, 1971) and has been developed by many others. But the most balanced and elegant account which is essential reading is Tyack (1974). There is also a growing related literature which is both historical and 'political' in nature, attempting to link changes in education to the broader patterns of social and economic power existing in American society. The most provocative, if problematic, analysis is Bowles and Gintis (1976). But Spring (1972, 1976), Greer (1973) and Violas (1978) are also helpful. Again Tyack (1976) has provided one of the most fascinating interpretations of many of these themes.

Policy studies

The literature on specific policy issues which have been faced in recent years is again large. School desegregation is obviously one of the most controversial which has generated a great deal of research; the literature is extensive. Perhaps the best guide is the work of Orfield (1969, 1975, 1979). Crain (1968) provides an earlier interpretation from a more conventional political science perspective. An equally troubling issue for the local schools systems has been the character and extent of financial support they have received from other levels of government. The debate about the impact of federal government aid for the schools is best captured by Berke and Kirst (1972). There has also been much work done on the politics of recent efforts to reform patterns of state financial support for school systems. Berke (1974), Reischauer and Hartman (1973), are the best introductions. Parkinson (1979) ties the two issues of finance and desegregation together as the most critical problems facing urban school systems over the next decade. No account of educational politics would be complete without a summary of the role of the courts in recent policy decisions. The best guide to this is Hogan (1974). Carnegie (1975a) is a good account of the genesis and problems of the policy of affirmative action in higher education. Lester (1974) is a more polemical analysis of the same issue. Breneman and Finn (1978) is a good set of essays on the impact of public policies upon the private sector in higher education; Carnegie (1975b) is also useful on this. Carnegie (1975c) and Cheit (1973) are helpful on the politics and problems of decline in higher education.

There is also some fascinating work available on a rather oblique angle of policy studies, the way in which ideas about education generated by social science research are incorporated into policy-makers' views of the world. As social science research into education has mushroomed in the past two decades and traditional 'common-sense' solutions to problems have been challenged, policy-makers have been presented with an increasingly uncertain intellectual environment in which to frame policies. A number of works have tried to examine the impact that changing ideas have had directly upon the decision-makers, as well as more generally upon the general climate of opinion within which they operate. McLaughlin (1975) is a particularly good study of the way in which policy-makers in Congress manipulated social scientists 'evaluation' studies of the important 1965 Federal ESEA legislation to justify policy positions which were not in fact suggested by the original studies. Cohen (1970) is also interesting, if now dated. Equally interesting is the work that has tried to assess the impact upon policy-makers of changing views that have been offered to them by the academic community about the nature of intelligence, its distribution across different racial, class and ethnic groups and its implications for public policies. Jensen (1969) is especially important as an attack upon the reformist policies of the 1960s based upon a conservative interpretation of the structure and distribution of intelligence across minority groups in America. Kamin (1974) is a fascinating critique of the genesis and impact of such ideas. Karier (1975) also contains much revealing material on these questions. Comparable analyses of the translation of research findings into public policies can be found in Moynihan and Mosteller's reassessment (1972) of Coleman's report (1966) on equality of opportunity in American schools, as well as in the special issue of the Harvard Educational Review (1973) dedicated to an analysis of Jenck's (1972) work which highlights some of the problems attached to 'forensic social research'. Another important piece is Pettigrew and Green's (1976) study of the politics of research in the controversial area of school desegregation, busing and so-called white flight from the cities. This issue, part of the broader area of the impact of cultural 'elites' upon decision-making, is one which seems fertile and worth developing.

Conclusion

Although there are almost as many citations of British as of American literature in this review, this is misleading. For whereas in the British case it represents virtually all of the literature, in the American case it is the tip of the iceberg. The richness and variety of the American scene still eludes us. The situation is changing in Britain as researchers have begun to address a wider range of questions in more depth and more subtly. However, much empirical and theoretical work along the lines suggested in the opening section remains to be done before we have a clear understanding of the politics of education and their impact upon the public at large.

References

Bailey, S. K. and Mosher, E. K. (1968) *E. S. E. A.: the Office of Education Administers a Law* (Syracuse University Press).

Barker, R. (1972) *Education and Politics 1900–51* (Clarendon Press).

Batley, R., O'Brien, O. and Parris, H. (1970) *Going Comprehensive* (Routledge & Kegan Paul).

Bendiner, R. (1964) *Obstacle Course on Capitol Hill* (McGraw Hill).

Benn, C. and Simon, B. (1972) *Half Way There* (Penguin Books).

Berke, J. S. (1974) *Answers to Inequity* (McCutchan).

Berke, J. S. and Kirst, M. (eds.) (1972) *Federal Aid to Education. Who Benefits? Who Governs?* (D.C. Heath).

Birley, D. (1970) *The Education Officer and His World* (Routledge & Kegan Paul).

Birley, D. and Dufton, A. (1971) *An Equal Chance* (Routledge & Kegan Paul).

Boaden, N. T. (1971) *Urban Policy-making* (Cambridge University Press).

Boaden, N. T. and Alford, R. A. (1969) 'Sources of diversity in English local government', *Public Administration*, **47**, pp. 203–24.

Bowles, S. and Gintis, H. (1976) *Schooling in Capitalist America* (Basic Books).

Boyle, E. and Crosland, A. (1971) *The Politics of Education* (Penguin).

Breneman, D. and Finn, C. (eds.) (1978) *Public Policy and Private Higher Education* (Brookings Institution).

Burgess, T. and Pratt, J. (1970) *Policy and Practice* (Allen Lane, The Penguin Press).

Byrne, D. S. and Williamson, W. (1975) *The Poverty of Education: a study in the politics of opportunity* (Rowman).

Carnegie Council (1975a) *Making Affirmative Action Work in Higher Education* (Jossey-Bass).

Carnegie Council (1975b) *The Federal Role in Post-secondary Education* (Jossey-Bass).

Carnegie Foundation (1975c) *More Than Survival: prospects for higher education in a period of uncertainty* (Jossey-Bass).

Cheit, E. (1973) *The New Depression in Higher Education - Two Years Later* (Jossey-Bass).

Cistone, P. (ed.) (1975) *Understanding School Boards* (D. C. Heath).

Coates, R. D. (1972) *Teachers' Unions and Interest Group Politics* (Cambridge University Press).

Cohen, D. K. (1970) 'Politics and research evaluation of social action programmes in education', *Review of Educational Research*, **40**, 2, pp. 213–38.

Coleman, J. S. *et al*. (1966) *On Equality of Educational Opportunity* (U. S. Government Printing Office).

Crain, R. L. (1968) *The Politics of School Desegregation* (Anchor Books).

David, M. E. (1977) *Reform, Reaction and Resources* (NFER).

Eidenberg, E. and Morey, R. D. (1969) *An Act of Congress: the legislative process and the making of education policy* (W.W. Norton).

Eliot, T. H. (1959) 'Towards an understanding of public school politics', *American Political Science Review*, **53**, 4, pp. 1032–50. Reprinted in A. Rosenthal (ed.) (1969) *Governing Education: a reader on politics, power and public school policy* (Anchor).

Fenwick, I. J. K. (1976) *The Comprehensive School 1944–70* (Methuen).

Fowler, G. (1974) 'Central government of education I' unit 2 Decision Making in British Educational Systems E.221 (Open University Press).

Fowler, G., Morris, V. and Ozga, J. (eds.) (1973) *Decision Making in British Education* (Heinemann Educational Books).

Glennerster, H. (1975) *Social Service Budgets and Social Policy* (Allen & Unwin).

Gove, S. K. and Wirt, F. (eds.) (1976) *Political Science and School Politics* (Lexington).

Greer, C. (1973) *The Great School Legend* (Viking Press).

Griffith, J. A. G. (1966) *Central Departments and Local Authorities* (Allen & Unwin).

Halsey, A. H. (ed.) (1972) *Educational Priority Volume 1* (HMSO).

Halsey, A. H. and Trow, M. A. (1970) *The New Academics* (Harvard University Press).

Heidenheimer, A. J., Heclo, H., Teich Adams, C. (1975) *Comparative Public Policy* (Macmillan).

Heidenheimer, A. J. and Parkinson, M. (1975) 'Equalizing educational opportunity in Britain and the United States: the politics of implementation', in W. Gwynn and G.C. Edwards (eds.) *Perspectives on Public Policy Making* (Tulane University Press) pp. 141–65.

Hogan, J. C. (1974) *The Schools, the Courts and the Public Interests* (D.C. Heath).

Jencks, C. (1972) *Inequality* (Harper).

Jennings, R. E. (1977) *Education and Politics: policy making in local education authorities* (Batsford).

Jensen, A. R. (1969) 'How much can we boost IQ and scholastic achievement?', *Harvard Educational Review*, **39**, 1, pp. 1–123.

Kamin, L. J. (1974) *The Science and Politics of I. Q.* (Halsted Press).

Kantor, P. (1974) 'The governable city: islands of power and political parties in London', *Polity*, **7**, 2, pp. 4–31.

Karier, C. (ed.) (1975) *Shaping the American Educational State 1900 to the Present* (Free Press).

Katz, M. B. (1968) *The Irony of Early School Reform* (Beacon Press).

Katz, M. B. (1971) *Class, Bureaucracy and Schools* (Praeger).

Killian, L. M. (1979) 'School busing in Britain', *Harvard Educational Review*, **49**, 2, pp. 185–206.

Kirp, D. L. (1979) *Doing Good by Doing Little: race and schooling in Britain* (University of California Press).

Kirst, M. W. (ed.) (1971) *State, School and Politics: research directions* (D. C. Heath).

Kogan, M. (1975) *Educational Policy-making* (Allen & Unwin).

Kogan, M. (1978) *The Politics of Educational Change* (Fontana).

Kogan, M. and Packwood, T. (1974) *Advisory Councils and Committees in Education* (Routledge & Kegan Paul).

Kogan, M. and van der Eyken, W. (1973) *County Hall* (Penguin).

Lester, R. A. (1974) *Antibias Regulation of Universities* (Jossey-Bass).

Litt, E. and Parkinson, M. (1979) *Politics and Policies in Education: Anglo-American perspectives* (Praeger).

Locke, M. (1974) *Power and Politics in the School System* (Routledge & Kegan Paul).

Lutz, F. N. and Iannacone, L. (1969) *Understanding Educational Organisations; a field study approach* (Charles E. Merrill).

McLaughlin, M. (1975) *Evaluation and Reform* (Ballinger).

Manzer, R. A. (1970) *Teachers and Politics* (Manchester University Press).

Masters, N. A., Salisbury, R. H. and Eliot, T. H. (1964) *State Politics and the Public Schools* (Alfred A. Knopf).

Meranto, P. (1967) *The Politics of Federal Aid to Education in 1965* (Syracuse University Press).

Meranto, P. (1970) *School Politics in the Metropolis* (Charles E. Merrill).

Moodie, G. C. and Rowland, E. (1974) *Power and Authority in British Universities* (McGill – Queens University Press).

Moynihan, D. P. and Mosteller, F. (eds.) (1972) *On Equality of Educational Opportunity* (Vintage).

Munger, F. J. and Fenno, R. F. (1962) *National Politics and Federal Aid to Education* (Syracuse University Press).

Murphy, J.T. (1971) 'Title I of E. S. E. A.: The politics of implementing federal education reform', *Harvard Educational Review*, **41**, 1, pp. 35–63.

Murphy, J. T. (1974) *State Education Agencies and Discretionary Funds* (D. C. Heath).

Newton, K. (1976) *Second City Politics* (Clarendon Press).

Orfield, G. (1969) *The Reconstruction of Southern Education* (John Wiley).

Orfield, G. (ed.) (1975) *Symposium on School Desegregation and White Flight* (Center for National Policy Review).

Orfield, G. (1979) *Must We Bus?* (Brookings Institution).

Parkinson, M. (1970) *The Labour Party and the Organisation of Secondary Education 1918–65* (Routledge & Kegan Paul).

Parkinson, M. (1979) 'Dilemmas for the city schools: racial isolation and fiscal stress', in G.A. Tobin (ed.) *The Changing Structure of the City* (Sage) pp. 157–76.

Peschek, D. and Brand, J. A. (1966) *Politics and Policies in Secondary Education* (Greater London Papers No. 11, London School of Economics).

Peterson, P. E. (1971) 'British interest group theory re-examined: the politics of comprehensive education in three cities', *Comparative Politics*, **3**, 2, pp. 381–402.

Peterson, P. E. (1974) 'The politics of American education', in F. Kerlinger (ed.) *Review of Research in Education Vol. 2* (Peacock), pp. 348–89.

Peterson, P. E. (1976) *School Politics Chicago Style* (Chicago University Press).

Peterson, P. E. and Kantor, P. (1976) 'Political parties and citizen participation in English city politics', *Comparative Politics*, **9**, 2, pp. 197–217.

Pettigrew, T. F. and Green, R. G. (1976) 'School desegregation in large cities: a critique of the Coleman "white flight" thesis', *Harvard Educational Review*, **46**, 1, pp. 1–53.

Pile, Sir W. (1979) *The Department of Education and Science* (Allen & Unwin).

Pratt, J., Burgess, T., Allemano, R. and Locke, M. (1973) *Your Local Education* (Penguin).

Raggatt, P. and Evans, M. (eds.) (1977) *Urban Education – the Political Context* (Ward Lock Educational).

Regan, D. E. (1979) *Local Government and Education* (Allen & Unwin).

Reischauer, R. D. and Hartman, R. W. (eds.) (1973) *Reforming School*

Finance (Brookings Institution).

Rogers, D. (1968) *110 Livingston Street* (Random House).

Rosenthal, A. (1969) *Pedagogues and Power: teacher groups in school politics* (Syracuse University Press).

Rubinstein, D. and Simon, B. (1973) *The Evolution of the Comprehensive School* (Routledge & Kegan Paul).

Salisbury, R. H. (1967) 'School politics in the big city', *Harvard Educational Review*, **37**, 3, pp. 408–24.

Saran, R. (1973) *Policy-making in Secondary Education* (Clarendon Press).

Saunders, P. (1979) *Urban Politics: a sociological perspective* (Hutchinson).

Scribner, J. (ed.) (1977) *The Politics of Education* (University of Chicago Press).

Spring, J. H. (1976) *The Sorting Machine* (McKay).

Spring, J. H. (1972) *Education and the Rise of the Corporate State* (Beacon Press).

Taylor, G. and Ayres, N. (1969) *Born and Bred Unequal* (Longman).

Thomas, N. C. (1975) *Education in National Politics* (McKay).

Thompson, J. T. (1976) *Policy Making in American Public Education* (Prentice Hall).

Tyack, D. (1974) *The One Best System* (Harvard University Press).

Tyack, D. (1976) 'Ways of seeing: an essay on the history of compulsory schooling', *Harvard Educational Review*, **46**, 3, pp. 355–89.

Various authors. (1973) 'Perspectives on inequality', *Harvard Educational Review*, **43**, 1, pp. 37–166.

Violas, P. C. (1978) *The Training of the Urban Working Class* (Rand McNally).

Weaver, T. (1979) 'Department of Education and Science: central control of education?' unit 2 The Control of Education in Britain E.222 (Open University Press).

Wirt, F. M. (1977) 'Education politics and policies', in H. Jacob and K. N. Vines (eds.) *Politics in the American States* (Little Brown) pp. 284–348.

Wirt, F. M. and Kirst, M. W. (1972) *The Political Web of American Schools* (Little Brown).

Zeigler, H. L. (1967) *The Political Life of American Teachers* (Prentice Hall).

Zeigler, H. L. and Johnson, K. (1972) *The Politics of Education in the States* (Bobbs-Merrill).

Zeigler, H. L., Kent Jennings, M. and Wayne Peak, G. (1974) *Governing American Schools: political interaction in local school districts* (Duxbury Press).

7 The ideological and policy response to black pupils in British schools
Barry Troyna

Introduction

In 1971, the Department of Education and Science (DES) published its 13th Education Survey; entitled *The Education of Immigrants*, it outlined the advice it had offered to HMIs on the education of immigrants (i.e. pupils of Afro-Caribbean and Asian origin) since 1963, and indicated that these various advisory notes were gradually developing into more coherent and definitive forms. The survey is particularly significant because it contained the assurance to LEAs that the Department intended to 'shape a coherent and practical policy' on this education issue (DES, 1971:15).

Since then however, the DES has been repeatedly criticised for failing to provide a uniform policy on the education of black pupils. In 1972, Felicity Bolton and Jennie Laishley asserted that 'the lack of a considered, *explicit* national policy' was one of the most significant factors associated with the growth of unrest amongst black youth (1972:1, original emphasis). The following year, the Select Committee on Race Relations and Immigration voiced a similar criticism of central government in its report on education: 'If . . . one conclusion stands out above all others, it is that we have failed to grasp, and are still failing to grasp the scale of what we have taken on' (1973:55: para. 227). And in 1976, the Chief Education Officers' report to the Community Relations Commission insisted that 'Little attempt appears to have been made either to formulate a national policy in other than the most general terms or to estimate the cost of an adequate ethnic minority education programme' (Community Relations Council 1976:6). However, perhaps the most severe indictment of central and local government attitudes appeared in a report on the West Indian community where it stated that the Select Committee had found 'a general lack of response by governments and local authorities to the Committee's previous recommendations' (1977).

On the face of it, these criticisms appear entirely valid. The most cursory perusal of government responses would reveal that, with one conspicuous exception[1] there have not been any centrally prescribed policies dealing specifically with the education of black pupils. Instead, public policy response has assumed two alternative forms. The first is the occasional publication of DES circulars and memoranda; these have dealt particularly with the issue of language provision for black, mainly Asian pupils. Secondly, there is the allocation of funds for schools in multiracial areas via broadly-based programmes such as Section II of the Local Government Act (1966) and the Urban Aid programme, launched in 1969 by the Local Government Grants (Social Need) Act. In short, policy has generally tended to proceed along 'racially inexplicit' lines, so that, with the obvious exception of language provision, the needs of black pupils are seen as indistinguishable from those of their residentially proximate white peers. As one commentator has recently remarked, the defining characteristic of educational policy in this area has been the notion of 'doing good by stealth' (Kirp 1980). As we have seen however, the refusal of central government to depart from this policy approach has led many critics to accuse it of inactivity.

In this paper I want to document central government responses to the education of black pupils (see Table 1) and to situate these on the context of changing conceptualisations of 'multicultural education'. I also want to suggest the the unwillingness of the DES to formulate a uniform policy on this subject has far more to do with its enduring commitment to an assimilationist perspective of blacks in Britain, than with the argument that it lacks the institutional power to prescribe such a policy. Put differently, the DES shares with other central government departments a conception of society as politically and culturally indivisible, and as a result perceives schools primarily as socialising, anglicising and integrating agencies. The nature and extent of 'cultural diversity' allowed in schools should, according to this view, have clearly defined limits. It will be tolerated only in so far as it does not threaten the fundamental values and assumptions of the educational system. If this central proposition is accepted, then inactivity in this context cannot be dismissed as a featureless non-event; on the contrary, it represents an explicit ideological position[2].

From 'assimilation' to 'cultural pluralism'

Offical rhetoric on the education of black pupils in British schools has shifted in emphasis over the past 20 years. The 'assimilationist' position which informed government thinking in the early 1960s has been gradually refined into an 'integrationist' and, more recently, 'cultural pluralist' model. Cultural pluralism is the most sophisticated and liberal variant of the earlier models, and directives based on the pluralist conception of 'multicultural education' propose that the curriculum be reappraised in recognition of the changing multiethnic, multicultural fabric of contemporary British society. The following extract from the 1977 Green Paper, *Education in Schools: A Consultative Document*, exemplifies this current idiom:

> Our society is a multicultural, multiracial one, and the curriculum should reflect a sympathetic understanding of the different cultures and races that now make up our society . . . (DES 1977:41, para. 10:11).

These three conceptual models are clearly useful for analysing the evolution of education policy in this area since the early 1960s. However, the following caveats are important; firstly, there has not been a neat and regular progression from one developmental stage to the other; and secondly, there may be a major discrepancy between the conceptual framework adopted by policy-makers and that used in the implementation of policy.

Assimilation
The assimilationist philosophy embraces a conception of the nation as a unitary whole which is indivisible both culturally and politically. To help maintain this world view, it was necessary in the early 1960s to control the potentially disruptive influence generated by the inflow of a comparatively large number of ethnically and culturally diverse groups into the society. Thus the period saw the first moves towards an exclusionist immigration policy which was legitimated on the grounds that assimilation would be facilitated if the number of black immigrants were kept at a containable level. Put simply, the state invoked the belief that 'keeping numbers down is good for race relations'. If this guiding philosophy were to retain credibility, however, it was important also for the state to encourage the black settlers to discard all traces of their cultural and ethnic identity; only then could they be receptive to and successfully internalise the values and assumptions of the majority culture. What this process entailed was vividly illustrated in an election speech given by George Partiger (former MP for Southall) in 1964:

> I feel that Sikh parents should encourage their children to give up their turbans, their religion and their dietary laws. If they refuse to integrate then we must be tough. They must be told they would be the first to go if there was unemployment and it should be a condition of being given National Assistance that the immigrants go to English classes (cited in Bagley 1973:304).

The role of the educational system under this regime was clear; schools were to actively discourage cultural diversity and were to act as the principal mechanism for assisting the assimilation of immigrants. As the second part of the Commonwealth Immigrants Advisory Council report put it:

> . . . a national system of education must aim at producing citizens who can take their place in a society properly equipped to exercise rights and perform duties which are the same as other citizens. If their parents were brought up in another culture or another tradition, children should be encouraged to respect it, but a national system cannot be expected to perpetuate the different values of immigrant groups (1964: 7, para. 10).

It would appear that classroom practice reflected an almost obsessive commitment to this philosophy. Jenny Williams reported from her study of schools in the Sparkbrook area of Birmingham that teachers conceived of their role as 'putting over a certain set of values (Christian), a code of behaviour (middle-class), and a set of academic and job aspirations in which white collar jobs have higher prestige than manual, clean jobs than dirty . . .' (1967: 237). Moreover, any radical departure from this perspective would, according to one head of a Humanities department, encourage divisiveness and sanction social and racial segregation: 'There are no courses in Asian history or geography, for example, since the whole aim of the school is towards social integration. We cannot account for practices in the home which may be towards segregation' (cited in Townsend and Brittan 1973:31).

The debate about policy for the education of black pupils, such as there was one in the early 1960s, proceeded along similar lines. In DES Circular 7/65, for instance, the task of education was defined as the 'successful assimilation of immigrant children', a process heavily dependent on 'a realistic understanding of the adjustments they have to make'. Significantly, the DES did not concede the need for any corresponding 'adjustments' in the education system. Instead, it focused its attention on the twin areas of 'language' and 'numbers', concerns which were related to the extent that both were seen to have the potential to inhibit assimilation (DES 1965).

In 1963, the DES published its first formal advice on this issue in pamphlet 43, *English for Immigrants*, in which it recommended the use of specifically trained teachers in English as a Second Language (E2L). The provision of E2L teachers was easy to justify within the DES's conceptualisation of the issue, as Street-Porter has commented:

... part of the philosophy underlying it was the theory that if immigrant children who could not speak English could quickly be taught it, they would equally quickly assimilate into the British educational system and ultimately into British society as a whole (1978:76).

Alan James has taken this point further: 'a dose of systematic language teaching would act as a lubricant'; after the successful completion of the course the immigrant pupil could be 'fed into the educational machine . . . without causing it to seize up' (1977:2). Following this line of approach, neither the DES nor individual LEAs felt impelled to prescribe any further modifications to the curriculum to ensure the 'successful assimilation of immigrant children'.

Nevertheless, the Department's awareness of the need for E2L teaching only went part of the way in placating the fears of white parents that the educational progress of their children in schools containing large numbers of immigrants was being impeded. In 1963, a group of white parents in Southall expressed their apprehensions to Sir Edward Boyle, then Minister of Education, who subsequently recommended to the government that no school should contain more than 30 per cent immigrant pupils. Boyle's rationale for this was two-fold. First, the concentration of immigrants in highly localised areas, and their children in one or two schools in those areas, was contrary to, and undermined the whole assimilationist philosophy. In June 1965 the DES gave its official sanction to the policy of 'dispersal', insisting that

> ... as the proportion of immigrant children in a school or class increases, the problems will become more difficult to solve and the chances of assimilation more remote . . . (DES Circular 7/65: 1965:4, para. 8).

Second, that the concentration of immigrant children in particular schools would lead to a reduction in education standards. So, in the same circular, the DES implored white parents to accept that some positive action was being taken to assuage their anxieties:

> *It will be helpful if the parents of non-immigrant children see that practical measures have been taken to deal with the problems in the schools, and that the progress of their own children is not being restricted by the undue preoccupation of the teaching staff with the linguistic and other difficulties of immigrant children* (1965:9, para. 8: original emphasis).

Needless to say, the formulation of a policy firmly rooted in the assimilationist mould paid little heed to the apprehensions and opinions of the immigrant parents.

The policy of 'dispersal' exemplified in the crudest terms the assumptions underpinning central government's assimilationist approach to 'race' related issues in this period, and it remains the only centrally endorsed, specific educational policy regarding 'race'. Why then did central government depart so far from what I have suggested is the conventional and politically expected course of 'doing "good" by stealth'?

The answer would seem to lie in the broader context of the Labour Party's decision to abandon its *laissez-faire* approach to 'race' and immigration after securing power in 1964. The precise reasons for this *volte-face* are difficult to pinpoint, although Crossman's reflections on the decision would suggest that it was first and foremost an electoral strategy, designed to appease the anti-immigration views of the electorate (see Butler and Stokes 1969:350). Thus:

> Ever since the Smethwick election it has been quite clear that immigration can be the greatest potential vote-loser for the Labour party if we are seen to be permitting a flood of immigration to come in and blight the central areas in our cities (Crossman 1975:149–50).

He continues: 'We felt we had to out-trump the Tories by doing what they would have done and so transforming their policy into a bi-partisan policy' (1975:299). The government White Paper, *Immigration From the Commonwealth* (Home Office 1965: Cmnd 2739) provided the electorate with clear evidence of Labour's 'about turn' and, significantly, the document included the gist of the statements of Circular 7/65. I am suggesting, then, that it was politically expedient in 1965 for central government to depart from its established policy approach to the education of black pupils and for it to actively promote a policy which on the one hand underlined its commitment to assimilation, and on the other reaffirmed to the electorate its decision to adopt a tougher line on the issue of 'race'. Significantly, we can infer from opinion polls in this period that the government's support for Circular 7/65 would have found approval amongst the electorate.

Integration

The policy of 'dispersal' had highlighted not only how crudely the assimilationist perspective was being operationalised in the early 1960s, but also the extent to which it was underpinned and sustained by racist assumptions and a belief in cultural superiority. As David Milner has indicated:

> ... 'immigrant' children were dispersed, irrespective of

whether they were immigrant or not, irrespective of whether they had language difficulties or not, including among them some West Indian children who, in contrast to what we now know, were then thought *not* to have language difficulties of the same order as Asians. In other words, the children were dispersed solely on the basis of colour . . . (1975:201).

Similarly, a spokesman for Ealing Community Relations Council insisted that the decision to sanction 'dispersal' illustrated 'an unspoken assumption that assimilation to the culture of the majority society should be an aim of educational policy'. But he continued: 'ethnic minorities may place greater value on their civil rights of freedom of choice and demand equality before the law'; what right then did the majority community have to 'over-ride the identity and culture of a minority within a multi-cultural society'? (cited in Killian 1979:203).

In the late 1960s and early 1970s such overt disregard for the black community in Britain became less prevalent, at least in educational matters, and 'integrationist' views came to be adopted as the working paradigm for educational policy and decision-makers. Essentially, however, the difference between the two conceptual frameworks was in degree rather than kind. Both, for instance, embraced the view that the absorption of the black communities into the majority culture should continue to be the national goal. The two models varied only in so far as integrationists did not advocate the total suppression of cultural differences; instead, they defined the aim as 'unity through diversity'. In other words, educationalists should encourage the retention and celebration of minority cultures in the classroom *providing* that this would neither be divisive nor threatening to the established aims and ethos of the educational system. For the first time then, gestures, albeit symbolic, were made towards the concept of 'multiculturalism' – a shift in emphasis which was neatly captured in Roy Jenkins' definition of integration as 'not a flattening process of assimilation but an equal opportunity accompanied by cultural diversity, in an atmosphere of mutual tolerance' (cited in Patterson 1969:113). The definition was, as Kirp remarks, 'as irrestistible as it was vague' (1980:46), and certainly did not provide any guidelines on how it could be effectively translated into classroom practice. Nor did the DES offer any clarification. Indeed, after the publication of Circular 7/65 it remained 'inactive' on this subject until 1971 when, in *Potential and Progress in a Second Culture* (Education Survey 10) it advised on methods of assessing the intelligence and academic attainment of 'immigrant' pupils. The only firm indication of DES receptivity to the integrationist philosophy was its drastic modification of the policy of 'dispersal' in *The Education of Immigrants* (Education Survey 13, 1971).

In the absence of any central directive, it was left to LEAs and individual schools to decide how best to translate the integrationist ideal into practice. Street-Porter provides the following overview of the practical response generated in this period:

> The late sixties saw the start of several small policies which reflected the views of the Jenkins statement and also the assimilation hangover. Teachers saw the need to become informed about the cultural background of the minority group children they taught . . . There was a mushrooming of courses and conferences to inform teachers about the homelands of such British-born children and there was an increasing number of advisory posts created to deal with the problems of "immigrant" education . . .' (1978:81).

Nevertheless, whilst there were signs that this shift in emphasis was being reflected at the 'chalk face', Kirp is empirically correct in reporting that 'local practice had changed less than national rhetoric' (1980:47). The Schools Council Project, *Education for a Multiracial Society*, shows that an attitude of 'benign neglect' continued to prevail in LEAs. Authorities with an ethnically homogeneous school population simply did not see any need to modify organisational procedures or curriculum content, whilst those with an ethnic mix in their schools continued to focus their attention on the linguistic needs of black – mainly Asian – pupils. In addition, the report pointed out that a significant number of teachers were resisting any attempt to modify their well-established 'colour blind' approach to teaching in multiethnic schools. One primary head teacher told the researchers:

> Having worked in a school with a large proportion of immigrants I wonder if too much emphasis should be given to racial differences. Children are children the world over. They meet and play on equal terms. Constant discussion of racial differences might lead to embarrassing situations (cited in Townsend and Brittan 1973:15).

In sum, the Schools Council Project had shown that the shift to an integrationist conception of the issue was far more in evidence at the level of national rhetoric than in LEAs and schools. Part of the reason for this may have been the non-intervention of the DES during much of this period. The absence of any formal DES policy (or advice) made it difficult for LEAs to formulate a cohesive and co-ordinated strategy based on integrationist assumptions. As Townsend reported, a wide array of differing, and in some instances contradictory, practices were taking place both at

Authority and school level (Townsend 1971). Clearly of greater significance though was the enduring commitment of LEAs and their schools to assimilationist postures and, as a corollary, their reluctance to recognise, even in a token form, the cultural differences of their black pupils; according to one head teacher, the process of adaptation was not negotiable, black pupils simply had to accept the values of the majority culture:

> I do not consider it the responsibility of an English State School to cater for the development of cultures and customs of a foreign nature. I believe our duty is to prepare children for citizenship in a free, democratic society according to British standards and customs (cited in Townsend and Brittan, 1973:13).

It is also possible to argue that the move towards integration did not entail any significant departure from the assumptions which had underlined assimilationist attitudes. Both clearly rested on Anglo-centric conceptions of the position of blacks in the society, both politically and economically. As the Select Committee on Race Relations and Immigration asserted in its response to demands for the inclusion of Black Studies in the school curriculum: 'Those who come here to settle must, to some extent, accept the ways of the country in which they are going to live and of whose society they form a part' (1973:23, para. 104). The difference was simply that while assimilationists had argued that the values and assumptions of the majority culture could only be maintained if minority cultural differences were suppressed, integrationists insisted that this end could best be ensured by minimal recognition of these differences, that is 'unity through diversity'. The Select Committee, again, was quite explicit on this:

> The demand for Black Studies has arisen because the content of education in Britain is seen as Anglo-centric and biased against black people. We can understand this. But we doubt whether Black Studies in the narrow sense would make a contribution to wider education and better race relations and we are not attracted by the idea of black teachers teaching pupils in separate classes or establishments. But the history, geography and cultures of the large minorities which now form part of British society are worthy of study and appreciation, not least by indigenous children. We are certainly not suggesting that curricula be turned upside down . . . (1973:28, para. 103).

Clearly, the means may have changed but the ends remained the same.

Cultural pluralism
Growing dissatisfaction amongst black pupils and their parents led

to a further refinement of the assimilationist model in the late 1970s. Schools were failing to nourish a positive group identity amongst their black pupils and this was seen to be causally related to their low academic performance. The disproportionately large number of black youngsters, mainly of West Indian origin, in the lower academic streams (Jelinek and Brittan 1976; Troyna 1978), in ESN schools (Coard 1971) and, more recently in disruptive units, or 'sin bins' (Francis 1979; St John Brooks 1981) clearly demonstrated the point. 'It has been clear that in order for black children to realise their full potential they must be respected as equal participants capable of full educational attainment' stated the first Annual Report of the Afro-Caribbean Education Resources (ACER) project, which began work in 1976. It went on:

> . . . the identity of a child or what he inherits is important to his or her self-esteem; to deny this is to deprive the individual of a basic human right. The school should become an enriched inter-cultural learning environment for the non-racist society that we all hope for (1977:4).

The failure of the schools to provide an 'appropriate' educational experience for its black pupils led to the setting up of supplementary education services for these pupils. The imperative was clear: supplementary schools would have the effect of balancing out the alleged 'white bias' in English education (see Cashmore and Troyna (forthcoming) for a fuller discussion). It has now been argued that whilst the supplementary schools provide a useful, temporary fill-in for black pupils, they avoid confronting the root of the problem, namely 'changing the thinking of the schools' (Mack 1977). This is perhaps only partly true; these forms of retaliatory action by black organisations helped to crystallise the inadequacies of the integrationist framework, and prompted the development of cultural pluralist conceptions of 'multicultural education'. This works along parallel lines to ACER's demands in prescribing 'multicultural materials' for all pupils and a 'well rounded educative experience for all pupils in their school life'. The integrationist's claim for the insertion of appendages such as Black Studies to the established curriculum is therefore eschewed in favour of the notion that an awareness of Britain's multiethnic society should permeate all aspects of the normal curriculum. According to the DES

> For the curriculum to have meaning and relevance for all pupils now in our schools, its content, emphasis and the values and assumptions contained must reflect the wide range of cultures, histories and life styles in our multi-racial society (White Paper 1978, Cmnd 7186:6).

Operationally, plans to integrate 'an awareness of Britain's mul-tiethnic society' into the curriculum have been inhibited by two crucial factors. Firstly, cultural pluralism is a diffuse concept which subsumes a diversity of educational objectives and strategies (Williams 1979) and, in the absence of any formal guidance from the DES, it has been interpreted in a variety of ways both in the formulation of LEA policy directives, and in pedagogic and class-room practices (Birley High School 1980). Secondly, and more significantly, the cultural pluralist model highlights the inherent conflict between autonomist and assimilationist elements of educa-tional policy. As McLean has suggested:

> In as far as they have an economic function and one of facilitat-ing social mobility, educational institutions must be assimilation-ist if they are to be consistent with social change (1980:9).

Put differently, the main purpose of schools is to provide pupils with the educational credentials necessary to secure employment and job security, and to assist the process of occupational and social mobility. Any attempt to disrupt this function will therefore be firmly resisted.

In this context it is possible to understand why LEAs and schools continue to define 'multicultural education' in terms of E2L provi-sion (Little and Willey 1981) and why a significant number of head teachers and their staff steadfastly refuse to reappraise the orienta-tion and content of their curricula (Brittan 1976; Giles 1977). In sum, cultural pluralism amounts to little more than modest token-ism, and like the earlier conceptual frameworks it takes as its starting point the assumption that the fundamental values of the school and society are impervious to change; cultural adaptation must take place within the black communities. It is a conception of 'multicultural education' which was exemplified in a recent article by Eric Bolton, an HMI and supporter of cultural pluralist approaches. In discussing the factors which have led to the changed awareness of what the objectives of a multiracial society might be, he writes:

> The most powerful drive has come from the growing belief that an individual needs to be secure in his own culture, and to see that culture respected by others if he is to be confident and *competent in a new society and if he is to move out of the ghetto and into the mainstream of ordinary life* (1979:6, emphasis added).

Conclusion
I have shown in this essay that the educational response to black pupils in British schools has not been orchestrated by centrally

prescribed policies, but has originated largely from the initiatives taken by LEAs and individual schools. One of the principal ways in which the DES has justified its decision not to prepare a uniform policy on this issue has been to stress its own lack of authority in a decentralised education system. It has argued that the formulation of a 'coherent and practical policy' at central government level would encroach on the 'freedom' and 'autonomy' of LEAs and undermine the diffusion of responsibility for policy decisions enshrined in the 1944 Education Act. In 1974, for example, the following response to the Select Committee's recommendation for the setting up of a central fund to which LEAs could apply 'for resources to meet the special educational needs' of black pupils and their parents was published:

> The public provision of education is, for the most part, the responsibility of the local education authorities. It is financed like any other local authority service largely through the rates and Rate Support Grant. It is the job of the local authority to decide how best to use its resources of staff and money to meet the needs of its area. If specific grants for particular aspects of education in which the local authorities have previously enjoyed discretion were to be introduced, the effect might be to reduce the scope of local responsibility (Home Office 1974: 13–14).

Not only does this response highlight the ambivalence about central and local government relationships, it also suggests that the power to formulate educational policy rests ultimately with LEAs. This representation of DES authority is not however entirely accurate; local authorities are not 'free' or 'autonomous' and neither are their schools (see Kogan and Van Der Eyken 1973; Lawton 1980). Indeed, from 1960 onwards there have been moves to reassert some central influence over educational policy generally, and the curriculum in particular[3]. The 1977 Green Paper clearly stipulated that whilst the responsibility for education is shared between the DES, LEAs and teachers, the distribution of power between them is neither static nor necessarily equable; it also indicated that a more positive approach from DES was to be characteristic of future policy:

> The Secretaries of State are responsible in law for the promotion of the education of the people of England and Wales. They need to know what is happening in the schools. *They must draw attention to national needs if they believe the education system is not adequately meeting them* (DES 1977:5, para. I.14, emphasis added).

Claims of institutional powerlessness therefore are largely untenable, and are certainly not sufficient to account for the reluctance of the DES to prescribe a 'coherent and practical policy' on the education of black pupils. Far more significant is its commitment to assimilation and a conception of the society as indivisible. Further, it insists that the cultural values and assumptions which underpin the society are non-negotiable. In refusing to formulate a policy based on the principle of multiculturalism, the DES acknowledges its reluctance, which is shared with central government, to concede any institutional or political power to the black communities. In the absence of negotiation and concession, and the continued pre-eminence of assimilation as a characteristic of DES and LEA approaches to this issue, multiculturalism in education remains a myth:

> Is (Britain) a society in which the best is taken from, say, West Indian, Asian and English culture to form a basis for a new culture? Is it a society in which the English culture must adapt itself to new and increasingly powerful voices of the different cultures? Are immigrant cultural forces sufficiently powerful to encourage the indigenous population to change its cultural heritage? Will a 'ghetto' situation contain immigrant cultures and cause the indigenous population to ignore and disregard immigrants, causing a multiracial society to remain really a racial one? (Head teacher cited in Townsend and Brittan 1973:16–17).

Notes

This section is based on a paper presented to the conference 'Policy in Education in a Period of Contraction' held at the Institute of Education, University of London, on 14th March 1981. I am grateful to Henry Miller, Frank Reeves and Sally Tomlinson for their comments on an earlier version of the paper.

[1] I am referring here to the policy of 'dispersal' or 'busing' which is dealt with later in this paper. For further details see also Killian (1979) and Kirp (1980).

[2] This interpretation of inaction as a conscious and deliberate decision derives from Steven Lukes' conceptual analysis of power. See Lukes (1974), particularly chapters 7 and 8.

[3] In 1960, the Conservative Minister of Education, David Eccles, announced his intention 'to make the Ministry's voice heard rather more often and positively and no doubt controversially' (cited in Lawton, 1980: 22).

Table 1   The educational response to black pupils in British schools and related policy initiatives on 'race' 1962—80

Year	Legislation	Educational policy	Action
1962	Commonwealth Immigrants Act		Commonwealth Immigrants Advisory Council is set up
1963		Ministry of Education agrees to 'dispersal' of 'immigrant' children	
1964			Bi-partisan policy on 'race' and immigration begins
1965	White paper on Immigration Race Relations Act	DES Circular 7/65 sanctions 'dispersal'	Race Relations Board is set up
1966	Section II of Local Government Act	Roy Jenkins defines 'integration' DES starts to collect statistics on 'immigrant' children	Local authorities with 'substantial numbers of immigrants' are eligible to apply for Section II grant
1967		DES Plowden Report adopts 'area based' approach The presence of immigrants in need of E2L regarded as a defining characteristic of an EPA	PEP report on racial discrimination published
1968	Commonwealth Immigrants Act Race Relations Act	Urban Aid Programme announced; funds to be made available to 'urban areas of general need'	Community Relations Commission set up
1969	Local Government Grants (Social Need) Act marks the start of UA Programme		Section II grants increase
1970			
1971	Immigration Act	DES Education Surveys 10 and 13 deal with the education of 'immigrants'	
1972		DES Education Survey on E2L needs of 'immigrants'	
1973		Select Committee Report: Education: 24 Recommendations	Schools Council Project Report: Education for a Multiracial Society

Year	Legislation	Educational policy	Action
1974		Government replies to Select Committee recommendations	Centre for Educational Disadvantage, and Assessment of Performance Unit set up Definition of 'immigrant' scrapped
1975		Bullock Committee of Enquiry publishes *Language of Life* report; see chapter 20	
1976	Race Relations Act		CRC and Race Relations Board scrapped; replaced by Commission for Racial Equality
1977		Select Committee reports on West Indian Community	
1978		Government response to 1977 Select Committee report	DES circulates *Education in Schools: A Consultative Document*
1979			Committee of Inquiry into the education of Ethnic Minority pupils set up under the Chairmanship of Rampton
1980	White Paper on Nationality		

Source: Adapted from National Association for Multiracial Education (1980:1–2); and Troyna (forthcoming)

References

Afro-Caribbean Educational Resources Project (1977) *First Annual Report* (ACER).

Bagley, C. (1973) 'The Education of Immigrant Children: A Review of Problems and Policies in Education' in *Journal of Social Policy*, **2**, 4, pp. 303–14.

Birley High School (1980) *Multi-Cultural Education in the 1980s* (City of Manchester Education Committee).

Bolton, E. (1979) 'Education in a Multiracial Society' in *Trends in Education*, no. 4, Winter, pp. 3–7.

Bolton, F. and Laishley, J. (1972) *Education for a Multiracial Britain* (Fabian Research Series 303).

Brittan, E. (1976) 'Multiracial Education – 2. Teacher Opinion on Aspects of School Life. Part 2: Pupils and Teachers' in *Educational Research*, **18**, 3, pp. 182–91.

Butler, D. and Stokes, D. (1969) *Political Change in Britain* (Macmillan).

Cashmore, E. and Troyna, B. (forthcoming) 'The Crisis of Black Youth' in E. Cashmore and B. Troyna (eds.), *Black Youth in Crisis* (Allen & Unwin).

Commonwealth Immigrants Advisory Council (1964) *Second Report* (Cmnd 2266 HMSO).

Coard, B. (1971) *How the West Indian Child is Made Educationally Sub-Normal in the British School System* (New Beacon Books).

Community Relations Council (1976), *Funding Multiracial Education: A National Strategy*, (Community Relations Council).

Crossman, R. (1975) *Diaries of a Cabinet Minister* (Hamish Hamilton// Jonathan Cape).

Department of Education and Science (1963) *English for Immigrants* (DES Pamphlet 43).

Department of Education and Science (1965) *The Education of Immigrants* (DES Circular 7/65, 14th June).

Department of Education and Science (1971) *Potential and Progress in a Second Culture* (DES Education Survey 10).

Department of Education and Science (1971) *The Education of Immigrants* (DES Education Survey 13).

Department of Education and Science (1977) *Education in Schools: A Consultative Document* (Green Paper Cmnd 6869, July, HMSO).

Francis, M. (1979) 'Disruptive Pupils: Labelling a New Generation' in *New Approaches in Multiracial Education*, **8**, 1, Autumn, pp. 6–9.

Giles, R. (1977) *The West Indian Experience in British Schools* (Heinemann Educational Books).

Home Office (1965) *Immigration From the Commonwealth* (Cmnd 2739, HMSO).

Home Office (1974) *Educational Disadvantage and the Educational Needs of Immigrants: Observations on the Report on Education of the Select Committee on Race Relations and Immigration* (Cmnd 5720, HMSO).

Home Office (1978) *The West Indian Community: Observations on the Report of the Select Committee on Race Relations and Immigration* (Cmnd 7186, HMSO).

James, A. (1977) 'Why Language Matters' in *Multiracial School*, **5**, 3, pp. 2–9.

Jelinek, M. M. and Brittan, E. (1976) 'Multiracial Education I: Inter-Ethnic Friendship Patterns' in *Educational Research*, **18**, 1, pp. 44–53.

Killian, L. M. (1979) 'School Bussing in Britain: Policies and Perceptions' in *Harvard Educational Review*, **49**, 2, pp. 185–206.

Kirp, D. (1980) *Doing Good By Doing Little* (University of California Press).

Kogan, M. and Van Der Eyken, W. (1973) *County Hall: The Role of the Chief Education Officer* (Penguin).

Lawton, D. (1980) *The Politics of the School Curriculum* (Routledge & Kegan Paul).

Little, A. and Willey, R. (1981) *Multi-ethnic Education: The Way Forward* (Schools Council Pamphlet 18).

Lukes, S. (1974) *Power: A Radical View* (Macmillan Studies in Sociology).

McLean, M. (1980) 'Cultural Autonomy and the Education of Ethnic Minority Groups' in *British Journal of Educational Studies*, **28**, 1, pp. 7–12.

Mack, J. (1977) 'West Indians and Schools' in *New Society*, 8th December, pp. 510–12.

Milner, D. (1975), *Children and Race* (Penguin).

National Association for Multiracial Education (1980) *Immigration, Race Relations and Multiracial Education* (unpublished paper).

Patterson, S. (1969) *Immigration and Race Relations in Britain: 1960–1967* (Oxford University Press for the Institute of Race Relations).

Schools Council (1973) *Education for a Multi-Racial Society* (Evans Bros// Methuen).

Select Committee On Race Relations and Immigration (1973) *Education: Vol. I. Report* (HMSO).

Select Committee on Race Relations and Immigration (1977) *The West Indian Community: Vol. I Report* (HMSO).

St John Brooks, C. (1981) 'What Should Schools Do With Their Problem Children?' in *New Society*, 8th January, pp. 44–6.

Street-Porter, R. (1978) *Race, Children and Cities: Open University Unit E361* (Open University).

Townsend, H. E. R. (1971) *Immigrant Pupils in England: The LEA Response* (NFER).

Townsend, H. E. R. and Brittan, E. (1973) *Multiracial Education: Need and Innovation* (Schools Council Working Paper 50).

Troyna, B. (1978) 'Race and Streaming: A Case Study' in *Educational Review*, **30**, 1, pp. 59–65.

Troyna, B. (forthcoming) 'A Question of Numbers: 'Race Relations', Social Policy and the Media' in P. Golding (ed.) *Mass Media and Social Policy* (Martin Robertson).

Williams, J. (1967) 'The Younger Generation' in J. Rex and R. Moore, *Race, Community and Conflict* (Oxford University Press for the Institute of Race Relations) pp. 230–57.

Williams, J. (1979) 'Perspectives on the Multicultural Curriculum' in *The Social Science Teacher*, **8**, 4, pp. 126–33.

8 Women and education
Sandra Acker

Introduction
We think of 'women and education', if at all, as a specialised though interdisciplinary topic. Yet it is a topic like no other – except, perhaps, 'men and education' (usually shortened to 'education'). A 'woman question' is potentially part of almost every other topic in sociology of education. Gender, however, has been at best a peripheral concern for the field (Acker 1981a). There are sex differences in educational experiences and outcomes as striking as the class differences which preoccupied sociologists for years (Blackstone 1976; King 1971). But sociologists of education have mostly failed to analyse ways in which schooling might support women's subordinate social and economic position.

Many of the studies discussed here are of recent origin and not well integrated into mainstream sociology of education. Constraints of space mean giving preference to sociological or quasi-sociological work, rather than popular debates, historical accounts, or psychological research on sex differences. Readers who wish fuller coverage of American work should consult bibliographies such as Rosenberg and Bergstrom (1975) and Stineman (1979).

Getting started
General textbooks on sociology of education contain limited discussions of women and education. A better start would be the recent texts and collections of readings specifically about the topic. Delamont (1980) is short, accessible, and includes vivid examples of sexism and stereotyping in schools. Byrne's (1978) longer text is polemical and punchy and aims to change attitudes and policies by providing extensive documentation of unequal opportunities. Those seeking an analysis of women's education in the context of capitalist society should read Deem (1978) or Sharpe (1976). Other introductions are Stockard *et al*. (1980) and Jones (1973).

Turning to 'readers', *Half the Sky* (Bristol Women's Studies Group 1979) contains short excerpts on women's education plus useful references. Spender and Sarah (1980) offer an interesting collection of articles linking the patriarchal order to school and classroom processes. Deem (1980) includes some excellent scholarly papers (Fuller; MacDonald; Shaw). Kelly (1981) effectively combines theoretical discussion, empirical research and personal experience. American readers include Mednick, Tangri and Hoffman (1975); Pottker and Fishel (1977); Stacey, Bereaud, and Daniels (1974).

Some special issues of journals can also be read as introductions to the field (*Educational Review* 1975; *Harvard Educational Review* 1979–80; *Women's Studies International Quarterly* 1978). Good single articles are Hannon 1979; Marks 1976; Shaw 1976; Wolpe 1974.

Contextualising women's education
Although many sociologists consider that education plays an important part in social and cultural reproduction, few have specifically analysed its role in the reproduction of gender relations and the sexual division of labour. Exceptions are Barrett (1980); David (1980); Deem (1978); MacDonald (1980); Wolpe (1978). All discuss women's education in the context of capitalism and/or patriarchy.

A number of writers use a socio-historical approach to contextualise women's education (Burstyn 1977; Delamont and Duffin 1978; Dyhouse 1977; Marks 1976; Purvis 1980). David (1980) shows how the state has used the family and education system together to sustain the sexual and social division of labour. Blunden (1980) is an original attempt to link sex-differentiated course provision in turn-of-the-century further education to the needs of the local economy.

Achievements, aspirations, adolescents
We have no concept of 'gender chances' analogous to 'class chances' in education, and have as yet paid little attention to ways in which schools and colleges influence aspirations, achievements, and opportunities for women. Government statistics give details on sex differences in subjects studied, exams taken, and school-leaver 'destinations' (DES 1980a, 1980b). Boys are more likely than girls to take three 'A' levels and go to university. For the majority of children who do not take 'A' levels, subject choice and destination are even more sex-stereotyped. Subjects typically studied by girls in effect disqualify them from further training in a great range of occupations (Byrne 1978). Women are very much under-represented on day-release and sandwich courses in further education. Men predominate on advanced and scientific/technical courses, while women pursue non-advanced nursing, catering and secretarial studies (Byrne 1978; DES 1980c; NATFHE 1980). Some colleges now provide special courses for mature women

'returners' (Stoncy and Reid 1980).

Even if one sees these patterns as simply 'underachievement' or low aspirations, why should 'underachievement' develop so dramatically during adolescence? Studies such as Sharpe's (1976) suggest adolescent girls' 'choices' must be interpreted in a context of media messages, peer pressures, institutional practices and limited economic opportunities. Moreover, girls are not a homogeneous group. Their aspirations and achievements are influenced in complex, interacting and sometimes unexpected ways by ability, class, region, ethnicity, and type of school attended (Byrne 1978; Fuller 1980; Sharpe 1976; Shaw 1980).

Socialisation, sexism, schools

To understand girls' aspirations and ultimately women's social position, it may help to examine social processes within schools. McDonald (1980) suggests schools transmit a 'gender code', and indeed gender seems to pervade school life. Tradition dictates that boys and girls be separated for registration, seating, queueing, physical education and craft subjects, and teachers make frequent statements reinforcing stereotyped sex roles (Clarricoates 1980; Delamont 1980; DES 1975; Fuller 1978; King 1978; Shaw 1976). Researchers report: timetabling policies which result in sex segregation; domination by boys of school resources, project topics, teacher attention and even space; highly restricted roles for women in children's books (Byrne 1978; Buswell 1981; Delamont 1980; Clarricoates 1978; Lobban 1975, 1978; Scott 1980; Wolpe 1977).

School organisation not only conveys messages about differentiation but also about power and hierarchy. Junior schools often have a mostly female staff but a male head teacher; in secondary schools, men more often than women hold headships and posts of responsibility, and teach high-prestige subjects and older children (Davies and Meighan 1975; Fuller 1978).

Some researchers find teachers 'prefer' girls (Hartley 1978; King 1978), others boys (Davies and Meighan 1975). Sexton (1969) argues that the 'feminised' primary school environment disadvantages boys. However, boys appear to get more teacher attention, both praise and punishment (Evans 1979; Lobban 1978), and girls' academic achievements are sometimes disparaged as products of hard work rather than talent (Buswell 1981; Clarricoates 1980; Davies 1979).

It is important to appreciate that sex may interact with class and race in influencing classroom events and teacher expectations (Clarricoates 1980; Fuller 1978; King 1978). We must also consider the attitudes and strategies of pupils themselves. Mixed sex groups seem unpopular with junior school children (Galton, Simon and Croll 1980). Shaw (1980) suggests the sexes see themselves as two separate reference groups: 'boys define themselves as being, whatever else, at least not a girl' (p. 71). Further investigation of the combined effects of school practices, teacher attitudes and pupil outlooks should increase our understanding of the contribution of schooling to the perpetuation of sexual divisions in society.

Women teachers

Although women are the majority of school teachers, men dominate the higher status posts (DES 1980d). Some writers blame women's reluctance to apply or lack of persistence for this (Hilsum and Start 1974), but there is also some evidence of sex discrimination (NUT 1980). Moreover, reductions in the size of the teaching force and the teacher training enterprise have had especially negative consequences for women (Bone 1980; Trown and Needham 1980). For discussions of women as school-teachers see Buchan (1980); Byrne (1978); Deem (1978); Delamont (1980); Trask and Gross (1976); Hope (1979); Lortie (1975); Partington (1975).

Women are a small minority of teachers in universities and colleges (DES 1980d and e) where they are concentrated at lower levels. Acker (1980) and Hochschild (1975) discuss some of the subtle barriers to success for women university teachers. Acker (1980) cites a number of other British and American studies; see also Rendel (1980). Bradley and Silverleaf (1979) and Scribbins (1977) discuss women teachers in further education.

Sources of change

Extensive American legislation has aimed at increasing women's educational opportunities (Fishel and Pottker 1977). Britain's Sex Discrimination Act contains provisions on education, but a number of ambiguities and exceptions limit its force (Acker 1981b; Harman 1978).

Another source of change is women's studies courses. De Wolfe (1980) considers the problems which may arise in reconciling feminist and academic objectives in such courses, and Guttentag and Bray (1976) discuss difficulties of changing children's stereotyped beliefs about sex roles. Adams and Laurikietis (1976), Bristol Women's Studies Group (1979) and Coussins (1979) are among those who have developed relevant materials for use in schools, colleges or universities.

Further references and resources

There are many areas it has not been possible to review in this section.

On the question of whether mixed or single sex schools are 'better' for girls, see Dale (1974); DES (1975); Lavigueur (1977); Kelly (1981); Okely (1978). Adolescent and preadolescent girls and their subcultures are discussed by Lambart (1976); Llewellyn (1980); McRobbie and Garber (1975) amd Meyenn (1980). Brah (1979), Fuller (1980), Sharpe (1976) and Wilson (1978) have written about the education of girls of West Indian and/or Asian descent. There is little British research on characteristics and experiences of women students in higher or further education (Preston 1977), but American literature is reviewed in Acker (1978).

Useful journals include *Signs, Women's Studies Abstracts, Resources for Feminist Research, Feminist Review, Women's Studies International Quarterly*. The newsletter *Women and Education* is available from 14 St Brendan's Road, Withington, Manchester. Women's Research and Resources Centre (190 Upper Street, London N1) has a good library, including unpublished papers, a women's studies syllabus collection, and a current research index. Several pamphlets on sex discrimination in education are available free from the Equal Opportunities Commission (Overseas House, Quay Street, Manchester).

Finally, for further reading about sex roles and women's position in society generally, see: Barker and Allen (1976a and b); Evans and Morgan (1979); Kanter (1977); Kuhn and Wolpe (1978); Mackie and Pattullo (1977); Rosaldo and Lamphere (1974); Stockard and Johnson (1980).

Conclusion

Considerable research on women and education is now taking place. Only slowly is this work becoming part of mainstream sociology of education; often it is still a fringe subject, 'for women only'. There are still many gaps and some of the research results need careful replication before we have more than very tentative conclusions. To the extent work of this kind is integrated into the sociology of education we may create a stronger field that does not rely on studies about half of humankind to reach conclusions about us all.

References

Acker, S. (1978) *Sex Differences in Graduate Student Ambition* (Ph.D. dissertation, unpublished, University of Chicago).
Acker, S. (1980) 'Women, the other academics', *British Journal of Sociology*

of Education, **1**, 1, pp. 81–91.

Acker, S. (1981a) 'No-woman's-land: British sociology of education 1960–1979', *Sociological Review*, **29**, 1, pp. 77–104.

Acker, S. (1981b) 'Sex discrimination in education: reply to Shaw', *Journal of Philosophy of Education*, **15**, 1, pp. 107–18.

Adams, C. and Laurikietis, R. (1976) *The Gender Trap* (Virago).

Barker, D. L. and Allen, S. (eds.) (1976a) *Dependence and Exploitation in Work and Marriage* (Longman).

Barker, D. L. and Allen, S. (eds.) (1976b) *Sexual Divisions and Society: Process and Change* (Tavistock).

Barrett, M. (1980) *Women's Oppression Today: Problems in Marxist Feminist Analysis* (Verso).

Blackstone, T. (1976) 'The education of girls today', in J. Mitchell and A. Oakley (eds.) *The Rights and Wrongs of Women* (Penguin) pp. 199–216.

Blunden, G. (1980) 'The whisky money and sexual inequality in nonadvanced further education 1890–1903', in *Proceedings of the Standing Conference on the Sociology of Further Education* (available from Coombe Lodge, Blagdon, Bristol).

Bone, A. (1980) *The Effect on Women's Opportunities of Teacher Training Cuts* (Equal Opportunities Commission).

Bradley, J. and Silverleaf, J. (1979) *Making the Grade: Careers in F. E. Teaching* (National Foundation of Educational Research).

Brah, A. K. (1979) *Inter-Generational and Inter-Ethnic Perceptions: A Comparative Study of South Asian and English Adolescents and Their Parents in Southall* (Ph.D. dissertation, unpublished, University of Bristol).

Bristol Women's Studies Group (ed.) (1979) *Half the Sky* (Virago).

Buchan, L. (1980) 'It's a good job for a girl (but an awful career for a woman!)', in D. Spender and E. Sarah (eds.) pp. 81–9.

Burstyn, J. (1977) 'Women's education in England during the nineteenth century: a review of the literature, 1970–1976', *History of Education*, **6**, 1, pp. 11–19.

Buswell, C. (1981) 'Sexism in school routines and classroom practices, *Durham and Newcastle Research Review*, **9**, 46, Spring, pp. 195–200.

Byrne, E. (1978) *Women and Education* (Tavistock).

Clarricoates, K. (1978) 'Dinosaurs in the classroom – a re-examination of some aspects of the hidden curriculum in primary schools', *Women's Studies International Quarterly*, **1**, 4, pp. 353–64.

Clarricoates, K. (1980) 'The importance of being Ernest . . . Tom . . . Jane. The perception and categorization of gender conformity and gender deviation in primary schools', in R. Deem (ed.) pp. 26–41.

Coussins, J. (1979) *Taking Liberties* (Virago).

Dale, R. (1974) *Mixed or Single Sex School?* vol. 3 (Routledge & Kegan Paul).

David, M. E. (1980) *The State, the Family and Education* (Routledge & Kegan Paul).

Davies, L. (1979) 'Deadlier than the male? Girls' conformity and deviance in school', in L. Barton and R. Meighan (eds.) *Schools, Pupils and Deviance* (Nafferton) pp. 59–73.

Davies, L. and Meighan, R. (1975) 'A review of schooling and sex roles with particular reference to the experience of girls in secondary schools', *Educational Review*, **27**, 3, pp. 165–78.

Deem, R. (1978) *Women and Schooling* (Routledge & Kegan Paul).

Deem, R. (ed.) (1980) *Schooling for Women's Work* (Routledge & Kegan Paul).

Delamont, S. (1980) *Sex Roles and the School* (Methuen).

Delamont, S. and Duffin, L. (eds.) (1978) *The Nineteenth Century Woman: Her Culture and Physical World* (Croom Helm).

Department of Education and Science (1975) *Curricular Differences for Boys and Girls in Mixed and Single-Sex Schools*, Education Survey 21 (HMSO).

Department of Education and Science (1980a) *Statistics of Education 1978 Vol. 1: Schools* (HMSO).

Department of Education and Science (1980b) *Statistics of Education 1978 Vol. 2: School Leavers CSE and GCE* (HMSO).

Department of Education and Science (1980c) *Statistics of Education 1977 Vol. 3: Further Education* (HMSO).

Department of Education and Science (1980d) *Statistics of Education 1978 Vol. 4: Teachers* (HMSO).

Department of Education and Science, University Grants Committee (1980e) *Statistics of Education 1977 Vol. 6: Universities* (HMSO).

Dyhouse, C. (1977) 'Good wives and little mothers: social anxieties and the schoolgirls' curriculum, 1890–1920', *Oxford Review of Education*, **3**, 1, pp. 21–36.

Educational Review (1975) **27**, 3, June.

Evans, M. and Morgan, D. (1979) *Work on Women: A Guide to the Literature* (Tavistock).

Evans, T. (1979) 'Creativity, sex-role socialisation and pupil-teacher interactions in early schooling', *Sociological Review*, **27**, 1, February, pp. 139–55.

Fishel, A. and Pottker, J. (1977) *National Politics and Sex Discrimination in Education* (Lexington Books).

Fuller, M. (1978) *Dimensions of Gender in a School* (Ph.D. dissertation, unpublished, University of Bristol).

Fuller, M. (1980) 'Black girls in a London comprehensive school', in R. Deem (ed.) op. cit., pp. 52–65.

Galton, M., Simon, B., and Croll, P. (1980) *Inside the Primary Classroom* (Routledge & Kegan Paul).

Guttentag, M. and Bray, H. (1976) *Undoing Sex Stereotypes: Research and Resources for Educators* (McGraw-Hill).

Hannon, V. (1979) 'Education for sex equality: What's the problem?', in D. Rubinstein (ed.) *Education and Equality* (Penguin) pp. 104–18.

Harman, H. (1978) *Sex Discrimination in School: How to Fight It* (National Council for Civil Liberties).

Hartley, D. (1978) 'Sex and social class: a case study of an infant school', *British Educational Research Journal*, **4**, 2, pp. 75–82.

Harvard Educational Review (1979–80) 'Women and Education' (special issue) Part I: **49**, 4, November and Part II: **50**, 1, February.

Hilsum, S. and Start, K. B. (1974) *Promotion and Careers in Teaching* (National Foundation for Educational Research).

Hochschild, A. (1975) 'Inside the clockwork of male careers', in F. Howe (ed.) *Women and the Power to Change* (McGraw-Hill) pp. 47–80.

Hope, A. (1979) *Up the Down Staircase: Careers of Women Teachers* (M.Ed.

dissertation, unpublished, University of Bristol).

Jones, K. (1973) 'Women's education' part 4 block V *Education Economy and Politics* E.352 (Open University Press).

Kanter, R. M. (1977) *Men and Women of the Corporation* (Basic Books).

Kelly, A. (ed.) (1981) *The Missing Half: Girls and Science Education* (University of Manchester Press).

King, R. (1971) 'Unequal access in education – sex and social class', *Social and Economic Administration*, **5**, 3, pp. 167–75.

King, R. (1978) *All Things Bright and Beautiful? A Sociological Study of Infants' Classrooms* (Wiley).

Kuhn, A. and Wolpe, A. M. (eds.) (1978) *Feminism and Materialism* (Routledge & Kegan Paul).

Lambart, A. (1976) 'The sisterhood', in M. Hammersley and P. Woods (eds.) *The Process of Schooling* (Routledge & Kegan Paul) pp. 152–9.

Lavigueur, J. (1977) *Equality of Educational Opportunity for Girls and its Relation to Co-education* (M.Ed. dissertation, unpublished, University of Sheffield).

Llewellyn, M. (1980) 'Studying girls at school: the implications of confusion' in R. Deem (ed.) op. cit., pp. 42–51.

Lobban, G. (1975) 'Sex roles in reading schemes', *Educational Review*, **27**, 3, pp. 202–10.

Lobban, G. (1978) 'The influence of the school on sex-role stereotyping', in J. Chetwynd and O. Harnett (eds.) *The Sex Role System* (Routledge & Kegan Paul) pp. 50–61.

Lortie, D. (1975) *Schoolteacher* (University of Chicago Press).

MacDonald, M. (1980) 'Socio-cultural reproduction and women's education', in R. Deem (ed.), op. cit., pp. 13–25.

McRobbie, A. and Garber, J. (1975) 'Girls and subcultures' in S. Hall and T. Jefferson (eds.) *Resistance Through Ritual* (Hutchinson) pp. 209–22.

Mackie, L. and Pattullo, P. (1977) *Women at Work* (Tavistock).

Marks, P. (1976) 'Femininity in the classroom', in J. Mitchell and A. Oakley (eds.) *The Rights and Wrongs of Women* (Penguin) pp. 176–98.

Mednick, M., Tangri, S., and Hoffman, L. (eds.) (1975) *Women and Achievement* (Hemisphere).

Meyenn, R. (1980) 'Schoolgirls' peer groups', in P. Woods (ed.) *Pupil Strategies* (Croom Helm).

National Association of Teachers in Further and Higher Education (1980) *The Education Training and Employment of Women and Girls* (NATFHE).

National Union of Teachers (1980) *Promotion and the Woman Teacher* (NUT).

Okely, J. (1978) 'Privileged, schooled and finished: boarding school education for girls', in S. Ardener (ed.) *Defining Females* (Croom Helm) pp. 109–39.

Partington, G. (1975) *Women Teachers in the Twentieth Century in England and Wales* (National Foundation for Educational Research).

Pottker, J. and Fishel, A. (eds.) (1977) *Sex Bias in the Schools: The Research Evidence* (Associated University Presses).

Preston, A. E. (1977) *Student Culture and the Perspectives of Women Students* (M.Ed. dissertation, unpublished, University of Bristol).

Purvis, J. (1980) 'Working class women and adult education in nineteenth-century Britain' *History of Education*, **9**, 3, pp. 193–212.

Rendel, M. (1980) 'How many women academics 1912–76?', in R. Deem (ed.), op. cit., pp. 142–61.

Rosaldo, M. Z. and Lamphere, L. (eds.) (1974) *Woman, Culture and Society* (Stanford University Press).

Rosenberg, M. B. and Bergstrom, L. V. (eds.) (1975) *Women and Society: a Critical Review of the Literature with a Selected Annotated Bibliography* (Sage).

Scott, M. (1980) 'Teach her a lesson: sexist curriculum in patriarchal education', in D. Spender and E. Sarah (eds.) pp. 97–120.

Scribbins, K. (1977) 'Women in education: some points for discussion', *Journal of Further and Higher Education*, **1**, 3, Winter, pp. 17–39.

Sexton, P. (1969) *The Feminized Male: Classrooms, White Collars, and the Decline of Manliness* (Vintage).

Sharpe, S. (1976) *Just Like a Girl* (Penguin).

Shaw, J. (1976) 'Finishing school', in D. L. Barker and S. Allen (eds.) *Sexual Divisions and Society* (Tavistock) pp. 133–49.

Shaw, J. (1980) 'Education and the individual: schooling for girls, or mixed schooling – a mixed blessing?', in R. Deem (ed.) op. cit., pp. 66–75.

Spender, D. and Sarah, E. (eds.) (1980) *Learning to Lose: Sexism and Education* (The Women's Press).

Stacey, J., Bereaud, S. and Daniels, J. (eds.) (1974) *And Jill Came Tumbling After: Sexism in American Education* (Dell).

Stineman, E. (1979) *Women's Studies: A Recommended Core Bibliography* (Libraries Unlimited).

Stockard, J. and Johnson, M. (1980) *Sex Roles* (Prentice-Hall).

Stockard, J. et al. (1980) *Sex Equity in Education* (Academic Press).

Stoney, S. M. and Reid, M. J. (1980) *Further Opportunities in Focus* (National Foundation for Educational Research and Further Education Curriculum Review and Development Unit).

Trask, A. and Gross, N. (1976) *The Sex Factor and the Management of Schools* (Wiley).

Trown, A. and Needham, G. (1980) *Reduction in Part-time Teaching: Implications for Schools and Women Teachers* (Equal Opportunities Commission and Assistant Masters and Mistresses Association).

Wilson, A. (1978) *Finding a Voice: Asian Women in Britain* (Virago).

de Wolfe, P. (1980) 'Women's studies: the contradictions for students', in D. Spender and E. Sarah (eds.), op. cit., pp. 49–54.

Wolpe, A. M. (1974) 'The official ideology of education for girls', in M. Flude and J. Ahier (eds.) *Educability, Schools and Ideology* (Croom Helm) pp. 138–59.

Wolpe, A. M. (1977) *Some Processes in Sexist Education* (Women's Research and Resources Centre).

Wolpe, A. M. (1978) 'Education and the sexual division of labour', in A. Kuhn and A. M. Wolpe (eds.) *Feminism and Materialism* (Routledge & Kegan Paul) pp. 290–328.

Women's Studies International Quarterly (1978) **1**, 4.

9 The sociology of adolescence and youth
David Marsland

Introduction: theoretical issues

In this section, I have limited my attention to adolescence and youth. In life-cycle terms, this involves neglecting childhood. My justification for this is provided by the practical and theoretical importance at the present time of the later phases of pre-adulthood, and the extent of their neglect by sociologists.[1]

In part the neglect of youth by sociologists must be attributed to the dominance in recent years of Marxist theory. As with sex and race, so with youth, Marxist analysis tends to derogate other differentiating variables aside from class to a position so secondary as to approach invisibility. At the end of the 1960s an analysis by Allen (1968) provided a definitive formulation of this characteristically Marxist dismissal of youth. The influence of her analysis, which has been reprinted and cited ubiquitously, can hardly be overestimated. Its influence has been strengthened by two other factors. First, the sociologist's parochial tendency to dismiss anything remotely psychological – as the concept of 'adolescence' has routinely been taken to be. Secondly, sociologists' generalised scepticism of anything so manifestly commonsensical as the concept of 'youth', which has been commonly treated as a concept for journalists and the person in the street and *ipso facto* inadequate for sociological analysis.

During the 1970s the undeniable significance of problems associated with young people – for example unemployment, education, delinquency – has constrained some revision of this *a priori* theoretical dismissal of youth. Indeed Marxist sociologists have been in the forefront of recent work on youth.

Their approach, most coherently expressed in the work of Stuart Hall *et al. Resistance Through Rituals* (1976), nevertheless maintains Allen's derogative view of the concept of youth and of the established approach to the sociological analysis of youth which has its roots in Eisenstadt (1956). In important respects Frank Musgrove's analysis (1964) supports the theoretical approach of Hall *et al.* (1976). It has remained throughout the 1970s as an influential source of conceptualisation for studies of young people, and *ipso facto* a source of distraction from the topic of youth in itself.

The key features of Marxist theorising about youth are most succinctly expressed in a recent paper by Hall *et al.* (1976). They conclude, among other things, that to construe youth as a stage of life is problematical; that there can be no 'sociology of youth'; that, as they say, 'youth as a concept is unthinkable'; that even as a social category it doesn't make much sense; and that in any case youth at best is a trivial, secondary phenomenon and normally dominated by class relations. In short, as in *Resistance Through Rituals*, they reject the concept and the theory associated with it.

I find all this exaggerated and less than persuasive. It denigrates the established knowledge we have about youth. It represents an account of youth which is compelled to deny falsely the significance of one set of forces in social life, the psychosocial forces organised in the age system, out of fear that their recognition may challenge the determinative pre-eminence of another set of such forces – those of class. I have attempted to present counter-arguments about the concept of youth along the following lines. First, the concept symbolises and demarcates an aspect of social reality which without it would remain uncharted and unexplicated. Secondly, it brings coherently into one analytical category a range of phenomena which, taken separately, would be incomprehensible. Thirdly, the concept provides, when properly constituted, a provisional theoretical model of the processes underlying the meaning and conditions of the life of young people, and of the forces controlling them (Marsland and Hunter 1976; Marsland 1978a).

On the basis of such arguments, a coherent rationale for the main theoretical alternative to the Marxist approach can be formulated. This approach grows out of the foundational work of Eisenstadt (1956, 1972), Coleman (1961, 1974) and Erikson (1963). It prescribes and justifies four main areas of requisite analysis in sociological research on young people:

1. the significance of peer groups in the life of young people;
2. the meaning, causes and functions of youth cultures and youth subcultures;
3. the causes, pattern, and consequences of intergenerational relations, or more specifically, of the cultural handling of relations between age groups;
4. the historical and political significance of the involvement of youth in transformational social change.

Overall these issues have not received during the 1970s the attention which they demand. This is due in part to the Marxist influence, which directs theoretical attention in different directions. Even more, however, it may be due to the effects of the third major theoretical approach in British sociological analysis of young people. This latter, which includes the work of some of the best and most influential researchers, such as Smith (1971) and Eggleston (1976) is typically *empiricist* and *eclectic*. It tends to minimise the significance of the level of issues pressed alike by Marxists and by the traditionally established sociology of youth. It could hardly be claimed that the work of the 1970s had attended to the resolution of issues at this level. On my reading of that work, such analysis cannot be postponed further, and must be a crucial item on the agenda of the 1980s.

In the meantime, since this theoretical level of argument has scarcely begun, it is not possible to articulate a review of research under coherent theoretical heads without imperialistically making illegitimate presumptions about the resolution of theoretical issues. Instead, I have organised my review here in terms of commonsensical, concrete and institutional spheres, each constituting an aspect of the cultural context of the life of young people.

Employment

During the 1960s, sociological studies of young people tended to focus on education and delinquency. Outside events have shifted the emphasis to the question of work. Unemployment among young people is manifestly structural. The effects of unemployment on young people are demonstrably serious. Among the research which has rapidly expanded during the 1970s in acknowledgement of these facts, the work of Ashton is especially important and valuable. In *Young Workers* Ashton and Field (1976) report on aspects of their on-going large-scale interview studies of young people's experience of 'the transition to work'. By contrast with most earlier studies, they succeed in locating this experience in the general social context of young people's lives. Their analysis is closely rooted in a coherent explication of the effects and meaning of family background, class, educational opportunities, and the structure of the job market. Besides providing a plausible account of these issues, their major contribution, which has been taken up and used extensively, is their development of a threefold typology of young people's perspectives on work. This divides young people into those headed for careers proper, who are presumptively 'middle-class'; those moving from a higher working-class background towards what they call 'short-term careers'; and the careerless. Their analysis, and specifically their typology, has had two beneficial effects. First, it grounds the analysis of young people and work firmly in contextual social variables. Secondly, it puts out of court that tendency to which British sociologists are peculiarly prone, of lumping all working-class young people haphazardly together. Or at least it ought to.

A second very valuable and important study to which attention should be drawn is Paul Willis' *Learning To Labour* (1977) which to some extent falls back into this trap, with its unpersuasive resurrection of the class homogeneity which Ashton and Field seek to dissipate. Despite this weakness, the meagre empirical data on which its analysis is based, and its flights of arcane theorising, it is undoubtedly a penetrating and valuable study. Better than any other recent study it explicates and displays the meaning, for young people themselves, of the limited and grossly limiting contexts of the work domain of life, for those most disadvantaged for competitive involvement in it.

It is precisely to the interests of such young people that the main research and development efforts of government have been directed in this decade. The weaknesses of the Job Creation Programme were evident. On the basis of this experience and considerable research, the Holland Report (1977) sought to find a way of doing better by unemployed and disadvantaged young people. The substantial expenditure on the Youth Opportunities Programme which the report argued for is certainly, despite criticisms of many sorts, an important practical innovation in this area. Research studies designed to evaluate aspects of the programme already constitute one of the most important bodies of research on young people and work, and many more are expected shortly. To date the study by Colin and Mog Ball (1979) is the most interesting and persuasive.[2] They do not stint criticism, and for the most part it is justified. The Youth Opportunities Programme takes far too little account of what studies such as Ashton and Willis have told us about the real situation, about the character and needs of disadvantaged young people, or about the structural character of youth employment. However, they are also more constructive than many other critics. Specifically, they open up the issue of the relations between education, work, and leisure in a way which has been largely neglected since Leigh's work (1971). If research on young people and work in the 1970s demonstrates anything, it is the necessity for imaginative large-scale organisational innovations which really get to grips with the inadequacies of teachers, careers officers and supervisors and managers in their dealings with young people (see Marsland 1978a on this point).

Education

Many of the studies of employment re-emphasise the problematics of the school, as currently conceived and organised, which earlier studies in the field of education had indicated (Hargreaves 1967). This line of critical work focusing on micro-interaction in the school, its determination by inappropriate curricula, and the apparent over-determining effect of family, class and community has continued. It is exemplified in the work of Hargreaves *et al.* (1975), Banks and Finlayson (1973), Holly (1971), King (1973), Murdock (1974), Welton (1977) and Murdock and Phelps (1973).

More recently however the benefits of a more systematic and global approach have become apparent, especially in the work of Michael Rutter and his associates in *15,000 Hours: Secondary Schools and their Effects on Children* (1979). This book seems to me likely to be among the few really influential studies of young people and education over the next ten years. It is, by contrast with most studies in this area, based on extensive and reliable data, and its arguments are logical and, to my mind, thoroughly persuasive. It demonstrates – what many earlier studies have denied – that the individual school can have a real and substantial effect on the commitment and achievement of pupils. It does this, as a result of careful research design, in a context which precludes its easy refutation by simple reference to class differences. Moreover, it locates the sources of the differential impact of schools in an unfashionable arena – the quality of leadership by heads and senior staff, the values and commitment of teachers, the clarity of curricular and other objectives, and the whole style and ethos of the school.

In my opinion, work such as Rutter's ought to serve as a model in terms of design, scope, data reliability, and self-discipline in interpretation for studies of education and young people. However, in the current climate of methodological and theoretical opinion, a quite different study may prove more influential. This is Paul Corrigan's *Schooling the Smash Street Kids* (1979). Based on Marxist axioms, it is a small-scale case study, with all the advantages and disadvantages of that genre. It purports to show, and certainly provides an interesting and plausible account of, how the educational system functions as a divisive apparatus of social control by the state. One can only hope that its pessimistic conclusions, rather than being seized with acclaim as warrant for its own initial assumptions, will be adopted by others as hypotheses, and tested carefully on an appropriate broader scale[3].

Community

If sociologists have tended in their analysis of work, education, and deviance to give perhaps too much attention to the community context at the risk of neglecting the specific effects of immediate organisational and interactional levels of context, it is equally true that we seem to lack studies of the community context itself and for its own sake. There are perhaps in the past ten years only two studies as penetrating as Willmott's classic *Adolescent Boys of East London* (1966).

The first of these is Howard Parker's *View From the Boys: A Sociology of Down-Town Adolescents* (1974). Like so many of the best studies in this period, this is a small-scale participant–observation study. We cannot altogether complain, since this is what the dominant methodological orthodoxy has constrained and warranted. But Cicourel, Becker and their British mediators have much to answer for.[4] Parker's study is beyond argument interesting, plausible, intelligent and important. Moreover, because of its interactionist theoretical underpinnings, we are spared the spurious dialectics which disfigure (without illuminating) so many recent case studies. 'The Boys' are a down-town gang of delinquent adolescents. Parker shows us their apprenticeship; their delinquent innovation in the face of the ubiquitous 'Them'; the skills and pleasures involved in stealing car radios; the way the Boys see 'Authority'; the persistent boredom of 'hanging around'; their occasional involvement in low-level manual work; and their pursuit of compensatory pleasure and excitement. The study confirms what most recent studies have shown, in the face of media exaggerations, about the mundane triviality of most juvenile deviance. On the other hand, a key argument in the book is that the life of such kids, even in these limiting circumstances, is active and intelligent and pursues its own defensible rationality and normalcy. The pity is that his methodology precludes any confident estimate either of how far his own evidence can be said to support his arguments, or of how far his findings are characteristic of other down-town areas of Liverpool, let alone other cities. In this case it is a considerable pity, since although it is a study of delinquency, and could have been reviewed as such here, it is much more than this. He enables us to see and understand the world as these kids see it. And beyond this again he provides a plausible account of precisely how and why this view arises and makes sense in a specific community context.

The second such study, Paul Willis' *Profane Culture* (1978), suffers, and perhaps to a greater extent, from the same methodological weaknesses. It also represents the same strengths in avoiding the spuriously abstracted empiricism of an earlier style of research on young people. Again we are shown powerfully and plausibly the seen and felt world of a group of young people, in this case bike-boys, and the community context which constitutes and explicates it. It is an important contribution to the programme of study of working-class youth sub-cultures called for by Mungham and Pearson (1976). People other than myself will no doubt be better satisfied than I am with Willis' theory work, which appears to ground his descriptions in forms of Marxism which are already subject to serious challenge even by other Marxists. Of the value of the descriptions, of the validity of the voice with which he enables them to speak, of the meaningfulness of his location of these voices and these lives in the specific type of community he evokes, there can be no doubt. Sadly, the specificity or generality of all this can only be the subject of speculative assertion and counter-assertion. For myself, I suspect these are as special and curious a group of young people as are the subjects of *Learning to Labour* (Willis, 1977). Among those who know that youth scene well some would agree with me, others would vociferously contradict me. Surely the lesson we have to learn is how to find ways of extending the scale and scope of such research without losing its penetrating depth?

Deviance

Ten years ago this section would have been headed 'Delinquency'. The change of name and the shift in methodological orientation which it announces is largely attributable to the National Deviancy Conference and in particular to two studies from the beginning of the 1970s. Their influence has continued to resonate through this field of sociological studies of young people. Stan Cohen's *Folk Devils and Moral Panics: The Creation of the Mods and Rockers* (1972) enunciated and explicated labelling theory for a sociological audience dissatisfied with 'Home Office Research' as powerfully and persuasively as is conceivable. What he purports to show (relying on theoretical analysis, some interviews and participant observation, and analysis of media treatment) is that what might seem to have been dangerous and threatening movements among young people were really creations, in the sense both of myths and social artifacts, of adults; that the threat in them was largely imaginary and fictional until it was fed back to young people by the media, the police, and the courts; and that the fundamental key to explicating youth movements and youth sub-cultures lies in the interests, attitudes, and reactions of adults.

Jock Young's *The Drugtakers* (1971) does a similar analytical job with a different set of deviant youth. If his influence has been somewhat less than Cohen's this is perhaps due to the relative modesty of his theoretical claims. At least he leaves us scope to believe that drug taking might have happened anyway, in some form, without the intrusion of labellers. For Cohen it seems that young people constitute as it were a cultural *tabula rasa* for labelling and shaping. No doubt the corrective influence of labelling theory has been necessary. But its weaknesses, despite the attractiveness and power of these key studies in this genre, are evident. One of these weaknesses has been attended to more recently by Marxists, both in *Resistance Through Rituals* (Hall and Jeffersen 1976) and especially in *Policing the Crisis* (Hall *et al*. 1978). See also Mungham and Pearson 1976. In this line of work the arbitrary grounding of adult labelling and handling of young people in an opaque and mysterious 'moral panic' is dismissed in favour of its specific location in the exigencies of a hegemonic ruling class faced with the task of managing economic crisis. Certainly this provides some sort of answer to labelling theory's primary weakness. In the end however it seems pretty unsatisfactory. This not only because of its practical futility, since it leaves us expecting revolution before amendment can even be hoped for, but also because of the incomplete plausibility of its own account, and the arbitrary use of evidence it seems persistently to depend on.

Meanwhile 'Home Office Research' has continued. This is exemplified at its best in work such as *The Delinquent Way of Life* by West and Farrington (1976).[5] In such work, the limitations of its theorising, the inadequate extent of its treatment of meaning and context, and the narrowing effects of its 'positivist' methodology are evident. On the other hand, it has two major advantages, which are surely necessary conditions of effective research in this area. First, it does attempt to explicate causes. Secondly, it is disciplined by coherent rules about the use of evidence and the grounds of inference. What seems to be needed is research disciplined along these lines which at the same time manages to take account of recent powerful conceptual analyses of general deviance such as those of Box (1971) and of Rock (1973).

This section ought also to take account of one of the most quoted studies of delinquent youth in this period. This is J. A. Patrick's *A Glasgow Gang Observed* (1972). More such straightforward studies might be of more value than any amount of contextualisation or theorisation.[6] Also properly a part of this section are studies of the 'treatment' and 'care' of deviant, including delinquent, young people. Two studies seem to me to warrant special attention. N. Tutt's *Care Or Custody* (1974) at least manages to open up the policy and practical issues without assuming that our only alternatives are repression or revolution. He is sadly somewhat less than unique in supposing that care and custody are incompatible. The second study, *After Grace – Teeth* by Spencer Millham *et al*. (1975), explores in a systematic comparative framework the residential experience of boys in approved schools (now community homes). It is a model of policy-oriented research. At the same time it succeeds, to an extent that critics of such work would presume impossible, in describing faithfully and believably the experience of the boys. Furthermore it concludes (p. 297) that 'contrary to much that has been previously written, residential care can be effective. Clearly some approved schools are good, and some far less so'.

Surely more of the research on deviance and young people ought to allow itself logical and methodological space to reach such conclusions where they are justified, and make commitments to identifying realistic routes to improvement and reform where this is feasible? Mere criticism is too easy, and as little help to the development of knowledge as to social advance. For a further review of the literature on deviance, see section 18 by Geoff Pearson.

Service of youth

In each of the spheres I have dealt with, there are adults charged with responsibilities for the care of young people. We need systematic evaluation in terms of the quality of personnel, resources, organisation and policy in each sphere. I cannot undertake that here. Instead I will refer briefly to a public service whose work on behalf of young people has been uncommonly neglected by sociologists – the Youth Service. Recently this neglect is beginning to be amended. In *Adolescence and Community* John Eggleston (1976) has explored through interview studies with young people, content analysis of policy documents, and case studies of innovative youth work, the pattern of operation and the effectiveness of the Service. On this basis he argues carefully and plausibly for some fundamental changes. These, in brief, would make the Youth Service more 'problem-oriented' and less 'developmental'. I happen to disagree with these arguments and have attempted to put the counter-case (Marsland 1980). Others may also disagree. The point is that Eggleston's work allows scope for such disagreement. By the nature of his evidence and his mode of argument, this research actually contributes to the strengthening of rational discussion about real and important issues. Surely we should be able to expect this of all research?

A more recent study, by Anthony Jeffs – *Young People and the Youth Service* (1979) – refuses this expectation. Throughout it tends to lean on a merely illustrative mode of evidence, without even the limited coherent empirical basis which Eggleston offers, and it maintains throughout a cynically critical tone. Surely the critical tradition of sociology ought not to be allowed to justify special pleading in any direction?

Conclusion

I have examined here no more than a few of the sociological studies of young people reported over the past ten years. I have intended by mentioning them to signal the value and importance of all the studies I have included, however critical I may have been of some of them. Even at the end of the 1970s there is still too little sociological research on youth as such, and it should be encouraged. But criticism with a positive intent is a proper way to conclude. My reading of this literature suggests to me three necessary levels of critique.

The first is at the level of *research method*. To my mind this research literature demonstrates the damaging effects of the so-called anti-positivism of the 1970s. We perhaps need to retrieve something of our ealier concern with reliability, validity, generalisability, systematic evidence, careful argument, willingness to prove ourselves wrong. But on the second level it is equally necessary to find ways of capitalising on studies of young people in different spheres by developing the still fragmentary and contentious *theory of youth*. It is futile to use basic concepts in *ad hoc* ways. Thirdly, what is to my mind the most important study of all those I have described, *Resistance Through Rituals* (Hall and Jefferson 1976) ought to be used as a bench-mark for measuring our own attitudes to young people and for evaluating the 'sense we make of the world' for young people when we involve ourselves in doing and reading research. This of course is to add a political and ethical level to the technical and theoretical levels of my critique. For in research concerning young people (and children) above all, our purposes and their moral justification matter. The sub-culture of youth, in its singularity and its many and changing varieties, is a major cultural phenomenon of modern society. How we interpret it and how we interpret the attempts of other adults in positions of influence and authority to interpret it and react to it, are matters of more than merely intellectual or academic significance. They matter in practice.

Acknowledgement
I am grateful to Philip Terpstra for help in the writing of this section.

Notes
[1] For an analysis of the issues touched on here, including the relations between childhood and youth, see 'Sociology of youth as an area of study', chapter 7, in Marsland (1978a).
[2] For one example of the practical evaluation of aspects of the Youth Opportunities Programme, in this case Community Service, see Marsland *et al*. 1980.
[3] I have not attended here, as I ought, to studies of tertiary education. Compared with the 1960s, sociological research on students has, for obvious if inadequate reasons, gone into recession. The continuing work of the Society for Research in Higher Education ought to be mentioned. But no better rationale for a systematic theorisation of the sociology of youth can be found than the absurd recent neglect of students, merely because, like drugs, they have dropped out of public concern.
[4] For an argument against rampant participant–observation, at least where knowledge claims are to be made, see 'On method in sociology', chapter 15, in Marsland (1978a).
[5] See also West (1973). Another example of such careful work, offering a complete contrast in this with some more fashionable studies, is Belson (1978). Compare, similarly, Plant (1975) with Young (1971).
[6] For an interesting study which falls into this danger see Marsh *et al*. (1978).

References
Allen, S. (1968) 'Some theoretical problems in the study of youth', *Sociological Review*, **16**, 3, pp. 319–31.
Anderson, D. (ed.) (1980) *The Ignorance of Social Intervention* (Croom Helm).
Ashton, D. N. and Field, D. (1976) *Young Workers: From School to Work* (Hutchinson).
Ball, C. and Ball, M. (1979) *Fit For Work: Youth, School, and Unemployment* (Writers and Readers Press).
Banks, O. and Finlayson, D. (1973) *Success and Failure in the Secondary School* (Methuen).
Belson, W. A. (1978) *Television Violence and the Adolescent Boy* (Saxon House).
Box, S. (1971) *Deviance, Reality and Society* (Holt, Rinehart & Winston).
Cohen, S. (1972) *Folk Devils and Moral Panics: The Creation of the Mods and Rockers* (Paladin).
Coleman, J. S. (1961) *The Adolescent Society* (Free Press).
Coleman, J. S. (eds.) (1974) *Youth: Transition to Adulthood* (University of Chicago Press).
Corrigan, P. (1979) *Schooling the Smash Street Kids* (Macmillan).
Day, M. and Marsland, D. (eds.) (1978) *Black Kids, White Kids, What Hope?* (National Youth Bureau).
Eggleston, J. (1976) *Adolescence and Community* (Edward Arnold).
Eisenstadt, S. N. (1956) *From Generation to Generation* (Free Press).

Eisenstadt, S. N. (1972) 'Archetypal patterns of youth', in P. K. Manning and M. Truzzi (eds.) *Youth and Sociology* (Prentice-Hall) pp. 15–30.

Erikson, E. H. (1963) *Childhood and Society* (Norton).

Hall, S. and Jefferson, T. (eds.) (1976) *Resistance Through Rituals: Youth Sub-Cultures in Post-War Britain* (Hutchinson).

Hall, S., Jefferson, T. and Clarke, J. (1976) 'Youth a stage of life?', *Youth in Society*, no. 17, pp. 17–19.

Hall, S. *et al.* (1978) *Policing the Crisis: Mugging, the State, and Law and Order* (Macmillan).

Hargreaves, D. H. (1967) *Social Relations in a Secondary School* (Routledge & Kegan Paul).

Hargreaves, D. H. *et al.* (1975) *Deviance in Classrooms* (Routledge & Kegan Paul).

The Holland Report (1977) *Young People and Work* (Manpower Services Commission, HMSO).

Holly, D. N. (1971) *Society, Schools, and Humanity: The Changing World of Secondary Education* (McGibbon & Kee).

Jeffs, A. J. (1979) *Young People and the Youth Service* (Routledge & Kegan Paul).

King, R. (1973) *School Organization and Pupil Involvement: a Study of Secondary Schools* (Routledge & Kegan Paul).

Leigh, J. (1971) *Young People and Leisure* (Routledge & Kegan Paul).

Marsh, P. *et al.* (1978) *The Rules of Disorder* (Routledge & Kegan Paul).

Marsland, D. (1978a) *Sociological Explorations in the Service of Youth* (National Youth Bureau).

Marsland, D. (1978a) 'Youth: a real force and an essential concept', in D. Marsland, 1978a, op. cit., chapter 6, pp. 72–89.

Marsland, D. (1978a) 'On method in sociology', in D. Marsland, 1978, op. cit., chapter 15, pp. 228–44.

Marsland, D. (1978b) 'Youth's problems and the problem of youth', in M. Day and D. Marsland (eds.), 1978, op. cit., chapter 11, pp. 93–104.

Marsland, D. (1980) 'Novelty, ideology, and reorganization', in D. Anderson (ed.) *The Ignorance of Social Intervention* (Croom Helm) chapter 3, pp. 21–43.

Marsland, D., Brelsford, P. and Terpstra, P. (1980) *Idea Into Practice: An Evaluation of Three Community Service Schemes* (Manpower Services Commission).

Marsland, D. and Hunter, P. (1976) 'Youth: a real force and an essential concept', *Youth in Society*, July, pp. 10–22.

Millham, S., Bullock, R. and Cherrett, P. (1975) *After Grace – Teeth* (Human Context Books).

Mungham, G. and Pearson, G. (eds.) (1976) *Working Class Youth Culture* (Routledge & Kegan Paul).

Murdock, G. (1974) *Cultures, Class, and Schooling* (Constable).

Murdock, G. and Phelps, G. (1973) *Mass Media and the Secondary School* (Macmillan).

Musgrove, F. (1964) *Youth and the Social Order* (Routledge & Kegan Paul).

Parker, H. J. (1974) *View from the Boys: A Sociology of Down-Town Adolescents* (David & Charles).

Patrick, J. A. (1972) *A Glasgow Gang Observed* (Methuen).

Plant, M. A. (1975) *Drugtakers in an English Town* (Tavistock).

Rock, P. (1973) *Deviant Behaviour* (Hutchinson).

Rutter, M. *et al*. (1975) *15,000 Hours: Secondary Schools and their Effects on Children* (Open Books).

Smith, C. S. (1971) *Adolescence* (Longmans).

Tutt, N. (1974) *Care or Custody: Community Homes and the Treatment of Delinquency* (Darton, Longman & Todd).

Welton, J. (1977) *Comprehensive Education: the Egalitarian Dream* (Frances Pinter).

West, D. J. (1973) *Who Becomes Delinquent?* (Heinemann Educational Books).

West, D. J. and Farrington, D. P. (1976) *The Delinquent Way of Life* (Heinemann Educational Books).

Willis, P. (1977) *Learning To Labour: How Working Class Kids Get Working Class Jobs* (Saxon House).

Willis, P. (1978) *Profane Culture* (Routledge & Kegan Paul).

Willmott, P. (1966) *Adolescent Boys of East London* (Routledge & Kegan Paul).

Young, J. (1971) *The Drugtakers* (Paladin).

10 Ideology and the curriculum
Michael Apple
Joel Taxel

The late Italian Marxist Antonio Gramsci showed considerable insight when he argued that the routine structures of our everyday lives, including our common-sense ideas and practices, can sustain class domination (Gitlin 1979). In such a perspective, cultural institutions like schools become rather consequential. As he argued, the control of the knowledge preserving and producing institutions is critical in enhancing the ideological hegemony of dominant classes, since these institutions are often the sites at which ideologies are produced within the common sense of students (Johnson 1979).

Gramsci is not alone in seeing the importance of cultural institutions in reproducing the ideological conditions necessary for unequal power and control. Louis Althusser (1971), for instance, makes a similar point when he distinguishes between 'repressive state apparatuses' and 'ideological state apparatuses'. The latter (with the school and family being important among them), though they have some degree of autonomy from the economy, help create the ideological pre-conditions for the continued expansion of capitalist social relations. While Althusser has been criticized for being overly deterministic (Erben and Gleeson 1977; Willis 1977), there is no doubt that to ignore the reproductive role of such ideological state apparatuses is unwarranted.

Now ideologies can be looked at in a number of ways. They can be more or less coherent sets of social beliefs that guide our actions and serve particular social interests (Apple 1979a). This position would lead us to focus on the beliefs of self-conscious groups – for example, political parties and organized classes – and the effect of these ideologies on schools.

Finn, Grant, and Johnson (1977), for example, analyze the implications and the history of the shifting ideologies about schooling in the recent past in the United Kingdom. They pay particular attention to the move to the right today, tracing this movement to the results of both economic and state crisis and the contradictions within social democratic ideologies of education. Donald (1979), as well, in an interesting use of discourse analysis, examines how public documents emanating from the state – here *The Green Paper* in England – help create the conditions necessary for bringing schools into closer correspondence with the ideological and 'man-power' needs of industry.

While exceptional, these studies are concerned more with ideologies *about* education, not ideologies *in* it. To look at ideologies in education we would have to shift our perspective on what the nature of ideology is. For ideologies cannot only be thought of as sets of beliefs that effect or generate state policy. They are also a complex assemblage of common-sense meanings and practices embodied within our institutions (Williams 1977; Apple 1979a). What would this mean in terms of unpacking the school's ideological role, especially the role of the curricular, pedagogical, and evaluative terrain of the school? In order to go any further into this question, we need to understand what it actually is that schools do as agencies of reproduction.

Even though there are serious differences among the many theorists of the social and ideological place of the school (see MacDonald 1977), most agree on a fundamental issue. They all see the institution as engaged in economic and cultural reproduction. Some will stress the economic role (Bowles and Gintis 1976); others will stress the cultural impact (Bernstein 1977; Bourdieu and Passeron 1977, 1979); while others will attempt to blend the two together (Apple 1979a and b). Basically, however, the various positions have argued the following points. Schools assist in selecting and certifying a work force for a hierarchical labor market and, it has been claimed, teach differential social messages by race, sex, and class depending on one's probable destination on that labor market (Bowles and Gintis 1976; Valance 1973/74). But schools do more than 'process people'; they 'process knowledge' as well (Young 1971). They help define certain groups' knowledge as legitimate, while other knowledge is considered inappropriate as school knowledge. This is not all, though. Schools also play a critical role in the *production* of knowledge. That is, our educational institutions are in part organized so that the technical/administrative knowledge needed for the division and control of labor, for expanding markets and stimulating needs, and for technical innovation is produced (Apple 1979a; Apple 1979b; Noble 1977).

This is clearly rather complex since taken together it sees schools as 'distributing' ideological norms and dispositions to students as it sorts them, as selecting and legitimating knowledge, and finally as producing knowledge that is economically important all at the same time. All of these complex functions may not be carried out totally smoothly, of course. One function may objectively contradict another at any given historical moment (Dale 1979). Yet all contribute in some very important ways to the creation of ideological hegemony.

Because of all this, if we are to understand the interconnections between ideology and the internal characteristics of schools, we need to go beyond the usual questions educators ask. We need not only to ask how a student can acquire more knowledge – the dominant question in our efficiency-minded field – but why and how particular aspects of the collective culture are presented as objective, factual knowledge. How do schools, in their day-to-day functioning, help in the reproduction of ideological hegemony?

Three areas of school life need to be interrogated if we are to understand the schools' role in ideological reproduction: (1) how the basic day-to-day regularities of schools contribute to students learning these ideologies; (2) how the form and content of curricular knowledge contribute to students learning these ideologies; and (3) how these ideologies are 'reflected' in the fundamental perspectives educators employ to guide and evaluate their own and students' activity (Apple 1979a).

Let us explain what each of these three questions entails. The first of these questions refers to the hidden curriculum in schools – the tacit teaching of social and economic norms, values, and dispositions to students that goes on simply by their living in and coping with the institutional expectations and routines day in and day out for years. The second question asks us to make curricular knowledge itself problematic, to pay much greater attention to the actual knowledge itself, to where this 'legitimate' knowledge comes from, whose knowledge it is, what social group or class it supports, and so on. It also asks us to examine not just the content but the way it is organized. Does the form itself embody ideological commitments? The final query asks us to become aware of the latent social commitments and implications that educators accept and promote by employing certain traditions and models – for example, systems management, a vulgar positivism, behavior modification, social labeling practices, and so on – in their own work.

We shall examine each of these three areas in turn, starting with the ideological role of the form and content of school knowledge. As we shall see, different *kinds* of ideological meanings and practices work through the overt and hidden curriculum in schools. Ideologies not only of class, but of race and gender relations interact within the institution.

Form and content in curriculum

Any meaningful accounting of the internal dynamics of schooling must illuminate the relationship between a society's dominant ideological forms and the curriculum itself. The content of the curriculum has not been ignored, of course. In fact, a body of research has amassed in recent years, seeking to determine the content of both trade and textbooks. Unfortunately, this research rarely ventures beyond description or asks why particular meanings evolve and 'get into' schools, while others are excluded. The fact that these studies lack a theoretical framework which might account for the consistency of their findings does *not*, however, prevent us from inserting these findings into a theory which seeks just such an explanation. A major basis of this theory can be found in Raymond Williams' (1961, 1977) idea of a 'selective tradition', the ability of certain groups to confer status and legitimacy on their knowledge, history, and culture, and to exclude that of others.

Drawing upon Williams, a fundamental starting point in the more theoretically cogent investigations of the relationship between ideology and curriculum is that stated by Young (1971): 'Those in positions of power will attempt to define what is taken as knowledge, how accessible to different groups any knowledge is, and what are accepted relationships between different knowledge areas and between those who have access to them and make them available'. Starting out from this statement, early work in England drew on social phenomenology and more structural forms of analysis to examine the stratification and social construction of school knowledge and social interaction in classrooms (Keddie 1971; Esland 1971). While more theoretically grounded than the content analyses noted earlier, there were a number of conceptual and political problems with some of this early work on the form and content of school knowledge. These included its overly relativistic perspective on knowledge, its tendency to overstate its arguments, and its lack of a clear political program (Bernbaum 1977; Karabel and Halsey 1977; Grierson 1978). However, many of these problems have been at least partly recognized and dealt with in later work such as Young and Whitty (1977) and in the studies of the relationship between ideology and various curriculum areas such as mathematics, English, music, media studies, and so on in Whitty and Young (1976). The increasing sophistication on the question of what is construed as socially legitimate knowledge and its ideological embeddedness is evident, though much more empirical work is needed. Ongoing rigorous work is being carried on by others. Bourdieu and Passeron's (1977) analyses of 'cultural capital' and 'symbolic violence' also suggest that the exclusive bestowal of legitimacy on the meanings of the dominant groups in society serves to disguise power relations which are, in fact, their ultimate source. In legitimizing the 'cultural capital' of only the dominant groups, Bourdieu (1971) argues that culture in general, and schools in particular, 'reproduce in transfigured, and therefore unrecognizable form, the structure of prevalent socio-economic relationships . . . which are consequently perceived as natural'. Significant conceptual work by Bernstein (1977) makes a similar point when suggesting that the 'form and content of educational transmissions embody class ideologies'. These important theoretical points become more comprehensible if we return to some of the extant analyses of past and current curricular materials that we alluded to earlier in this section.

Elson's (1964) analysis of over 1,000 19th century American textbooks painstakingly documents the kinds of economic and political ideals with which early textbook writers sought to 'indoctrinate' their immature readers and thereby 'train citizens in character and proper principles'. She shows that the texts unabashedly provided legitimacy for the 'conquest and subordination of inferior races', the total dominance of men over women, and for the necessity of the importance, and continuation, of class distinctions. These points were all substantiated by Mosier's (1965) analysis of the McGuffey Readers, one of the most influential textbooks produced in the annals of American educational history.

The past few decades have been marked by intense, at times violent, controversy over the nature and composition of curricular materials used in classrooms. Especially significant is the fact that many of the groups which have been historically subject to slander, stereotyping, and outright omission have struggled for greater recognition of their history and culture. Fitzgerald's (1979) provocative account of controversy and change in the American textbook industry is the most detailed, but suffers from a lack of a unifying theoretical perspective. Taxel's (1978/79) discussion of alleged attempts to 'censor' materials deemed racist and sexist goes further theoretically, seeing these disputes as related to competing claims over ideology and social justice.

Despite the important strides which have been made in eliminating the blatant racism, sexism, and classism characteristic of earlier texts in Canada, England, and the United States, studies indicate that text materials continue to reflect the perspectives of the groups which dominate society. Among the better studies are the California Department of Education (1964); Kruz (1970); the Council on Interracial Books for Children (1977), Broderick (1973), Swanson (1977) and Byler (1974).

Numerous studies have documented the persistance of ideologies of gender relations in curricula. Among the most notable is a study of basal readers by the Women on Words and Images (1972); Saario *et al.* (1973) document pervasive sexism in educational achievement tests, the differential curricular requirements imposed on males and females, as well as stereotyping in basal readers. Deem (1978) argues persuasively that quite similar tendencies exist within the British system of education.

Other studies have focused less on the formal corpus of school knowledge and more on children's literature. Among the notable studies of sexism in children's literature are Lieberman (1972-3), Weitzman *et al.* (1972), Nilsen (1971), and Dixon (1977a and b).

But what of the selective tradition concerning class domination? That American textbooks have long reflected the perspectives of business interests, over those of the working class, is documented in early research by Donnally (1938). This is not all. Apple (1971) and Popkewitz (1977) demonstrate that various curricular materials tend to 'flatten reality' by over-emphasizing harmony and consensus while minimizing the existence of social problems and conflict. More recently, Anyon (1979) views the treatment of economic history and concepts in recent American history texts as a more general problem in the creation of ideological hegemony. She argues that 'the school curriculum has contributed to the formation of attitudes that make it easier for powerful groups to manage and control society' – a thesis advanced on a more theoretical level by Eggleston (1977) and Williams (1961).

Nearly all of the studies discussed above are limited to the analysis of either curriculum, text, or tradebook content. In doing so they have overlooked the fact that the 'forms' in which these materials are manifest carry important ideological messages (Apple 1978a and b; Eagleton 1976). Unlike analyses of curriculum content, work on curricular form is relatively recent. For example, employing Wright's (1975) analysis of the ideological structure of narrative form, Taxel (1980) examined both form and content of a sample of children's fiction, showing that they 'reflected' in some very important ways changes in the economic and ideological structures in society. In a similar vein, Beyer's (1979) work in the field of aesthetic education has sought to demonstrate the manner in which the form and content of aesthetic curricula combine and serve to legitimate the current social order.

The focus on the form into which knowledge is organized is continued in other significant work. Bernstein (1977) and Grace (1978), for example, argue that the form the curriculum takes is basically dependent upon ideological conflicts within the middle class. The importance of examining form is reiterated by Apple (1980b) who shows that the increasing use of commercially pro- duced, pre-packaged curricular 'systems' which are organized around 'individualized learning' documents both the ability of capital to enter into schools in subtle ways and the increasing power of ideologies of segments of the middle class in education.

Most of these later, more thereotically grounded studies of ideology and curricular form and content have been influenced by Marxist approaches to the study of culture. While there is some debate over whether a Weberian rather than a Marxist model can account for some of the findings (Collins 1977), there is agreement that a selective tradition, one related to the process of economic and cultural reproduction, is operating in the form and content of curricula.

The hidden curriculum

As was suggested earlier, any attempt to illuminate the ideological role of schooling must consider not only the nature of the know- ledge transmitted via the formal corpus of social knowledge, but also the values, attitudes, and predispositions taught by the hidden curriculum. While pieces such as Parsons (1959), Dreeben (1968) and Jackson (1968) were major contributions to the literature on the internal dynamics of schooling, they do not suggest any rela- tionship between the specific values taught in schools and those 'required' in an advanced industrial society. The dominant values were accepted as given and inquiry focused relatively uncritically into how the schools, as agents of 'society', socialized children into the 'shared' set of norms, dispositions and rules. Apple and King (1977) and Cagan (1978) go beyond this, critically examining the relationships between the values actually taught in schools and the 'requirements' of an unequal society.

A considerable segment of research into the hidden curriculum has been descriptive and concerned with the manner in which pupil identities are formed and social reality constructed in class- rooms (e.g. Rist 1970; Esland 1971; Keddie 1971; Rosenbaum 1976; Woods and Hammersley 1977). While providing important information about the reality of British and American classrooms, this research failed to adequately explore how and why 'reality comes to be constructed in particular ways' (Whitty 1974; Apple 1978b). The need to situate the often ahistorical, phenomenologi- cally informed descriptions of classroom life in a more critical structural perspective has been repeatedly argued, however (Sharp and Green 1975; Apple 1978b; Dale *et al*. 1976; Woods and Hammersley 1977).

One of the most important analyses of the hidden curriculum is that of Bowles and Gintis (1976). They focus on the 'correspondence' between the social relations of schooling (i.e. the hidden curriculum) and the social relations of production. While they contribute a good deal to our understanding of the political economy of schooling, they treat schools as 'black boxes'. That is, they take for granted, rather than investigate in detail, day-to-day classroom life. They leave little room for conflict and contradiction within the school or between the school and the economy. Also left unmentioned is the important role played by the form and content of school knowledge in the reproductive process they wish to describe. Finally, they ignore the fact that, as a state institution, schools are a site of conflict between classes and class segments (Bernstein 1977; Finn, Grant, and Johnson 1977; Wright 1978). Hence these institutions do not necessarily directly reflect the needs of capital.

This is quite an important issue. Much of the research seeking to establish the relationship between cultural and economic reproduction has been informed by a far too mechanistic correspondence theory between ideology, mode of production, and the culture of the school. Such a perspective ignores the fact that hegemony is always contested (Johnson 1979), the fact that schools and classrooms, just like the workplace (Edwards 1979), are scenes of contestation and struggle.

As Willis (1977) and Apple (1980a and c) have shown, schools and culture have some degree of 'relative autonomy'. They are the sites of complex ideological struggles, not passive reflections of bourgeois values.

Educators' ideological perspectives

Now that we have examined some, though certainly not all, of the issues involved in the relationships between the form and content of the curriculum, the hidden curriculum, and ideological reproduction, we need to investigate one final area, the perspectives that educators employ to order, guide, and give meaning to their own and students' activity. These perspectives, though ideally aimed at helping, often serve as mechanisms of social and economic control (Edelman 1977).

Many of the models of research and evaluation that dominate the curriculum field and education in general have their roots in less than neutral soil. For example, the tradition of behavioral objectives, while considered neutral today, was originally proposed by individuals who sought to pattern schools after the needs of industry (Kliebard 1971; Franklin 1974). Furthermore, the proponents were also committed to the principles of the popular eugenics movement (Karier, Violas and Spring 1973). More currently, the use of techniques such as systems management for the organization and control of what happens in schools speaks to the continued dominance of corporate ideology. As Braverman (1974) has shown, these techniques were not neutral, but were instituted to increase the power of capital over labor.

Questions have also been raised about the actual curricular research techniques which have become standard. Apple (1974, 1979a) has argued that the categories used to collect data and design curricula – categories such as 'gifted students', 'slow learners', 'disadvantaged', and so on – accept existing social regularities as given. In a similar vein, Karabel and Halsey (1977) and Wexler (1976) show how the various research traditions of examining academic achievement have tended to neglect the economic and ideological issues surrounding such research. On an even more abstract level, critical social theorists such as Habermas (1971) have sought to show that the logics which dominate the positivistic science practised in advanced industrial societies, when used in policy-oriented fields such as education, lead toward the substitution of technical criteria for what should be ethical and political debate. They thus serve the interests of both the administrative managers of institutions and those who have economic and cultural power, and cover more fundamental social conflicts about what social institutions like schools should be accomplishing (Apple 1974). As Young (1971) has noted, as long as we 'take' the taken-for-granted perspectives and problems of schools, rather than 'make' them ourselves, we shall be caught in this ideological dilemma.

Conclusion

In this conclusion, we shall briefly point to areas in need of further work. We have noted throughout this chapter that there is a danger of an overly functionalist and deterministic position in a large portion of the literature on ideology and curriculum, due in part to their treatment of schools as black boxes and to their lack of sophistication on the nature of contradictions, mediations, and resistances. Because of this, ethnographic investigations similar to Willis (1977) which focus on the lived culture of students and how resistances – which may differ by race, class and sex – are manifest in day-to-day life are essential. Also helpful here is the literature on resistances among blue and white collar workers (Edwards 1979), so that we may see how teachers, for instance, may resist the rationalizing ideologies that pervade the school.

On the issue of the form and content of school knowledge, much work needs to be done using techniques drawn from discourse analysis, semiotics, and structural analysis of texts if we are to become more sophisticated in unpacking how curricula work ideologically. Recent critical analyses of the political economy and ideological role of television (Gitlin 1979), mass-media, films (Wright 1975) and advertising (Ewen 1976) could also provide important insights into the relationships between the material conditions of a society and its cultural apparatus.

Finally, there is the question of practice. A number of individuals have documented the fact that there were alternative models of what might be called 'working-class' or 'socialist' curriculum and pedagogy at one time; however, these have slowly atrophied. The development of such alternative models is essential to go beyond the analyses we have reviewed here.

References

Althusser, L. (1971) 'Ideology and ideological state apparatuses', in L. Althusser (ed.) *Lenin and Philosophy and Other Essays* (New Left Books) pp. 127–86.

Anyon, J. (1979) 'Ideology and United States history textbooks', *Harvard Educational Review*, **49**, pp. 361–86.

Apple M. W. (1971) 'The hidden curriculum and the nature of conflict', *Interchange*, **2**, 4, pp. 27–40.

Apple, M. W. (1974) 'The process and ideology of valuing in educational settings', in M. W. Apple *et al.* (eds.) *Educational Evaluation: Analysis and Responsibility* (McCutchan) pp. 3–34.

Apple, M. W. (1978a) 'Ideology and form in curriculum evaluation', in G. Willis (ed.) *Qualitative Evaluation* (McCutchan) pp. 495–521.

Apple, M. W. (1978b) 'The new sociology of education: analyzing cultural and economic reproduction', *Harvard Educational Review*, **48**, pp. 495–503.

Apple, M. W. (1979a) *Ideology and Curriculum* (Routledge & Kegan Paul).

Apple, M. W. (1979b) 'The production of knowledge and the production of deviance in schools', in L. Barton and R. Meighan (eds.) *Schools, Pupils and Deviance* (Nafferton Books) pp. 113–31.

Apple, M. W. (1980a) 'Analyzing determinations: understanding and evaluating the production of social outcomes in schools', *Curriculum Inquiry*, **10**, 1, pp. 55–76.

Apple, M. W. (1980b) 'The other side of the hidden curriculum', *The Journal of Education*, **162**, 1, pp. 47–66.

Apple, M. W. (1980c) 'Curriculum form and the logic of technical control: building the possessive individual', paper presented to Sociology of Education Conference, Westhill College, Birmingham, England, January.

Apple, M. W. and King, N. (1977) 'What do schools teach?', *Curriculum Inquiry*, **6**, 4, pp. 341–69.

Bernbaum, G. (1977) *Knowledge and Ideology in the Sociology of Education* (Macmillan).

Bernstein, B. (1977) *Class, Codes and Control vol. III: Towards a Theory of Educational Transmissions* (Routledge & Kegan Paul).

Beyer, L. E. (1979) 'Aesthetic theory and the ideology of educational institutions', *Curriculum Inquiry*, **9**, 1, pp. 13–26.

Bourdieu, P. (1971) 'The thinkable and the unthinkable', *Times Literary Supplement*, October 15, 1971, pp. 1255–6.

Bourdieu, P. and Passeron, J. C. (1977) *Reproduction in Education, Society and Culture* (Sage Publications).

Bourdieu, P. and Passeron, J. (1979) *The Inheritors* (University of Chicago Press).

Bowles, S. and Gintis, H. (1976) *Schooling in Capitalist America* (Basic Books).

Braverman, H. (1974) *Labor and Monopoly Capital* (Monthly Review Press).

Broderick, D. (1973) *Image of the Black in Children's Literature* (Bowker).

Byler, M. (1974) 'The image of American indians projected by non-indian writers', *School Library Journal*, **20**, pp. 36–9.

Cagan, E. (1978) 'Individualism, collectivism, and radical educational reform', *Harvard Educational Review*, **48**, 2, pp. 227–66.

California Department of Education (1964) *The Negro in American History Texts* Eric Document Reproduction Service No. Ed 017 586.

Collins, R. (1977) 'Some comparative principles of educational stratification', *Harvard Educational Review*, **47**, pp. 1–27.

Council on Interracial Books for Children (1977) *Stereotypes, Distortions, and Omissions in U.S. History Textbooks* (The Racism and Sexism Resource Center for Educators).

Dale, R. (1979) 'The politicization of school deviance', in L. Barton and R. Meighan (eds.) *Schools, Pupils and Deviance* (Nafferton) pp. 95–112.

Dale, R. *et al.* (eds.) (1976) *Schooling and Capitilism* (Routledge & Kegan Paul).

Deem, R. (1978) *Women and Schooling* (Routledge & Kegan Paul).

Dixon, B. (1977a) *Catching them Young, Volume 1: Sex, Race and Class in Children's Fiction* (Pluto Press).

Dixon, B. (1977b) *Catching them Young, Volume 2: Political Ideas in Children's Fiction* (Pluto Press).

Donald, J. (1979) 'Green paper: noise of a crisis', *Screen Education*, **30**, Spring, pp. 13–49.

Donnally, W. (1938) 'The haymarket riot in secondary school textbooks', *Harvard Educational Review*, **8**, pp. 205–16.

Dreeben, R. (1968) *On What is Learned in Schools* (Addison-Wesley).

Eagleton, T. (1976) *Marxism and Literary Criticism* (University of California Press).

Edelman, M. (1977) *Political Language* (Academic Press).

Edwards, R. (1979) *Contested Terrain: The Transformation of the Workplace in the Twentieth Century* (Basic Books; also Heinemann Educational Books 1980).

Eggleston, J. (1977) *The Sociology of the School Curriculum* (Routledge & Kegan Paul).

Elson, R. M. (1964) *Guardians of Tradition: American Schoolbooks of the Nineteenth Century* (University of Nebraska Press).

Erben, M. and Gleeson, D. (1977) 'Education as reproduction', in M. Young and G. Whitty (eds.) *Society, State and Schooling* (The Falmer Press) pp. 73–92.

Esland, G. (1971) 'Teaching and learning as the organization of knowledge', in M. Young (ed.) (1971) pp. 70–115.

Ewen, S. (1976) *Captains of Consciousness* (McGraw-Hill).

Finn, D., Grant, N. and Johnson, R. (1977) 'Social democracy, education and the crisis', *Working Papers in Cultural Studies*, **10**, pp. 147–98.

Fitzgerald, F. (1979) *America Revised: History School Books in the Twentieth Century* (Little, Brown).

Franklin, B. (1974) *The Curriculum Field and the Problem of Social Control, 1918–1938* (University of Wisconsin, Ph.D. dissertation, unpublished).

Gitlin, T. (1979) 'Prime time ideology', *Social Problems*, **26**, 3, pp. 251–66.

Grace, G. (1978) *Teachers, Ideology and Control* (Routledge & Kegan Paul).

Grierson, P. C. (1978) 'An extended review of *Knowledge and Control, Explorations in the Politics of School Knowledge*, and *Society, State and Schooling*', *Educational Studies*, **4**, pp. 67–84.

Habermas, J. (1971) *Knowledge and Human Interests* (Beacon Press).

Jackson, P. W. (1968) *Life in Classrooms* (Holt, Rinehart & Winston).

Johnson, R. (1979) 'Three problematics: elements of a theory of working class culture', in J. Clarke, C. Critcher and R. Johnson (eds.) *Working Class Culture: Studies in History and Theory* (Hutchinson).

Karabel, J. and Halsey, A. H. (eds.) (1977) *Power and Ideology in Education* (Oxford University Press).

Karier, C., Violas, P. and Spring, J. (1973) *Roots of Crisis* (Rand-McNally).

Keddie, N. (1971) 'Classroom knowledge', in M. Young (ed.) (1971) pp. 133–60.

Kliebard, H. (1971) 'Bureaucracy and curriculum theory', in V. Haubrich (ed.) *Freedom, Bureaucracy and Schooling* (Assoc. for Supervision and Curriculum Development).

Kruz, M. M. (1970) 'Freedom and racial equality: a study of "revised" high school history texts', *School Review*, **78**, pp. 297–354.

Lieberman, M. (1972) 'Some day my prince will come: female acculturation through the fairy tale', *College English*, **34**, pp. 383–95.

MacDonald, M. (1977) 'The curriculum and cultural reproduction', units 18, 19 and 20 of block III Schooling and Society E.202 (Open University Press).

Mosier, R. (1965) *Making the American Mind: Social and Moral Ideas in the McGuffey Readers* (Russell & Russell).

Nilsen, A. P. (1971) 'Women in children's literature', *College English*, **32**, pp. 918–26.

Noble, D. (1977) *America by Design: Science, Technology and the Rise of Corporate Capitalism* (Alfred Knopf).

Parsons, T. (1959) 'The school class as a social system: some of its functions in American society', *Harvard Educational Review*, **29**, pp. 297–318.

Popkewitz, T. (1977) 'The latent values of the discipline centered curriculum', *Theory and Research in Social Education*, **5**, 1, pp. 41–60.

Rist, R. (1970) 'Student social class and teacher expectation: the self-fulfilling prophecy in ghetto education', *Harvard Educational Review*, **40**, pp. 411–51.

Rosenbaum, J. E. (1976) *Making Inequality: the Hidden Curriculum of High School Tracking* (John Wiley).

Saario, T., Jacklin, C. and Tittle, C. (1973) 'Sex stereotyping in the public schools', *Harvard Educational Review*, **43**, pp. 386–415.

Sharp, R. and Green, A. (1975) *Education and Social Control: A Study in Progressive Primary Education* (Routledge & Kegan Paul).

Swanson, C. (1977) 'The treatment of the American Indian in high school history texts', *The Indian Historian*, **10**, pp. 28–37.

Taxel, J. (1978/79) 'Justice and cultural conflict: racism, sexism and instructional materials', *Interchange*, **9**, 1, pp. 56–84.

Taxel, J. (1980) *The Depiction of the American Revolution in Children's Fiction: A Study in the Sociology of School Knowledge* (University of Wisconsin, Ph.D. dissertation, unpublished).

Vallance, E. (1973/74) 'Hiding the hidden curriculum', *Curriculum Theory Network*, **4**, 1, pp. 5–21.

Weitzman, L., Eifler, D., Hokada, E. and Rose, C. (1972) 'Sex-role socialization in picture books for pre-school children', *American Journal of Sociology*, **72**, pp. 1125–50.

Wexler, P. (1976) *The Sociology of Education: Beyond Equality* (Bobbs-Merrill).

Whitty, G. (1974) 'Sociology and the problem of radical educational change', in M. Flude and J. Ahier (eds.) *Educability, Schools and Ideology* (John Wiley) pp. 112–37.

Whitty, G. and Young, M. (eds.) (1976) *Explorations in the Politics of School Knowledge* (Nafferton Books).

Williams, R. (1961) *The Long Revolution* (Chatto & Windus).

Williams, R. (1977) *Marxism and Literature* (Oxford University Press).

Willis, P. (1977) *Learning to Labour* (Saxon House).

Women on Words and Images (1972) *Dick and Jane as Victims: Sex Stereotyping in Children's Readers* (Princeton: Women on Words and Images).

Woods, P. and Hammersley, M. (eds.) (1977) *School Experience: Explorations in the Sociology of Education* (St. Martin's Press).

Wright, E. O. (1978) *Class, Crisis and the State* (New Left Books).

Wright, W. (1975) *Sixguns and Society* (University of California Press).

Young, M. (ed.) (1971) *Knowledge and Control* (Collier-Macmillan).

Young, M. and Whitty, G. (eds.) (1977) *Society, State and Schooling* (Falmer Press).

11 Ideology, psychology and the biological sciences
Ken Richardson

Introduction

Probably one of the most far-reaching discoveries of intellectual debate over the last two decades is the realisation that at the root of every ideological, philosophical, social, political and educational system is a specific conception of the nature of human beings. The point has also been made that the prevailing conceptions of the nature of human nature, and indeed of nature generally, are themselves embedded in the prevailing modes of production, that is the operations and relations through which human labours are combined, in specific ways, to transform nature in specific ways.

Much of the recent literature in the philosophy of science and in the sociology of knowledge has been concerned to make these points (see section 5 for a resume of the literature). The point of the present section is to illustrate this quality of intellectual manufacture in the literature concerned, at its roots, with the *relations* of production – that is in the fields of psychology, the human biological sciences and, of course, in education. In particular it is hoped to illustrate the coherence between the literature of biology and psychology on the one hand and the dominant relations of production on the other, and between both of these and the guiding precepts of education. This may also indicate where future critical efforts need to be directed.

The roots of psychology

This intellectual interdependence is buried deep in modern history. It is no accident that the very philosophers who laid the foundations of the modern science of nature were the very same persons who established the fundamental presuppositions of modern psychology, the science of the mind. The crucial event here was the transformation of the conception of the nature of humanity in response to the rise of capitalism in the 17th century, and with it the fabrication of competitive individualism. Thus the conception of exploitable humans became integrated with the scientific conception of the nature of nature in the 17th and 18th centuries. To understand this there is probably no substitute for returning to the primary sources, and many recent commentaries and/or collections of works exist; Smith (1966) on Descartes; Yolton (1977) on Locke; Peters (1956) on Hobbes; and Cohen (1965) on Hume. Through these conceptions, in the subsequent centuries, education became increasingly geared to the labour market.

For psychology and for biology the 19th century was important in two ways. First was the rise of positivism and the increasing utilitarian view of nature and of people. John Stuart Mill wrote the first positivist programme for psychology and the social sciences, complaining of their backward state as 'a blot on the face of science' and urging that 'the same processes through which the laws of many simpler phenomena have by general acknowledgement been placed beyond dispute must be consciously and deliberately applied to these more difficult enquiries' (quoted by Hearnshaw 1964, p. 5). A key aspect of Mill's vision of society was compulsory state education with mental tests and exams being used for occupational selection.

Secondly, the psychology of competitive individualism found expression in evolutionary theory, as in Darwin (1859) and Spencer (1855). As Marx wrote in a letter to Engels,

> It is remarkable how Darwin recognises among beasts and plants his English society with its division of labour, competition, opening up of new markets, "inventions", and the Malthusian "struggle for existence". It is Hobbes's "bellum omnium contra omnes" (quoted by Sahlins 1976; see also Hofstadter 1959 for further discussion of this process of ideological diffusion).

The resulting interplay of psychology and biology then led in several directions. Here we shall consider the two most dominant developments. It is worth pointing out in passing, however, that by this time many socialistic psychological and educational ideas were being developed based on antithetical presuppositions (for a recent overview and assessment, see Castles and Wüstenberg 1979).

The psychology of imperialism and class domination

First in Spencer and then in Galton, competitive individualism became translated, via evolutionary theory, into competition among individuals varying in 'natural talent'. At home this became the psychology of class domination. Extended to the colonies it became the psychology of imperialism. In both, exploitation was legitimised by reference to inexorable biological 'laws', which were used specifically to reconcile democratic ideals with the requirements for bourgeois progress. This has been well discussed lately by Chase (1977).

This crudely biological psychology resulted logically in the eugenics movement, in which Galton saw in the ploys of the dog-breeders the basis for the improvement of the whole of human society. The history of the eugenics movement from Galton up to the present time, and especially its influence on psychology, genetics and politics (national socialism) has been well documented in a series of papers in a recent issue of the journal *Annals of Science* (vol. 36, 1979) which contains extensive bibliographies. It was in this movement that intelligence testing first became actively promoted. The role of the intelligence test in eugenics propaganda, especially in the passing of 'race protection' and immigration acts in America, in the first 30 years of this century, and of the leading psychologists engaged in the propaganda, have been reviewed recently by several authors (Karier 1972; Pickens 1968; Kamin 1975; Hirsch 1971).

The contemporary expression of this movement is, of course, the phenomenon known as Jensenism, the chief literature being Jensen (1969, 1974) and Herrnstein (1973) in the United States, and Eysenck (1971) in the United Kingdom. There were a large number of fairly immediate responses to these writings (e.g. *Harvard Educational Review* Reprint Series no. 2, devoted entirely to the matter; and contributions in Richardson *et al*. 1972). Responses in the last five years have been increasingly forceful. The most sensational aspect of these has been the revelation of Sir Cyril Burt's fabrication of the data which were one of the main props of Jensenism (Kamin 1975; Dorfman 1978; Hearnshaw 1979). Similarly, the nature of the whole business of intelligence test construction and application has been increasingly subject to critical scrutiny (Blum 1978; Lawler 1978; Block and Dworkin 1976; Rose and Rose 1978).

The psychology of imperialism and class domination has had wide repercussions in education, mainly in the form of preconceptions and low expectations concerning the educability of non-white/non-middle-class groups. Some of the best evidence is found in the reports of the successive Education Commissions; for example, the justification for early selection in the Spens Report of 1937:

Psychological Evidence

Intellectual development during childhood appears to progress as if it were governed by a single central factor, usually known as 'general intelligence', which may be broadly described as innate all-round intellectual ability. It appears to enter into everything which the child attempts to think, or say, or do, and seems on the whole to be the most important factor in determining his work in the classroom. Our psychological witnesses assured us that it

can be measured approximately by means of intelligence tests
. . . We were informed that, with few exceptions, it is possible at a
very early age to predict with some degree of accuracy the
ultimate level of a child's intellectual powers. (Quoted from
Maclure 1965).

The low measure 'intelligence' of working-class children came to
have a powerful hold on the minds of educators as a quasi-scientific
vindication of their own intuitions about 'bright' and 'dull' children
(which in fact had been the basis of the construction of the intelligence tests in the first place, though the circularity usually goes
unrecognised), and even on those of its chief victims, who left
school actually believing they had little in the way of brains. The
race concept was avidly embraced not only by psychometrists but
by the earliest educational psychologists at the turn of the century
who saw, in the developing child, a recapitulation of racial history
which education may accelerate. In pursuit of these ideas journals
were founded (e.g. the *Journal of Genetic Psychology* by G. Stanley
Hall) and longitudinal studies of child development and educational attainment were instigated in which, as Piaget (1973) noted,
there appeared 'admirable documents compiled year after year on
the same school children . . . as assessed by all the known tests,
though their painstaking and scholarly authors had no idea what
they were going to get from this'.

Similar ideas prevail today, in which the blame for educational
failure is located in the insular individual and his or her genetic
endowment or personal environment, instead of in the very *social*
process which organised education represents. The phenomenon
of Jensenism – with its educational corollaries of differential
treatment and expectations, segregation, and so on – represents
the resilience of the race concept in education, even though it is
now *quite* clear that there are no such things as human 'races' in the
genetic or biological sense of the word (Lewontin 1974a; Latter
1980).

These ideas have, of course, interacted strongly with the biological discipline of genetics – especially population and quantitative
genetics – so much of which is based on Galtonian concepts and
presuppositions. Advances in this field are often used, in turn, by
'hereditarians' in psychology, especially in psychometry, to support the logic, if not the substance, of their arguments. The frequent use by psychologists of the concept of heritability – a statistic
which, it is alleged, informs us about the degree of 'genetic determination' of a character – is undoubtedly the best example of this
conceptual cross-fertilisation. Professors of education are in fact
renowned for their sloppy equating of heritability and educability.

In fact, it needs to be stressed that quantitative genetics remains in a very backward state where complex characters are concerned, and that in order to meet the demands psychology makes of it, it has had to resort to the most improbable simplifications. This point has been made most strongly in connection with the concept of heritability (e.g. Lewontin 1974a; Layzer 1974; Feldman and Lewontin 1975; Kempthorne 1977). The more general point is one well expressed at the recent International Conference on Quantitative Genetics, especially by Kempthorne in his paper 'The status of quantitative genetic theory' (Pollack *et al.* 1977). After first noting that the genetic model adopted by psychologists and behaviour geneticists (and, implicitly at least, by many educators) 'is highly naive genetically and, more critically, environmentally', he goes on to declare that 'it is surely obvious that the model of the nuclear genotype plus random environment is so naive as to vitiate any substantive conclusions, but the use of such models can thicken journals and lead in some cases to totally unnecessary deep societal conflict' (Kempthorne 1977). Further points in a similar vein can be found elsewhere in the *Proceedings*, which volume also contains an extensive bibliography (Pollack *et al.* 1977). Thus, far from enlightening the problems of psychology and education from an objective position, it seems that quantitative genetics has itself been severely handicapped by presuppositions arising from *within* psychology.

Comparative psychology

Darwin himself was among the first to attempt to bridge the behavioural gap between humans and other species in his comparative studies of behaviour (Darwin 1871, 1873). There has been considerable interest lately in this aspect of Darwin's work, especially as it laid the foundations of comparative psychology (Gruber 1974). Evolutionary theory subsequently inspired the burgeoning work in 'animal psychology' started by Romanes, Morgan and Thorndike; or, as William James put it, 'so it has come to pass that the instincts of animals are ransacked to throw light on our own' (James 1890). Right up until fairly recent years attempts to construct a *scala natura* of animal intelligence continued, though with little success. The reasons for the disappointment have been well discussed by Lockard (1971).

Two other major strands developed from these origins, however, and highly influential ones at that. These are behaviourism and sociobiology.

Behaviourism

Thorndike's 'laws' of learning, which, thanks to the going conception of evolution, were considered to be applicable to the whole of the animal kingdom, led to the advent of behaviourism (with additional inputs from the work of Bechterev and Pavlov, in Russia, on conditioning). Psychology thus imbued with positivism became the science of behaviour. The landmark text is Watson (1924). Behaviourism swept America in the 1930s and led to the development of diverse versions by individual theorists. For the history and development of behaviourism see especially Murphy (1949); Hearnshaw (1964); and Richardson (1980). After the Second World War the 'operant' behaviourism of B. F. Skinner came to dominate (Skinner 1972, 1974).

Behaviourism has undoubtedly had important ramifications in education, behavioural biology, and even in theories of brain function; and especially in clinical psychology where (in the guise of behaviour therapy) it has, in the 1970s, enjoyed a major boom with 'all the accompanying exaggerated claims and inadequately trained therapists jumping on the bandwagon' (Adams *et al*. 1973). The symposium proceedings edited by Wann (1964) probably remain one of the best sets of critical analyses of behaviourism as an idiosyncratic philosophy of science. The manipulative and/or totalitarian implications of behaviourism have been severely criticised throughout the 1970s both by non-behaviourists (e.g. Chomsky 1973; Rose 1974) and behaviourists themselves (e.g. Holland 1975, 1978).

However, the grossly ideological quality of behaviourist learning theory itself has received scant attention. Yet there is, in such theory, a most glaring correspondence between intellectual manufacture and relations of human social production. For 'learning' as seen by the behaviourist – the conditioning of reliable responses to fixed stimuli for certain rewards – corresponds to only *one* human condition, namely the ideal, compliant worker in factory or office: another turn of the lever, another penny in the pay packet! Beyond *fixed* stimuli and *fixed* responses, behaviourism is quite incapable of dealing with human learning, even though the vast majority of human behaviour (and probably that of all complex animals) takes place in quite *novel* situations with the production of quite *novel* responses, a point which was made long ago in the sphere of language learning (cf. Chomsky's 1959 review of Skinner's *Verbal Behaviour*) and now being increasingly taken up in discussions of concept learning (e.g. Lasky and Kallio 1978; Schmidt 1975; Weiner-Ehrlich *et al*. 1980, and contributions in Anderson 1977). Nonetheless the archetypal and almost universal organisation of learning in schools – the conditioning of the fixed, preconceived responses of individuals, who have no control over the learning process nor over the goal of what is learned, for specific rewards – clearly reflects an interaction with behaviourist learning theory *and* the human social relations on which it is based.

Sociobiology

The concept of instinct as an indelible behavioural tendency implanted in species in the course of evolution had a momentous impact on psychology. Although the concept had, of course, existed within psychology since the 17th century (or indeed long before that) it was now being given a much clearer, biological rationale. William McDougall's *Social Psychology* (1905) signalled the new trend, and it became common practice to explain all manner of behaviours by simply labelling them instincts (see Murphy 1949). Thus arose a major controversy with the behaviourists, although as Beach (1955), in summarising this debate, has noted, '. . . this war over instinct was fought more with words and inferential reasoning than with behavioural evidence . . . from the armchair in the study rather than the laboratory'.

In the 1930s, however, the debate was carried to the field by behavioural biologists like Lorenz and Tinbergen, and the instinct concept became incorporated into a new discipline called ethology. The new behavioural data emanating from field studies led, in the 1960s and 1970s, to two successive waves of popularisation. The first arose in the 1960s with titles like *The Territorial Imperative* (Ardrey 1967), *On Aggression* (Lorenz 1966); *The Naked Ape* (Morris 1967) and *The Imperial Animal* (Tiger and Fox 1971). All of these, with their common themes, have received classic rebuttals: see, for example, Alland (1972) and contributions in Montagu (1973); and Mayr (1974) has criticised, on evolutionary grounds, the 'typological thinking' that governs the instict–learning dichotomy.

The second wave was a rather more sophisticated up-dating of McDougall's *Social Psychology*, based on the recent development of concepts in neo-Darwinism applied to social species, and consequently to human beings. This was the famed 'new synthesis' of sociobiology. Works by the early architects (Hamilton 1964; Trivers 1971; Wilson 1975) have inspired in the last few years a virtual avalanche of books and papers. Perhaps the best known of these – and, in its own way, an apotheosis of competitive individualism – is Dawkins' (1976) *The Selfish Gene*. For recent representations and discussions see Freedman (1979), Barash (1977) and contributions in Jones and Reynolds (1978). Among the many refutations of these views are Lewontin (1979); Sahlins (1976); Washburn (1978a and b); and Kamin *et al*. (in press).

Apart from galvanising racism (however unintentionally) one of the most conspicuous spin-offs of sociobiological theory, and one likely to have further repercussions in education, is the 'scientific' counterblast to the women's movement. These writings assert the biologically-ordained submissiveness of women, and their shortfall in typical 'masculine' cognitive capacities (as deduced from 'intelligence' and related tests), all loosely packed together by shallow appeals to differential structuring of the brain (cerebral lateralisation) or hormone levels during development. Representative books on this subject include Maccoby and Jacklin (1974); Hutt (1972), Wittig and Peterson (1979), Weitz (1977), and Lloyd and Archer (1976). Some of these attempt some criticism of the overtly sexist principles enshrined in this movement; others can be found in sections 8 and 10 of this book. However, it can probably be said that no comprehensive attack on the presuppositions underlying these theories has yet been mounted, although, especially in the domains of evolutionary biology and cognition, they should be eminently possible.

Conclusion

Hopefully these two or three strands will suffice to draw attention to the nature of the literature surrounding psychology and human biological sciences, and to illustrate the ideological reflection of certain presuppositions corresponding to a certain mode of production in a certain historical epoch. A complete review would have to include, for example: child psychology, especially the longitudinal studies and Piagetian studies, and recent reactions to them; cognitive psychology, especially its reflection in theories of brain function; and, of course, Freudian psychology.

It only remains to be stressed that the ideas thus articulated to create a simple logic of the nature of humanity entered education with the foundations and growth of the state system, since when there has been continual cross-fertilisation between education and the human sciences. Thus today it is not difficult to find in education several dominant principles as the reflections of the presuppositions articulated through psychology and the biological sciences. These include: education as the cultivation of natural talent; natural talent distributed in the population in the same way as height and weight, according to the curve of normal distribution; the most productive talents largely confined to males and supportive talents largely confined to females (with, in some minds at least, a similar distinction between 'races'); education as an overwhelmingly (and necessarily) individualistic and competitive business; learning necessitating conditioning or reinforcement (through what is called extrinsic as opposed to intrinsic motivation); and humans in general, and children in particular, in possession of an irrational streak, thus necessitating large degrees of coercion or constraint.

References

Adams, H. E., Heyse, H. and Meyer, V. (1973) 'Issues in the clinical application of behaviour therapy', in H. E. Adams and I. P. Umkil (eds.) *Issues and Trends in Behaviour Therapy* (Charles C. Thomas).
Alland, A. (1972) *The Human Imperative* (Columbia University Press).
Anderson, R. C. (ed.) (1977) *Schooling and the Acquisition of Knowledge* (New Jersey: Lawrence Erlbaum).
Annals of Science, **36**, 1979.
Ardrey, R. (1967) *The Territorial Imperative* (Heron Books).
Barash, D. P. (1977) *Sociobiology and Behaviour* (Elsevier).
Beach, F. A. (1955) 'The descent of instinct', *Psychological Review*, **62**, pp. 401–10.
Block, L. and Dworkin, N. (eds.) (1976) *The IQ Controversy* (Quaver Press).
Blum, J. M. (1978) *Pseudo-science and Mental Ability* (Monthly Review Press).
Castles, S. and Wustenberg, E. (1979) *The Education of the Future* (Pluto Press).
Chase, A. (1977) *The Legacy of Malthus: the Social Costs of the New Scientific Racism* (Alfred Knopf).
Chomsky, N. (1959) Review of Skinner's *Verbal Behaviour*, *Language*, **35**, pp. 26–58.
Chomsky, N. (1973) *For Reasons of State* (Fontana).
Cohen, R. (ed.) (1965) *Essential Works of David Hume* (Bantam Books).
Darwin, C. (1859) *On the Origin of Species* (Murray, reprinted by Watts and Co. 1950).
Darwin, C. (1871) *The Descent of Man and Selection in Relation to Sex* (John Murray).
Darwin, C. (1873) *The Expression of the Emotions in Man and Animals* (Appleton).
Dawkins, R. (1976) *The Selfish Gene* (Oxford University Press).
Dorfman, D. D. (1978) 'The Cyril Burt affair: new findings', *Science*, **201**, pp. 1177–83.
Eysenck, H. J. (1971) *Race, Intelligence and Education* (Temple Smith).
Feldman, M. W. and Lewontin, R. C. (1975) 'The heritability hang-up', *Science*, **193**, pp. 1163–8.
Freedman, D. G. (1979) *Human Sociobiology* (The Free Press).
Gruber, H. E. (ed.) (1974) *Darwin on Man* (Wildwood House).
Hamilton, W. D. (1964) 'The genetic evolution of social behaviour', *Journal of Theoretical Biology*, **7**, pp. 1–52.
Harvard Educational Review, Reprint Series no. 2.
Hearnshaw, L. S. (1964) *A Short History of British Psychology* (Methuen).
Hearnshaw, L. S. (1979) *Cyril Burt: Psychologist* (Hodder & Stoughton).
Herrnstein, R. (1973) *IQ in the Meritocracy* (Houghton Mifflin).

Hirsch, J. (1971) 'Behaviour-genetic analysis and its biosocial consequences', in R. Canero (ed.) *Intelligence: Genetic and Environmental Influences* (Grune & Stratton) pp. 88–106.

Hofstadter, R. (1959) *Social Darwinism in American Thought* (Braziller).

Holland, J. G. (1975) 'Behaviour modification for prisoners, patients and other people', *Mexican Journal of Behavior Analysis*, **1**, pp. 81–95.

Holland, J. G. (1978) 'Behaviourism: part of the problem of part of the solution?', *Journal of Applied Behavior Analysis*, **11**, pp. 163–74.

Hutt, C. (1972) *Males and Females* (Penguin).

James, W. (1890) *The Principles of Psychology* (Dover Books).

Jensen, A. R. (1969) 'How much can we boost IQ and scholastic achievement?', *Harvard Educational Review*, **39**, pp. 1–123.

Jensen, A. R. (1974) *Genetics and Education* (Methuen).

Jones, N. B. and Reynolds, V. (eds.) (1978) *Human Behaviour and Adaptation* (Taylor and Francis).

Kamin, L. (1975) *The Science and Politics of IQ* (John Wiley).

Kamin, L., Lewontin, R. C. and Rose, S. P. R. (in press) *Biological Myths: Social Realities* (Penguin).

Karier, C. (1972) 'Testing for order and control in the corporate liberal state', *Educational Theory*, **22**, 2, pp. 154–80.

Kempthorne, O. (1977) 'Status of quantitative genetic theory', in E. Pollock *et al.* (1977), op. cit.

Lasky, R. E. and Kallio, K. D. (1978) 'Transformation rules in concept learning', *Memory and Cognition*, **6**, pp. 491–5.

Latter, B. D. H. (1980) 'Genetic differences within and between populations of the major human sub-groups', *American Naturalist*, **116**, pp. 220–37.

Lawler, J. M. (1978) *IQ. Heritability and Racism* (Lawrence & Wishart).

Layzer, D. (1974) 'Heritability of IQ scores: science or numerology?', *Science*, **183**, pp. 1259–65.

Lewontin, R. C. (1974a) *The Genetics of Evolutionary Change* (New York: Columbia University Press).

Lewontin, R. C. (1974b) 'The analysis of variance and the analysis of causes', *American Journal of Human Genetics*, **26**, pp. 400–11.

Lewontin, R. C. (1979) 'Sociobiology as an adaptationist program', *Behavioural Science*, **24**, pp. 5–14.

Lloyd, B. and Archer, J. (eds.) (1976) *Exploring Sex Differences* (Academic Press).

Lockard, R. B. (1971) 'Reflections on the fall of comparative psychology: is there a message for us all?', *American Psychologist*, **26**, pp. 168–79.

Lorenz, K. (1966) *On Aggression* (Methuen).

Maccoby, E. E. and Jacklin, C. N. (1974) *The Psychology of Sex Differences* (Stanford University Press).

Maclure, J. S. (ed.) (1965) *Educational Documents* (Methuen).

McDougall, W. (1905) *Introduction to Social Psychology* (Methuen).

Mayr, E. (1974) 'Behavior programmes and evolutionary strategies', *American Scientist*, **62**, pp. 650–9.

Montagu, A. (ed.) (1973 2nd edn.) *Man and Aggression* (Oxford University Press).

Morris, D. (1967) *The Naked Ape* (Cape).

Murphy, G. (1949) *Historical Introduction to Modern Psychology* (Routledge & Kegan Paul).

Peters, R. S. (1956) *Hobbes* (Pelican).

Piaget, J. (1973) *Main Trends in Psychology* (George Allen & Unwin).

Pickens, D. K. (1968) *Eugenics and the Progressives* (Vanderbilt University Press).

Pollack, E., Kempthorne, O. and Bailey, T. B. (eds.) (1977) *Proceedings of the International Conference on Quantitative Genetics* (Iowa State University Press).

Richardson, K. (1980) 'Motivation and learning', block 3 Personality and Learning E.201 (Open University Press).

Richardson, K., Spears, D. and Richards, M. P. M. (eds.) (1972) *Race, Culture and Intelligence* (Penguin).

Rose, H. and Rose, S. (1978) 'The IQ myth', *Race and Class*, **20**, 1, pp. 63–74.

Rose, S. (1974) *The Conscious Brain* (Weidenfeld & Nicolson).

Sahlins, M. (1976) *The Use and Abuse of Biology* (Tavistock).

Schmidt, R. A. (1975) 'A schema theory of discrete motor skill learning', *Psychological Review*, **82**, pp. 225–60.

Skinner, B. F. (1972) *Beyond Freedom and Dignity* (Jonathan Cape).

Skinner, B. F. (1974) *About Behaviourism* (Jonathan Cape).

Smith, N. K. (1966) *New Studies in the Philosophy of Descartes* (Macmillan).

Spencer, H. (1855) *The Principles of Psychology* (Longman, Brown, Green & Longmans).

Tiger, L. and Fox, R. (1971) *The Imperial Animal* (Holt, Rinehart & Winston).

Trivers, R. L. (1971) 'The evolution of reciprocal altruism', *Quarterly Review of Biology*, **46**, pp. 35–57.

Wann, T. W. (ed.) (1964) *Behaviourism and Phenomenology* (University of Chicago Press).

Washburn, S. L. (1978a) 'Animal behaviour and social anthropology', *Society*, **15**, 6, pp. 35–41.

Washburn, S. L. (1978b) 'Human behavior and the behavior of other animals', *American Psychologist*, **33**, pp. 405–18.

Watson, J. B. (1924) *Behaviourism* (Norton).

Weiner-Ehrlich, W. K., Bart, W. M. and Millward, R. (1980) 'An analysis of generative representation systems', *Journal of Mathematical Psychology*, **21**, pp. 219–46.

Weitz, S. (1977) *Sex Roles: Biological, Psychological and Sociological Foundations* (Oxford University Press).

Wilson, E. O. (1975) *Sociobiology: the New Synthesis* (Harvard University Press).

Wittig, M. A. and Peterson, A. C. (1979) *Sex-related Differences in Cognitive Functioning* (Academic Press).

Yolton, J. W. (ed.) (1977) *The Locke Reader* (Cambridge University Press).

12 The use of case studies in applied research and evaluation
Rob Walker

The purpose of this section is to review selectively some of the uses made of case studies in the areas of applied research, action research and evaluation in recent years. The self-conscious designation of 'applied research', 'action research' and 'evaluation' is itself a relatively recent phenomenon in educational studies, although the terms have been widely and variously used in social science for much longer (see, for example, Kemmis 1980 for the history of the term 'action research' in psychology). There is also considerable overlap between the applications of the terms, 'applied research' being a predominantly English usage, 'action research' more commonly used in Australia, and 'evaluation' in the USA.

I shall not attempt here to enter into debates about definition and usage, but shall treat the terms loosely and interchangeably as referring to educational research that seeks to have a direct relationship with attempts to improve educational practice. While it is true to say that all educational research has some implications for practice, the studies considered here, for the most part, seek to work in a close, often service, relationship to those who are the subjects of study and those who commission it. To use an analogy, these studies aspire to be more like engineering than physics, more like medical research than physiology; more directly, they intend to contribute to education rather than to social science.

The applied tradition in educational studies has tended to run parallel to conventional fields of study, often drawing its practitioners from a variety of areas. Its development was closely associated with the curriculum development movement in the 1960s and 1970s which had the incidental effect of drawing into universities and colleges people with first-hand experience of the process of project-initiated curriculum innovation. The studies reviewed here therefore touch on areas of sociology, psychology, history, philosophy, linguistics and even anthropology; but they are not easily contained by any one of them. For the most part they aspire to be synthetic rather than analytic, holistic rather than fragmentary, balanced rather than biased.

Although many of the studies referred to are limited in circulation or difficult to obtain, this section takes the view that this is a new area of research with important implications for the organisation, practice and teaching of educational studies, and not simply a specialised addition to the field in general.

Uses of case studies

The term 'case study' as applied to institutions or action programmes has generally been used in educational research in four different senses:

1. The 'typical' case

This studies one instance in detail, but in such a way as to emphasise the relevance of the particular case to more general issues and concerns. While the writer will often connect the particularities of the case to a wider context, the belief is that a process of 'naturalistic generalisation' (Stake 1975a) will allow the reader to extrapolate and to relate the study to cases known from experience. Thus Peshkin's study of the community of Mansfield and its High School '. . . is intended to portray the integral relationship between school and community in a rural area' (Peshkin 1978, p. 8). And Wolcott sees his study of a Kwakiutl village school as simultaneously concerned with the particular and the general:

> The people and the situation represented in these pages are unique and yet highly representative . . . A comparable study of even the closest neighbouring village would reveal the kinds of differences that give each village and each school a personality in some ways unique. Still, those who have taught or observed in schools with other Indian children, or among children in certain sections of the big cities of North America, or among children in other parts of the world where a Western-oriented curriculum is being introduced under conditions of cultural stress, will recognise similarities in the behaviour of pupils, parents and teachers to those reported here. (Wolcott 1967, p. viii).

2. The 'critical' case

This attempts to test a theoretical proposition or the accepted wisdom of practitioners. Again the case is defined by its relation to a 'class' which it is taken to typify, but it is also seen to have particularities which coincide in such a way as to make it of special interest. Thus Smith and Keith (1971) set their study of Kensington School in the context of the claims being made about radical innovations in schooling, while Sharp *et al.* (1975) present a case study of Mapledene Lane School which they claim can be read 'as a piece of critical sociology' (p. ix). In both cases the aspiration of the writers is to go beyond providing detailed description or documentary evidence in order to test policies or theories.

3. The case study as a simulation or as a teaching aid

There are several examples of school case studies developed as simulation exercises, for example ILEA (n.d.) have produced a case study for pupils, Saville (1981) has brought out some studies for teachers and Jenkins (1977) has written a case study of a simulation. In this context an interesting example is Ianni (1975), who has produced a graduate course in educational administration developed from the field notes made in conducting ten school case studies. The course focuses on the task of 'problem identification', and aims to give administrators 'as close a simulated experience of doing a field study of a school as we could without sending them out into schools'. (Ianni 1975, p. 10).

4. The 'holistic' case study

Rather than beginning with a 'class' and studying a sample of N = 1, this begins with the study of a case and asks questions about its representativeness and significance as the study procedes or concludes. This approach tends to deny the choice of case study as a purely technical or methodological decision (Kemmis 1976) and to celebrate the idiosyncracy of the case (MacDonald and Walker 1975). It is an approach most often used in evaluation studies, where selection of the case for study may be in the hands of others, or where sampling is seen to be an inappropriate device.

The use of the term 'case study' to cover studies of individuals, for example the work of Erlwanger (1973), Driver (1973) and other students of Easley and Witz (Easley and Witz 1972) is not included in this review, which limits itself to studies of the contexts of learning rather than learning itself.

Applied research and evaluation and conventional educational research

Conventionally in educational research emphasis is placed on the bounding and defining of the case – on its typicality or criticality – for only in this way can the case be interpreted and its contribution to conventional educational theory be appreciated. Indeed the connection between the case study and established theory is what makes the study available for critical appraisal. But in applied research and evaluation, by definition, the emphasis is less on theoretical explication than on the management and practice of a particular programme, classroom, school or innovation. The

emphasis tends to fall much more on the idiosyncracies and particularities of the case – the qualities of people, and the immediacy
of events, the irreversibility of the arrow of time – the very things
that constitute background noise, or surface ephemera when the
stress is on drawing out significance in the light of conventional
theory.

The distinction is perhaps best made using the analogy of 'figure
and ground' experiments in perceptual psychology. In many standard psychology texts drawings can be found which are interpreted differently according to the way the observer looks at them
– a picture of a Grecian urn can also be a double profile of human
faces. In conventional educational research a case study is looked at
in such a way that theoretical issues constitute the figure and the
immediate surface of events constitutes the ground, but in applied
research and evaluation the picture is reversed and theoretical
concerns are seen as ground. The difference is in the way we look,
not in what we are looking at.

I have, perhaps pretentiously, inserted the word 'conventional'
in referring to theory because it is often assumed that educational
theory is necessarily an aspect of social science theory, and that
educational research is necessarily social science research. For a
number of applied research and evaluation specialists this is coming to be a contentious issue, and I will refer to it again at a later
point.

Case study in applied research and evaluation (Britain)
In Britain case study research in education derives from two traditions; one long-established, practice-related and developed mainly
by Her Majesty's Inspectorate (HMI); the other recent, academic
and developed mainly in response to the curriculum development
movement of the 1960s and 1970s.

The inspectorial tradition is scarcely mentioned in the academic
literature, but is highly influential in government reports (for
example in Plowden and Newsom reports, and in the more recent
primary and secondary school surveys). Observation in schools is
the key method used, and the experience of the observer the main
claim to reliability and validity, but the actual practice of observation, recording and analysis tends to remain obscure and its practitioners secretive. Even though HMI has recently made the writing of reports a greater priority, and has begun publishing shorter
studies and discussion documents, the accounts given in Thomas
(1980), Tanner (1977) and DES (1977) are as close as HMI gets to
revealing the ways in which they work.

The academic tradition has developed from studies made by

those evaluating the curriculum developments of the 1960s; for example, Shipman *et al*. (1974) and MacDonald (1979c) both produced studies of curriculum development projects which, in their detailing of particularities, took them beyond the testing of preordinate propositions. The 'case' became seen as worthy of study in and for itself, becoming more in the character of contemporary history (e.g. Shipman), or documented narrative (e.g. MacDonald): two styles that have recently been reworked by Stenhouse (1979), and termed 'oral history' (with a heavy reliance on interview methods) and 'ethnography' (with a reliance on participant observation), thus emphasising their methodological distinctiveness.

While Shipman and MacDonald were both at work on their studies a paper by Parlett and Hamilton (1972), originally published in mimeo (and incidentally rejected by a number of journal editors) gained considerable circulation and was quoted regularly at conferences, in articles and course reading lists. This paper developed a critique of conventional evaluation strategies and advocated the use of mixed methods in order to illuminate the programme being studied. 'Illuminative methods' rapidly penetrated professional vocabularies and became a feature of a number of research and evaluation studies. A conference (reported in MacDonald and Parlett 1973) produced a widely quoted 'manifesto' for the 'new evaluation', and subsequently a book (Hamilton *et al*. 1977). Drafted by Stake, the manifesto read as follows:

1. That past efforts to evaluate (educational) practices have, on the whole, not adequately served the needs of those who require evidence of the effects of such practices, because of:
   (i) an under-attention to educational processes including those of the learning milieu;
   (ii) an over-attention to psychometrically measurable changes in student behaviour (that to an extent represent the outcomes of the practice, but which are a misleading over-simplification of the complex changes that occur in students); and
   (iii) the existence of an educational research climate that rewards accuracy of measurement and generality of theory but overlooks both mismatch between school problems and research issues and tolerates ineffective communication between researchers and those outside the research community.
2. That future efforts to evaluate these practices be designed so as to be:
   (i) responsive to the needs and perspectives of differing audiences;
   (ii) illuminative of the complex organisation, teaching and learning processes at issue;

(iii) relevant to public and professional decisions forthcoming; and

(iv) reported in language which is accessible to their audiences.

3. More specifically they recommended that, increasingly,

(i) observational data, carefully validated, be used (sometimes in substitute for data from questioning and testing);

(ii) the evaluation be designed so as to be flexible enough to allow for response to unanticipated events (progressive focusing rather than preordinate design); and that

(iii) the value positions of the evaluator, whether highlighted or constrained by the design, be made evident to the sponsors and audiences of the evaluation.

4. Though without consensus on the issues themselves, it was agreed that considered attention by those who design evaluation studies should be given to such issues as the following:

(i) the sometimes conflicting roles of the same evaluator as expert, scientist, guide and teacher of decision-makers on the one hand, and as technical specialist, employee and servant of decision-makers on the other;

(ii) the degree to which the evaluator, his sponsors and his subjects, should specify in advance the limits of inquiry, the circulation of findings, and such matters as may become controversial later;

(iii) the advantages and disadvantages of intervening in educational practices for the purpose of gathering data or of controlling the variability of certain features in order to increase the generalisability of the findings;

(iv) the complexity of educational decisions which, as a matter of rule, have political, social and economic implications; and the responsibility that the evaluator may or may not have for exploring these implications;

(v) the degree to which the evaluator should interpret his observations rather than leave them for different audiences to interpret.

It was acknowledged that different evaluation designs will serve different purposes and that even for a single educational programme many different designs could be used (Hamilton *et al.* 1977).

The important thing to note about the manifesto is less its advocacy of qualitative research methods than its stance in relation to research and practice. The manifesto was important because it indicated the possibility of a political shift in the power relations between evaluators and practitioners, opening up the opportunity for teachers and administrators to enter into what were often previously considered to be evaluator's (or researcher's) areas of authority. The effect of attempting to implement the manifesto was to establish rights for participants in the evaluation/research process.

Although the 'new evaluation' set itself up as a counter to conventional evaluation, conventional evaluation itself barely existed in Britain at the time. As with many innovations, the new practice filled areas created by sudden expansion rather than by displacing an established and institutionalised practice. As a result the new evaluation developed with more than a sideways glance at the massive and continuing American investment in conventional evaluation. Also the arguments made by Parlett and Hamilton and others expressed a sense of unease felt by researchers outside the field of evaluation, and so were broadened into a general critique of the educational research enterprise. This caused some confusion, especially among sociologists, for there is in fact little novelty in the methods used by illuminative evaluation. Most of the ground has previously been covered by writers like Becker (1971), Glaser and Strauss (1967) and by the Chicago School.

Why did evaluation and applied research provide a significant area for rethinking educational research at this time? In part because in a time of general expansion, and later contraction, evaluation was seen by policy-makers as worth encouraging, especially given the poor record of conventional research in contributing to professional practice. But there were other reasons too that related to the expansion of higher education and the structural divisions among educational faculties in British Universities. Most university departments of education (and many colleges) reveal a primary cleavage between theory and practice, with educational research dominated by those with specialised training in the social sciences. Conventional practice in educational research demands that research problems can only be approached from a social science discipline base, indeed that 'educational research' only exists, not as a field of research in its own right, but as an applied area defined by the overlap of the educational interests of psychology, sociology, history and philosophy. The growth of curriculum studies in the 1960s was handled not by rethinking these divisions so much as by 'adding on' (often rather uneasily) chairs of curriculum and specialist associations and journals.

The frequent references made by Parlett and Hamilton and others to ethnography as an important and neglected source for educational evaluation has sometimes been taken to signify a bid being made to raise the status of anthropology amongst the educationally relevant social sciences. There are however few references to the relevance of anthropological theory to education (a rare exception is Adelman (1976), which uses theories of material culture in reporting on the uses made of objects in a nursery class); more often ethnographic methods are used as an example of the possibilities that exist for research outside the range of standard techniques available in educational psychology.

A number of evaluation studies were set up in the second half of the 1970s which involved those people who had advocated the new evaluation, and which, in their extensive use of case studies, put many of the ideas to the test (see Adelman *et al*. 1976). For example, in Britain, Barry MacDonald set up an evaluation of a £2.5m government initiative in computer-assisted learning (MacDonald *et al*. 1975; MacDonald *et al*. [in preparation]); an evaluation of an EEC-sponsored programme in careers education (MacDonald 1979a); and evaluation of a British Library project attempting to develop information skills in secondary schools (MacDonald 1979b); and a case study evaluation of bilingual education in the USA (MacDonald *et al*. 1980). David Hamilton evaluated an individualised science project designed for use in small, remote rural schools (Hamilton 1975), and conducted a study of an open-plan primary school (Hamilton 1977). Clem Adelman carried out a study of three colleges' responses to the introduction of a course-unit system (Adelman and Gibb 1979). John Elliott designed an experimental accountability system for schools which is currently being tested (Elliott [in preparation]). David Jenkins evaluated a social studies curriculum which was designed to bring about mutual understanding between Catholic and Protestant in Northern Ireland secondary schools (Jenkins and O'Connor 1979). Helen Simons wrote an evaluation of native-language programmes for immigrant children set up by one LEA using EEC funds (Simons 1979).

The range of these studies is considerable, and reflects the flexibility required of the evaluator in moving into unfamiliar areas. Although the studies mentioned constitute the growing tradition of work in this area, they are mostly available only in limited editions and by application to the authors. A public, published corpus of work has yet to emerge. As a result the studies mentioned tend to enjoy an underground or ingroup circulation, but not to be widely known outside evaluation circles; indeed some, like Simons (1979) and Jenkins and O'Connor (1979) are only available to limited audiences.

In the area of applied/action research are, for example, Elliott and Adelman's *Ford Teaching Project*, and a series of DES courses run by John Elliott at the Cambridge Institute of Education; the publication problems are similar. What is published tends to be methodological rather than substantive accounts, which circulate only in mimeographed form.

The use of qualitative methods in evaluation (USA)

Alongside the British developments I have described, a number of American evaluation studies began to turn to qualitative methods of inquiry. There was in America a stronger tradition of empirical work in the anthropology of education (e.g. Wolcott 1967; 1973; Warren 1967; Spindler 1955, 1974; Singleton 1974), to which evaluation could turn for inspiration. There were also studies made by people with other backgrounds who became, as it were, self-trained in educational ethnography (Jackson 1968; Smith and Geoffrey 1968; Smith and Keith 1971), and it was often these 'marginal' people who were among the first to apply ethnographic techniques to evaluation problems (Smith and Pohland 1974; Brauner 1974; Stake and Gjerde 1974), or to incorporate the methods as one strand in multiple-approach studies that more nearly conformed to the illuminative ideal (e.g. Fox *et al*. 1976).

Just as Parlett and Hamilton's paper captured and crystallised the interest that was developing in Britain in the use of qualitative methods in evaluation, so a series of papers by Stake became the key point of reference in the USA. It was Stake who established that an evaluation should be an evaluation of a *programme*, in all its complex particularities, rather than an evaluation of products or of generalised abstractions (Stake (1967). Once taken, this step broadens the interest of the evaluator away from gains on test scores, or responses to curriculum materials, to take account of the social processes, institutions and contexts implicated in any social action programme. Stake has argued (1972) for an approach to the study of educational programmes that emphasises what he has called 'portrayal' rather than 'analysis'; and later 'seeing' rather than 'measurement' (1978b). He has also advocated 'responsive evaluation' (1975a and b), requiring the evaluator to take seriously the requirements, expectations and understandings of specified audiences for the evaluation report, and so devaluing the importance sometimes given to the evaluator's own interpretations, theorising or judgement (Stake and Scheyer 1976).

While Stake's writings chimed well with those of the 'illuminative' evaluators they have to be seen against the background of the more established and larger scale enterprise that evaluation in the USA represents. Nevertheless, in recent years a number of case study evaluations have been funded in the USA, often involving teams of observers working in scattered, multi-site studies (Stake and Easley 1978; Herriott 1977). Amongst the problems raised by these studies have been those of management and organisation (Miles 1978) and condensation (Stake 1979).

Current issues

It would be wrong to claim too much for this emerging tradition of educational study; clearly the present situation is largely one where reach has exceeded grasp. Much of what has been claimed remains contentious and often partially understood, inside and outside the field. In order to preserve some sense of the precariousness of the field I close this section, not with a summary or conclusions, but with a brief survey of some of the current internal debates and contentious issues which characterise the field.

Fairness vs truth

A recurring concern, expressed most strongly in MacDonald's 'Democratic Model' (MacDonald and Walker 1974, Norris 1977) is for the development of procedures for the conduct of case study research which stress the rights of participants. Evaluators, Mac-Donald argues, are caught between 'the public right to know and the participants' right to privacy', a balance that is pushed to a critical point in some of MacDonald's own studies, which emphasise the role of individuals in the educational process but offer them control over the uses made by the evaluation of 'private' data.

In conventional research truth is generally rated more important than fairness, the significance of the role played by individuals being left until they are dead (history), or deemed superficial (journalism). An evaluation study can be prepared to compromise on its claims to truth if it sees itself as offering competitive interpretations with claims no stronger than the evidence will sustain.

Generalisation vs particularity

Evaluation and applied research studies are defined by the boundaries of an innovation, action programme or institution. They are necessarily more concerned with particularities than conventional research studies. Nevertheless there is some contention as to the degree of abstraction that is desirable (Stake 1972; MacDonald and Walker 1974).

Reliability of the observer

A common criticism of case study methods rests on their dependence on single observers, multi-observer studies being generally used to multiply the observations rather than to cross-check. Fensham and Ingvarson (1977) report on a study where different observers reported 'blind' on the same classrooms.

Stenhouse (1978) has argued that behind each case study ought to lie a case record or archive to which scholars may turn in developing a critique of the study.

Validity vs reliability

Advocates of case studies have tended to stress the significance of face validity, considering measurement studies, whether in testing or survey research, to be strong on reliability but weak on validity. Measurement studies, they have argued, produce technically reliable data which may be replicable but which is difficult to interpret. Case studies are seen as essentially non-replicable, but the process of interpretation is more open to the reader to test against experience (Walker 1974).

Science vs art

Some advocates of the new evaluation have seen the possibility that 'practice-oriented inquiry', which starts from the study of specific educational situations, practices, programmes or institutions, might lead eventually to a specifically educational theory, different in character to the disciplines of the social sicences (e.g. Stenhouse 1979). Others have been prepared to look to the concepts and methods of research in the arts and humanities, and in other applied fields of professional endeavour like journalism, so breaking the longstanding assumption that educational research should necessarily be bound by the conventions of the social sciences (Eisner 1976; Fox *et al.* 1978; Walker [in press]).

A common criticism (e.g. Delamont 1978) has been that the resulting eclecticism is likely to lead to a cul-de-sac for general theory. There seems though a general consensus amongst those in the field that even if theoretical progress is possible or desirable (both points being at issue), it will only emerge gradually as a residual accumulation from the collection of case studies. Most remain sceptical about the need to put a high priority on theoretical development at the present time.

Note

Written in part as a contribution to an SSRC project: Exemplary Case Records, directed by Lawrence Stenhouse, CARE, University of East Anglia.

References

Adelman, C. (1976) *The Use of Objects in the Education of Children of 3–5 Years* (Final Report to the SSRC, CARE, University of East Anglia, Norwich, England).

Adelman, C. and Gibb, I. (1979) *A Study of Student Choice in the Context of Institutional Change* (Bulmershe College of Higher Education, Reading, England).

Adelman, C., Jenkins, D. and Kemmis, S. (1976) 'Rethinking case study:

notes from the second Cambridge conference', *Cambridge Journal of Education*, **6**, pp. 139–50.

Becker, H. S. (1961) *Boys in White* (University of Chicago Press).

Becker, H. S. (1971) *Sociological Work* (Allen Lane, The Penguin Press).

Brauner, C. (1974) 'The first probe', in D. Sjorgren (ed.) *Four Evaluation Examples: AERA Monograph series No 7* (Rand McNally).

Delamont, S. (1978) *Sociology and the Classroom* unpublished conference paper (Westhill College, Birmingham, England).

Department of Education and Science (1977) *Ten Good Schools: A Secondary School Survey* (HMSO).

Driver, R. P. (1973) *The Representation of Conceptual Frameworks of Young Adolescent Science Students* Ph.D. thesis, unpublished (University of Illinois).

Easley, J. A. and Witz, K. G. (1972) *Analysis of Cognitive Behaviour in Children* (Report Project 0-0216 US Office of Health Education and Welfare).

Eisner, E. W. (1976) 'On the use of educational connoisseurship and educational criticism for evaluating classroom life', *Teachers College Record*, **78**, 7, pp. 345–58.

Elliott, J. (in preparation) *Responsive Accountability project* (Cambridge Institute of Education).

Elliott, J. and Adelman, C. (eds.) (1975) *Ford Teaching Project* (Cambridge Institute of Education).

Erlwanger, S. H. (1973) 'Benny's conception of rules and answers in IPI mathematics', *Journal of Children's Mathematical Behaviour*, **1**, 2, pp. 7–26.

Fensham, P. and Ingvarson, L. (1977) *Case Study Research in Science Classrooms* (Australian Association for Research in Education, conference paper, Faculty of Education, Monash University).

Fox, G. T. *et al*. (1976) *1975 CMTI Impact Study* (Madison, Wisconsin USA: University of Wisconsin).

Fox, G. T. *et al*. (1978) *Residual Impact of the 1975 Impact Study* (Madison, Wisconsin USA: University of Wisconsin).

Glaser, B. G. and Strauss, A. (1967) *The Discovery of Grounded Theory* (Aldine Press).

Hamilton, D. (1975) *Big Science: Small School* (Conference paper, Association for Applied Anthropology, Amsterdam).

Hamilton, D. (1977) *In Search of Structure: A case study of a new Scottish open plan primary school* (Hodder & Stoughton).

Hamilton, D. *et al*. (eds.) (1977) *Beyond the Numbers Game: A reader in educational evaluation* (Macmillan Education).

Hamilton, D. and Dockerell, T. (eds.) (1980) *Rethinking Educational Research* (Hodder & Stoughton).

Herriott, R. E. (1977) *Ethnographic Case Studies in Federally-funded Multidisciplinary Policy Research* (Cambridge, Mass., USA: Abt Associates).

Ianni, F. A. J. (1975) *Studying Schools as Social Systems: A manual for field research in education* (Horace Mann-Lincoln Institute, Teachers College, Columbia University).

ILEA *Selecting a Headteacher* (Media Resources Centre, Inner London Education Authority).

Jackson, P. (1968) *Life in Classrooms* (Holt, Rinehart & Winston).

Jenkins, D. (1977) 'Business as usual: the "skills of bargaining" course at the London Business School', in G. Willis (ed.) *Qualitative Education: concepts and cases in curriculum criticism* (McCutchan).

Jenkins, D. and O'Connor, S. (1979) *Chocolate Cream Soldiers: final report of the Schools Cultural Studies Project* (New University of Ulster).

Kemmis, S. (1976) *The Imagination of the Case and the Invention of the Study* (CARE, University of East Anglia, Norwich, England).

Kemmis, S. (1980) *Research on Action Research Project: annual review* (mimeo, Deakin University, Australia).

MacDonald, B. and Parlett, M. (1973) 'Rethinking evaluation: notes from the Cambridge Conference' *Cambridge Journal of Education* vol. 3, no. 2, pp. 74–82.

MacDonald, B. (1974) 'Evaluation and the control of education', in B. MacDonald and R. Walker (eds.), op. cit., pp. 9–22.

MacDonald, B. and Walker, R. (eds.) (1974) *Innovation, Evaluation, Research and the Problem of Control* (CARE, University of East Anglia, Norwich, England).

MacDonald, B. and Walker, R. (1975) 'Case study and the social philosophy of educational research', *Cambridge Journal of Education*, **5**, pp. 2–11.

MacDonald, B. *et al*. (1975) *The Programme at TWO* (CARE, University of East Anglia, Norwich, England).

MacDonald, B. (1979a) *Careers Guidance Observed: a proposal to the DES* (CARE, University of East Anglia, Norwich, England).

MacDonald, B. (1979b) *Information Skills and the Curriculum: an evaluation proposal to the British Library* (CARE, University of East Anglia, Norwich, England).

MacDonald, B. (1979c) *The Experience of Innovation* (CARE, University of East Anglia, Norwich, England).

MacDonald, B. *et al*. (1980) *Bilingual Education in the USA: an independent study* (CARE, University of East Anglia, Norwich, England).

MacDonald, B. *et al*. (in preparation) *Understanding Computer Assisted Learning* (CARE, University of East Anglia, Norwich, England).

Miles, M. (1978) *Ethnographic Methods and their Problems* (Center for Policy Research).

Norris, N. (ed.) (1977) *Safari Interim Papers* II *Theory in Practice* (CARE, University of East Anglia, Norwich, England).

Parlett, M. and Hamilton, D. (1972) *Evaluation as Illumination: a new approach to the study of innovatory programmes* Occasional Paper no. 9 (Centre for Research in the Educational Sciences, University of Edinburgh), reprinted in D. Hamilton *et al*. (eds.) (1977) pp. 6–22.

Peshkin, A. (1978) *Growing Up American: schooling and the survival of community* (University of Chicago Press).

Saville, C. (1981) *Is it Possible for an Adviser to do Research?* Ph.D. dissertation (CARE, University of East Anglia, Norwich, England).

Sharp, R., Green, A. and Lewis, J. (1975) *Education and Social Control: a study of progressive primary education* (Routledge & Kegan Paul).

Shipman, M. D., Bolam, D. and Jenkins, D. (1974) *Inside a Curriculum Project: a case study in the process of curriculum change* (Methuen).

Simons, H. (1979) *Mother-tongue and Culture* (Cambridge Institute of Education).

Singleton, J. (1974) 'Education as a social process: essay review', *Reviews in Anthropology*, pp. 145–51.

Smith, L. M. (1978) 'An evolving logic of participant observation, educational ethnography and other case studies', in L. Shulman (ed.) *Review of Research in Education* (Peacock) pp. 145–51.

Smith, L. M. and Geoffrey, W. (1968) *The Complexities of an Urban Classroom* (Holt, Rinehart & Winston).

Smith, L. M. and Keith, P. M. (1971) *Anatomy of an Educational Innovation* (Wiley).

Smith, L. M. and Pohland, P. A. (1974) 'Education, technology and the rural highlands', in D. Sjogren (ed.) *Four Evaluation Examples: anthropological, economic, narrative and portrayal* (Rand McNally) pp. 5–54.

Spindler, G. D. (ed.) (1955) *Education and Anthropology* (Stanford University Press).

Spindler, G. D. (eds.) (1974) *Education and Cultural Process: towards an anthropology of education* (Holt, Rinehart & Winston).

Stake, R. E. (1967) 'The countenance of educational evaluation', *Teachers College Record*, **68**, pp. 523–40.

Stake, R. E. (1972) *An Approach to the Evaluation of Instructional Programs (Program Portrayal vs Analysis)* (CIRCE, School of Education, University of Illinois, USA).

Stake, R. E. (1975a) 'To evaluate an arts programme' in R. E. Stake (ed.) *Evaluating the Arts in Education* (Charles E. Merrill).

Stake, R. E. (1975b) 'Program evaluation; particularly responsive evaluation' (Occasional papers no. 5: West Michigan University, Kalamazoo) reprinted in D. Hamilton and T. Dockerell (eds.), 1980, pp. 72–87.

Stake, R. E. (1978a) 'The case study method in social inquiry', *Educational Researcher*, **7**, 2, February, pp. 5–8.

Stake, R. E. (1978b) 'On seeing and measuring', *Journal of Curriculum Studies*, **10**, 3, p. 265.

Stake, R. E. (1979) *The Validity of Policy Research* (CIRCE, University of Illinois, USA).

Stake, R. E. and Easley, J. A. (eds.) (1978) *Case Studies in Science Education* (CIRCE, University of Illinois, USA).

Stake, R. E. and Gjerde, C. (1974) 'T. city evaluation', in D. Sjorgren (ed.) *AERA Monograph Series No. 7 Four Evaluation Examples* (Rand McNally) pp. 99–139.

Stake, R. E. and Scheyer, P. (1976) 'A self-evaluation portfolio', *Studies in Educational Evaluation*, **55**, 3, pp. 52–79.

Stenhouse, L. (1978) 'Case studies and case records: towards a contemporary history of education', *British Educational Research Journal*, **4**, 2, pp. 21–41.

Stenhouse, L. (1979) *The Study of Samples and the Study of Cases* (Presidential address to annual conference of BERA).

Tanner, R. (1977) *The Way We Have Come* (The Plowden Conference, Bishop Grosseteste College, Lincoln, England).

Thomas, N. (1980) 'The primary school survey: methods and findings', *Journal of Curriculum Studies*, **12**, 1, (in press).

Walker, R. (1974) 'The conduct of educational case studies: ethics, theory and procedures', reprinted in D. Hamilton and T. Dockerell (eds.) (1980) op. cit., pp. 30–63.

Walker, R. (in press) 'On the uses of fiction in educational evaluation – and I don't mean Cyril Burt', in D. Smetherham (ed.) *Inside Evaluation* (Nafferton Books).

Warren, R. L. (1967) *Education in Rebhausen, a German Village* (Holt, Rinehart & Winston).

Wolcott, H. (1967) *A Kwakiutl Village and School* (Holt, Rinehart & Winston).

Wolcott, H. (1973) *The Man in the Principal's Office: an ethnography* (Holt, Rinehart & Winston).

13 The sociology of language and education
A. D. Edwards

Introduction

Answering their own question 'What has the sociology of language to say to the teacher?', Fishman and Salmon (in Cazden *et al*. 1972) argued against the exclusion from classrooms of non-standard varieties of language. Such varieties were socially constructed barriers to learning where the linguistic intolerance of teachers made them so, or where they were used by pupils as a 'sign of rebellion' against cultural indoctrination. They therefore cited the acceptance of regional dialects in the schools of Swabia as an example to those insisting on standard American even in classrooms largely populated by speakers of Black Vernacular. The argument is typical of the reaction at that time against associating linguistic 'difference' with cognitive 'deficit'. Two other related 'messages to teachers' can be extracted from the book in which their analysis appears – that different ways of *using* language reflect and reinforce different conditions of life, and that classrooms make distinctive communicative demands which children from certain social class and ethnic backgrounds may be unable or unwilling to meet (Cazden *et al*. 1972).

These three themes, with some variations, continue to provide the most directly relevant applications of sociolinguistic research to educational problems. But it must be emphasised that sociolinguistics has had such a short active life that solutions cannot reasonably be expected. Until the 1960s, sociologists seemed to show as little interest in language as most linguists did in how language was used in social life, a point made by Giglioli in introducing one of three useful anthologies published in the same year (Giglioli 1972; Pride and Holmes 1972; Gumperz and Hymes 1972). Both the rapid accumulation of work in 'social-linguistics', and its multidisciplinary character, are further exemplified in Trudgill (1974a), Dittmar (1976), Gregory and Carroll (1978) and Giles and St. Clair (1979). There is an overt concern with educational problems in Trudgill (1975), Stubbs (1976a) and Edwards (1976a). Despite the title of this section, then, much of the work reviewed is not distinctively sociological. What it has in common is an interest in language *as* social behaviour and *in* its social and cultural settings. The scope of that common interest is displayed in the journal 'Language in Society', launched in 1972 and still edited by one of the 'founders' of sociolinguistics, Dell Hymes. The range of his own work is evident in Hymes (1977).

Social class and modes of communication

The sequence in which the three main sociolinguistic themes were introduced will be altered in recognition of what was for some years a splendid exception to sociologists' neglect of language. Bernstein's theory of sociolinguistic codes is a natural starting point for this more detailed review because it represents both a general account of how culture is transmitted and reproduced through everyday uses of language, and a more particular diagnosis of how and why language differences contribute to educational failure. The theory preceded, guided, and was then modified by an intensive programme of research into social class differences in what language is habitually used to do, and into some of the consequent discontinuities in communicative experience between home and school (Bernstein 1974; Lee 1973). Parts of that programme are briefly reported in Bernstein (1973), and its later development can be sampled in Adlam (1977) and Hawkins (1977).

The extraordinary influence of the theory in teacher training (Shafer and Shafer 1975), and the over-simplified 'apocryphal' versions of it generated from Bernstein's own obscure and sometimes contradictory expositions, produced an understandably strong reaction. Indeed, the fervour of some critics is a tribute to the perceived importance of their target (Rosen 1974; Dittmar 1976, pp. 4–78; Stubbs 1976a, pp. 39–50; Jackson 1977; Robinson 1978). Evidence for and against the theory can be found in Pap and Pleh (1974), Wootton (1974), Edwards (1976b), Tough (1977) and Rushton and Young (1975). The 'opposition' has tended to emphasise how elaborated working-class speech and writing can be when the context seems to require it. But Bernstein himself has insisted that he is not arguing social class differences in what children *can do* with language, only in the kinds of selection they are disposed to make 'from the same linguistic resources' in specifiable contexts. He has therefore denounced any association of his work with theories of 'verbal deprivation'. There is a considerable overlap, however, with the long research tradition of showing lower-class children as lacking (or at best inexperienced in) certain uses of language which seem necessary for educational success –

for example, the use of language to make ideas verbally explicit, to explain rather than merely describe, to generalise, and to display an appropriate sense of what the listener needs to know (Hess and Shipman 1972; Halliday 1975; Tough 1977). Such research suggests that socially disadvantaged children have 'an established disposition to use language in a limiting way' (Tough 1977). But the diagnosis has been strongly challenged by those aware of the difficulties of measuring communicative competence, of the likelihood that any sample performance will be strongly influenced by the context in which it was elicited, and of the impossibility of simply presenting a predetermined task to young children on the assumption that they will perceive its demands as the researcher intends (Cazden 1972; Cicourel *et al*. 1974; Donaldson 1978). Relatively naturalistic recording in settings where children have scope to define the communicative situation for themselves has shown them able to, for example, switch roles and display sensitivity to the listener's needs in ways which most earlier studies could not have recognised (Cazden 1977; many of the papers in Ervin-Tripp and Mitchell-Kernan 1977; Garnica and King 1979). As will be argued later, this new sensitivity to the situation in which data is collected also drew attention to classroom constraints on pupils' communicative options.

Speech style, communicative repertoire, and scholastic success

The research just cited focuses on children's functional repertoire, and on the semantic complexity 'evident' in their use of language. Critics of that research have sought to demonstrate that non-standard varieties are linguistically no less systematic or complex than their standard equivalents, and have argued that superficial differences cannot be taken as evidence of different levels or styles of thinking. The most influential of these critics was Labov (1972, 1976), and there is a useful sample of related American work in Williams (1971). John Edwards (1979) provides an excellent overview of the controversy (see also Robinson 1975; Edwards 1976a, chapter 4).

Denying the inherent inferiority of non-standard forms of speech is obviously not incompatible with recognising that *sounding* disadvantaged will often have serious consequences. 'Sociological dialectology' showed in detail how groups ranked hierarchically on some scale of socio-economic status will be ranked in the same order by the frequency with which they use or avoid certain stigmatised features of pronunciation, vocabulary and grammar, and thereby provided unusually hard evidence of social mobility, status anxiety, and social aspirations (Labov 1977; Trudgill 1974b;

Trudgill 1978). It also drew attention to the importance of such differences as a resource for displaying, for example, rank or ethnic loyalty, and for locating the present status and future prospects of others (Giles and Powesland 1975). The educational relevance of such stereotyping is argued by Trudgill (1975) and Williams (1976) and is indicated in the empirical work of Seligman *et al.* (1972), Macauley (1977) and V. Edwards (1978). Briefly, speech differences may shape teachers' judgements about a pupil's ability or ambition which go far beyond the 'evidence' which those differences are supposed to provide.

Sociolinguistic investigation of communicative competence also extended the notion of 'interference' between the language of home and school to the whole 'etiquette of communication' (Ervin-Tripp 1973; Wells 1977). Such studies have highlighted the culture-shock which pupils and teachers from markedly different backgrounds may experience when their respective rules for speaking appropriately are in conflict, and the real possibility that pupils' ignorance or defiance of what is 'proper' in classrooms may be misread as proving a general unfitness for learning (V. Edwards 1978; Foster 1974; and the chapters by Philips and by Dumont in Cazden *et al.* 1972). Some of this work broadened into more sociologically (and anthropologically) oriented analysis of the inequalities produced by monocultural forms of schooling in polycultural societies, and was presented as carrying important lessons for the schooling of working-class children in 'middle-class schools' (Keddie 1975). The investigation of 'whose language counts' in such critical contexts as classrooms has been readily assimilated into some recent studies of how schooling functions to reproduce social hierarchies. For example, several contributors in Giles (1977) treat the educational exclusion of a minority language as an exercise in 'cultural colonisation' (see also MacKinnon 1977).

Theoretically similar analyses have also been made of socially privileged styles of communication within the same language, one group's ways of speaking being imposed as the best of all those possible and then taken as evidence of the 'natural' superiority of those with the relevant facility with words (Bisseret 1979; Bourdieu and Passeron 1977, pp. 77–105). But these analyses wait on a great deal more evidence than is currently available about the forms and functions of classroom communication.

Language in classroom interaction

It is assumed in much of the research just cited that classroom language is normally standard and rather formal, and that marked deviations from it are likely to be excluded from the serious business of instruction. There has also been some inquiry, still more speculative than empirical, into the forms and functions of language which may be associated with particular subjects and used as a test or badge of academic identity (Barnes *et al*. 1971; Edwards 1976a, pp. 150–57; Edwards 1978; Richards 1978). Much more extensive, as Hammersley's contribution to this present volume indicates, has been the investigation of how classroom talk is organised as discourse – how orderly interaction and semantic coherence are maintained in settings with a large number of potential (but often unwilling) participants. Some of this research has arisen from a 'pure' sociolinguistic interest in how talk is organised in settings with clearly defined role-relationships (Coulthard 1977), or in how meanings are embedded in a particular context (Gumperz and Herasimchuk 1975), or in how social scientists may be persuaded to adopt a more linguistically sophisticated approach to verbal interaction than they usually employ (Stubbs 1981). Some of the most interesting classroom research has also been the product of ethnomethodologists' concern with the structuring of interaction and with how social relationships are routinely constituted and displayed (Cicourel *et al*. 1974; Mehan 1978), or more specifically with the organisation of turns and topics in status-marked settings (McHoul 1978; Edwards 1980). There has also been a rapidly growing interest in the communicative relationships of adults and children, and in the possibly common features which these relationships display (Speier 1976; Snow and Ferguson 1977; Ervin-Tripp and Mitchell-Kernan 1977; French and MacLure 1981).

The most directly applied research has concentrated on the communicative consequences of the teacher's transmission of information and skills (Barnes 1976; Edwards and Furlong 1978). Because it is so much easier to record and transcribe, formal teaching has perhaps received a disproportionate share of researchers' attention. It is in the context of class teaching that McHoul examines how the teacher's 'right' to allocate, terminate and reallocate turns is displayed and conceded, Sinclair and Coulthard (1975) show how certain kinds of initiating turn are virtually monopolised, and Stubbs (1976b) argues that this monopoly is especially evident in the frequency of those 'formulations' through which the teacher defines what is, what has been, and what will be happening during the course of the lesson. The complementary assumptions of teacher-knowledge and pupil-ignorance underlie the characteristic question–answer sequences in which the relevance, correctness and adequacy of each pupil contribution is likely to be indicated, and in which those answers are progressively 'shaped' to the appropriate outcome through the provision of increasingly heavy cues and clues (Hammersley 1977; Mehan 1978; French and MacLure 1979).

Research of this kind helps to identify those activities which constitute class teaching, the conditions necessary (if not sufficient) for less teacher-controlled discourse, and the features which such discourse might be expected to display (Barnes and Todd 1977; Edwards and Furlong 1978). It also raises some difficult methodological questions. Can the researcher select features which have a special interactional and pedagogic significance, or should the entire discourse be systematically analysed (Stubbs 1981)? Because much of what is meant need not be put into words, how is the researcher to capture what teacher and pupils 'must be' assuming in order to talk as they do? How is a recognition of what constitutes communicative competence in classrooms to avoid explaining away pupils' nonconformity as incompetence when it may be an expression of resistance? These remain open questions. But sociolinguistics has already made important contributions to the perennial investigation of 'educability' and the more recent investigation of 'cultural bias' in the processes of schooling. It has also reinforced more linguistically sensitive approaches to the study of classroom interaction than the varieties of systematic observation which dominated in the 1960s. And if it has had much 'to say to teachers', it has also had much to learn from studying how language is used in classrooms. Recognition of this reciprocal relationship has led the sociolinguist Dell Hymes to become Dean of a University Faculty of Education, and to comment that 'with a bit of luck and a lot of initiative, education may find itself a major force in shaping the study of language' (Hymes 1979).

References

Adlam, D. (1977) *Code in Context* (Routledge & Kegan Paul).
Barnes, D. *et al*. (1971) *Language, the Learner and the School* (revised edn.) (Penguin).
Barnes, D. (1976) *From Communication to Curriculum* (Penguin).
Barnes, D. and Todd, F. (1977) *Communication and Learning in Small Groups* (Routledge & Kegan Paul).
Bernstein, B. (ed.) (1973) *Class, Codes and Control* vol. 2 (Routledge & Kegan Paul).
Bernstein, B. (1974) *Class, Codes and Control* vol. 1 (2nd edn.) (Routledge & Kegan Paul).
Bisseret, N. (1979) *Education, Class Language and Ideology* (Routledge & Kegan Paul).
Bourdieu, P. and Passeron, J-P. (1977) *Reproduction in Education, Society and Culture* (Sage).
Cazden, C. (1972) 'The situation: a neglected source of social class differ-

ences in language use', in J. Pride and J. Holmes *Sociolinguistics* (Penguin) pp. 294–313.

Cazden, C. (1977) 'Concentrated versus contrived encounters: language assessment in early childhood', in A. Davies (ed.) *Language and Learning in Early Childhood* (Heinemann Educational Books) pp. 40–59.

Cazden, C. *et al.* (eds.) (1972) *The Functions of Language in the Classroom* (Teachers' College Press).

Cicourel, A. *et al.* (1974) *Language Use and School Performance* (Academic Press).

Cooper, B. (1976) *Bernstein's Codes: a Classroom Study* (University of Sussex Occasional Papers no. 16).

Coulthard, M. (1977) *An Introduction to Discourse Analysis* (Longman).

Dittmar, N. (1976) *Sociolinguistics: a Critical Survey of Theory and Application* (Arnold).

Donaldson, M. (1978) *Children's Minds* (Fontana).

Edwards, A. D. (1976a) *Language in Culture and Class* (Heinemann Educational Books).

Edwards, A. D. (1976b) 'Speech codes and speech variants: social class and task differences in children's speech', *Journal of Child Language*, **3**, 1, pp. 247–65.

Edwards, A. D. (1978) 'The language of history and the communication of historical knowledge', in A. Dickinson and P. Lee *History Teaching and Historical Understanding* (Heinemann Educational Books) pp. 54–71.

Edwards, A.D. (1980) 'Patterns of power and authority in classroom talk', in P. Woods *Teacher Strategies: Explorations in the Sociology of the School* (Croom Helm) pp. 237–53.

Edwards, A. D. and Furlong, V. J. (1978) *The Language of Teaching* (Heinemann Educational Books).

Edwards, J. (1979) *Language and Disadvantage* (Arnold).

Edwards, V. (1978) 'Language attitudes and underperformance in West Indian children', *Educational Review*, 30, pp. 51–8.

Edwards, V. K. (1979) *The West Indian Language Issue in British Schools: challenges and responses* (Routledge & Kegan Paul).

Ervin-Tripp, S. (1973) *Language Acquisition and Communicative Choice* (Stanford University Press).

Ervin-Tripp, S. and Mitchell-Kernan, C. (eds.) (1977) *Child Discourse* (Academic Press).

Foster, H. (1974) *Ribbin', Jivin' and Playin' the Dozens: the unrecognised dilemma of inner-city schools* (Bollinger).

French, P. and MacLure, M. (1979) 'Getting the right answer and getting the answer right', *Research in Education* no. 22, pp. 1–23.

French, P. and MacLure, M. (eds.) (1981) *Adult-Child Conversation* (Croom Helm).

Garnica, O. K. and King, M. L. (eds.) (1979) *Language, Children and Society: the effect of social factors on children learning to communicate* (Pergamon Press).

Giglioli, P. (ed.) (1972) *Language and Social Context* (Penguin).

Giles, H. (ed.) (1977) *Language Ethnicity and Intergroup Relations* (Academic Press).

Giles, H. and Powesland, P. (1975) *Speech Style and Social Evaluation* (Academic Press).

Giles, H. and St. Clair, R. (eds.) (1979) *Language and Social Psychology* (Blackwell).

Gregory, M. and Carroll, S. (1978) *Language and Situation* (Routledge & Kegan Paul).

Gumperz, J. and Hymes, D. (eds.) (1972) *Directions in Sociolinguistics: the Ethnography of Communication* (Holt, Rinehart & Winston).

Gumperz, J. and Herasimchuk, E. (1975) 'The conversational analysis of social meaning: a study of classroom interaction', in M. Sanchez and B. Blount (eds.) *Sociocultural Dimensions of Language Use* (Academic Press) pp. 81–116.

Halliday, M. (1975) *Learning How to Mean* (Arnold).

Hammersley, M. (1977) 'School learning: the cultural resources required by pupils to answer a teacher's question', in P. Woods and M. Hammersley *School Experience* (Croom Helm) pp. 57–86.

Hawkins, P. (1977) *Social Class, the Nominal Group and Verbal Strategies* (Routledge & Kegan Paul).

Hess, R. and Shipman, V. (1972) 'Early experience and the socialization of cognitive modes in children', in A. Cashdan *et al. Language in Education* (Routledge & Kegan Paul/Open University Press) pp. 169–77.

Hymes, D. (1977) *Foundations in Sociolinguistics: an Ethnographic Approach* (Tavistock).

Hymes, D. (1979) 'Language in education: forward to fundamentals', in O. Garnica and O. King *Language, Children and Society* (Pergamon) pp. 1–19.

Jackson, L. A. (1977) 'The myth of restricted and elaborated code', in B. R. Cosin *et al. School and Society: a Sociological Reader* (Routledge & Kegan Paul and Open University Press) pp. 163–71.

Keddie, N. (ed.) (1975) *Tinker, Tailor . . . : the Myth of Cultural Deprivation* (Penguin).

Labov, W. (1972) 'The logic of non-standard English', in P. Giglioli *Language and Social Context* (Penguin) pp. 179–215.

Labov, W. (1976) *Language in the Inner-City* (University of Pennsylvania Press).

Labov, W. (1977) *Sociolinguistic Patterns* (University of Pennsylvania Press).

Lee, V. (1973) 'Social relationships and language: some aspects of the work of Basil Bernstein' block 3 Language and Learning E. 262 (Open University Press).

Macauley, R. K. (1977) *Language, Social Class and Education: a Glasgow study* (Edinburgh University Press).

McHoul, A. (1978) 'The organisation of turns at formal talk in the classroom', *Language in Society*, **7**, 2, pp. 183–213.

MacKinnon, K. (1977) *Language, Education and Social Processes in a Gaelic Community* (Routledge & Kegan Paul).

Mehan, H. (1978) 'Structuring school structure', *Harvard Educational Review*, **48**, 1, pp. 32–64.

Pap, M. and Pleh, C. (1974) 'Social class differences in the speech of six-year old Hungarian children', *Sociology*, **8**, pp. 267–75.

Pride, J. and Holmes, J. (eds.) (1972) *Sociolinguistics* (Penguin).

Richards, J. (1978) *Classroom Language: What Sort?* (Allen & Unwin).

Robinson, W. (1975) 'The dialogue of deficit and difference in language proficiency', *International Journal of Psycholinguistics*, **3**, pp. 27–40.

Robinson, W. P. (1978) *Language Management in Education: the Australian Context* (Allen & Unwin).

Rosen, H. (1974) 'Language and class: a critical look at the theories of Basil Bernstein', in D. Holly (ed.) *Education and Domination* (Arrow) pp. 58–87.

Rushton, J. and Young, G. (1975) 'Context and complexity in working-class language', *Language and Speech*, **18**, 4, pp. 366–87.

Seligman, C. *et al*. (1972) 'The effects of speech style and other attributes on teachers' attitudes towards pupils', *Language and Society*, **1**, 1, pp. 131–42.

Shafer, R. and Shafer, S. (1975) 'Teacher attitudes towards children's language in West Germany and England', *Comparative Education*, **11**, pp. 43–61.

Sinclair, J. and Coulthard, M. (1975) *Towards an Analysis of Discourse: the English of Teachers and Pupils* (Cambridge University Press).

Snow, C. and Ferguson, C. (eds.) (1977) *Talking to Children: Language Input and Acquisition* (Cambridge University Press).

Speier, M. (1976) 'The child as conversationalist', in M. Hammersley and P. Woods (eds.) *The Process of Schooling* (Routledge & Kegan Paul and Open University Press) pp. 98–103.

Stubbs, M. (1976a) *Language, Schools and Classrooms* (Methuen).

Stubbs, M. (1976b) 'Keeping in touch: some functions of teacher-talk', in M. Stubbs and S. Delamont *Explorations in Classroom Observation* (Wiley) pp. 151–172.

Stubbs, M. (1981) 'Linguistic date in educational research', in Adelman, C. *Uttering and Muttering: reporting and using talk in social and educational research* (Bullmershe College) 1981, Grant McIntyre.

Tough, J. (1977) *The Development of Meaning* (Allen & Unwin).

Trudgill, P. (1974a) *Sociolinguistics: an Inroduction* (Penguin).

Trudgill, P. (1974b) *The Social Differentiation of English in Norwich* (Cambridge University Press).

Trudgill, P. (1975) *Accent, Dialect and the School* (Arnold).

Trudgill, P. (ed.) (1978) *Sociolinguistic Patterns in British English* (Arnold).

Wells, G. (1977) 'Language use and educational success', *Research in Education*, no. 18, pp. 9–34.

Williams, F. (ed.) (1971) *Language and Poverty* (Markham).

Williams, F. (1976) *Explorations of the Language Attitudes of Teachers* (Newbury).

Wootton, A. (1974) 'Talk in the homes of young children', *Sociology*, **8**, pp. 277–95.

14 Sociological approaches to the teaching profession
Eric Hoyle

'A man's work is as good a clue as any to the course of his life, and to his social being and identity' (Hughes 1958). Although one would perhaps wish to expand this statement to include women's work and to refer to the significance of the *lack* of work, the assertion remains valid and points to the importance of the sociology of work. In spite of Hughes' pioneering studies, and the significance of work in the life of the individual, the sociology of work has been somewhat slow to develop. However, there are signs of an accelerating interest.

In the literature one often finds a coupling of 'the sociology of work and occupations'. This may appear to involve a redundant term, and this is often the case, but studies of 'work' and of 'occupations' *can* imply somewhat different concerns. The sociology of work is principally concerned with the nature of work experience itself: the routines, relationships and responsibilities of the workplace, and in particular the *meaning* of this experience for the individual. This approach has been followed in detailed case studies, often by an observer–participant but sometimes from the outside, of the work situation of clerks, car workers, scientists, lorry drivers and deep-sea fishermen amongst others. The sociology of occupations is concerned with the structure of the occupation as a whole: its place in the labour market, social status, career patterns, occupational associations etc., and such cultural factors as dominant values, beliefs and ideologies. But, to repeat, this distinction should not be pressed too hard and many studies embrace both elements. Reviews of the whole field of work and occupational sociology are those of Berger (1964), Hall (1969), Pavalko (1971) and Elliott (1972).

Professions are studied in the same way as other occupations, but they have often been of special interest to the sociologist because the characteristics attributed to the professions are held to have a special social significance. Durkheim (1957), for example, held that professional ethics had a moral significance for society as a whole. Much more recently, Halmos (1965) has taken the same view, though his emphasis differs from that of Durkheim. And Parsons (1951) drew heavily on the characteristics of the professions in formulating his theory of how the social system sustains itself.

A study of the sociology of the teaching profession enables the teacher to clarify in his own mind some of the many issues which he confronts as a practitioner. Such a study is more relevant to all those concerned with policy issues in education. Some issues are: Does the teacher actually *need* a body of theoretical knowledge? Has the steady extension of the period of teacher education increased the level of skills or has its main purpose been to enhance the status of the profession? Is industrial action compatible with professional responsibility? Should the teacher back his professional judgement to the degree of defying educational authorities when he believes his pupils will benefit? Is success in the classroom sufficiently closely related to career success? Does a professional stance require a degree of detachment and objectivity towards pupils? How should the teacher be professionally accountable, to whom and for what? Needless to say there are no definitive answers to such questions, nor can a study of the teaching profession provide them directly, but at least teachers and others would be better prepared to confront such issues by drawing on the sociology of the teaching profession.

Theoretical and methodological issues

Three broad approaches to the study of professions can be identified: *functionalist*, *symbolic interactionist* and *radical-critical*.

Functionalist assumptions can be summarised – perhaps to the point of caricature – as follows. Professions perform an essential public service requiring the exercise of high-level skills based on a body of theoretical knowledge. This skill and knowledge can be acquired only through a lengthy period of higher education during which trainees also internalise a set of professional values and acquire a professional identity. These values may be general, for example, the primacy of client interest; or specific to a particular profession and perhaps made explicit in a code of ethics. As the exercise of professional knowledge is a matter of judgment, the practitioner functions most effectively when he enjoys a high degree of autonomy. This autonomy needs the protection of strong associations which would also have the function of controlling entry to the profession and influencing government policy in its sphere of interest. Individuals are induced to acquire the necessary degree of skill and knowledge, exercise responsibility and subjugate personal to client interest in return for high social status and financial reward.

Parsons (1951, 1958, 1968) developed a sophisticated functionalist approach to the professions, but there had been an implicit functionalist perspective in the many studies which attempted to identify the criteria which distinguished professions from other occupations. Many taxonomies have been produced which address themselves to the question: What is the nature of a profession? (see Flexner 1915; Cogan 1953; Greenwood 1957; Becker 1962 and Goode 1969). Not all such studies have been overtly functionalist but they have taken for granted the concept of profession as indicating a unique type of occupation. Other studies were concerned with the question: Is *x* a profession? This was frequently asked of the teaching profession, for example by Lieberman (1956) and Inlow (1956). Initially occupations were implicitly divided into 'professions' and 'other occupations', but the more common approach is to conceive a continuum, at one end of which are the established professions and along which are ranged what are variously referred to as quasi-emergent, marginal or semi-professions; Etzioni (1969) includes teaching in the latter category. Hickson and Thomas (1969) scaled the criteria of professions and allocated scores to occupations according to the degree to which they meet the criteria.

Of itself, the taxonomising of occupations would be a somewhat sterile activity if it did not generate substantive questions about professional functions. In particular it raises issues concerned with *professionalisation*. This is the process by which occupations move along the hypothetical continuum as they progressively meet more of the criteria to a higher degree. This is often treated as a unitary process, but it can be conceived of as having two components: *professionalism*, that is, the strategy and rhetoric used by an organised occupation as it seeks to move along the continuum; and *professionality*, that is, the exercise of professional skill and knowledge (Hoyle 1974). The improvement of status and of skill can provide *pari passu*, but professionalism (self-interest) could diverge from professionality (client-interest).

The functionalist perspective is associated with a methodological stance which views professions as social systems, that is, as having a structure of roles, an organisation, an institutionalised pattern of handling problems, and a culture incorporating its values and norms. This system is viewed 'from the outside' and speculations about it are based on the data which are usually drawn upon in an institutional analysis, official statistics, surveys, documents and so on.

The *symbolic interactionist* approach owes much to the influence of Everett Hughes at the University of Chicago (Hughes

1958) who treated *profession* as a symbolic rather than a descriptive category, 'a symbol of a desired conception of one's work and, hence, of one's self'. He was therefore concerned less with the social functions of the professions than with what it means to engage in professional work. This concern with the meaning of work was associated with a methodological approach which used observation and interviews to ascertain how participants defined their work situation and to help the sociologist to interpret these meanings.

I have used the term *radical/critical* to indicate a broad category embracing a number of approaches which are critical of functionalist assumptions. Johnson (1972), for example, argues that functionalist arguments simply conceal the fact that the pre-eminence of the established professions owes more to the power which they have been able to wield than to the rewards for service bestowed by a grateful society. But more pertinent to the teaching profession is the work of radical critics who advocate the de-professionalisation of the existing professions (Halmos 1973). Their criticism is directed particularly towards the knowledge-base and autonomy arguments of the functionalists. Although not an advocate of total de-professionalisation, Halmos (1965, 1970) argues that the theoretical knowledge held to be necessary to practice in those professions, such as teaching, which are concerned with bringing about changes in people are greatly exaggerated, since the essence of professional practice is the personal relationship between practitioners and client. Reiff (1971) and Bennett and Hockenstad (1973) argue that the systematic, rationalistic knowledge-base of the professions is perhaps less significant than intuitive, interpretative, experienced-based knowledge. Haug (1973) takes the same view of the professional knowledge-base and also argues that the autonomy claimed to be necessary is simply a device for maintaining distance between practitioner and client and also for avoiding accountability to the client and to laymen generally.

This perspective has considerable implications for the teaching profession in that it raises questions about its knowledge-base which are often concealed in the perennial debate about the theory–practice relationship (Hoyle 1980) and relates to the professionalism–professionality issue mentioned earlier. There is no distinctive methodology associated with the radical/critical perspective, although potentially a phenomenological study of the work situation of teachers could contribute to this approach.

Additional reading can be found in Ben-David (1963), Vollmer and Mills (1966), Jackson (1970) and Freidson (1971).

Studies of the teaching profession

This section will be relatively short, since it is concerned only with studies of the teaching profession as a whole.

Two American studies deal with the world of the schoolteacher. Waller (1932) simply 'sociologised' about school-teaching with such insight that his study has remained a widely-read and relevant classic. Insofar as it can be categorised, the approach is within the symbolic interactionist framework. In the introduction to his recent study of the schoolteacher, Lortie (1975) hopes that it is in the tradition of Waller in providing documentation of genuine insights into the nature of teaching as an occupation. Thus Lortie draws on historical and survey data and also on his own observational and interview data gathered from fieldwork on teachers in five cities. Jackson (1968) came to the study of 'life in classrooms' unencumbered with any constraining sociological perspective, but brought great insight to his interpretation of how elementary school teachers define the classroom world.

Lieberman (1956) offers an overview of the American teaching professions 'from the outside' by drawing on a wide range of survey material and documentation. The material is integrated around a number of perennial issues: status, autonomy, control and the tension between self-interest and client-interest. As such, the work is a model of integration. A more recent analysis of the American teaching profession is that of Dorros (1968). Finally, an excellent chapter-length review of some of the characteristics of the teaching profession which raises a number of interesting issues is Leggatt (1970). Though a philosophical rather than a sociological approach, Langford (1978) raises issues about responsibility, service, codes of conduct and so on.

Additional reading is provided by Gerstl (1967), Kelsall and Kelsall (1969), Dreeben (1970) and Lortie (1973).

Selected aspects of teaching as a profession

1. Status

Status is a perennial concern both of members of the professions and the sociologists who study them. The desire for status is held to be a motivational factor according to functionalist analysis. The radical/critical view accepts the pull of status but suggests that it detracts from client-interest. The 'facts' of the status of teaching as determined by surveys of the social ranking of occupations can be gathered from the many comparative studies of occupational prestige both between different occupations within the same country and between the same profession in different societies.

Bernbaum, Noble and Whiteside (1969), as well as reporting an empirical study, review the literarture on intraoccupational prestige, for example between graduates and non-graduates. A generalisation which can be derived from the literature on the status of teaching is that it has broadly the same relative prestige in most industrialised societies for which data are available.

The determinants of prestige are complex and there is no study undertaking the difficult task of weighting the factors which might be held to affect it. There is, however, much speculative discussion and the following groups of factors help to determine the prestige of a teacher: (1) characteristics of teachers, for example class background, sex, qualifications; (2) characteristics of clients, for example age, social class background, degree of voluntariness; (3) characteristics of the work situation, for example organisational setting, clients and, in groups, daily contact with clients. These characteristics are frequently used to contrast teachers unfavourably with the established professions since the general desire for professionalisation tends to encourage such a perspective rather then to embrace teaching with non-professionai organisations. Leggatt (1970) and Hoyle (1969a) both explore the determinants of the prestige of teachers.

Some of the determinants of status are amenable to change. For example, the length of the teacher education course in England and Wales has been extended from two to four years since the early 1960s, and has now moved rapidly to an all-graduate profession as in Scotland. But unlike its Scottish counterpart, the teaching profession in England and Wales has been unable to have established a General Teaching Council to control entry in spite of the recommendations of the Weaver Report (HMSO 1970).

Hall, Hans and Lauwerys (1953), Floud and Scott (1961) and Groff (1962) provide further reading.

2. Career
The concept of career usually connotes the process whereby an individual moves up an occupational hierarchy. However, Hughes (1958) takes a broader view and sees a career as a person 'managing his life' in the sense of making choices, establishing commitments, laying side-bets. Although work remains a central component of a teacher's life, and few are untouched by career concerns in the narrower sense of the term, it is seen in a broader context. Studies of careers in the narrower sense tend to be based on survey material and correlate promotion with such factors as age, sex, qualifications and experience. The career *structure* of the teacher in England and Wales can be derived from official statistics (DES 1979).

One important policy issue which arises from the increasing *differentiation* and *stratification* of the teaching profession is which of these processes (Bucher and Strauss 1961) are the result of the 'pull' of needed specialisation or the 'push' of the salary scale. A detailed national study of careers (Hilsum and Start 1974) explored the factors leading to promotion, LEA policies, and teachers' attitudes to promotion. Amongst the most salient factors to emerge was that women were promoted less than proportionally to men. Married women teachers tend to have abbreviated, interrupted or intermittent careers and this raises considerable policy issues about the use of trained professional capacity. Kelsall (1963) explored the problem of women's careers by following up a sample of college leavers. The question of women's careers raises social, cultural and political questions which are beyond the scope of this review. Falling rolls are likely to exacerbate the problem of women's careers since the opportunity of part-time and intermittent careers will be curtailed.

The approach to careers stemming from Hughes concentrates on the meaning and management of careers. Becker's (1952) study of the Chicago schoolteacher illustrated a pattern of lateral movement from downtown to suburban schools. Geer (1966) explored the factors leading to a relatively low commitment of teachers to their profession. A British study of the careers of British teachers which takes an interpretive approach has been undertaken by Lyons. Although the complete material is at present unpublished, an account of the work is given in Lyons and McCleary (1980).

See Charters (1967), Purvis (1973) and Hoyle (1981) for further reading.

3. Control

The literature frequently juxtaposes two models of control: the *professional*, in which the practitioner enjoys a high degree of autonomy and is controlled by his peers via collegial authority and, ultimately, by the law; and the *bureaucratic*, in which the practitioner is controlled by the detailed rules and hierarchical authority exercised by a superior. This conflict has been explored by Corwin (1965, 1970), who has identified a militant professionalism as a response to bureaucratic control, and by McKay (1966), Moeller and Charters (1966) and Boyan (1967). However, a number of theorists see schools as a mixture of hierarchical control in relation to goals, and professional autonomy in relation to classroom practice, and have been concerned with exploring the balance between the two; see Bidwell (1965), Litwak and Meyer (1974) and Lortie (1969). These discussions raise some quite crucial issues relating to the potential degree of participation in decision-making which teachers might enjoy, and link closely with the current debate about patterns of accountablility (Kogan 1978).

For further reading, see Abrahamson (1967), Lortie (1964), Marcus (1971) and Becher and McClure (1978).

4. Satisfaction

Many of the issues touched upon above – status, career, authority – lead on to the question of the job satisfaction of the teacher. Insofar as policy issues are generated by study of the teaching profession these will turn on the possibilities of initiating changes which will enhance teacher satisfaction. The concept of satisfaction is much disputed, but there is general research support for Herzberg's 'two factor theory' of satisfaction which holds that the factors leading to job satisfaction and dissatisfaction form distinct clusters (Herzberg, Mausner and Snyderman 1959). This theory has been substantiated for teachers via a specific test of Herzberg's theory (Sergiovanni 1967). This view can also be inferred from a variety of studies using different theoretical approaches and techniques. The factors which lead to satisfaction are implicit to the task of teaching: that is, intrinsic factors of classroom context and relationships with pupils. Dissatisfaction arises from such *extrinsic* factors as status, authority, structure and remuneration. There are a number of studies of teacher satisfaction using questionnaires of various kinds (e.g. Rudd and Wiseman 1962) but perhaps more interesting material is provided by interviews (e.g. Jackson 1968; Lortie 1975). These studies again point to classroom factors as a source of satisfaction, and to career and remuneration factors as a source of dissatisfaction. An important future area of possible dissatisfaction is the advent of falling rolls which will reduce the opportunity structure in teaching. One should not perhaps equate high opportunities for promotion with satisfaction and low opportunities with dissatisfaction (Hoyle 1969b), but the sudden reduction of promotion prospects is likely to lead to dissatisfaction in the short run and probably exacerbate the tension between two kinds of success: in terms of professionality and in terms of public recognition and promotion (Parsons 1951).

For additional reading, see Mumford (1970).

Further areas of study

Inevitably many issues have had to be omitted from this brief review. Some other important areas for study are:

Occupational choice: Guba, Jackson and Bidwell (1963),

Morton-Williams, Finch and Poll (1966), Butler (1968), and Ashley *et al*. (1970).

Professional socialisation: Shipman (1967), Edgar and Warren (1969), Taylor (1969) and Lacey (1977).

Work situation: Bidwell (1970), Morrison and MacIntyre (1973), Hilsum and Cane (1971), Hilsum and Strong (1978) and Hargreaves (1978).

Professional associations: Tropp (1957), Cole (1969), Blum (1969), Manzer (1970), Coates (1972), Gosden (1972), Tipton (1974) and Bloomer (1980).

Conclusion

The sociology of the teaching profession is a sub-division of the sociologies of both work and education. Its significance as a field lies in the fact that it relates to a number of substantive policy issues: the length and content of teacher education, the influence of the organised profession on decisions about educational provision, the enhancement of job satisfaction amongst teachers, career opportunities for women, the freedom of the teacher, the accountability of the profession to the community and so on. Many of these are perennial issues, but from time to time there arise specific issues to which the theory and research sociology of the teaching profession can contribute. A current example is that of falling rolls, the effects of which have consequences for recruitment, promotion, the teacher's work, the structure of the profession, job satisfaction, remuneration and so on. Thus there is a strong case for the continued development of this field of sociological inquiry.

References

Abrahamson, M. (ed.) (1967) *The Professional in the Organization* (Rand McNally).

Ashley, B. *et al*. (1970) 'A sociological analysis of students' reasons for becoming teachers', *Sociological Review*, **18**, 1, pp. 53–69.

Becher, T. and McClure, S. (eds.) (1978) *Accountability in Education* (SSRC/NFER).

Becker, H. S. (1952) 'The career of the Chicago schoolteacher', *American Journal of Sociology*, **57**, pp. 470–7. Reprinted in M. Hammersley and P. Woods (eds.) (1976) *The Process of Schooling: a sociological reader* (Routledge & Kegan Paul and Open University Press) pp. 75–80.

Becker, H. S. (1962) 'The nature of a profession', in *Education for the Professions* (National Society for the Study of Education) pp. 27–46.

Ben-David, J. (1963) 'Professions in the class system of present day society: a trend report and bibliography', *Current Sociology*, **12**, 3, pp. 246–330.

Bennett, W. S. and Hockenstad, M. C. (1973) 'Full-time people workers and conceptions of the "professional" ', in P. Halmos (ed.) *Profes-*

sionalization and Social Change: Sociological Review Monograph 20 (University of Keele) pp. 21–45.

Berger, P. L. (1964) *The Human Shape of Work: Studies in the sociology of occupations* (Macmillan).

Bernbaum, G., Noble, G. and Whiteside, T. (1969) 'Intra occupational prestige differentiation in teaching', in S. J. Eggleston (eds.) *Paedagogica Europaea* vol. 5 (W. and R. Chambers) pp. 41–59.

Bidwell, C. E. (1965) 'The school as a formal organization', in J. G. March (ed.) *Handbook of Organizations* (Rand McNally) pp. 972–1022.

Bidwell, C. E. (1970) 'Students and schools: some observations on client trust in client-serving organizations', in W. R. Rosengren and M. Lefton (eds.) *Organizations and Clients: essays in the sociology of service* (Merrill) pp. 37–70.

Bloomer, K. (1980) 'The teacher as a professional trade unionist', in E. Hoyle and J. Megarry (eds.) *World Yearbook of Education, 1980: The Professional Development of Teachers* (Kogan Page).

Blum, A. A. (ed.) (1969) *Teachers' Unions and Associations* (University of Illinois Press).

Boyan, N. J. (1967) 'The emergent role of the teacher in the authority structure of the school', in R. Allen and J. Schmid (eds.) *Collective Negotiations and Educational Administration* (Arkansas Press) pp. 1–20. Reprinted in F. D. Carver and T. J. Sergiovanni (eds.) (1969) *Organizations and Human Behaviour: focus on schools* (McGraw Hill) pp. 200–211.

Bucher, R. and Strauss, A. (1961) 'Professions in process', *American Journal of Sociology*, **65**, pp. 325–34. Reprinted in M. Hammersley and P. Woods (eds.) (1976) *The Process of Schooling: a sociological reader* (Routledge & Kegan Paul and Open University Press) pp. 19–26.

Butler, J. R. (1968) *Occupational Choice: Science Policy Studies No. 2* (HMSO).

Charters, W. W. (1967) 'Some "obvious" facts about the teaching career', *Educational Administration Quarterly*, **3**, 2, pp. 183–93.

Coates, R. D. (1972) *Teachers' Unions and Interest Group Politics* (Cambridge University Press).

Cogan, M. L. (1953) 'Towards a definition of a profession', *Harvard Educational Review*, **23**, pp. 33–50.

Cole. S. (1969) *The Unionization of Teachers: a study of the UFT* (Praeger).

Corwin, R. G. (1965) *A Sociology of Education* (Appleton-Century-Crofts).

Corwin, R. G. (1970) *Militant Professionalism: a study of organizational conflict in high schools* (Appleton-Century-Crofts).

Department of Education and Science (1970) *A Teaching Council for England and Wales: report of the working party appointed by the Secretary of State for Education and Science* (HMSO).

Department of Education and Science (1979) *Statistics of Education, 1977, Vol. 5 Teachers* (HMSO).

Dorros, S. (1968) *Teaching as a Profession* (Ohio University Press).

Dreeben, R. (1970) *The Nature of Teaching* (Scott Foresman).

Durkheim, E. (1957) *Professional Ethics and Civic Morals* (Routledge & Kegan Paul).

Edgar, D. E. and Warren, R. L. (1969) 'Power and autonomy in teacher socialization', *Sociology of Education*, **42**, 4, pp. 386–99.

Elliott, P. (1972) *The Sociology of the Professions* (Macmillan).

Etzioni, A. (ed.) (1969) *The Semi Professions and their Organization* (Free Press).

Flexner, A. (1915) 'Is social work a profession?', in *Proceedings, National Conferences of Charities and Corrections*, pp. 576–90.

Floud, J. and Scott, W. (1961) 'Recruitment to teaching in England and Wales', in A. H. Halsey, J. Floud and C. A. Anderson (eds.) *Education, Economy and Society* (Free Press) pp. 527–44.

Freidson, E. (ed.) (1971) *The Professions and their Prospects* (Sage).

Geer, B. (1966) 'Occupational commitment and the teaching profession', *School Review*, **77**, 1, pp. 31–47.

Gerstl, J. (1967) 'Education and the sociology of work', in D. A. Hansen and J. Gerstl (eds.) *On Education: sociological perspectives* (Wiley) pp. 224–61.

Goode, W. J. (1969) 'The theoretical limits of professionalization', in A. Etzioni (ed.) *The Semi Professions and their Organization* (Free Press) pp. 266–308.

Gosden, P. H. J. H. (1972) *The Evolution of a Profession* (Blackwell).

Greenwood, E. (1957) 'Attributes of a profession', *Social Work*, **2**, pp. 45–55.

Groff, P. J. (1962) 'The social status of teachers', *Journal of Educational Sociology*, **36**, 1, pp. 20–25.

Guba, E. G., Jackson, P. W. and Bidwell, C. E. (1959) 'Occupational choice and the teaching career', *Educational Research Bulletin*, **38**, pp. 1–12. Reprinted in W. W. Charters and N. L. Gage (eds.) (1963) *Readings in the Social Psychology of Education* (Allyn and Bacon) pp. 271–8.

Hall, R. H. (1969) *Occupations and the Social Structure* (Prentice-Hall).

Hall, R. K., Hans, N. and Lauwerys, J. (1953) 'The social position of teachers', in R. K. Hall, N. Hans and J. Lauwerys (eds.) *Yearbook of Education, 1953* (Evans) pp. 1–29.

Halmos, P. (1965) *The Faith of the Counsellors* (Constable).

Halmos, P. (1970) *The Personal Service Society* (Constable).

Halmos, P. (1973) *Professionalization and social change*, Sociological Review Monograph No. 20 (University of Keele).

Hargreaves, D. H. (1978) 'What teaching does to teachers', *New Society*, **43**, 805, pp. 540–2.

Haug, M. (1973) 'De-professionalization: an alternate hypothesis for the future', in P. Halmos (ed.) (1973) op. cit., pp. 195–211.

Herzberg, F., Mausner, B. and Snyderman, B. (1959) *The Motivation to Work* (Wiley).

Hickson, D. J. and Thomas, M. W. (1969) 'Professionalization in Britain: a preliminary measurement', *Sociology*, **3**, 1, pp. 37–53.

Hilsum, S. and Cane, B. (1971) *The Teacher's Day* (NFER).

Hilsum, S. and Start, K. B. (1974) *Promotion and Careers in Teaching* (NFER).

Hilsum, S. and Strong, C. (1978) *The Secondary Teacher's Day* (NFER).

Hoyle, E. (1969a) *The Role of the Teacher* (Routledge & Kegan Paul).

Hoyle, E. (1969b) 'Professional stratification and anomie in the teaching profession', in S. J. Eggleston (ed.) *Paedagogica Europaea Vol. 5* (W. and R. Chambers) pp. 60–72.

Hoyle, E. (1974) 'Professionality, professionalism and control in teaching', *London Educational Review*, **3**, 2, pp. 13–19.

Hoyle, E. (1980) 'Professionalization and deprofessionalization in education', in E. Hoyle and J. Megarry (eds.) *World Yearbook of Education, 1980: the Professional Development of Teachers* (Kogan Page).

Hoyle, E. (1981) 'The teacher's career' section 2 block 6 Management and the School (Open University Press).

Hughes, E. C. (1958) *Men and their Work* (Free Press).

Inlow, G. (1956) 'Is teaching a profession?', *School Review*, **66**, 6, pp. 256–9.

Jackson, J. A. (ed.) (1970) *Professions and Professionalization* (Cambridge University Press).

Jackson, P. W. (1968) *Life in Classrooms* (Holt, Rinehart & Winston).

Johnson, T. J. (1972) *Professions and Power* (Macmillan).

Kelsall, R. K. (1963) *Women and Teaching* (HMSO).

Kelsall, R. K. and Kelsall, H. M. (1969) *The Schoolteacher in England and the United States: the findings of empirical research* (Pergamon).

Kogan, M. (1978) 'The impact and policy implications of monitoring procedures', in T. Becher and S. McClure (eds.) *Accountability in Education* (SSRC/NFER) pp. 113–26.

Lacey, C. (1977) *The Socialization of Teachers* (Methuen).

Langford, G. (1978) *Teaching as a Profession: an essay in the philosophy of education* (Manchester University Press).

Leggatt, T. (1970) 'Teaching as a profession', in J. A. Jackson (ed.) *Professions and Professionalization* (Cambridge University Press) pp. 155–77.

Lieberman, M. (1956) *Education as a Profession* (Prentice-Hall).

Litwak, E. and Meyer, H. J. (1974) *School, Family and Neighbourhood: the theory and practice of school-community relations* (Columbia University Press).

Lortie, D. C. (1964) 'The teacher and team teaching: suggestions for long range research', in J. S. Shaplin and H. F. Olds (eds.) *Team Teaching* (Harper) pp. 270–305.

Lortie, D. C. (1969) 'The balance of control and autonomy in elementary school teaching', in A. Etzioni (ed.) *The Semi-Professions and their Organization* (Free Press) pp. 1–53.

Lortie, D. C. (1973) 'Observations on teaching as work', in R.M.W. Travers (ed.) *Second Handbook of Research on Teaching* (Rand McNally) pp. 474–97.

Lortie, D. C. (1975) *Schoolteacher: a sociological study* (University of Chicago Press).

Lyons, G. and McCleary, L. (1980) 'Careers in teaching', in E. Hoyle and J. Megarry (eds.) *World Yearbook of Education, 1980: The Professional Development of Teachers* (Kogan Page) pp. 98–111.

McKay, D. A. (1966) 'Using professional talent in a school organization', *Canadian Education and Research Digest*, **6**, pp. 342–52. Reprinted in T. D. Carver and T. J. Sergiovanni (eds.) (1969) *Organizations and Human Behaviour: focus on schools* (McGraw Hill) pp. 228–34.

Manzer, R. A. (1970) *Teachers and Politics* (Manchester University Press).

Marcus, P. M. (1971) 'Schoolteachers and militant conservatism', in E. Freidson (ed.) *The Professions and their Prospects* (Sage) pp. 191–216.

Mason, W., Dressel, P. J. and Bain, R. K. (1959) 'Sex role and career orientation of beginning teachers', *Harvard Educational Review*, **29**, 4, pp. 370–83.

Moeller, G. H. and Charters, W. W. (1966) 'Relation of bureaucratization to sense of power among teachers', *Administrative Science Quarterly*, **10**, pp. 444–65. Reprinted in F. D. Carver and T. J. Sergiovanni (eds.) (1969) *Organizations and Human Behaviour: focus on schools* (McGraw Hill) pp. 235–48.

Morrison, A. and McIntyre, D. (1973) *Teachers and Teaching* (2nd edn.) (Penguin).

Morton-Williams, R., Finch, S. and Poll, C. (1966) *Undergraduates' Attitudes to Teaching as a Career* (Central Office of Information).

Mumford, E. (1970) 'Job satisfaction: a new approach derived from an old theory', *Sociological Review*, **18**, 1, pp. 71–101.

Parsons, T. (1951) *The Social System* (Routledge & Kegan Paul).

Parsons, T. (1958) *Essays in Sociological Theory* (revised edn.) (Free Press).

Parsons, T. (1968) 'Professions', in *International Encyclopaedia of the Social Sciences* (Collier Macmillan) pp. 536–47.

Pavalko, R. L. (1971) *The Sociology of Occupations and Professions* (F. E. Peacock).

Purvis, J. (1973) 'Schoolteaching as a professional career', *British Journal of Sociology*, **24**, 1, pp. 43–57.

Reiff, R. (1971) 'The danger of the techni-pro: democratizing the human service professions', *Social Policy*, **2**, pp. 62–4.

Rudd, W. G. A. and Wiseman, S. (1962) 'Sources of dissatisfaction amongst a group of teachers', *British Journal of Educational Psychology*, **32**, 3, pp. 275–91.

Sergiovanni, T. J. (1967) 'Factors which affect satisfaction and dissatisfaction of teachers', *Journal of Educational Administration*, **5**, pp. 66–82. Reprinted in F. D. Carver and T. J. Sergiovanni (eds.) (1969) *Organizations and Human Behaviour: focus on schools* (McGraw Hill) pp. 249–60.

Shipman, M. (1967) 'Education and college culture', *British Journal of Sociology*, **18**, 4, pp. 425–34.

Taylor, W. (1969) *Society and the Education of Teachers* (Faber and Faber).

Tipton, B. (1974) 'The hidden side of teaching: the teachers' unions', *London Educational Review*, **3**, 2, pp. 20–30.

Tropp, A. (1957) *The Schoolteachers* (Heinemann Educational Books).

Vollmer, H. M. and Mills, D. L. (eds.) (1966) *Professionalization* (Prentice-Hall)

Waller, W. (1932) *The Sociology of Teaching* (Wiley).

15 The sociology of classrooms
Martyn Hammersley

Introduction
The classroom is a key site in which to explore the nature of schooling and the impact upon it of changing social conditions. It is where the real work of education occurs. Yet, curiously, it is only relatively recently that sociologists of education have shown interest in studying classroom processes. Moreover, even now many exhibit a preference for speculation rather than empirical research in this area. This is perhaps because the classroom is so familiar, it is one of the few institutional settings of which virtually everyone has extensive experience. However, such familiarity is not a sound basis for knowledge (Delamont 1981). As soon as we begin to look closely at classroom interaction it becomes clear that the various parties to it have sharply differing, and sometimes surprising, perspectives; that features of it which seem unremarkable are by no means 'natural' or inevitable; and that the form and content of classroom process is structured by a complex set of conditions which have developed over time and which derive from the nature of the wider society.

There is now quite a considerable literature in this field, but two general points should be borne in mind:

1. *The wide range of approaches*
The different approaches are: 'positivist' (e.g. Flanders 1970)A[1]; functionalist (e.g. Young and Beardsley 1968)A; Marxist (Willis 1977); cultural anthropological (Dumont and Wax 1977)A; symbolic interactionist (Woods 1979); social phenomenological (Keddie 1971); sociolinguistic (Phillips 1972)A; and ethnomethodological (Payne 1976). (For introductions to these various theoretical traditions see Giddens 1976; Worsley 1977, ch. 9; Morris 1977; Coulthard 1977; and Cuff and Payne 1979.) The positivist, sociolinguistic and ethnomethodological approaches constitute relatively isolated traditions, hardly drawn on by, and drawing little on, the others. Research in the other categories tends to be more eclectic, for example seeking to combine interactionism and phenomenology (Hargreaves, Hester and Mellor 1975; Pollard 1980), or interactionism/phenomenology and Marxism (Sharp

and Green 1975; Willis 1977).

The different approaches vary considerably in the volume of work produced. Some, most notably the functionalist, provide very few examples, while the positivist category actually contributes more than half the literature on classroom interaction; though much of it is of a psychological character. The central interest of this work is identifying 'good' teaching by providing quantitative pictures of the frequency of different types of teacher action and relating these to differential pupil achievement. In terms of recent growth the interactionist, sociolinguistic, ethnomethodological and Marxist approaches are in the forefront. A common feature of these is their opposition to the central methodological and theoretical features of 'positivist' research. They argue that it employs crude, pre-given categories in a way which neglects the complexity of both participant perspectives and the process of classroom interaction itself; and that it fails to examine the social origins and wider consequences of particular forms of teaching and learning (Walker 1971, 1972; Hamilton and Delamont 1976; Walker and Adelman 1975c; Sharp and Green 1975; Coulthard 1977).

These alternative approaches usually adopt or recommend some form of ethnographic methodology. For general reading on this, see Atkinson (1979) and Hammersley (1979a and b); Walker and Adelman (1975a) is a handbook detailing one such approach to classroom observation; Stubbs (1977b) provides a sociolinguistic, and Anderson (1979) an ethnomethodological, perspective on method; and see Delamont (1976b) for an attempt to combine positivist and ethnographic methods.

2. The settings

A large proportion of the research has taken place in fairly 'traditional' state secondary school classrooms. However, the following document research in 'progressive' secondary, middle and primary schools: Gracey (1972)A; Sharp and Green (1975); Berlak *et al*. (1975), and Berlak and Berlak (1976); Hannan (1975); Bennett (1976); Boydell (1978); A. Hargreaves (1978, 1979); Edwards and Furlong (1978). (For convenience I have used the relatively crude distinction between 'traditional' and 'progressive' teaching, but see Berlak *et al*. 1975 and Hammersley 1977a). Middle, primary and nursery school classrooms provide the settings for the following studies: Smith and Geoffrey (1968)A; Dixon (1972)A; Gracey (1972)A; McPherson (1972)A; Kanter (1972)A; Nash (1973); Mackay (1973)A; Willes (1977, 1980); A. Hargreaves (1978, 1979); King (1978); Pollard (1979, 1980); French and MacLure (1979); Bossert (1979)A; MacLure and French (1980); Meyenn (1980a and b).

There is little research on classroom interaction in post-compulsory education, but see Atkinson (1975), (1976) and (1977), and the applied work of Abercrombie and Terry (1978), Rudduck (1978) and Parlett (1967)A.

General texts
The Open University course E282 School and Society (1971) provides an early account of the phenomenological orientation in this field, while Block Two of its replacement, E202 Schooling and Society (1977), presents an interactionist overview of the area. Robinson (1974) is an early review of the ethnographic literature; Delamont (1976a) is a more extended outline of the field, again from a basically ethnographic point of view. Stubbs (1976a) provides a good discussion from a sociolinguistic perspective, as does Coulthard (1977) at a more advanced level. Furlong and Edwards (1977) compare and contrast three different approaches to the analysis of classroom talk. Edwards and Furlong (1978) give a readable and systematic summary of current findings regarding the structure of classroom interaction. For the most recent reviews of the sociolinguistic, positivist and ethnographic literature see Edwards (1980b), McIntyre (1980) and Hammersley (1980c) respectively.

There are several collections bringing together important articles: Cazden, John and Hymes (1972)A; Chanan and Delamont (1975); Stubbs and Delamont (1976); Hammersley and Woods (1976); Cosin *et al.* (1977); Woods and Hammersley (1977); Barton and Meighan (1979); Eggleston (1979); Woods (1980a and b); and Furlong (forthcoming).

The structure of classroom interaction
The positivist tradition focuses almost exclusively on this area, usually producing statistical generalisations about the typical frequencies of different kinds of classroom acts (Flanders 1970)A, but also some rather more sophisticated accounts pinpointing typical sequences and their functions: Bellack (1966)A; Smith *et al.* (1967)A; Kounin (1970)A and Lundgren (1974).

Sociolinguistic and ethnomethodological research also falls under this heading. Sinclair and Coulthard (1975) provide the most developed sociolinguistic account of the structure of classroom interaction (see Burton 1980 for an up-dated summary, Hammersley 1980b for an ethnographic critique, and Stubbs 1977a for a sociolinguistic critique of ethnographic work). Willes (1977, 1980) presents an interesting application of the Sinclair and Coulthard model to the socialisation of reception-class children into competent classroom participants. Wells and Montgomery (1980) outline a rather different model, using it to compare adult–child interaction in the home and at school (see Drew 1980 for an ethnomethodological critique of this, and by implication of other sociolinguistic models). For other examples of a sociolinguistic approach see Gumperz and Herasimchuk (1972)A; Cazden, John and Hymes (1972)A; and Stubbs (1975, 1976a and b).

Among ethnomethodological work McHoul (1978) compares formal classroom interaction with ordinary conversation pointing to the role of pre-allocation of turns to speak, and the resulting asymmetry of interactional rights between teachers and pupils. Mehan (1978, 1979)A provides a much more extensive analysis, identifying the major sequential patterns of classroom interaction and also the topical organisation of lessons. For other examples of ethnomethodological analysis see Mackay (1973), Payne (1976), Payne and Hustler (1980), and Cuff and Hustler (1980). Some recent work in this tradition has attempted to provide an integrated account of verbal and nonverbal aspects of classroom behaviour: McDermott (1976)A; McDermott and Aron (1977)A; and McDermott, Gospodinoff and Aron (1978)A. McDermott investigated social interaction in two first grade reading groups, seeking to document the self-fulfilling processes involved in the 'success' of one group and the 'failure' of the other. A promising recent development of this approach is its application to interaction in 'alternative' schools: Moore (1978)A.

Those working within interactionism, phenomenology and Marxism have given rather little attention to the structure of classroom interaction itself. However, see Barnes (1969, 1976), Hammersley (1974, 1976), Torode (1977) and Edwards and Furlong (1978); Pollard's (1979) and (1980) analysis of negotiated order in the classroom and its relation to teacher and pupil interests; and Ball (1980) on the establishment of patterns of classroom interaction in initial encounters in secondary schools.

Some attention, displaying a wide variety of approaches but little co-ordination, has been given to the implications of different patterns and features of classroom interaction for pupil learning and careers and for social reproduction, especially the reproduction of class (and also gender) divisions: Kanter (1972)A; McDermott (1976)A; Vulliamy (1976); Hardy (1976); Morgan (1977)A; Mehan (1979)A; Bossert (1979)A; Clarricoates (1980).

Teacher perspectives and strategies
Waller (1932)A and Becker (1951, 1952a and b, 1953)A are classic general accounts of teacher perspectives. Waller emphasises the

conflictual character of teacher–pupil relations and also examines the impact of teaching on the teacher. Becker looks to the relationships of teachers with pupils, parents, colleagues and principals as the source of their occupational problems and as a key to their characteristic perspectives. Lortie (1975)A is a more recent contribution along similar lines which examines the recruitment and socialisation patterns of teachers and their career and work rewards. Smith and Geoffrey (1968)A is an early and rather neglected account of the process of teaching provided by the collaboration of a researcher and teacher studying the latter's lessons. They present a detailed account of the process of classroom interaction against the background of school-wide events and seek to generate a formalised theory of teacher decision-making. Much recent work has focused on the recurrent problems and dilemmas facing teachers in the classroom and the strategies they use to deal with them: Dixon (1972)A; McPherson (1972)A; Stebbins (1975)A; Berlak *et al.* (1975); Berlak and Berlak (1976); Sharp and Green (1975); Delamont (1976a); Wegmann (1976)A; Hammersley (1976); Doyle (1977)A; Woods (1979, 1980a); Lacey (1977); Metz (1978a and b)A; A. Hargreaves (1978, 1979); Edwards and Furlong (1978); Reynolds and Sullivan (1979); Pollard (1979, 1980); and French and MacLure (1979). Much of this concentrates on the problem of classroom order, but Stebbins, Delamont, Berlak *et al.*, Edwards and Furlong, and French and MacLure discuss instructional strategies of various kinds.

There have also been a number of attempts to relate these problems and strategies to the institutional and societal context: Leacock (1969)A examines the constraints operating on teachers in four different schools and how the teachers' practices diverge from their ideals and contribute to class reproduction. Warren (1973)A, Stebbins (1976)A and Denscombe (1977, 1980a and b) examine the role of school organisation and architecture in shaping teachers' classroom concerns and strategies; and D. H. Hargreaves (1980) discusses the mediating role of the occupational culture. Gracey (1972)A points to the effects of bureaucracy in the school system and in the school, while Sharp and Green (1975), A. Hargreaves (1978) and Woods (1979) provide more wide-ranging accounts appealing to the contradictions of capitalism (Sharp and Green; A. Hargreaves) and increasing rationalisation in modern industrial society (Woods).

An aspect of teacher perspectives given much attention in recent years is teacher typifications of pupils: Rist (1970, 1973)A; Nash (1973); Mehan (1973)A; Cicourel *et al.* (1974)A; Sharp and Green (1975); Hargreaves, Hester and Mellor (1975); Gouldner (1978)A.

This interest arises on the one hand from claims about the effects of teachers' expectations on pupil achievement (Rosenthal and Jacobson 1968A; Good and Brophy 1978A) and on the other from the application of labelling theory to the school situation (Cicourel and Kitsuse 1963, 1977A; Hargreaves, Hester and Mellor 1975). D. H. Hargreaves (1977) provides an analytic overview of much of this literature.

Pupil adaptations and strategies

Early studies in this field adopted a subcultural approach, identifying pro- and anti-school subcultures among pupils, and relating the development of these to streaming and to class cultures: D. H. Hargreaves (1967) and Lacey (1970). Willis (1976, 1977), Lambart (1976), Ball (1978, 1981), Corrigan (1979) and Meyenn (1980a and b) represent modifications and developments of this basic model. Woods (1979) provides an alternative, adaptation model in which he locates various aspects of pupil experience in state secondary schools, such as being 'shown up' and 'having a laugh'. Also, where Willis (1977) interprets pupil culture within a Marxist model of class reproduction, Woods adopts a neo-Weberian approach, relating it to trends in western society towards bureaucratisation and rationalisation.

Both the subculture and adaptation models were developed originally from functionalism (see Cohen 1955 and Merton 1957). Birksted (1976), Delamont (1976a), Furlong (1976), Werthman (1977)A, Woods (1978a and b), Davies (1979), Pollard (1979), Denscombe (1980b), Ball (1980) and Turner (forthcoming) are phenomenological and interactionist accounts which emphasise the complexity and contextual variability of pupil action. Woods (1979), Davies (1978, 1979), and Hammersley and Turner (1980) attempt to bridge the interactional and adaptation levels.

Marsh, Rosser and Harré (1978) present an unusual approach, looking at the rules underlying the accounts pupils give of their classroom behaviour with a view to revealing the structure of their motivation in the classroom.

Research has tended to focus on white, male, deviant pupils in fairly traditional, state secondary schools. Lambart (1976), Furlong (1976), Delamont (1976a), Davies (1978, 1979), Fuller (1980), Llewellyn (1980), and Meyenn (1980a and b) are exceptions, dealing with 'conformist' and 'deviant' girls, (and in the case of Furlong and Fuller, West Indian girls) in an unstreamed grammar school (Lambart), a private school (Delamont) and a middle school (Meyenn), as well as in secondary modern (Furlong) and comprehensive schools (Davies, Fuller, Llewellyn). Hammersley and

Turner (1980) discuss the issue of conformity; Fuller and Llewellyn that of gender; and Davies (1979) both. There has been little research on the adaptations of pupils under 'progressive' teaching (though see Novak 1974, 1975A; Hannan 1975; and Ball 1978, 1981) and virtually none at all on the adaptations and strategies of primary school pupils (but see Pollard 1979).

The obverse of the research on teacher typifications of pupils looks at pupil reactions to labelling: D. H. Hargreaves (1976) and Bird (1980). Conversely, Gannaway (1976) and Furlong (1977) have investigated pupil typifications of teachers. There is little work on pupils' typifications of one another, but see Harré (1975), Morgan, O'Neill and Harré (1979) and Turner (forthcoming).

An area of major importance where much work remains to be done is pupil and student learning strategies: Becker *et al.* (1961, 1968)A; Holt (1970)A; Miller and Parlett (1974); Barnes (1976); Barnes and Todd (1977); Woods (1978a and b); and MacLure and French (1980).

Conclusion

One of the key problems in this area is the fragmentation of theoretical and methodological approaches. This has resulted not only in rather restricted communication among those working in the field, but also in a lack of overall co-ordination of research and therefore limited cumulative development. This is especially unfortunate given the substantive and methodological complementarities the various approaches display. Thus, for example, the sociolinguistic and ethnomethodological work on classroom interaction fills an important gap in the interactionist, phenomenological and Marxist literature (Hammersley 1980c); and the concern of the positivists with frequencies cannot be entirely escaped by those working in the other traditions, witness for example the centrality to their overall argument of Sharp and Green's (1975) claim about the differential frequency of teacher–pupil contacts for different types of pupil. There are, of course, serious theoretical and methodological disagreements between approaches, though they have often been exaggerated.

Two issues are particularly important. Firstly, there is the split between discipline-oriented and policy-oriented research. Many classroom ethnographers rejected not only the theory and methodology of positivist research, but also its applied orientation. Others developed a separate, applied tradition of 'illuminative evaluation' (Hamilton 1977a and b; Walker and Adelman 1975b). However, while 'pure' and 'applied' research are certainly different in nature, they are nonetheless complementary and many of the theoretical and methodological problems faced in each are similar.

The other major problem area is that of relating analyses of classroom interaction to macro-accounts of the functioning of educational and social systems. As a result of commitment to theoretical approaches which pay relatively little attention to the macro-level, or even deny its validity, classroom researchers have in general provided little explicit foundation for relating macro- and micro-levels of analysis; though see Sharp and Green (1975), Willis (1977), A. Hargreaves (1978, 1979) and Woods (1979) for attempts to 'bridge the gap'. On the other side, those working at the macro-level have also paid insufficient attention to the problem, making little use of the micro-literature. Once again there are serious theoretical and practical problems involved here, but these are increasingly being given attention: for example D. H. Hargreaves (1978), Edwards (1980a and c); A. Hargreaves (1980); and Hammersley (1980a).

The literature on classroom interaction provides an extremely important corrective to the common-sense assumptions often made about classroom processes in sociological work and educational theory. With increased theoretical and methodological co-ordination and the development of linkages between 'pure' and 'applied', macro- and micro-research, this field promises to make a major contribution to our understanding of, and perhaps control over, educational processes.

Notes
[1] 'A' signifies research on North American settings.

References

Abercrombie, M. L. J. and Terry, P. M. (1978) *Talking to Learn: improving teaching and learning in small groups* (Research into Higher Education Monographs, Society for Research into Higher Education, University of Surrey).

Adelman, C. (ed.) (1977) *Uttering, Muttering: collecting, using and reporting talk for social and educational research* (Bulmershe College of Higher Education, Reading, England); 2nd ed. Grant McIntyre 1981.

Anderson, D. C. (1979) *Evaluation by Classroom Experience* (Nafferton).

Atkinson, P. (1975) 'In cold blood: bedside teaching in a medical school', in G. Chanan and S. Delamont (eds.) 1975, pp. 163–82.

Atkinson, P. (1976) *The Clinical Experience: an ethnography of medical education* unpublished Ph.D. thesis (University of Edinburgh).

Atkinson, P. (1977) 'The reproduction of medical knowledge', in R. Dingwall *et al*. (eds.) *Health Care and Health Knowledge* (Croom Helm).

Atkinson, P. (1979) 'Research design in ethnography' part 5 block 3

Research Methods in Education and the Social Sciences DE304 (Open University Press) pp. 41–81.

Atkinson, P. and Delamont, S. (1976) 'Mock ups and cock ups: the stage-management of guided discovery learning', in P. Woods and M. Hammersley (1977) pp. 87–108.

Ball, S. (1978) *Processes of Comprehensive Schooling* unpublished Ph.D. thesis (University of Sussex).

Ball, S. (1980) 'Initial encounters in the classroom and the process of establishment', in P. Woods (ed.), 1981, pp. 143–61.

Ball, S. (1981) Beachside Comprehensive: a case study of secondary schooling (Cambridge University Press).

Barnes, D. (1969) 'Language in the secondary classroom', in D. Barnes *et al. Language, the Learner and the School* (Penguin) pp. 9–77.

Barnes, D. (1976) *From Communication to Curriculum* (Penguin).

Barnes, D. and Todd, F. (1977) *Communication and Learning in Small Groups* (Routledge & Kegan Paul).

Barton, L. and Meighan, R. (eds.) (1979) *Schools Pupils and Deviance* (Nafferton).

Becker, H. S. (1951) *Role and Career Problems of the Chicago Public School Teacher* unpublished Ph.D. thesis (University of Chicago).

Becker, H. S. (1952a) 'The career of the Chicago public schoolteacher', *American Journal of Sociology*, **57**, pp. 470–77. Reprinted in H. S. Becker (1971) *Sociological Work* (Allen Lane) and in M. Hammersley and P. Woods (eds.) (1976).

Becker, H. S. (1952b) 'Social-class variations in the teacher-pupil relationship', *Journal of Educational Sociology*, **25**, 4, pp. 451–65. Reprinted in H. S. Becker (1971) *Sociological Work* (Allen Lane) and in B. R. Cosin *et al.* (eds.), 1977.

Becker, H. S. (1953) 'The teacher in the authority system of the public school', *Journal of Educational Sociology*, **27**, pp. 128–41. Reprinted in H. S. Becker (1971) *Sociological Work* (Allen Lane) and in M. Hammersley and P. Woods (eds.), 1976.

Becker, H. S. *et al.* (1961) *Boys in White* (University of Chicago Press).

Becker, H. S. *et al.* (1968) *Making the Grade* (Wiley).

Bellack, A. *et al.* (1966) *The Language of the Classroom* (Teachers College Press).

Bennett, N. (1976) *Teaching Styles and Pupil Progress* (Open Books).

Berlak, A. *et al.* (1975) 'Teaching and learning in English primary schools', *School Review*, **83**, 2, pp. 215–43. Reprinted in M. Hammersley and P. Woods (eds.), 1976.

Berlak, H. and Berlak, A. (1976) 'Towards a political and social psychological theory of schooling: an analysis and interpretation of English informal primary schools', *Interchange*, **6**, 3, pp. 11–22.

Bird, C. (1980) 'Deviant labelling in school: the pupils' perspective', in P. Woods (ed.), 1980b, pp. 94–107.

Birksted, I. K. (1976) 'School versus pop culture: a case study of adolescent adaptation', *Research in Education*, no. 16, pp. 13–23.

Bossert, S. T. (1979) *Tasks and Social Relationships in Classrooms* (Cambridge University Press).

Boydell, D. (1978) *The Primary Teacher in Action* (Open Books).

Burton, D. (1980) 'The sociolinguistic analysis of spoken discourse', in P.

French and M. MacLure (eds.), pp. 21–46.

Cazden, C. B., John, V. P. and Hymes, D. (eds.) (1972) *Functions of Language in the Classroom* (Teachers College Press).

Chanan, G. and Delamont, S. (eds.) (1975) *Frontiers of Classroom Research* (NFER).

Cicourel, A. V. and Kitsuse, J. I. (1963) *The Educational Decision-makers* (Bobbs-Merrill).

Cicourel, A. V. and Kitsuse, J. I. (1977) 'The social organisation of the high school and deviant adolescent careers', in B. R. Cosin *et al.* (eds.), pp. 114–21.

Cicourel, A. V. *et al.* (1974) *Language Use and School Perfomance* (Academic Press).

Clarricoates, K. (1980) ' "The Importance of Being Ernest . . . Emma . . . Tom . . . Jane": the perception and categorisation of gender conformity and gender deviation in primary schools', in R. Deem (ed.), pp. 26–41.

Cohen, A. K. (1955) *Delinquent Boys* (Routledge & Kegan Paul).

Corrigan, P. (1979) *Schooling the Smash Street Kids* (Macmillan).

Cosin, B. R. *et al.* (eds.) (1977) *School and Society* (Routledge & Kegan Paul).

Coulthard, M. (1977) *An Introduction to Discourse Analysis* (Longman).

Cuff, E. C. and Hustler, D. (1980) 'Stories and story time in an infant classroom', in P. French and M. MacLure (eds.), pp. 111–41.

Cuff, E. C. and Payne, G. C. F. (1979) *Sociological Perspectives* (George Allen & Unwin).

Davies, L. (1978) 'The view from the girls', *Educational Review*, **30**, 2, pp. 103–9.

Davies, L. (1979) 'Deadlier than the male? Girls' conformity and deviance in school', in L. Barton and R. Meighan (eds.), pp. 59–73.

Deem, R. (ed.) (1980) *Schooling for Women's Work* (Routledge & Kegan Paul).

Delamont, S. (1976a) *Interaction in the Classroom* (Methuen).

Delamont, S. (1976b) 'Beyond Flanders' Fields', in M. Stubbs and S. Delamont (eds.).

Delamont, S. (1981) 'All too familiar: a decade of classroom research', *Educational Analysis*, **3**, 1.

Denscombe, M. (1977) *The Social Organisation of Teaching* unpublished Ph.D. thesis (University of Leicester).

Denscombe, M. (1980a) ' "Keeping 'em quiet": the significance of noise for the practical activity of teaching', in P. Woods (ed.) (1980a) pp. 61–83.

Denscombe, M. (1980b) 'Pupil strategies and the open classroom', in P. Woods (ed.) 1980b, pp. 50–73.

Denscombe, M. (1981) *The Social Organisation of Classroom Control* (Nafferton).

Dixon, C. (1972) 'Guided options as a pattern of control in a Headstart Program', *Urban Life and Culture*, **1**, 2, pp. 203–16.

Doyle, W. (1977) 'Learning the classroom environment: an ecological analysis', *Journal of Teacher Education*, **28**, 6, pp. 51–5.

Dreitzel, H. P. (ed.) (1973) *Recent Sociology No. 5 Childhood and Socialisation* (Collier-Macmillan).

Drew, P. (1980) 'Adults' corrections of children's mistakes: a response to

Wells and Montgomery', in P. French and M. MacLure (eds.), pp. 244–67.

Dumont, R. V. and Wax, M. L. (1977) 'Cherokee school society and the intercultural classroom', in B. R. Cosin *et al.* (eds.), pp. 70–78.

Edwards, A. (1980a) 'Patterns of power and authority in classroom talk', in P. Woods (ed.), 1980a, pp. 237–53.

Edwards, A. (1980b) 'Perspectives on classroom language', *Educational Analysis*, **2**, 2, pp. 31–46.

Edwards, A. D. (1980c) 'Analysing classroom talk', in P. French and M. MacLure (eds.), pp. 291–306.

Edwards, A. and Furlong, J. F. (1978) *The Language of Teaching* (Heinemann Educational Books).

Eggleston, J. (ed.) (1979) *Teacher Decision-making in the Classroom* (Routledge & Kegan Paul).

Flanders, N. (1970) *Analyzing Teaching Behaviour* (Addison-Wesley).

French, P. and MacLure, M. (1979) 'Getting the right answer and getting the answer right', *Research in Education*, no. 22, pp. 1–23.

French, P. and MacLure, M. (1980) *Adult–Child Conversation: studies in structure and process* (Croom Helm).

Fuller, M. (1980) 'Black girls in a London comprehensive school', in R. Deem (ed.), pp. 52–65.

Furlong, V. J. (1976) 'Interaction sets in the classroom: towards a study of pupil knowledge', in M. Stubbs and S. Delamont (eds.), pp. 23–44.

Furlong, V. J. (1977) 'Anancy goes to school: a case study of pupils' knowledge of their teachers', in P. Woods and M. Hammersley (eds.), pp. 162–85.

Furlong, V. J. (forthcoming) *Contemporary Research with School Pupils* (Nafferton).

Furlong, V. and Edwards, A. (1977) 'Language in classroom interaction: theory and data', *Educational Research*, **19**, pp. 122–8.

Gannaway, H. (1976) 'Making sense of school', in M. Stubbs and S. Delamont (eds.), pp. 45–82.

Giddens, A. (1976) *New Rules of Sociological Method* (Hutchinson).

Good, T. L. and Brophy, J. E. (1978) *Looking in Classrooms* (Harper & Row).

Gouldner, H. (1978) *Teachers' Pets, Troublemakers and Nobodies* (Greenwood Press).

Gracey, H. L. (1972) *Curriculum or Craftsmanship: elementary school teachers in a bureaucratic system* (University of Chicago Press).

Gumperz, J. and Herasimchuk, E. (1972) 'The conversational analysis of social meaning: a study of classroom interaction', in R. Shuy (ed.) *Sociolinguistics* (Georgetown Monograph Series on Language and Linguistics no. 25).

Hamilton, D. (1977a) *In Search of Structure* (Hodder & Stoughton for the Scottish Council for Research in Education).

Hamilton, D. (ed.) (1977b) *Beyond the Numbers Game* (Macmillan).

Hamilton, D. and Delamont, S. (1976) 'Classroom research', in M. Stubbs and S. Delamont (eds.), pp. 3–20.

Hammersley, M. (1974) 'The organisation of pupil participation', *Sociological Review*, **22**, 3, pp. 355–68.

Hammersley, M. (1976) 'The mobilisation of pupil attention', in M. Hammersley and P. Woods (eds.), 1976, pp. 104–15.

Hammersley, M. (1977a) 'Teacher perspectives', units 9–10 of Schooling and Society (E202) (Open University Press) pp. 5–114.

Hammersley, M. (1977b) 'School learning: the cultural resources required to answer a teacher's question', in P. Woods and M. Hammersley (eds.), 1977, pp. 57–86.

Hammersley, M. (1979a) 'Data collection in ethnographic research' part 3 Block 4 Research Methods in Education and the Social Sciences DE.304 (Open University Press) pp. 89–177.

Hammersley, M. (1979b) 'Analyzing ethnographic data' part 1 of Block 6 Research Methods in Education and the Social Sciences DE.304 (Open University Press) pp. 9–40.

Hammersley, M. (1980a) 'On interactionist empiricism', in P. Woods (ed.), 1980b, pp. 198–213.

Hammersley, M. (1980b) 'Putting competence into action: some sociological notes on a model of classroom interaction', in P. French and M. MacLure (eds.), 1980, pp. 47–58.

Hammersley, M. (1980c) 'Classroom ethnography', *Educational Analysis*, **2**, 2, pp. 47–74.

Hammersley, M. and Turner, G. (1980) 'Conformist pupils?', in P. Woods (ed.), 1980b, pp. 29–49.

Hammersley, M. and Woods, P. (eds.) (1976) *The Process of Schooling* (Routledge & Kegan Paul).

Hannan, A. (1975) 'The problem of the "unmotivated" in an open school. A participant observation study', in G. Chanan and S. Delamont (eds.), 1975, pp. 146–62.

Hardy, J. (1976) 'Textbooks and classroom knowledge: the politics of explanation and description', in G. Whitty and M. F. D. Young (eds.), 1976, pp. 87–98.

Hargreaves, A. (1978) 'The significance of classroom coping strategies', in L. Barton and R. Meighan (eds.) *Sociological Interpretations of Schooling and Classrooms: a reappraisal* (Nafferton) pp. 73–100.

Hargreaves, A. (1979) 'Strategies, decisions and control: interaction in a middle school classroom', in J. Eggleston (ed.), 1979, pp. 134–69.

Hargreaves, A. (1980) 'Synthesis and the study of strategies: a project for the sociological imagination', in P. Woods (ed.), 1980b, pp. 162–97.

Hargreaves, D. H. (1967) *Social Relations in a Secondary School* (Routledge & Kegan Paul).

Hargreaves, D. H. (1976) 'Reactions to labelling', in M. Hammersley and P. Woods (eds.), 1976, pp. 201–7.

Hargreaves, D. H. (1977), 'The process of typification in the classroom: models and methods', *British Journal of Educational Psychology*, **47**, pp. 274–84.

Hargreaves, D. H. (1978) 'Whatever happened to symbolic interactionism', in L. Barton and R. Meighan (eds.) *Sociological Interpretations of Schooling and Classrooms: a reappraisal* (Nafferton) pp. 7–22.

Hargreaves, D. H. (1980) 'The occupational culture of teachers' in P. Woods 1980a, op. cit., pp. 125–48.

Hargreaves, D. H. Hester, S. and Mellor, F. (1975) *Deviance in Classrooms* (Routledge & Kegan Paul).

Harré, R. (1975) 'The origins of social competence in a pluralist society', *Oxford Review of Education*, **1**, 2, pp. 151–8.

Holt, J. (1970) *How Children Fail* (Penguin).

Kanter, R. M. (1972) 'The organisation child: experience management in a nursery school', *Sociology of Education*, **45**, pp. 186–212.

Keddie, N. (1971) 'Classroom knowledge', in M. F. D. Young (ed.) *Knowledge and Control* (Collier-Macmillan) pp. 133–60.

King, R. (1978) *All Things Bright and Beautiful* (Wiley).

Kounin, J. S. (1970) *Discipline and Group Management in Classrooms* (Holt, Rinehart & Winston).

Lacey, C. (1970) *Hightown Grammar* (Manchester University Press).

Lacey, C. (1977) *The Socialization of Teachers* (Methuen).

Lambart, A. (1976) 'The sisterhood', in M. Hammersley and P. Woods (eds.), 1976, pp. 152–9.

Leacock, E. B. (1969) *Teaching and Learning in City Schools: a comparative study* (Basic Books).

Llewellyn, M. (1980) 'Studying girls at school', in R. Deem (ed.), 1980, pp. 42–51.

Lortie, D. C. (1975) *Schoolteacher: a sociological study* (University of Chicago Press).

Lundgren, U. P. (1974) 'Pedagogical roles in the classroom', in J. Eggleston (ed.) *Contemporary Research in the Sociology of Education* (Methuen) pp. 200–13.

McDermott, R. P. (1976) *Kids Make Sense: an ethnographic account of the interactional management of success and failure in one first grade classroom* Ph.D. thesis (Stanford University).

McDermott, R. P. and Aron, J. (1977) 'Pirandello in the classroom: on the possibility of equal educational opportunity in American culture', in M. Reynolds (ed.) *The Futures of Education for Exceptional Children* (Council for Exceptional Children) pp. 41–64.

McDermott, R. P., Gospodinoff, K. and Aron, J. (1978) 'Criteria for an ethnographically adequate description of concerted activities and their contexts', *Semiotica*, **24**, 3/4, pp. 245–75.

McHoul, A. (1978) 'The organisation of turns at formal talk in the classroom', *Language in Society*, **7**, pp. 183–213.

McIntyre, D. (1980) 'Systematic observation of classroom activities', *Educational Analysis*, **2**, 2, pp. 3–30.

Mackay, R. W. (1973) 'Conceptions of children and models of socialisation', in H. P. Dreitzel (ed.), 1973, pp. 27–43. Reprinted in R. Turner (1974) *Ethnomethodology* (Penguin).

MacLure, M. and French, P. (1980) 'Routes to right answers: on pupils' strategies for answering teachers' questions', in P. Woods (ed.), 1980b, pp. 74–93.

McPherson, G. A. (1972) *Small Town Teacher* (Harvard University Press).

Marsh, P., Rosser, E. and Harré, R. (1978) *The Rules of Disorder* (Routledge & Kegan Paul).

Mehan, H. (1973) 'Assessing children's school performance', in H. P. Dreitzel (ed.), 1973, pp. 240–64. Reprinted in Hammersley and Woods (eds.), 1976.

Mehan, H. (1978) 'Structuring school structure', *Harvard Educational Review*, **48**, 1, pp. 32–64.

Mehan, H. (1979) *Learning Lessons* (Harvard University Press).

Merton, R. K. (1957) *Social Theory and Social Structure* (Free Press).

Metz, M. H. (1978a) *Classrooms and Corridors: the crisis of authority in desegregated secondary schools* (University of California Press).

Metz, M. H. (1978b) 'Order in the secondary school: strategies for control and their consequences', *Sociological Inquiry*, **48**, 1, pp. 59–69.

Meyenn, H. J. (1980a) 'School girls' peer groups', in P. Woods (ed.), 1980b, pp. 108–42.

Meyenn, R. J. (1980b) 'Peer networks among middle school pupils', in A. Hargreaves and L. Tickle (eds.) *Middle Schools: origins, ideology and practice* (Harper & Row) pp. 247–76.

Miller, C. M. L. and Parlett, M. (1974) *Up to the Mark: a study of the examination game* (Society for Research into Higher Education, Monograph 21).

Mishler, E. G. (1972) 'Implications of teacher strategies for language and cognition: observations in first grade classrooms', in C. B. Cazden *et al.* (eds.), 1972, pp. 267–98.

Moore, D. T. (1978) 'Social order in an alternative school', *Teachers College Record*, **79**, 3, pp. 437–51.

Morgan, E. P. (1977) *Inequality in Classroom Learning* (Praeger).

Morgan, J., O'Neill, C. and Harré, R. (1979) *Nicknames: their origins and social consequences* (Routledge & Kegan Paul).

Morris, M. (1977) *An Excursion into Creative Sociology* (Blackwell).

Nash, R. (1973) *Classrooms Observed* (Routledge & Kegan Paul).

Novak, M. (1974) 'Living and learning in the free school', *Interchange*, **5**, 2, pp. 1–10.

Novak, M. (1975) *Living and Learning in the Free School* (McClelland & Stewart).

Parlett, M. (1967) *Classroom and Beyond* (Education Research Center, Massachusetts Institute of Technology).

Payne, G. C. F. (1976) 'Making a lesson happen: an ethnomethodological analysis', in M. Hammersley and P. Woods (eds.), 1976, pp. 33–40.

Payne, G. and Hustler, D. (1980) 'Teaching the class: the practical management of a cohort', *British Journal of Sociology of Education*, **1**, 1, pp. 49–66.

Phillips, S. U. (1972) 'Participant structures and communicative competence: Warm Springs children in community and classroom', in C. B. Cazden *et al.* (eds.), 1972, pp. 370–94.

Pollard, A. (1979) 'Negotiating deviance and "getting done" in primary school classrooms', in L. Barton and R. Meighan (eds.), 1979, pp. 75–94.

Pollard, A. (1980) 'Teacher interests and changing situations of survival threat in primary school classrooms', in P. Woods (ed.), 1980a, pp. 34–60.

Reynolds, D. (1976a) 'The delinquent school', in M. Hammersley and P. Woods (eds.), 1976, pp. 217–29.

Reynolds, D. (1976b) 'When teachers and pupils refuse a truce', in G. Mungham and G. Pearson (eds.) *Working Class Youth Culture* (Routledge & Kegan Paul) pp. 124–37.

Reynolds, D. and Sullivan, M. (1979) 'Bringing schools back in', in L. Barton and R. Meighan (eds.), 1979, pp. 43–58.

Rist, R. (1970) 'Student social class and teacher expectations', *Harvard Educational Review*, **40**, 3, pp. 411–51.

Rist, R. (1973) *The Urban School: a factory for failure* (MIT Press).
Robinson, P. (1974) 'An ethnography of classrooms', in J. Eggleston (ed.) *Contemporary Research in the Sociology of Education* (Methuen) pp. 251–66.
Rosenthal, R. and Jacobson, L. (1968) *Pygmalion in the Classroom* (Holt, Rinehart & Winston).
Rudduck, J. (1978) *Learning Through Small Group Discussion* (Research into Higher Education Monographs, Society for Research into Higher Education, University of Surrey).
School and Society (E.282) (1971) (Open University Press).
Schooling and Society (E. 202) (1977) (Open University Press).
Sharp, R. and Green, A. (1975) *Education and Social Control* (Routledge & Kegan Paul).
Sinclair, J. McH. and Coulthard, R. M. (1975) *Towards an Analysis of Discourse* (Oxford University Press).
Smith, B. O. *et al.* (1967) *A Study of the Strategies of Teaching* (Research Report, U.S. Office of Education, University of Illinois).
Smith, L. M. and Geoffrey, P. (1968) *The Complexities of an Urban Classroom* (Holt, Rinehart & Winston).
Stebbins, R. A. (1975) *Teachers and Meaning: definitions of classroom situations* (E. J. Brill).
Stebbins, R. A. (1976) 'Physical context influences on behaviour: the case of classroom disorderliness', *Environment and Behaviour*, 5, 3, pp. 291–314. Reprinted in M. Hammersley and P. Woods (eds.), 1976.
Stubbs, M. (1975) 'Teaching and talking: a sociolinguistic approach to classroom interaction', in G. Chanan and S. Delamont (eds.), 1975, pp. 233–46.
Stubbs, M. (1976a) *Language Schools and Classrooms* (Methuen).
Stubbs, M. (1976b) 'Keeping in touch: some functions of teacher talk', in M. Stubbs and S. Delamont (eds.), 1976.
Stubbs, M. (1977a) 'Linguistic data in educational research', in C. Adelman (ed.), 1977, pp. 47–73.
Stubbs, M. (1977b) 'Collecting conversational data: notes on sociolinguistic methodology', in C. Adelman (ed.), 1977, pp. 229–64.
Stubbs, M. and Delamont, S. (eds.) (1976) *Explorations in Classroom Observation* (Wiley).
Torode, B. (1977) 'Interrupting intersubjectivity', in P. Woods and M. Hammersley (eds.), 1977, pp. 109–28.
Turner, G. (forthcoming) ' "Swots" and "dossers": a decision-making approach to pupil orientation', in V. J. Furlong (ed.), forthcoming.
Vulliamy, G. (1976) 'What counts as school music?', in G. Whitty and M. F. D. Young (eds.), 1976, pp. 19–34.
Walker, R. (1971) *The Social Setting of the Classroom: a review of observational studies and research* M.Phil. thesis (University of London).
Walker, R. (1972) 'The sociology of education and life in the school classrooms', *International Review of Education*, 18, pp. 32–41.
Walker, R. and Adelman, C. (1975a) *A Guide to Classroom Observation* (Methuen).
Walker, R. and Adelman, C. (1975b) 'Developing pictures for other frames: action research and case study', in G. Chanan and S. Delamont (eds.), 1975, pp. 220–32.

Walker, R. and Adelman, C. (1975c) 'Interaction analysis in informal classrooms: a critical comment on the Flanders system', *British Journal of Educational Psychology*, **45**, 1, pp. 73–6.

Waller, W. (1932) *The Sociology of Teaching* (Wiley).

Warren, R. L. (1973) 'The classroom as a sanctuary for teachers: discontinuities in social control', *American Anthropologist*, **75**, pp. 280–91.

Wegmann, R. (1976) 'Classroom discipline: an exercise in the maintenance of social reality', *Sociology of Education*, **49**, pp. 71–9.

Wells, G. and Montgomery, M. (1980) 'Adult–child interaction at home and at school', in P. French and M. MacLure (eds.), 1980, pp. 210–43.

Werthman, C. (1977) 'Delinquents in schools: a test for the legitimacy of authority', in B. R. Cosin *et al.* (eds.), 1977, pp. 34–43.

Westbury, I. (1973) 'Conventional classrooms, "open" classrooms and the technology of teaching', *Journal of Curriculum Studies*, **5**, 2, pp. 95–121.

Whitty, G. and Young, M. F. D. (eds.) (1976) *Explorations in the Politics of School Knowledge* (Nafferton).

Willes, M. (1977) 'Early lessons learned too well', in C. Adelman (ed.), 1977, pp. 173–95.

Willes, M. (1980) 'Learning to take part in classroom interaction', in P. French and M. MacLure (eds.), 1980, pp. 73–90.

Willis, P. (1976) 'The class significance of school counter-culture', in M. Hammersley and P. Woods (eds.), 1976, pp. 188–200.

Willis, P. (1977) *Learning to Labour* (Saxon House).

Woods, P. (1978a) 'Relating to schoolwork: some pupil perceptions', *Educational Review*, **30**, 2, pp. 167–75.

Woods, P. (1978b) 'Negotiating the demands of schoolwork', *Curriculum Studies*, **10**, 4, pp. 309–27.

Woods, P. (1979) *The Divided School* (Routledge & Kegan Paul).

Woods, P. (ed.) (1980a) *Teacher Strategies* (Croom Helm).

Woods, P. (ed.) (1980b) *Pupil Strategies* (Croom Helm).

Woods, P. and Hammersley, M. (eds.) (1977) *School Experience* (Croom Helm).

Worsley, P. (ed.) (1977) *Introducing Sociology* (Penguin).

Young, T. R. and Beardsley, P. (1968) 'The sociology of classroom teaching: a micro-functional analysis', *Journal of Educational Thought*, **2**, 3, pp. 175–86.

16 Organisational theory and schools
Brian Davies

It would not be difficult to show that organisational theory has been among the more conservative and moribund reaches of the social sciences. Its international house journal the *Administrative Science Quarterly* shows remarkable stability and sameness over 25 years of publication. There are at least two reasons for this state of affairs. Firstly, the study of organisations is complex and has drawn upon the ideas of the whole range of the social sciences – psychology, economics and so on – as well as sociology. As we saw in section 2, one of the complexities we encounter is that there are many 'sociologies', so in organisational studies that difficulty is increased by the addition of these other disciplinary perspectives. This makes the field potentially fascinating, but it also makes it almost impossible to synthesise. We simply do not know how to 'convert' psychology, sociology and economics 'into' one another. The second factor is that organisational studies of behaviour very often tend to be looking for 'one best way' of running organisations. From the very earliest days of systematic organisational theorising in the early part of this century, there have been close links between theory, research and organisational consultancy. A good deal of the work has been paid for by industrial and commercial organisations wanting guidance as to their efficiency. There is, therefore, a persistent 'managerial' tone and much recent criticism of it in the literature.

Both difficulties and possibilities are not, then, to be underestimated. More than most social science areas, it displays great difficulties in naming its objects, let alone successfully analysing and relating them. Its tendency, therefore, is to oversimplification in the face of a highly complex reality. It is shot through with special pleading as to the the 'real' basis of organisational functioning both on its sociological and other fronts. This special pleading takes the form of one analyst after another arguing that he/she has located *the* 'key dimension' of organisational process, *the* best place to start analysis, *the* clearest vantage point from which to view how the organisation works. These are illustrated in (2) below, where some argue for technology as the key dimension, others for human relations, decision-making, and so on. Moreover, in a far-reaching sense, such insights as it provides have still only been applied in very limited fashion to the study of educational establishments. When they have, as often as not, it has been a partial by-product of other analytical concerns – predominantly to do with the selective and allocatory (distributional), that is, the 'who gets picked for what' aspect of school processes, the public administration of school systems and the understanding of teaching and learning processes. This has produced a situation at the present time when there is much more material available which is relevant to an understanding of schools as organisations than there is codification of this work.

Streaming, pastoral systems, subjects, examinations and assessment and so on are all aspects of their organisational properties They have been researched a good deal but there has been little effort to co-ordinate or think through in systematic ways the information which we have on them. It is rather like having several jigsaws, all with pieces missing, distributed in a number of boxes. We tend to miss the importance at the organisational level, going all too often for either individual or group (in and out of school) 'explanations' of educational phenomena. For example, a widely held belief is that variations in children's attainment are related to different styles of teaching. In such work, attention is rarely paid to curriculum content, child grouping, and so on. The quality of the analysis would make most industrial organisational theorists blanch. With this in mind, the student must be recommended to acquire a basic literacy in the general sociology of organisations in order to maximise the possibilities of grasping the relevance of the fragmentary corpus on schooling. The very business of the quality of the teaching–learning which is possible in classrooms will be largely determined, I would argue, by the constraints and possibilities generated at the level of school organisation. What resources (physical and human) are provided, and what shape of arrangements people will work in, are questions settled in the main beyond the power of single persons or factions.

1. Overviews of the sociology of organisations

There are several very good texts and readers available. Burrell and Morgan (1979) succeeds better than any of its predecessors in clarifying the links between varieties of sociological theory and organisational approaches. Indeed it could be read as a highly compact introduction to sociological theory itself. Particularly, it lays proper emphasis on the societal embeddedness of organisational form. Clegg and Dunkerley (1977, 1980) go even further in 'speaking this silence' in the literature and attempt to develop a political economy of organisations. The excesses of their 'radicalism' are well criticised by Bradley and Wilkie (1980). Among earlier works, Mouzelis (1975), with an important revision of his earlier Parsonian view, Silverman (1970) with his pre-'analytic' argument for an action approach, Blau and Schoenherr (1971) and Champion (1975) with a useful, condensed version of organisational models can be recommended. Dunkerley (1972) is, if anything, too short even as an introduction. Jehenson (1973) presents a phenomenological introduction, while Novikov (1972) represents an eastern European Marxist critique of bourgeois foundationing while, characteristically, leaving unformed the preferred shape of the materialist alternatives. Burns (1967) typifies in a more sensitive way than usual the taxonomic urge deep in the organisational analytic bones. Among the very many readers available, March (1965) is still classic, while Salaman and Thompson (1973) is excellent and its use is specially recommended in conjunction with Open University course DT352. Pugh *et al.* (1975) present a workmanlike overview of British research.

2. Some particular schools of thought
All of the texts mentioned cover, more or less efficiently, the historical succession of dominant emphases in the sociology of organisations, albeit from very varying points of view. On a highly selective basis the following works have heuristic value in evoking ideas relevant to education.

(i) On bureaucracy: the literature since Weber has much to with survey attempts to purify it as conceptualisation or to use it as a basis for taxonomising. However, two long-established case studies, Gouldner (1954) and Crozier (1964), read along with Clegg (1977) have considerable general force in evoking thought about power and control which can be thought through in school terms. Much of school behaviour is highly rule-bound (indeed it is *about* legitimising rules of all sorts) and power-soaked. It is also about one group of people – staff – deliberately changing the attributes of the other – pupils/students. The combination of these tendencies gives to school organisation its curious 'loose-limbed' texture: bureaucratised up to a point, but also cellular, disjointed, having its bounded realities within classrooms, departments and between schools themselves and outside.

(ii) On human relations: research is available in abundance on the effects of organisational structure and technology on group formation and culture. From two very differing strands within this

sub field, Roy (1960) shows how people evoke meaning even in the most daunting work situations, while Argyris (1964) provides a more social psychological exemplar of Maslovian man's battle against organisation needs. In education, nearly all the 'streaming' research, for example, belongs in this box without knowing it.

(iii) On decision-making: at the conceptual level, Cyert and March (1964) produce an economics-cultured view of organisational objectives while Dalton (1959) is a case study of a proto-interactionist type of managerial groupings and cliques. More studies are needed of how decisions are made at levels from staff-room to chalkface, and they are slowly emerging.

(iv) On systems approaches: two strands are worth taking up: Parsons (1958) and an example of socio-technicism in Miller and Rice (1967). By and large, schools have resisted taking advice from systems theorists (who make most of their living through consul-tancy) as successfully as they resist advice from most people. After all, if school goals are multiple, overlapping and contradictory, there are liable to be several equally 'justifiable' ways of doing most things, or at least interested parties will argue that is the case.

(v) On technology: the literature is again vast but Perrow (1967) stands as overview and a good example of an argument for the primacy of 'how the work is done' in organisational process. This approach is highly promising in relation to schools.

(vi) Against reification: using linguistic, ethnomethodological and 'radical' arguments in partly similar ways, Silverman (1976) and Clegg (1975) report fieldwork that pinpoints growing doubt in the traditional categories of organisational analysis. More work is needed in this perspective and it should be applied to educational establishments in a systematic way.

3. Overviews and typologies of schools as organisations

Bidwell (1965) and Corwin (1967) were the first to produce worth-while systematisations of the field. Katz (1964) argues more nar-rowly around the concept of functional autonomy. Musgrove (1973) and Dale (1973) comment broadly on the sociology of the school. Hoyle (1973) and Davies (1973, 1976) and Tyler (1973) provide further British development of the earlier American work. Bell (1980) and Davies (1981) attempt to sum up the present state of the literature. Turner (1969) reports briefly on a field study but in a broadly-based way and Weick (1976) in a curiously-written article succeeds, in effect, in pulling together the running themes that schools are loose federations within and, in some ways, weakly linked without. The importance of the links between schools and their environments as a basis for typologising also runs through Parsons (1958), Carlson (1964) and Litwack and Meyer (1965).

4. Aspects of schools as organisations

If nothing else, the problem of codifying the literature on schools as organisations raises in sharpest form the issue of levels of analysis and possible interactions between them in sociological work. If our starting point is that schools are distinctive organisations, that is to say that they have real tasks to be performed, different from those belonging to any other institutions, then we face not only the problems of delineating their nature but of how their form has been socio-historically produced, how they relate to other aspects of social structure and of how they function within. The literature is either recent or thin or both on many aspects of these issues. A great deal of it has been devoted merely to taking those aspects of school structure and process that have seemed important in influencing the selective and allocatory functions of school systems. Therefore we have relatively rich seams of literature on issues like ability and classroom interaction, and thin veins elsewhere.

(*i*) *The social context of school organisations*: the way that schools are produced historically has recently come into sharper sociological focus with the growth of Marxist and 'critical' attention. In America the earlier work of Cremin (1961) is now supplemented by, for example, that of Callahan (1962), Katz (1971) and Spring (1972). In British terms, this interesting contrast can be roughly paralleled by comparing Banks (1955) and Musgrove (1971) with Miller (1973) and Wardle (1974). Musgrove (1979) responds to the Marxist class thesis.

At the more specific conceptual level of the relative autonomy of schooling (and school organisations), Bourdieu and Passeron (1977), and Bernstein (1977) in his later essays, along with the Bowles and Gintis (1976) thesis, are indispensable. In this context Sharp and Green (1975) may be read as an attempt to instance Althusser at the organisational level. That mixture of social speculation and revelatory journalism which has become known as the alternative or de-schooling impulse can be read in Goodman (1971) and Illich (1971). It owes a great deal to Reimer (1971).

(*ii*) *The administrative matrix of schools*: the American tradition in school administrative studies has long been aware of social science. Good examples of its changing emphases are found in Halpin

(1958) and Owens (1970). Gross and Herriott (1965) is a good example of the approach hybridised with a focus on schools as sources of ability output. The present state of the art is well encompassed in Open University course E321 *Management in Education*, the readers for which are Houghton *et al.* (1975) and Dobson *et al.* (1975). The direct focus on organisational theory and schools in the course, represented by the set book by Bennett (1974) and the unit by Davies (1976) is rather unstrenuous. Morgan (1976) and Boyd-Barrett *et al.* (1976) are other units worth attention.

(iii) Schools as organisations: some of the key categories of organisational theory at large have been applied to the sociology of the schools, but much of the connection is indirect and hazy. On the bureaucratic properties of schools see Anderson (1968), Moeller (1964), Watson (1969) and Bidwell (1965). As a wide corpus which attempts to say something of the structure, goals and culture of public schools in Britain, see Lambert (1966), Lambert and Millham (1968), and Lambert *et al.* (1973, 1975).

The mainstream is much narrower. It has tended to focus on the effects on pupil performance of a single aspect of school structure, grouping by ability, and to embed this structural effect in its human relations concomitants. An early overview is found in Yates (1966). A discussion of the research tradition in general exists in Corbishley (1977). Cicourel and Kitsuse (1963) is a durable American empirical study. The British stream can be characterised by Brandis and Young (1967), Lunn (1970), Hargreaves (1967) and Lacey (1970). An interesting contrast of focus on grouping for pastoral purposes is found in Corbishley and Evans (1980). While these studies are only narrowly organisational, they do share a common focus on a limited aspect of schools as differentiators. In overlap with this latter emphasis, but looking for rather differently conceived structural effects, we also have Barker and Gump (1964), strangely our only major study as to the effect of school size and badly under-conceptualised, Rutter *et al.* (1979) with more measurement (and 'message') than theory, and Reynolds (1976a and b) which may be used as access to the work on the 'delinquency producing' properties of schools.

Spilling out of both ends of the 1960s, we also have a fascinating but diffuse bunch of case studies of educational organisations that all in some degree see them as penetrated by societal influences as well as generating characteristic lives of their own. Gordon (1957) is first, and still full of interest, focusing mainly on how the grade system dominates pupil-teacher relations in an American high school. Becker *et al.* (1968) is its student-centred, college level counterpart. The grade system's effect is also the secret message of Coleman's (1961) delineation of high school student subcultures and Clark's (1960) classic delineation of junior college. King (1969) and Tipton (1973) are viable British studies. The decisional and systemic properties of educational establishments can be fully followed in the Open University course E321. Richardson (1973) stands clear as a case study embodying the cloying properties of Freud plus task. Eggleston (1979) contains a number of insights on teacher decision-making. If 'how the work is done' is an important feature of organisational analysis, then educational theories in this area need to take on the sociology of teaching and learning with new seriousness. Waller (1967) remains important while Schlechty (1976) argues precisely the case for organisational theories of instruction, and Davies and Evans (forthcoming) review this field and its overlap with schools as organisations. The base data for school 'technology' is to be found predominantly in classroom studies. Here curriculum overt and hidden (Henry 1971 had the concept, Jackson 1968 named it) intermingle, in highly characteristic group socialisation processes (Wheeler 1966 pre-dates Perrow's insights on these) which we know to be highly suffused by pupil and teacher typificatory practices and work strategies. These are fully annotated elsewhere in this bibliography, and one might mention only Nash (1973), King (1978), Mehan (1979) and Woods (1980a and b) as contrasting exemplars of the work. Finally, Lundgren (1972) and Westbury (1978) – compare with Westbury and Bellack (1971) – and Westbury (1980) come closest to grasping the central importance of the interplay between the societal determinants of school work and its relationships to wider school organisation. The time is ripe for pursuing the idea that the organisational level of schooling must be thought of as the focusing-point for a great deal that is exciting in modern sociology of education. Classrooms exist in schools; curricula, overt and hidden, are transmitted in them; staff and pupils are inputs, the limits to whose strategies are in a vital way set by the details of the structure set over time within which the varying processes which make up schooling occur. It is in school organisations that the drama of the dull and bright, the struggles about control and assessment, the motivating and the trimming, all occur. If we take these processes less for granted we shall educate better.

References

Anderson, J. G. (1968) *Bureaucracy in Education* (John Hopkins Press).

Argyris, C. (1964) *Integrating the Individual and the Organization* (John Wiley).

Banks, O. (1955) *Parity and Prestige in English Secondary Education* (Routledge & Kegan Paul).

Barker, R. G. and Gump, P. V. (1964) *Big School, Small School* (Stanford University Press).

Becher, H. S., Geer, B. and Hughes, E. C. (1968) *Making the Grade* (John Wiley).

Bell, L. A. (1980) 'The school as an organisation: a reappraisal', *British Journal of the Sociology of Education*, **1**, 2, pp. 183–92.

Bennett, S. J. (1974) *The School: An Organizational Analysis* (Blackie).

Bernstein, B. (1977) *Class, Codes and Control* vol. 3 (Routledge & Kegan Paul).

Bidwell, C. E. (1965) 'The school as a formal organisation', in J. G. March (ed.) *Handbook of Organisations* (Rand McNally) pp. 972–1022.

Blau, P. M. and Schoenherr, R. A. (1971) *The Structure of Organisations* (Basic Books).

Bourdieu, P. and Passeron, J. C. (1977) *Reproduction in Education, Society and Culture* (Sage Publications).

Bowles, S. and Gintis, H. (1976) *Schooling in Capitalist America* (Routledge & Kegan Paul).

Boyd-Barrett, O., McHugh, R. and Morgan, C. (1976) 'The manager and groups in the organisation' units 14–15 *Management in Education* E.321 (Open University Press).

Bradley, D. A. and Wilkie, R. (1980) 'Radical organization theory – a critical comment', *British Journal of Sociology*, **31**, 4, pp. 574–9.

Brandis, W. and Young, D. (1967) 'Two types of streaming and their probable application in comprehensive schools', in B. R. Cosin, I. R. Dale, G. M. Esland and D. F. Swift (eds.) *School and Society* (1971) (Routledge & Kegan Paul and Open University Press) pp. 148–51.

Burns, T. (1967) 'The comparative study of organisations', in V. H. Vroom (ed.) *Method of Organisational Research* (University of Pittsburg Press).

Burrell, G. and Morgan, G. (1979) *Sociological Paradigms and Organisational Analysis* (Heinemann Educational Books).

Callahan, R. E. (1962) *Education and the Cult of Efficiency* (University of Chicago).

Carlson, D. (1964) 'Environmental constraints and organizational consequences: the public school and its clients', in D. E. Griffiths (ed.) *Behavioural Science and Educational Administration* (National Society of the Study of Education 63rd Yearbook Part 2) pp. 262–76.

Champion, D. J. (1975) *The Sociology of Organizations* (McGraw-Hill).

Cicourel, A. V. and Kitsuse, J. I. (1963) *The Educational Decision Makers* (Bobbs Merrill).

Clark, B. R. (1960) *The Open Door College* (McGraw Hill).

Clegg, S. (1975) *Power, Rule and Domination* (Routledge & Kegan Paul).

Clegg, S. (1977) 'Power, organisation theory, Marx and critique', in S. Clegg and D. Dunkerley (eds.) *Critical Issues in Organisations* (Routledge & Kegan Paul) pp. 21–40.

Clegg, S. and Dunkerley, D. (eds.) (1977) *Critical Issues in Organizations* (Routledge & Kegan Paul).

Clegg, S. and Dunkerley, D. (1980) *Organisation, Class and Control* (Routledge & Kegan Paul).

Coleman, J. S. (1961) *The Adolescent Society* (Free Press).

Corbishley, P. (1977) 'Research findings on teaching groupings in secondary schools', in B. Davies and R. G. Cave (eds.) *Mixed Ability Teaching in the Secondary School* (Ward Lock) pp. 11–17.

Corbishley, P. and Evans, J. (1980) 'Teachers and pastoral care: an empirical comment', in A. R. Best, C. B. Jarvis and P. M. Ribbins (eds.) *Perspectives on Pastoral Care* (Heinemann Educational Books).

Corwin, R. G. (1967) 'Education and the sociology of complex organisations', in D. A. Hansen and J. E. Gerstl (eds.) *On Education: Sociological Perspectives* (John Wiley) pp. 156–223.

Cremin, L. A. (1961) *The Transformation of the School: Progressivism in American Education 1876–1957* (Knopf).

Crozier, M. (1964) *The Bureaucratic Phenomenon* (Tavistock).

Cyert, R. M. and March, J. G. (1964) 'A behavioural theory of organisational objectives', in W. W. Cooper, F. Shelley and H. Leavitt (eds.) *New Perspectives in Organisational Research* (John Wiley) pp. 289–305.

Dale, I. R. (1973) 'Phenomenological perspectives on the sociology of the school', *Educational Review*, **25**, 3, pp. 175–89.

Dalton, M. (1959) *Men Who Manage* (John Wiley).

Davies, B. (1973) 'On the contribution of organisational analysis to the study of educational institutions' in R. Brown (ed.) *Knowledge, Education and Cultural Change* (Tavistock) pp. 249–95.

Davies, B. (1976) *Social Control and Education* (Methuen).

Davies, B. (1981) 'Schools as organisations and the organisation of schooling', *Educational Analysis*, **3**, 1, pp. 47–67.

Davies, B. and Evans, J. (forthcoming) 'Bringing teachers back in'.

Davies, D. (1976) 'Schools as organisations' unit 3 *Management in Education* E.321 (Open University Press).

Dobson, L., Gear, T. and Westoby, A. (eds.) (1975) *Management in Education: Reader 2* (Ward Lock Educational and Open University Press).

Dreeben, R. (1968) *On What Is Learned In School* (Addison Wesley).

Dunkerley, D. (1972) *The Study of Organisations* (Routledge & Kegan Paul).

Eggleston, J. (ed.) (1979) *Teacher Decision-making in the Classroom* (Routledge & Kegan Paul).

Goodman, P. (1971) *Compulsory Miseducation* (Penguin).

Gordon, C. W. (1957) *The Social System of the High School* (Free Press).

Gouldner, A. W. (1954) *Patterns of Industrial Bureaucracy* (Free Press).

Gross, N. and Herriott, R. E. (1965) *Staff Leadership in Public Schools* (John Wiley).

Halpin, A. W. (ed.) (1958) *Administrative Theory in Education* (Macmillan).

Hargreaves, D. H. (1967) *Social Relations in a Secondary School* (Routledge & Kegan Paul).

Henry, J. (1971) *Essays on Education* (Penguin).

Houghton, V. P., McHugh, G. A. R. and Morgan, C. (eds.) (1975) *Management in Education Reader 1: The Management of Organisations and Individuals* (Ward Lock and Open University Press).

Hoyle, E. (1973) 'The study of schools as organisations', in V. Houghton, R. McHugh and C. Morgan (eds.) (1975) *Management in Education: Reader 1* (Ward Lock Educational and Open University Press) pp. 85–108.

Illich, I. (1971) *Deschooling Society* (Calder and Boyers).

Jackson, P. W. (1968) *Life in Classrooms* (Holt, Rinehart & Winston).

Jehenson, R. (1973) 'A phenomenological approach to the study of a formal organisation', in G. Psathas (ed.) *Phenomenological Sociology* (John Wiley) pp. 219–47.

Katz, F. E. (1964) 'The school as a complex organisation', *Harvard Educational Review*, **34**, 3, pp. 428–55.

Katz, M. B. (1971) *Class, Bureaucracy and Schools* (Praeger).

King, R. (1969) *Values and Involvement in a Grammar School* (Routledge & Kegan Paul).

King, R. (1978) *All Things Bright and Beautiful* (John Wiley).

Lacey, C. (1970) *Hightown Grammar: the School as a Social System* (Manchester University Press).

Lambert, R. (1966) 'The public schools: a sociological introduction', in G. Kalton (ed.) *The Public Schools* (Longmans) pp. xi–xxxii.

Lambert, R., Bullock, R. and Millham, S. (1973) 'The informal social system', in R. Brown (ed.) *Knowledge, Education and Cultural Change* (Tavistock) pp. 297–316.

Lambert, R., Bullock, R. and Millham, S. (1975) *The Chance of a Lifetime: A Study of Boarding Education* (Weidenfeld & Nicolson).

Lambert, R. and Millham, S. (1968) *The Hothouse Society* (Weidenfeld & Nicolson).

Litwak, E. and Meyer, M. J. (1965) 'Administrative styles and community linkages of public schools: some theoretical considerations', in A. J. Reiss (ed.) *Schools in a Changing Society* (Free Press) pp. 49–98.

Lundgren, U. P. (1972) *Frame Factors and the Teaching Process* (Allfoto i Göteberg A. B.).

Lunn, J. B. (1970) *Streaming in the Primary School* (NFER).

March, J. G. (ed.) (1965) *Handbook of Organisations* (Rand McNally).

Mehan, H. (1979) *Learning Lessons* (Harvard University Press).

Miller, P. J. (1973) 'Factories, monitorial schools and Jeremy Bentham: the origins of the "management syndrome" in popular education', *Journal of Educational Administration and History*, **V**, 2, pp. 10–20.

Miller, E. J. and Rice, A. K. (1967) *Systems of Organization* (Tavistock).

Moeller, G. H. (1964) 'Bureaucracy and teachers' sense of power', *School Review*, **72**, 3, pp. 137–57.

Morgan, G. (1976) 'Management in education – dissimilar or congruent?' unit 1 *Management in Education* E.321 (Open University Press).

Mouzelis, N. P. (1975) *Organisation and Bureaucracy* (Routledge & Kegan Paul).

Musgrove, F. (1971) *Patterns of Power and Authority in English Education* (Methuen).

Musgrove, F. (1973) 'Research on the sociology of the school and of teaching', in W. Taylor (ed.) *Research Perspective in Education* (Routledge & Kegan Paul) pp. 154–71.

Musgrove, F. (1979) *School and the Social Order* (John Wiley).

Nash, R. (1973) *Classrooms Observed* (Routledge & Kegan Paul).

Novikov, N. (1972) *Organisational Society: Social Mechanisms and Ideology* (Novosti Press).

Owens, R. G. (1970) *Organisational Behaviour in Schools* (Prentice-Hall).

Parsons, T. (1958) 'Some ingredients of a general theory of formal organisation', in A. W. Halpin (ed.) *Administrative Theory in Education* (Macmillan) pp. 40–72.

Perrow, C. (1967) 'A framework for the comparative analysis of organisations', *American Sociological Review*, **32**, 2, pp. 194–208.

Pugh, D., Mansfield, R. and Warner, M. (1975) *Research in Organisational Behaviour: A British Survey* (Heinemann Educational Books).

Reimer, E. (1971) *School is Dead* (Penguin).

Reynolds, D. (1976a) 'The delinquent school', in M. Hammersley and P. Woods (eds.) *The Process of Schooling* (Routledge & Kegan Paul and Open University Press) pp. 217–29.

Reynolds, D. (1976b) 'When pupils and teachers refuse a truce', in G. Mungham and G. Pearson (eds.) *Working Class Youth Culture* (Routledge & Kegan Paul) pp. 124–37.

Richardson, E. (1973) *The Teacher, the School and the Task of Management* (Heinemann Educational Books).

Roy, F. (1960) ' "Banana time": job satisfaction and informal interaction', *Human Organisation*, **18**, pp. 158–68.

Rutter, M. *et al.* (1979) *Fifteen Thousand Hours* (Open Books).

Salaman, G. and Thompson, K. (eds.) (1973) *People and Organisations* (Longman and Open University Press).

Schlechty, P. C. (1976) *Teaching and Social Behaviour* (Allyn & Bacon).

Sharp, R. and Green, A. G. (1975) *Education and Social Control* (Routledge & Kegan Paul).

Silverman, D. (1970) *The Theory of Organisations: A Sociological Framework* (Heinemann Educational Books).

Silverman, D. (1976) *Organisational Work* (Collier Macmillan).

Spring, J. H. (1972) *Education and the Rise of the Corporate State* (Beacon Press).

Tipton, B. F. A. (1973) *Conflict and Change in a Technical College* (Hutchinson).

Turner, C. M. (1969) 'An organisational analysis of a secondary modern school', *Sociological Review*, **17**, 1, pp. 67–86.

Tyler, W. (1973) 'The organisational structure of the secondary school', *Educational Review*, **25**, 3, pp. 223–36.

Waller, W. (1967) *The Sociology of Teaching* (John Wiley).

Wardle, D. (1974) *The Rise of the Schooled Society* (Routledge & Kegan Paul).

Watson, L. E. (1969) 'Office and expertise in the secondary school', *Educational Research*, **11**, 2, pp. 104–12. Reprinted in D. F. Swift (ed.) (1970) *Basic Readings in the Sociology of Education* (Routledge & Kegan Paul) pp. 136–49.

Weick, K. E. (1976) 'Educational organizations as loosely-coupled systems', *Administrative Science Quarterly*, **21**, March, pp. 1–19.

Westbury, I. (1978) 'Research into classroom processes: a review of ten years' work', *Journal of Curriculum Studies*, **10**, 4, pp. 283–308.

Westbury, I. (1980) 'Schooling as an agency of education: some implications for curriculum theory', in W. B. Dockrell and D. Hamilton (eds.) *Rethinking Educational Research* (Hodder & Stoughton) pp. 88–114.

Westbury, I. and Bellack, A. A. (1971) *Research into Classroom Processes* (Teachers College, Columbia University).

Wheeler, S. (1966) 'The structure of formally organized socialisation sellings', in O. G. Brim and S. Wheeler *Socialisation After Childhood* (John Wiley) pp. 51–107.

Woods, P. (ed.) (1980a) *Pupil Strategies: explorations in the sociology of the school* (Croom Helm).
Woods, P. (ed.) (1980b) *Teacher Strategies: explorations in the sociology of the school* (Croom Helm).
Yates, A. (ed.) (1966) *Grouping in Education* (John Wiley).

The sociology of special schooling, deviance and social control: editorial note

In section 17, David Thomas and Patsy Taylor argue that two areas of study for the sociology of special education should be deviance and marginality 'subsumed under the general umbrella of misfit sociology' (p. 261). In section 18, Geoffrey Pearson examines the general sociological area of deviance and social control. He presents a detailed account of the literature and enables educational discussions to be placed within the intellectual and historical framework of this area of sociology. Deviance raises a number of issues for educational studies, and some of these are discussed in the introduction to this book. The books listed below consider deviance in specifically educational contexts.

References
Barton, L. and Meighan, R. (eds.) (1979) *Schools, Pupils and Deviance* (Nafferton Books).
Barton, L. and Tomlinson, S. (1981) *Special Education: Policy, Practices and Social Issues* (Harper & Row).
Hargreaves, D. H., Hester, S. K. and Mellor, F. J. (1975) *Deviance in Classrooms* (Routledge & Kegan Paul).

17 The sociology of special schooling
David Thomas
Patsy Taylor

Introduction

The sociology of special schooling is waiting to be invented. There are few texts in which 'special education' and 'sociology' are juxtaposed in their titles, an exception being Milofsky (1976) though there are a number of papers which indicate that the relationship could be a positive one. We hope to suggest some sociological perspectives which might illuminate theory and practice and to comment on the neglect of this area of education by sociologists.

What is special schooling?

According to the DES (1971) special schooling provides a regime to overcome the learning difficulties of handicapped pupils through the provision of a generous teacher–pupil ratio, various forms of therapy and special teaching facilities. The aim of such schooling is to produce children who, as far as is possible, become self-reliant and responsible adults. Special schooling as traditionally conceived is for pupils who are handicapped by blindness, deafness, physical handicaps, epilepsy, maladjustment, education sub-normality (mild and severe), speech defects, and also for those who are 'delicate' and autistic. Though the major provider of resources is the LEA, there is also an important independent and voluntary sector. Special schooling for handicapped pupils is offered in segregated day and residential schools, as well as in ordinary (mainstream) schools, through special classes or units or via individual teaching. There are also teaching facilities in children's hospitals and home tuition. The separate special schools provide places for about 170,000 pupils in approximately 1,500 schools in England and Wales. The number of pupils in each category of disability varies considerably, ranging from about 500 places for autistic children to over 100,000 for educationally subnormal pupils. Some categories/places remain fairly constant over the years, while others show significant changes – for example maladjustment with 517 places in 1950 and 13,653 in 1976. Within categories significant changes in composition can take place, as for example the current dominance of pupils with spina bifida in schools for the physically handicapped, reflecting changes in medical practice and skills.

Until fairly recently there was an almost universal agreement that the direction of special schooling was to match incidence figures with placement figures, and to expand and refine the classificatory system. Since 1945 we have seen a substantial expansion of places based on the belief that placing pupils in special schools with others carrying a similar diagnostic label was an effective method of meeting needs. These assumptions were challenged, and Section 10 of the Education Act confirmed and underlined a belief that the optimum educational location for a child was in his or her ordinary school, and that special schooling was only to be contemplated when satisfactory integration could not take place. This view was substantially upheld by the Warnock Committee (1978).

The change in ideology and policy was induced by a number of factors. These included:

1. cumulative evidence that the academic attainments of pupils in special classes were not superior to those of comparable pupils in ordinary classes (Goldstein *et al.* 1965);
2. the prevailing orthodoxy of classifying pupils by medical symptoms was challenged (Younghusband 1970);
3. the technical adequacy of tests used for selection purposes came under attack (Salvia and Ysseldyke 1978);
4. the ethnic and social class bias in selection procedures was highlighted (Mercer 1973; Coard 1971); and
5. the placement of pupils in special schools was seen (especially in the USA) as a violation of childrens' rights (US Public Law 94–142; and Hobbs 1975).

Sociological aspects
The bulk of the literature on special schooling derives from medicine, psychology or education in which there is a particular emphasis on individual pathology. The centrality of this clinical ideology has muted the search for a wider theoretical perspective and indeed such an ideology is intuitively hostile to sociological viewpoints. Not only has special schooling failed to develop an indigenous sociological view of itself, but it has been neglected by sociologists. A partial explanation of this neglect may reside in the marginality of special education, perceiving itself to be a residual

and discrete operation, presenting itself as a branch of the health or welfare services and unconsciously ascribing to schools and professionals something of the stigma which attaches to its clients. Part of the neglect may also be due to the pressing preoccupations of sociologists with the radical debate that has gone on within the sociology of education about the direction, concern and approaches to the sociology of education which has deflected interest from the more marginal areas such as special schooling.

Special schooling
Among the few sociological studies of special schooling is King, Reynes and Tizard's (1971) examination of structure, attitudes and regimes in institutions for the mentally retarded; this can be supplemented by Oswin's (1971) account of the weekend life of such children. Studies of maladjusted children and their schools are more frequent but not always with a clear sociological stance (Bridgeland 1971). A rare and hence most valuable source on physically handicapped young people is Miller and Gwynne's *A Life Apart* (1971), while many insights from the socialisation of the handicapped adult which could be applied to pupils may be found in Scott (1969); and while it should perhaps be classed as 'literature' rather than 'social science', there is Wakefield's *Special School* (1977). A major gap in the literature is the lack of detailed studies of the organisational structure of special schools, the nature of formal and informal networks and of intensive investigation into the content of teacher–pupil interaction (a rare example of the latter being provided by Craig and Collins 1970).

If substantial research on special schools as social systems is lacking, we at least have the beginnings of a theoretical perspective, provided by Willower (1970). Recognising the dominance of medicine and psychology in this field, he argues for the examination of stable collectivities (special school or special class) focusing upon the norms, roles and expectations within each social system; the socialisation of special educators, patterns of authority, leadership-style and relationship between mainstream and special education. He would also include the social status and occupational prestige of teachers (Sharples and Thomas 1969), reasons for wanting to teach the handicapped and job satisfaction. Willower also suggests that we look at the coping mechanism employed by pupils in stigmatised settings which could be examined alongside such aspects as self-esteem, social status of handicapped children in special and regular classes (Bryan and Pflaum, 1978) and the factors affecting successful and unsuccessful integration (Anderson 1973).

While sociological studies of special schools are few and far between, the most intensively developed area is that of the family. Farber's (1959) initial contribution has stood the test of time and has been supplemented by work on families coping with children with different handicaps (Hewett 1970); cerebral palsy (Gregory 1976); deafness (Woodburn 1975); and spina bifida (see also Burton 1975 and Kew 1975). The effects of a handicapped child on family cohesion and community relations have also been the subject of much concern (McAllister *et al*. 1973). Many of these studies have been concerned to rehabilitate the family of the handicapped child from its earlier ascribed status as a pathological social unit. The most highly developed sociological approaches are those of Voysey (1972, 1975) and Booth (1978). In the catalogue of sociological aspects of special schooling that await attention, the curriculum of special schools stands out as requiring analysis. The assumptions that underpin practices like behaviour modification and token economies, prescriptive teaching and so on, could be a worthwhile area of investigation.

Special education is remarkable in its pervasive use of the 'medical model' in an educational context. The belief that a child's physical condition implies a specific educational need continues to flourish. Medical criteria seldom constitute valid criteria of educational needs. Sociologically the treatment of handicapped children has generally followed the traditional image of deviance. Mental or physical handicap was seen as a sufficient condition for explaining behaviour or personality. Pearson (1975) has outlined a variety of perspectives within the sociology of deviance (which he re-names 'misfit sociology') and these could be usefully employed in the study of handicap.

'Misfit' sociology draws on a variety of approaches within sociology including exchange theory, labelling symbolic interactionalism as well as ethnomethodology and phenomenology. The central and unifying idea within 'misfit' sociology is the view of deviance as a socially constructed event, not as a property inherent in any particular type of behaviour. Hence the emphasis within the misfit paradigm on micro-sociological aspects is that it is concerned with the intricacies and complexities of social interaction and the ways in which these shape human conduct.

Milofsky (1974, 1976) has argued that the concept of marginality is of particular relevance to special education and can be seen operating in school systems where special educators are divided, fragmented, unable to define their roles in unambiguous ways and are easily exploited by more socially cohesive and powerful groups.

By maintaining the rhetoric of the clinical model and failing to control the conditions under which children are labelled, special education serves as a means for stigmatizing children and blaming institutional failure on innocent students. Given the chronic marginality of special education one must ask whether it is constructive to allow such programmes to continue. (1976, p. 67).

So far we have suggested two main themes for the sociology of special education – marginality and deviance. From these positions we could move on to examine the concept of the professionalisation of special educators – the manner in which teachers are socialised into their roles, and particularly the function of professional knowledge which enables teachers to surround themselves with a body of specialised knowledge, skills and therapeutic techniques that legitimise their roles, justifying their isolation and separation from mainstream teaching.

An equally important area for study is the relationship between special and ordinary schools. One perspective would suggest that special schooling operates as a device for perpetuating the mainstream's self-erecting definitions of the types of pupils it rightfully regards as its own. Special education becomes not so much the location for the accurate placement of pupils with special needs, but a convenient depository for the unwanted (White and Charry 1966). It then becomes essential to translate this into an affirmative view of a monopoly of care (Deno 1970) and both systems become locked in a symbiotic relationship (Milofsky 1974).

There have been several pleas for the incorporation of a sociological perspective on special schooling (McMaster 1973) for the illumination of such aspects as labelling, family dynamics and community involvement. Broad structural aspects such as social class have received attention from Broadhead (1972) and Rutter, Tizard and Whitmore (1970). The socialisation of the handicapped child has been looked at by Thomas (1978), Zigler *et al.* (1973), Richardson (1973) and Scott (1973). On matters relating to sub groups or categories of children there are a few studies with an overt sociological orientation such as Conrad (1975) on the 'medicalization of deviance' (hyperactivity), Schrag and Divoky (1975) on hyperactivity, Divoky (1974) on learning disabilities and Davis (1956) on children in hospital.

There are several issues of a sociological nature which are of relevance to the study of handicapped children. These include the nature and quality of social interactions between normals and disabled (Davis 1961), including the spread of courtesy stigma (Birenbaum 1970; Voysey 1972), the use and manipulation of personal space, the cognitive and behavioural aspects of pro-social behaviour and such intriguing findings as the capacity of retarded individuals to manipulate their IQ scores according to perceptions of positive or negative outcomes of testing (Braginsky and Braginsky 1971). Much of these disparate research efforts could be usefully incorporated into a construct like 'identity formation', and how children are transformed into the social status of 'handicapped child' (Goffman 1963; Edgerton 1967).

Conclusion

We have suggested that concepts of marginality and deviance subsumed under the general umbrella of misfit sociology would seem to hold the greatest potential for the study of special education. To this we would add the social system perspective advocated by Willower. Problem children were placed in the context of social systems that define the problem. We need to shift the debate in order to query the construction, attribution and acceptance of deviance, and to ask whether such deviance is pathology in the individual or in the system. The older view of handicapped children tended to neglect the socio-political contexts in which 'problems' were defined. An examination of teacher training and key textbooks and official rhetoric which attempts to legitimise the clinical perspective would be of interest; and in addition to the contribution which the 'deviance' approach could make, special education could usefully draw upon the sociology of medicine, professionalisation and of the curriculum. The manner in which mainstream teaching now appears to believe itself confident and competent to deal with 'problems' it formerly felt were the prerogative of special schooling would also be revealing.

References

Anderson, E. (1973) *The Disabled Schoolchild* (Methuen).

Birenbaum, A. (1970) 'On managing a courtesy stigma', *Journal of Health and Social Behavior*, **11**, June, pp. 196–206.

Booth, T. A. (1978) 'From normal baby to handicapped child: unravelling the idea of subnormality in families of mentally handicapped children', *Sociology*, **12**, 2, pp. 203–21.

Bridgeland, M. (1971) *Pioneer Work with Maladjusted Children* (Staples Press).

Braginsky, D. and Braginsky, B. M. (1971) *Hansels and Gretels* (Holt, Rinehart & Winston).

Broadhead, G. (1972) 'Social class factors and special education', *Journal of Biological Science*, **4**, pp. 315–24.

Bryan, T. and Pflaum, S. (1978) 'Social interactions of learning disabled children', *Learning Disabilities*, **1**, 3, pp. 70–79.

Burton, L. (1975) *The Family Life of Sick Children* (Routledge & Kegan Paul).

Coard, B. (1971) *How the West Indian Child is made Educationally Subnormal in the British School System* (New Beacon).

Conrad, P. (1975) 'The medicalization of deviance in American culture', *Social Problems*, **23**, 1, pp. 12–21.

Craig, W.N. and Collins, J.L. (1970) 'Analysis of communicative interaction in classes of deaf children', *American Annals of the Deaf*, **115**, 2, pp.79–85.

Davis, F. (1956) 'Definitions of time and recovery in paralytic polio convalescence', *American Journal of Sociology*, **61**, pp. 582–7.

Davis, F. (1961) 'Deviance disavowal: the management of strained interaction by the visibly handicapped', *Social Problems*, **9,** pp. 120–32.

Deno, E. (1970) 'Special education as developmental capital', *Exceptional Children*, **37**, 3, pp. 229–38.

Department of Education and Science (1971) *The Educational System of England and Wales* (DES).

Divoky, D. (1974) 'Education's latest victim: the L.D. kid', *Learning*, **3**, 5, pp. 20–25.

Dunn, L.M. (1968) 'Special education for the mildly retarded: is much of it justifiable?', *Exceptional Children*, **35**, pp. 5–22.

Edgerton, R. B. (1967) *The Cloak of Competence: stigma in the lives of the mentally handicapped* (University of California Press).

Farber, B. (1959) *Effects of a Severely Mentally Retarded Child on Family Integration* (Child Development Publication: Monograph of the Society for Research in Child Development. Serial 71).

Goffman, E. (1963) *Stigma: notes on the management of spoiled identity* (Prentice-Hall).

Goldstein, H., Moss, J. W. and Jordan, L.J. (1965) *The Efficacy of Special Class Training on the Development of Mentally Retarded Children* (University of Illinois).

Gregory, S. (1976) *The Deaf Child and his Family* (Allen & Unwin).

Hewett, S. (1970) *The Family and the Handicapped Child* (Allen & Unwin).

Hobbs, N. (ed.) (1975) *Issues in the Classification of Children* (2 vols.) (Jossey-Bass).

Kew, S. (1975) *Handicap and Family Crisis* (Pitman).

King, R.D., Reynes, N.V. and Tizard, J. (1971) *Patterns of Residential Care* (Routledge & Kegan Paul).

McAllister, R. J., Butler, E. W. and Lei, T-J. (1973) 'Patterns of social interaction among families of behaviorally retarded children', *Journal of Marriage and the Family*, **35**, 1, pp. 93–100.

McMaster, J. M. (1973) *Towards an Educational Theory for the Mentally Handicapped* (Arnold).

Mercer, J. (1973) *Labelling the Mentally Retarded* (University of California Press).

Miller, E.J. and Gwynne, G. V. (1971) *A Life Apart* (Tavistock).

Milofsky, C. (1974) 'Why special education isn't special', *Harvard Educational Review*, **44**, 4, pp. 437–58.

Milofsky, C. (1976) *Special Education: a Sociological Study of California Programs* (Praeger Publications).

Oswin, M. (1971) *The Empty Hours* (Allen Lane).

Pearson, G. (1975) *The Deviant Imagination* (Macmillan).

Richardson, S. A. (1973) 'The effect of physical disability on the socialization of a child', in D. A. Goslin, (ed.) *Handbook of Socialization Theory and Research* (Rand McNally) pp. 1047–64.

Rutter, M., Tizard, J. and Whitmore, K. (1970) *Education, Health and Behaviour* (Longman).

Salvia, J. and Ysseldyke, J. E. (1978) *Assessment in Special and Remedial Education* (Houghton Mifflin).

Schrag, P. and Divoky, D. (1975) *The Myth of the Hyperactive Child and other means of Child Control* (Pantheon).

Scott, R. A. (1969) *The Making of Blind Men* (Russell Sage Foundation).

Scott, R. A. (1970) 'The construction of conceptions of stigma by professional experts', in J. D. Douglas (ed.) *Deviance and Respectability* (Basic Books) pp. 254–90.

Scott, R. A. (1973) 'The socialization of blind children', in D. A. Goslin (ed.) *Handbook of Socialization Theory and Research* (Rand McNally) pp. 1025–45.

Sharples, D. and Thomas, D. (1969) 'The perceived prestige of normal and special teachers', *Exceptional Children*, **35**, pp. 473–9.

Thomas, D. (1978) *The Social Psychology of Childhood Disability* (Methuen).

Voysey, M. (1972) 'Impression management by parents with disabled children', *Journal of Health and Social Behavior*, **13**, pp. 80–89.

Voysey, M. (1975) *A Constant Burden* (Routledge & Kegan Paul).

Wakefield, T. (1977) *Special School* (Routledge & Kegan Paul).

Warnock, M. (1978) Special Education Needs: report of the Committee of Enquiry into the education of handicapped children and young people Cmd. 7212 (HMSO).

White, M. A. and Charry, J. (1966) *School Disorder, Intelligence and Social Class* (Teachers College Press Columbia University).

Willower, D. (1970) 'Special education: organization and administration', *Exceptional Children*, **36**, pp. 591–4.

Woodburn, M. F. (1975) *Social Implications of Spina Bifida* (NFER).

Younghusband, E. (ed.) (1970) *Living with Handicap* (National Bureau for Co-operation in Child Care).

Zigler, E. and Harter, S. (1973) 'The socialization of the mentally retarded', in D. A. Goslin (ed.) *Handbook of Socialization Theory and Research* (Rand McNally) pp. 1065–1102.

18 The sociology of deviance and social control
Geoffrey Pearson

It is difficult to describe any precise boundaries to the field of 'deviance' studies, because it intersects with such a wide range of intellectual and practical concerns. These include criminology and psychiatry, social work, and various kinds of institutions such as prison, reformatories and mental hospitals, as well as education and schooling.

The word 'deviance' is usually taken to mean conduct which deviates from the 'norm' within a given society. However, this formulation contains hidden difficulties because 'normality' itself covers an enormously rich patchwork of diverse (and hence deviating) standards and practices. What is judged to be 'normal' or 'deviant' varies cross-culturally and across history, and even within a given social order different people hold to different definitions of what is 'deviant'. The sociology of deviance therefore occupies difficult moral and political terrain (Pearson 1975; Young 1971a, ch. 3; Matza 1969; Szasz 1961, 1973). Particulary since the new directions opened out by the work, for example, of Becker (1963) and Matza (1969) there has been a lively debate on the nature and necessity of moral and political commitment within this sphere (Becker 1967b; Gouldner 1968; Cohen 1975, 1979; Downes and Rock 1979; National Deviancy Conference 1980).

There is little theoretical harmony within the sociology of deviance. The main traditions are those of the Chicago School (Anderson 1923; Shaw 1930; Whyte 1943); various kinds of social strain or 'anomie theory' (Merton 1938, 1957; Cohen 1955, 1965); the interactionist or 'labelling theory' perspective (Becker 1963, 1964; Lemert 1972; Schur 1971); and different forms of 'conflict theory' including Marxism (Taylor *et al*. 1973, 1975; Fine *et al*. 1979). The range of theoretical positions is reviewed by Lemert (1972, ch. 1), and Taylor *et al*. (1973).

Useful introductions to the contours of the subject are provided by Becker (1963), Box (1971), Lemert (1972) and L. Taylor (1971). There are also collected editions of research studies which indicate the broad scope of the sociology of deviance: Rubington and

Weinberg (1973); Merton and Nisbet (1971), Cohen (1971), Taylor and Taylor (1973), Filstead (1972) and Douglas (1970).

What is deviance?

The term 'deviance' is used to encompass an enormously varied range of human conduct. Here, for example, are a few central areas of concern.

1. Certain forms of sexual conduct

These include prostitution (Davis 1937; Bryan 1965; McIntosh 1978); rape (Amir 1971; Schwendinger and Schwendinger 1974) and homosexuality (Plummer 1975). There is also a sociology of 'normal' as well as 'deviant' sexual conduct (Gagnon and Simon 1973; Gagnon 1977) and the debate on sexual deviance and normality has been enlivened by a growing feminist literature (Smart 1976; Smart and Smart 1978; McIntosh 1978).

2. Drug use

Areas of concern include marijuana (Becker 1963; Young 1971a and b); heroin and cocaine (Stimson 1973; Musto 1973); LSD (Becker 1967a); drunken vagrancy (Archard 1979) as well as 'respectable' upper-class alcoholism and addiction (Roman 1974; Hessler 1974).

3. Youth problems

Troublesome youths have provided a major focus within the social sciences and public life (Pearson 1981). There are innumerable studies of gang life and delinquency (Whyte 1943; Shaw 1930; Cohen 1955; Miller 1958; Cloward and Ohlin 1960; Matza 1964; Downes 1966; Parker 1974; Corrigan 1979); delinquency and schools (Willis 1977; Reynolds 1976; Hargreaves 1967); vandalism and rowdyism (Ward 1973; Cohen 1968, 1974; Pearson 1976a and b); football hooliganism (Taylor 1971; Ingham *et al.* 1978; Marsh *et al.* 1978); and youth sub-cultures and 'deviant' styles (Rock and Cohen 1970; Hebdige 1979; Hall *et al.* 1976; Mungham and Pearson 1976; Willis 1978; Robins and Cohen 1978; P. Cohen 1972; S. Cohen 1973; Brake 1980).

4. Madness and neurosis

Scheff (1967) and Spitzer and Denzin (1968) provide overviews of the literature on mental patients and madness. There are two central emphases within the sociology of madness. The first explores the relationships between mental disorders and social-structural variables such as social class, housing, work, gender and so on (Faris and Dunham 1939; Hollingshead and Redlich 1958; Brown and Harris 1978). A second approach examines what Goffman (1959) calls the 'moral career' of the mental patient and how the experience of madness is shaped and structured by its social setting (Erikson 1957; Lemert 1962; Goffman 1968; Rosenhan 1973) and this approach is developed into a systematic sociological theory of chronic mental disorder by Scheff (1966). There are affinities between the sociology of madness and the 'anti-psychiatry' movement associated with Laing (1967), Cooper (1970), and others (Pearson 1975; Hemingway and Pearson 1978).

So, what is deviance? 'Deviance' is a remarkably flexible word, in so far as it is used to describe such things as madness, crime, sexual conduct, drug use or youth sub-cultures which have very little else in common. Different authorities define the boundaries of 'deviance' differently: for example, Clinard (1968) includes marital conflict and divorce, ethnic minorities and old age within his classification of 'deviant behaviour'. Another area of deviancy studies (Goffman 1963; F. Davis 1961; Scott 1969, 1970; Lemert 1951) focuses on physical handicaps and blindness involving the notion of illness as 'deviance', whereas Lemert (1972, chs. 10 and 11) has considered stuttering as an instance of deviant conduct.

There is also a literature which concerns itself with the marginal or exotic fringes of 'deviance', such as bohemians and pool-hall hustlers (Polsky 1971); hippies (F. Davis 1967); night-club strippers (Boles and Garbin 1974); topless barmaids (Ames *et al.* 1970); or nudist camps (Weinberg 1965).

Blind spots and weaknesses
Even within this straggling literature, where it sometimes seems that almost anything might be defined as 'deviance', there are a number of obvious blind spots and biases.

1. The hidden contours of class
There are, for example, marked class biases within the study of crime and criminals. The bulk of criminology looks at working-class crime and petty, often unsuccessful crime, while 'white collar crime', business crime, and the crimes of the powerful are largely neglected (Chapman 1968; Thio 1973; Liazos 1972; Pearce 1976; Leigh 1981; Levi 1981). There are similar class distortions within the literature on youth and youth culture (Murdock and McCron 1976).

There is very little work of any substance on organised crime and racketeering (McIntosh 1975; Klockars 1974; Walsh 1977; Pearce 1976). In the case of 'white collar crime' the work of Sutherland

(1940, 1941, 1945 and 1949) stood in splendid isolation for many years, although there is a revival of interest in such things as the 'hidden economy' of perks, fiddles and other respectable illegalities (Henry 1978; Ditton 1977, 1979).

2. *Women and deviance*

There are comparable weaknesses and biases in the literature on female crime and deviance, involving specific (but often unacknowledged) sub-definitions of what is 'normal' for women, and hence what is 'deviant' (Smart 1976; Wilson 1977). For example, within the vast literature on youth, girls are almost entirely ignored (McRobbie 1978; McRobbie and Garber 1975; Brake 1980). By comparison, women are over-represented among mental patients, and large tracts of the psychiatric literature have a specific (but once again unacknowledged) orientation towards the definition of women's problems (Smart 1976; Chesler 1974; Smart and Smart 1978; Brown and Harris 1978).

Definition and control: morality and politics

Variations in what is defined as deviant, together with the biases incorporated into various definitions, remind us that 'deviance' and 'normality' are subject to social (and historical) definition and redefinition, and that the definition of the boundaries of deviance is a moral–political issue (Horowitz and Liebowitz 1968; Becker 1967b). The field of vision of the sociology of deviance is considerably widened by this recognition, in that it requires that attention be paid not only to the deviant, but also to those social processes by which definitions of deviance are constructed, maintained and also possibly altered (cf. Erikson 1966).

The social control apparatus is an obvious focus of interest here: the police (Bordua 1967; Skolnick 1965; Piliavin and Briar 1964; Holdaway 1979; Punch 1979; Young 1971b); prisons (Sykes 1958; Cohen and Taylor 1972; Fitzgerald and Sim 1979); mental hospitals (Stanton and Schwartz 1954; Stotland and Kobler 1965; Goffman 1968; Scull, 1977a and b); the justice system (Cicourel 1976; Carlen 1976; Matza 1964; Brown and Bloomfield 1979). The mass media have also been scrutinised in this context (Cohen and Young 1973; Chibnall 1977; Winick 1978) with particular interest focusing on the news media's orchestration of 'moral panics' (S. Cohen 1973; Hall *et al.* 1978; Hall 1976; Fishman 1978).

The creation or alteration of 'norms' and regulations also involves pressure groups, professional rivalries, and the activities of 'moral entrepreneurs': the creation of drug laws (Becker 1963; Dickson 1968; Musto 1973; Galliher and Walker 1977); the temperance movement (Gusfield 1963); homosexual politics (Weeks 1977); moral crusades against 'permissiveness' (Tracey and Morrison 1979; Cliff 1979); social panics about juvenile crime (Platt 1969; Gillis 1974, 1975; Springhall 1977; Pearson 1981); the failure of reformist legislation (National Deviancy Conference 1980); or client struggles such as prison riots (Fitzgerald 1977; Ignatieff 1979) and claimant unions (Rose 1974).

A new historical dimension has also been added to the study of deviance and social non-conformity: the birth of the prison and mental asylum (Ignatieff 1979; Foucault 1967, 1977; Scull 1977b); the advance of medical ideologies which annexed madness to medicine (Scull 1975, 1976); the origins of legal ideologies and the 'rule of law' (Thompson 1975a; Hay 1975); and various studies of social problems such as 'riot', unruly apprentices, poaching and the game laws, machine-wrecking, arson and anonymous threatening letters (Thompson 1971, 1975b; Hay *et al*. 1975; Davis 1971; Smith 1973; Pearson 1978, 1979; Forster and Ranum 1978).

References

Ames, R. G. *et al*. (1970) 'Breakfast with topless barmaids', in J. D. Douglas (ed.) *Observations of Deviance* (Random House) pp. 35–52.

Amir, M. (1971) *Patterns in Forcible Rape* (Chicago University Press).

Anderson, N. (1923) *The Hobo* (University of Chicago).

Archard, P. (1979) *Vagrancy, Alcoholism and Social Control* (Macmillan).

Becker, H. S. (1963) *Outsiders* (Free Press).

Becker, H. S. (ed.) (1964) *The Other Side* (Free Press).

Becker, H. S. (1967a) 'History, culture and subjective experience: an exploration of the social bases of drug-induced experiences', in H. S. Becker, 1970, *Sociological Work* (Allen Lane) pp. 307–27.

Becker, H. S. (1967b) 'Whose side are we on?', *Social Problems*, **14**, pp. 239–47.

Boles, J. and Garbin, A. P. (1974) 'Stripping for a living: an occupational study of the night club stripper', in C. D. Bryant (ed.) *Deviant Behaviour: Occupational and Organisational Bases* (Rand McNally) pp. 312–35.

Bordua, D. (1967) *The Police* (Wiley).

Box, S. (1971) *Deviance, Reality and Society* (Holt, Rinehart & Winston).

Brake, M. (1980) *The Sociology of Youth Culture and Youth Subcultures* (Routledge & Kegan Paul).

Brown, G. W. and Harris, T. (1978) *Social Origins of Depression: a study of psychiatric disorder in women* (Tavistock).

Brown, P. D. and Bloomfield, T. (1979) *Legality and Community: the politics of juvenile justice in Scotland* (Aberdeen People's Press).

Bryan, J. H. (1965) 'Apprenticeship in prostitution', *Social Problems*, **12**, 3, pp. 287–97.

Carlen, P. (1976) *Magistrates' Justice* (Martin Robertson).

Chapman, D. (1968) *Sociology and the Stereotype of the Criminal* (Tavistock).

Chesler, P. (1974) *Women and Madness* (Allen Lane).

Chibnall, S. (1977) *Law-and-Order News* (Tavistock).

Cicourel, A. V. (1976) *The Social Organisation of Juvenile Justice* (Heinemann).

Cliff, D. (1979) 'Religion, morality and the middle class', in R. King and N. Nugent (eds.) *Respectable Rebels* (Hodder & Stoughton) pp. 127–52.

Clinard, M. B. (1968) *Sociology of Deviant Behaviour* (3rd edn.) (Holt, Rinehart & Winston).

Cloward, R. A. and Ohlin, L. E. (1960) *Delinquency and Opportunity: A Theory of Delinquent Gangs* (Free Press).

Cohen, A. K. (1955) *Delinquent Boys: the Culture of the Gang* (Free Press).

Cohen, A. K. (1965) 'The sociology of the deviant act: anomie theory and beyond', *American Sociological Review*, **30**, 1, pp. 5–14.

Cohen, P. (1972) 'Subcultural conflict and working class community', *Working Papers in Cultural Studies*, **2**, pp. 5–52.

Cohen, S. (1968) 'Who are the vandals?', *New Society*, no. 324, pp. 872–8.

Cohen, S. (ed.) (1971) *Images of Deviance* (Penguin).

Cohen, S. (1973) *Folk Devils and Moral Panics* (Paladin).

Cohen, S. (1974) 'Breaking out, smashing up and the social context of aspiration', *Working Papers in Cultural Studies*, **5**, pp. 37–63.

Cohen, S. (1975) 'It's alright for you to talk: political and sociological manifestos for social action', in R. Bailey and M. Brake (eds.) *Radical Social Work* (Edward Arnold) pp. 76–95.

Cohen, S. (1979) 'Guilt, justice and tolerance: some old concepts for a new criminology', in D. Downes and P. Rock (eds.) *Deviant Interpretations* (Martin Robertson) pp. 17–51.

Cohen, S. and Taylor, L. (1972) *Psychological Survival* (Penguin).

Cohen, S. and Young, J. (eds.) (1973) *The Manufacture of News. Deviance, Social Problems and the Mass Media* (Constable).

Cooper, D. (1970) *Psychiatry and Anti-Psychiatry* (Paladin).

Corrigan, P. (1979) *Schooling the Smash Street Kids* (Macmillan).

Davis, F. (1961) 'Deviance disavowal: the management of strained interaction by the visibly handicapped', *Social Problems*, **9**, pp. 120–32.

Davis, F. (1967) 'Why all of us may be hippies some day', *Trans-action*, **5**, 2, pp. 10–18.

Davis, K. (1937) 'The sociology of prostitution', *American Sociological Review*, **2**, pp. 744–55.

Davis, N. Z. (1971) 'The reasons of misrule: youth groups and charivaris in sixteenth century France', *Past and Present*, **50**, pp. 41–75.

Dickson, D. T. (1968) 'Bureaucracy and morality: an organisational perspective on a moral crusade', *Social Problems*, **16**, 2, pp. 143–56.

Ditton, J. (1977) *Part-time Crime* (Macmillan).

Ditton, J. (1979) *Controlology: Beyond the New Criminology* (Macmillan).

Douglas, J. D. (ed.) (1970) *Deviance and Respectability* (Basic Books).

Downes, D. (1966) *The Delinquent Solution* (Routledge & Kegan Paul).

Downes, D. and Rock, P. (eds.) (1979) *Deviant Interpretations* (Martin Robertson).

Erikson, K. T. (1957) 'Patient role and social uncertainty – a dilemma of the mentally ill', *Psychiatry*, **20**, pp. 263–74.

Erikson, K. T. (1966) *Wayward Puritans* (Wiley).

Faris, R. and Dunham, W. (1939) *Mental Disorders in Urban Areas* (University of Chicago).

Filstead, W. J. (ed.) (1972) *An Introduction to Deviance: Readings in the Process of Making Deviants* (Markham).

Fine, B. *et al.* (eds.) (1979) *Capitalism and the Rule of Law* (Hutchinson).

Fishman, M. (1978) 'Crime waves as ideology', *Social Problems*, **25**, 5, pp. 531–43.

Fitzgerald, M. (1977) *Prisoners in Revolt* (Penguin).

Fitzgerald, M. and Sim, J. (1979) *British Prisons* (Blackwell).

Forster, R. and Ranum, O. (eds.) (1978) *Deviants and the Abandoned in French Society* (John Hopkins University Press).

Foucault, M. (1967) *Madness and Civilisation* (Tavistock).

Foucault, M. (1977) *Discipline and Punish: the birth of the prison* (Allen Lane).

Gagnon, J. (1977) *Human Sexualities* (Scott, Foresman).

Gagnon, J. and Simon, W. (1973) *Sexual Conduct: the social sources of human sexuality* (Aldine).

Galliher, J. and Walker, A. (1977) 'The puzzle of the social origins of the Marijuana Tax Act of 1937', *Social Problems*, **24**, 3, pp. 367–77.

Gillis, J. (1974) *Youth and History* (Academic Press).

Gillis, J. (1975) 'The evolution of juvenile delinquency in England 1890–1914', *Past and Present*, **67**, pp. 96–126.

Goffman, E. (1959) 'The moral career in the mental patient', *Psychiatry*, **22**, 2, pp. 123–42. Reprinted in E. Goffman (1968) *Asylums* (Penguin) pp. 117–55.

Goffman, E. (1963) *Stigma: notes on the management of spoiled identity* (Prentice Hall).

Goffman, E. (1968) *Asylums* (Penguin).

Gouldner, A. W. (1968) 'The sociologist as partisan: sociology and the welfare state', *American Sociologist*, **3**, 2, pp. 103–16.

Gusfield, J. (1963) *Symbolic Crusade: Status Politics and the American Temperance Movement* (University of Illinois).

Hall, S. (1976) 'Violence and the media', in N. Tutt (ed.) *Violence* (HMSO).

Hall, S. *et al.* (eds.) (1976) *Resistance Through Rituals* (Hutchinson).

Hall, S. *et al.* (1978) *Policing the Crisis: mugging, the state and law and order* (Macmillan).

Hargreaves, D. H. (1967) *Social Relations in a Secondary School* (Routledge & Kegan Paul).

Hay, D. (1975) 'Property, authority and the criminal law', in D. Hay *et al.* (1975), op. cit., pp. 17–63.

Hay, D. *et al.* (1975) *Albion's Fatal Tree: crime and society in eighteenth century England* (Allen Lane).

Hebdige, D. (1979) *Subculture: the meaning of style* (Methuen).

Hemingway, L. and Pearson, G. (1978) 'Psychiatry and society', unit 25 block 7 Social Work, Community Work and Society DE.206 (Open University Press).

Henry, S. (1978) *The Hidden Economy* (Martin Robertson).

Hessler, R. M. (1974) 'Junkies in white: drug addiction among physicians', in C. D. Bryant (ed.) (1977) *Deviant Behaviour: occupational and organisational bases* (Rand McNally) pp. 146–53.

Holdaway, S. (ed.) (1979) *The British Police* (Edward Arnold).

Hollingshead, A. B. and Redlich, F. (1958) *Social Class and Mental Illness* (Wiley).

Horowitz, I. L. and Liebowitz, M. (1968) 'Social deviance and political marginality: toward a redefinition of the relation between sociology and politics', *Social Problems*, **15**, 3, pp. 280–96.

Ignatieff, M. (1979) *A Just Measure of Pain: the penitentiary in the Industrial Revolution* (Macmillan).

Ingham, R. et al. (1978) *Football Hooliganism: the wider context* (Inter-Action).

Klockars, C. B. (1974) *The Professional Fence* (Tavistock).

Laing, R. D. (1967) *The Politics of Experience* (Penguin).

Leigh, L. H. (1981) *Commercial Fraud in Britain* (Heinemann Educational Books).

Lemert, E. M. (1951) *Social Pathology* (McGraw-Hill).

Lemert, E. M. (1962) 'Paranoia and the dynamics of exclusion', *Sociometry*, **25**, pp. 2–25.

Lemert, E. M. (1972) *Human Deviance, Social Problems and Social Control* (2nd edn.) (Prentice-Hall).

Levi, M. (1981) *The Phantom Capitalists: the organization and control of long-firm fraud* (Heinemann Educational Books).

Liazos, A. (1972) 'The poverty of the sociology of deviance: nuts, sluts and perverts', *Social Problems*, **20**, 1, pp. 103–20.

McIntosh, M. (1975) *The Organisation of Crime* (Macmillan).

McIntosh, M. (1978) 'Who needs prostitutes? the ideology of male sexual needs', in C. Smart and B. Smart (eds.) *Women, Sexuality and Social Control* (Routledge and Kegan Paul) pp. 53–64.

McRobbie, A. (1978) 'Working class girls and the culture of femininity', in Women's Studies Group, Centre for Contemporary Cultural Studies *Women Take Issue: aspects of women's subordination* (Hutchinson), pp. 96–108.

McRobbie, A. and Garber, J. (1975) 'Girls and subcultures: an exploration'. Reprinted in S. Hall *et al.* (eds.) (1976) *Resistance Through Rituals* (Hutchinson) pp. 209–22.

Marsh, P. et al. (1978) *The Rules of Disorder* (Routledge & Kegan Paul).

Matza, D. (1964) *Delinquency and Drift* (Wiley).

Matza, D. (1969) *Becoming Deviant* (Prentice-Hall).

Merton, R. K. (1938) 'Social structure and anomie', *American Sociological Review*, **3**, pp. 672–82.

Merton, R. K. (1957) *Social Theory and Social Structure* (Free Press).

Merton, R. K. and Nisbet, R. (eds.) (1971) *Contemporary Social Problems* (3rd edn.) (Harcourt Brace Jovanovich).

Miller, W. B. (1958) 'Lower-class culture as a generating milieu of gang delinquency', *Journal of Social Issues*, **15**, pp. 5–19.

Mungham, G. and Pearson, G. (eds.) (1976) *Working Class Youth Culture* (Routledge & Kegan Paul).

Murdock, G. and McCron, R. (1976) 'Youth and class: the careers of a confusion', in G. Mungham and G. Pearson (eds.) *Working Class Youth Culture* (Routledge & Kegan Paul) pp. 10–26.

Musto, D. (1973) *The American Disease: origins of narcotics control* (Yale University Press).

National Deviancy Conference (eds.) (1980) *Permissiveness and Control: the fate of the sixties legislation* (Macmillan).

Parker, H. J. (1974) *View From the Boys* (David & Charles).

Pearce, F. (1976) *Crimes of the Powerful: Marxism, crime and deviance* (Pluto Press).

Pearson, G. (1975) *The Deviant Imagination* (Macmillan).

Pearson, G. (1976a) 'In defence of hooliganism', in N. Tutt (ed.) *Violence* (HMSO) pp. 192–220.

Pearson, G. (1976b) ' "Paki-bashing" in a North East Lancashire cotton town: a case study and its history', in G. Mungham and G. Pearson (eds.) *Working Class Youth Culure* (Routledge & Kegan Paul) pp. 48–81.

Pearson, G. (1978) 'Goths and vandals – crime in history', *Contemporary Crises*, **2**, pp. 119–39. Reprinted in S. L. Messinger and E. Bittner (eds.) *Criminology Review Yearbook*, vol. I. 1979, pp. 242–62.

Pearson, G. (1979) 'Resistance to the machine', in H. Nowotny and H. Rose (eds.) *Counter-movements in the Sciences. Sociology of the Sciences Yearbook, 1979* (Reidel) pp. 185–220.

Pearson, G. (1981) *The British Hooligan. A History of Respectable Fears* (Macmillan).

Piliavin, I. and Briar, S. (1964) 'Police encounters with juveniles', *American Journal of Sociology*, **70**, pp. 206–14.

Platt, A. M. (1969) *The Child Savers: the invention of juvenile delinquency* (Univeristy of Chicago).

Plummer, K. (1975) *Sexual Stigma* (Routledge & Kegan Paul).

Polsky, N. (1971) *Hustlers, Beats and Others* (Penguin).

Punch, M. (1979) *Policing the Inner City* (Macmillan).

Reynolds, D. (1976) 'When pupils and teachers refuse a truce: the secondary school and the creation of delinquency', in G. Mungham and G. Pearson (eds.) *Working Class Youth Culture* (Routledge & Kegan Paul) pp. 124–58.

Robins, D. and Cohen, P. (1978) *Knuckle Sandwich: growing up in the working class city* (Penguin).

Rock, P. and Cohen, S. (1970) 'The Teddy Boys', in V. Bogdanor and R. Skidelsky (eds.) *The Age of Affluence, 1951—1964* (Macmillan) pp. 288–320.

Roman, P. M. (1974) 'Setting for successful deviance: drinking and deviant drinking among middle- and upper-level employees', in C. D. Bryant (ed.) *Deviant Behaviour: occupational and organisational bases*, 1977 (Rand McNally) pp. 109–28.

Rose, H. (1974) 'Up against the welfare state: the claimant unions', in R. Miliband and J. Saville (eds.) *The Socialist Register 1973* (Merlin Press) pp. 179–203.

Rosenhan, D. L. (1973) 'On being sane in insane places', *Science*, **179**, 4070, pp. 250–58.

Rubington, E. and Weinberg, M. S. (eds.) (1973 2nd edn.) *Deviance: the interactionist perspective* (Macmillan).

Scheff, T. J. (1966) *Being Mentally Ill* (Aldine).

Scheff, T. J. (ed.) (1967) *Mental Illness and Social Processes* (Harper & Row).

Schur, E. M. (1971) *Labelling Deviant Behaviour* (Harper & Row).

Schwendinger, J. and Schwendinger, H. (1974) 'Rape myths: in legal, theoretical and everyday practice', *Crime and Social Justice*, **1**, 1, pp. 18–26.

Scott, R. A. (1969) *The Making of Blind Men* (Russell Sage).

Scott, R. A. (1970) 'The construction of conceptions of stigma by professional experts', in J. D. Douglas (ed.) *Deviance and Respectability* (Basic Books) pp. 225–90.

Scull, A. T. (1975) 'From madness to mental illness: medical men as moral entrepreneurs', *Archives of European Sociology*, **16**, 2, pp. 218–61.

Scull, A. T. (1976) 'Mad-doctors and magistrates: English psychiatry's struggle for professional autonomy in the nineteenth century', *Archives of European Sociology*, **17**, 2, pp. 279–305.

Scull, A. T. (1977a) *Decarceration: community treatment and the deviant* (Prentice Hall).

Scull, A. T. (1977b) 'Madness and segregative control: the rise of the insane asylum', *Social Problems*, **24**, 3, pp. 337–51.

Shaw, C. R. (1930) *The Jack-Roller: a delinquent boy's own story* (University of Chicago).

Skolnick, J. (1965) *Justice Without Trial* (Wiley).

Smart, C. (1976) *Women, Crime and Criminology: a feminist critique* (Routledge & Kegan Paul).

Smart, C. and Smart, B. (eds.) (1978) *Women, Sexuality and Social Control* (Routledge & Kegan Paul).

Smith, S. R. (1973) 'The London apprentices as seventeenth century adolescents', *Past and Present*, **61**, pp. 149–61.

Spitzer, S. P. and Denzin, N. K. (eds.) (1968) *The Mental Patient* (McGraw-Hill).

Springhall, J. (1977) *Youth, Empire and Society: British youth movements, 1883–1940* (Croom Helm).

Stanton, A. H. and Schwartz, M. S. (1954) *The Mental Hospital* (Basic Books).

Stimson, G. V. (1973) *Heroin and Behaviour* (Irish University Press).

Stotland, E. and Kobler, A. (1965) *Life and Death of a Mental Hospital* (University of Washington).

Sutherland, E. H. (1940) 'White collar criminality', *American Sociological Review*, **5**, pp. 1–12.

Sutherland, E. H. (1941) 'Crime and business', *Annals of the American Academy of Political and Social Science*, **217**, pp. 112–18.

Sutherland, E. H. (1945) 'Is "white collar crime" crime?', *American Sociological Review*, **10**, pp. 132–9.

Sutherland, E. H. (1949) *White Collar Crime* (Dryden Press).

Sykes, G. M. (1958) *Society of Captives* (Princeton University Press).

Szasz, T. S. (1961) *The Myth of Mental Illness* (Harper & Row).

Szasz, T. S. (1973) *The Manufacture of Madness* (Paladin).

Taylor, I. (1971) 'Soccer consciousness and soccer hooliganism', in S. Cohen (ed.) *Images of Deviance* (Penguin) pp. 134–64.

Taylor, I. and Taylor, L. (eds.) (1973) *Politics and Deviance* (Penguin).

Taylor, I., Walton, P. and Young, J. (1973) *The New Criminology* (Routledge & Kegan Paul).

Taylor, I., Walton, P. and Young, J. (eds.) (1975) *Critical Criminology* (Routledge & Kegan Paul).

Taylor, L. (1971) *Deviance and Society* (Nelson).

Thio, A. (1973) 'Class bias in the sociology of deviance', *American Sociologist*, **8**, 1, pp. 1–12.

Thompson, E. P. (1971) 'The moral economy of the English crowd in the eighteenth century', *Past and Present*, **50**, pp. 76–136.

Thompson, E. P. (1975a) *Whigs and Hunters: the origin of the Black Act* (Allen Lane).

Thompson, E. P. (1975b) 'The crime of anonymity', in D. Hay *et al.* (1975), op. cit., pp. 255–344.

Tracey, M. and Morrison, D. (1979) *Whitehouse* (Macmillan).

Walsh, M. E. (1977) *The Fence: a new look at the world of property theft* (Greenwood).

Ward, C. (ed.) (1973) *Vandalism* (Architectural Press).

Weeks, J. (1977) *Coming Out: homosexual politics in Britain from the nineteenth century to the present* (Quartet).

Weinberg, M. S. (1965) 'Sexual modesty, social meanings and the nudist camp', *Social Problems*, **12**, pp. 311–18.

Whyte, W. F. (1943) *Street Corner Society* (Chicago University Press).

Willis, P. (1977) *Learning to Labour: how working class kids get working class jobs* (Saxon House).

Willis, P. (1978) *Profane Culture* (Routledge & Kegan Paul).

Wilson, E. (1977) *Women and the Welfare State* (Tavistock).

Winick, C. (ed.) (1978) *Deviance and Mass Media* (Sage).

Young, J. (1971a) *The Drugtakers* (Paladin).

Young, J. (1971b) 'The role of the police as amplifiers of deviance, negotiators of reality and translators of fantasy', in S. Cohen (ed.) *Images of Deviance* (Penguin) pp. 27–61.

19   Sociology and physical education
Charles Jenkins

The term 'physical education' gives rise to semantic, conceptual and substantive problems. For example it overlaps with, but needs to be distinguished from physical recreation and competitive sport. For present purposes the field of physical education includes all teaching, learning and participation (compulsory or voluntary) in physical activities which is planned, guided or encouraged by educational institutions, whether carried on inside or outside a formal timetable. It includes all extra-curricular physical activities, intra and inter-mural competition, all representative sport and other involvement in physical activities to the extent that these enjoy at least 'moral' support as serving educational ends in educational settings.

The sociological study of physical education
In the most general sense the sociological study of physical education is concerned with the application of sociological theories and methods to the study of social influences on involvement in physical activities, and to the development of understanding of the meaning systems in which these activities are embedded in educational contexts. More specifically it includes investigation of:

1. the ways in which social institutions shape the development of physical education ideology and the implementation of this ideology in constructing physical education curricula;
2. the ways in which social relationships structure participation in physical education situations;
3. the ways in which physical education experiences may effect the social and moral development of individuals, and reciprocally, how the individual's perception of reality affects his interpretation of these experiences;
4. the contribution of physical education systems to the maintenance of social structures at the micro- and macro- levels; and
5. the professionalisation of physical education.

Hoyle (1977) and Loy (1972) have outlined approaches to the

sociological analysis of physical education, within which to examine conceptually unrelated social facts about participation in physical activities and insights into the operation of physical education systems, many of which have been derived eclectically from sociological studies that have touched on physical education incidentally. But there is not, as yet, a coherent sociology of physical education, nor has the field been developed sufficiently to merit the status of a sub-discipline.

Development of the field

Progress towards a sociology of physical education, which is all that can be claimed, has been made within the theoretical contexts of the sociology of education and the sociology of sport. Evolving interest reflects the dominating concerns of the parent disciplines, in which the emphasis has shifted from a 'systems' to an action paradigm (Hoyle 1977, Whitson 1978).

The 'systems' paradigm

Initially, in this country, academic and professional interest was focused on the 'social justice' and 'pool of ability' issues in physical education which were revealed incidentally by the Crowther (1959), Albemarle (1960) and Newsom (1963) reports. These reports and studies of streaming and tripartitism in the 1960s showed that the social class background of children articulated with differentiating processes in the school to affect voluntary involvement in physical activities during school life and afterwards. Early leavers were shown to be particularly vulnerable to the problem, as it came to be defined, of drop-out from voluntary participation in physical recreations and sport. This problem was labelled initially the 'Albemarle Gap' and the issue was taken up by the Wolfenden Committee on Sport (1960) which identified a sports version of 'drop-out' known popularly as the 'Wolfenden Gap'.

The physical education profession was worried by this evidence of pupil apathy and drop-out and responded with sociographic studies of participation which confirmed that voluntary participation was stream and class related, especially for girls (Emmett 1971, Saunders and White 1976, Bond 1977, Hendry 1978).

Concurrently academic interest in physical education as a feature of organisational life and in the role of the teacher was aroused by structural–functional approaches to the sociology of the school, which drew attention to the social control potential of physical education as an agency of socialisation and social integration. In functionalist terms physical education, as a vital element in

the expressive culture of the school, performed pattern maintenance, tension management and integrative functions. Hargreaves's (1967) study, though not functionalist, recognised the
integrated potential of physical education and is important for its
analysis of the processes in the school which led to the statistical
relationship between class and streaming. Physical education
teachers, although found to be victims of role strain, role conflict,
marginality and status inconsistency, were identified as the elite
amongst expressive leaders in the school (Whitehead and Hendry
1976). The potential dysfunctions of athletics were noted by Waller
(1967) and Coleman (1961).

The physical education profession was ambivalent in its
response to these insights, which simultaneously threatened establishment ideology and had the potential to provide an explicit
sociological rationale to complement, or as an alternative to, the
obsolescent health, fitness and character training ideology. These
contradictions were gradually resolved, and a more explicit version
of the inherently conservative 'systems' paradigm was assimilated
by physical education ideology.

A further stimulus to sociological thinking about physical education was provided by sociological treatment of the history of education, which has led to studies of the role of games in elite socialisation and the social, political, economic and military influences on
curriculum development in state schools (e.g. Smith 1974). Generally, the development of physical education systems in this and
other countries has been analysed as a response to political,
economic and social exigencies (Koch 1975; McIntosh 1957; Mandell 1972; Kolatch 1972; Riordan 1977, 1978 and Brohm 1978),
articulated through the setting of instrumental goals for physical
education which reflect currently defined social problems. In different historical contexts these goals have included military and
industrial fitness and discipline (labour and defence in the Soviet
Union), health, citizenship, personal development, and recently
'leisure'. The means have included military and Swedish drill,
German gymnastics, team games, educational gymnastics, outdoor
pursuits and a proliferation of physical recreation options in
schools. The ends and means are typically adapted to social class
specific 'needs' and roles as these are defined and legitimated by
the established order. In the 19th century the English middle and
upper class 'needed' leadership and character training; the incal-
citrant working classes 'required' obedience training and discipline. Quite different physical education systems were developed
for the 'Two Nations' (McIntosh 1957, 1976, 1979; Kane 1976;
Smith 1974).

Studies of the Victorian public school have also produced interesting data on the social control and socialisation functions of the team games tradition, which can be reworked sociologically within the systems paradigm. Rich sources of sociological insight into the role that games were believed to play in elite socialisation and social control can be found in the works of de S. Honey (1977), Gathorne-Hardy (1977), Simon and Bradley (1974), Delamont and Duffin (1978) and Dunning and Sheard (1979).

Until the mid-1970s the treatment of social issues in physical education was dominated by the 'systems' perspective and functionalism, which have a powerful 'elective affinity' with 'traditional' physical education ideology, the latter comprising a fascinating (if not altogether coherent) amalgam of conservatism, idealism and empiricism which is sufficiently loose to assimilate eclectically elements of different perspectives, methodology, and extrinsic and intrinsic values.

The social action paradigm
Reflecting the shift in education from instrumental to intrinsic values, physical educationists have been influenced by social action approaches to the sociology of education, the implications of which are discussed by Hoyle (1977). Hoyle identifies the major features of phenomenological sociology and shows how the perspective focuses on the social world of the individual as he perceives it and treats taken-for-granted assumptions, including sociological constructs, as problematical. In contrast to the systems approach, which is concerned with phenomena external to the individual such as social order, socialisation, and educational wastage, the social action paradigm focuses on the face-to-face interaction of pupils and teachers (in physical education situations), treats as problematic the existence of physical education as a curriculum subject and examines the gap between ideology, theory and practice. Hoyle goes on to discuss in more detail the implications of this paradigm for the sociology of curriculum development in physical education, and makes the interesting point that the radical stance which is intrinsic to social phenomenology may not be readily assumed by physical educationists who are strongly committed to professional ideology. However, symbolic interaction, especially Goffman's dramaturgical analysis, has had a particular appeal to dance specialists, but this professional interest has not led to any major publications.

Critical theory
The implications of critical theory for the study of physical educa-

tion have attracted interest since the mid-1970s, but this and other neo-Marxist approaches conflict with physical education ideology. Indeed physical education teachers who embrace critical theory tend to abandon the profession, as they begin to perceive themselves as agents of oppression and as part of the apparatus of social control and social reproduction which maintains capitalist hegemony (Brohm 1978, Helmes 1978). According to Hargreaves (1975), physical education is inherently conservative and functionalist in its ideology and operation, socialising youngsters into conformity with the competitive mores, dominant rules and values of the hegemonic culture of both capitalism and communism. Landers (1976) and Loy *et al.* (1978) refuted Waller's (1967) contention that competitive sport had a conservative influence on the athletically inclined and Stevenson (1975) could not discover any socialisation effects. Generally, character training claims, which once occupied an important place in the professional ideology of physical education, have not been supported by empirical studies (Roberts *et al.* 1974, Clifford and Clifford 1972).

However, in a depoliticised form this radical critique, reinforced by influences from social theory, is beginning to stimulate more radical thinking about the operation of physical education systems, and there is growing need for ethnographic studies of what Paul Willis (1980) labelled 'the physical route to social control'. Few marginal or alienated young people appear to be brought into the mainstream of school life through physical education, which may be both integrative and divisive for children from different presenting cultures. Physical education may have the latent function of contributing to differentiating processes in the school (Hargreaves 1967; Loy *et al.* 1978, Rehberg and Cohen 1975; Saunders and White 1976; Bend and Petrie 1977; Schafer 1969; Landers *et al.* 1978), especially where working class youngsters react against the middle class hegemony exercised over school physical education.

Ethnographic studies of the interests, attitudes and values of 'youth sub-cultures', especially the sub-cultures of deviant or disadvantaged groups provide insights into 'different ways of understanding social institutions' (Hendry 1978) which can help physical education teachers to understand 'drop-out' and pupil hostility to physical education (Daniel and McGuire 1972; Mungham and Pearson 1976; Willis 1978; Cohen 1980).

The institutional context
The attempt to absorb sociological perspectives into the professional knowledge of physical education has occurred in the context of changes in teacher education since 1972, which have brought

physical education, a previously vocational, practical subject, into the mainstream of higher education. This status crisis has produced a massive process of academic drift, which has increased the academic content of courses and pressured physical education lecturers to upgrade their qualifications to legitimate the existence of physical education, human movement studies, sports science, dance and recreation studies in higher education, and to meet the validation criteria of universities and the CNAA. The process through which sociological 'knowledge' has been absorbed into the professional knowledge of physical education has not been investigated in any detail, nor is there space to pursue the issue. Several interesting leads into the sociology of the physical education profession, however, can be found in the work of Whitehead and Hendry (1976), Pooley (1975) and Hartnett and Naish (1978). In this context the 'human movement' movement in the post-James era is worthy of study (Kane 1976, 1977).

The historical isolation of the physical education profession from the academic and research tradition of the university partly explains the undeveloped nature of the field and it would be presumptuous, in view of the lack of theoretical cohesion and the paucity of research, to write of a sociology of physical education. With one or two exceptions, for example Mangam (1973), Saunders and White (1976), McPherson (1979), Loy (1972) and Hendry (1978), which give useful introductions, the major contribution has been made, often incidentally, by sociologists whose ideas have been followed up by physical educationists.

At its present stage of development the sociological study of physical education can do little more than stimulate the sociological imagination of physical educationists to read more widely in the discipline of sociology and undertake their own sociologically oriented research. Students and practitioners with little background in sociology and the sociology of education are advised, therefore, to read sections 2, 3 and 9 of the present volume; and it is suggested that further reading should be undertaken concurrently in the sociology of play, sport, leisure and comparative studies, which overlap with much of the substance of a sociology of physical education.

This brief review must be treated as no more than an attempt to define a field and to identify issues of sufficient sociological interest to merit attention.

References

Ball, D. W. and Loy, J. (eds.) (1978) *Sport and Social Order* (Addison-Wesley).

Bend, E. and Petrie, B. M. (1977) 'Sport participation, scholastic success and social mobility', *Exercise and Sport Science Reviews* (USA), **5**, pp. 1–44.

Bond, J. R. (1977) 'Sporting achievements: schoolboy attitudes', *British Journal of Physical Education*, **8**, 1, pp. 15–16.

Brohm, J. M. (1978) *Sport: A Prison of Measured Time* (Ink Links).

Clifford, E. and Clifford, M. (1972) 'Self concepts before and after survival training', units 8–10 of Open University course *Personality Growth and Learning* E281 (Open University Press) pp. 147–54.

Cohen, S. (1980) *Folk Devils and Moral Panics* (Martin Robertson).

Coleman, J. S. (1961) *The Adolescent Society: The Social Life of the Teenager and its Impact on Education* (Free Press).

Daniel, S. and McGuire, P. (1972) *The Paint House: Words from an East End Gang* (Penguin).

Delamont, S. and Duffin, L. (1978) *The Nineteenth Century Woman: Her Cultural and Physical World* (Croom Helm).

Dunning, E. and Sheard, K. (1979) *Barbarians, Gentlemen and Players* (Martin Robertson).

Emmett, I. (1971) *Youth and Leisure in an Urban Sprawl* (Manchester University Press).

Gathorne-Hardy, J. (1977) *The Public School Phenomenon* (Hodder).

Hargreaves, D. H. (1967) *Social Relations in a Secondary School* (Routledge & Kegan Paul).

Hargreaves, J. (1975) 'The political economy of mass sport', in S. Parker *et al.* (eds.) *Sport and Leisure in Contemporary Society* (Polytechnic of Central London).

Hartnett, A. and Naish, M. (1978) 'Knowledge, pseudo-knowledge, methods of legitimation: some speculations about professional status with particular reference to teachers of physical education', *Physical Education Review*, **1**, 2, pp. 76–88.

Helmes, R. C. (1978) *Ideology and Social Control in Canadian Sport: A Theoretical Review* (School of Physical and Health Education, Queen's University, Kingston, Canada).

Hendry, L. B. (1978) *School, Sport and Leisure: Three Dimensions of Adolescence* (Lepus Books).

de S. Honey, J. R. (1977) *Tom Brown's Universe* (Millington).

Hoyle, E. (1977) 'New directions in the sociology of education and implications for physical education', in J. E. Kane (ed.) *Movement Studies and Physical Education* (Routledge & Kegan Paul) pp. 111–24.

Kane, J. E. (ed.) (1976) *Curriculum Development in Physical Education* (Crosby Lockwood Staples).

Kane, J. E. (ed.) (1977) *Movement Studies and Physical Education* (Routledge & Kegan Paul).

Koch, H. W. (1975) *The Hitler Youth* (McDonald & Jane).

Kolatch, J. (1972) *Sport, Politics and Ideology in China* (G. David).

Landers, D. M. (ed.) (1976) *Social Problems in Athletics* (Chicago University Press).

Landers, D. M. *et al.* (1978) 'Socialisation via interscholastic athletics: its affects on education attainment', *Research Quarterly* (USA), **49**, 4, December, pp. 475–83.

Loy, J. (1972) 'Sociology and physical education', in R. N. Singer *et al.* (eds.)

Physical Education: An Interdisciplinary Approach (Macmillan).

Loy, J., McPherson, B. D. and Kenyon, G. (1978) *Sport and Social Systems* (Addison-Wesley).

McIntosh, P. C. *et al.* (eds.) (1957) *Landmarks in the History of Physical Education* (Routledge & Kegan Paul).

McIntosh, P. C. (1976) 'The curriculum of physical education', in J. E. Kane (ed.) op. cit., pp. 13–46.

McIntosh, P. C. (1979) *Fair Play: Ethics in Sport and Education* (Heinemann Educational Books).

McPherson, B. D. (1979) 'Avoiding chaos in the sociology of sport brick-yard', *Quest*, **30**, Summer, pp. 72–9.

Mandell, D. (1972) *The Nazi Olympics* (Souvenir Press).

Mangam, J. A. (ed.) (1973) *Physical Education and Sport: Sociological and Cultural Perspectives* (Blackwell).

Mungham, G. and Pearson, G. (eds.) (1976) *British Working Class Youth Cultures* (Routledge & Kegan Paul).

Pooley, J. C. (1975) 'The professional socialisation of physical education students in the United States and England', *International Review of Sports Sociology*, **10**, 3–4, pp. 97–108.

Rehberg, R. A. and Cohen, M. (1975) 'Athletes and scholars: an analysis of the compositional characteristics and image of these two youth cultures', *International Review of Sport Sociology*, **10**, 1, pp. 91–108.

Riordan, J. (1977) *Sport in Soviet Society* (Cambridge University Press).

Riordan, J. (1978) *Sport under Communism* (C. Hurst).

Roberts, K. *et al.* (1974) *The Character Training Industry* (David & Charles).

Saunders, E. D. and White, G. B. (1976) *Social Investigation in Physical Education and Sport* (Lepus Books).

Schafer, W. E. (1969) 'Participation in interscholastic athletics and delinquency: a preliminary study', *Social Problems*, **17**, (1), pp. 10–47.

Simon, B. and Bradley, I. (eds.) (1974) *The Victorian Public School* (Gill-/Macmillan).

Smith, W. D. (1974) *Stretching their Bodies* (David & Charles).

Stevenson, C. L. (1975) 'Socialisation effects of participation in sport. A critical review of the research', *Research Quarterly*, **46**, 3, pp. 287–301.

Waller, W. (1967) *The Sociology of Teaching* (Wiley).

Whitehead, N. J. and Hendry, L. B. (1976) *Teaching Physical Education in England: Description and Analysis* (Lepus Books).

Whitson, D. (1978) *Research Methodology*. Sociology of Sport, Monograph Series (Canada: Cahper).

Willis, P. (1978) *Learning to Labour: How working class kids get working class jobs* (Saxon House).

Willis, P. (1980) Unpublished lecture (University of Birmingham).

20 Towards a sociology of curricular innovation
Ray Derricott

Over the last 20 years considerable attention has been focused on attempts to change the curricula of schools. During this period, national and regional curriculum development projects have produced innovations and have endeavoured to get these adopted in schools. However, schools, like many other organisations, have shown a propensity to resist change. Curricular change usually is accompanied by organisational change, which together disturb established routines and make new demands of teachers. In trying to make sense of the effects upon schools of new ideas, new materials and teaching methods and new forms of organisation, concepts from many branches of the social sciences have been used. If, from an increasing body of literature, a sociology of curricular innovation is to emerge, it will need to provide a conceptual framework which enhances our understanding in the following areas:

1. processes involved in the communication of innovation from the initiator or developer to potential users;
2. processes involved in the adoption, adaptation and implementation (i.e. the putting into practice) of innovations in schools and wider educational systems such as local authorities;
3. processes involved in the generation of school-based or school-focused innovation; and
4. ways of evaluating the effectiveness of innovation.

Such a sociology of innovation would not only be concerned with retrospective analysis of what happened to innovations but should also have predictive power and be useful to innovators contemplating action within the educational system. It cannot be claimed that we have arrived at this level of understanding but the works included in this section hold considerable promise.

The literature reviewed below focuses on efforts made to change the curricula of schools as the result of national, regional and local development projects or as the result of school-based activity. Firstly, attention is drawn to literature which attempts to clarify and define some of the concepts associated with curricular innovation. This is followed by an assessment of some of the models, mainly drawn from systems analysis, that have been used to describe, evaluate and explain the many research development and diffusion projects, both British and American, that were a feature of the 1960s and 1970s. The third sub-section considers the interaction between changes in theoretical perspective represented by an increasing emphasis on phenomenology and, accompanying this, an increasing conviction that a micro-analysis of what happens in individual schools and classrooms holds the key to our understanding of the process of innovation. A final sub-section explores the correlation between changes in theoretical perspectives and the search for new foundations upon which to base innovations in teaching.

The clearest introductory discussions of innovation and related ideas are to be found in Hoyle (1972), Stenhouse (1975), Mac-Donald and Walker (1976) and Cooper (1978).

Many of the concepts associated with curricular innovation are used inconsistently, which is not surprising as this literature is itself drawn from a wide range of differing sources and traditions of inquiry. The most frequently occurring definition is that used by Katz *et al.* (1963) who see innovation as

> (1) acceptance (2) over time (3) of some specific item, idea or practice, (4) by individuals, groups or other adopting units, linked by (5) specific channels of communication, (6) to a social structure and (7) to a given system of values or culture.

Hoyle (1972) sees innovation as being encompassed under the generic term 'change' which he points out can vary in its degree. In the same analysis Hoyle distinguishes between innovation used as a common noun to refer to a new object, idea or practice, and as an abstract noun which refers to the processes involved in adopting innovation. Miles (1964), Shipman *et al.* (1974) and Hoyle (1970, 1972 and 1975) explore the differences between innovation and change and the relationships between innovation, invention, development, diffusion and adoption. All these writers agree that the faithful adoption of an innovation rarely occurs and that adaptation usually accompanies adoption. This process of adaptation is seen in terms of negotiation by MacDonald and Walker (1976) and as mutual adaptation between developers and users by Fullan and Pomfret (1977).

Attempts to distinguish between the 'diffusion' and 'dissemination' of innovations will be found in MacDonald and Walker (1976), Humble and Simons (1978), Cooper (1978) and Blyth *et al.* (1976). All agree that dissemination is part of a planned strategy for the spreading of information and ideas whereas diffusion is a haphazard, unstructured process.

Systems analysis and curricular innovation

Bolam (1975) in searching for a conceptual framework within which to study innovation indicates the dynamic nature of the concept and defines innovation as an open system. Bolam claims that general systems theory 'has much to offer as a means of ordering data from various social sciences, as a model of an organisation and its environment and as a powerful heuristic device'. This view is given general support by Hoyle (1972), Fullan (1972) and Katz and Kahn (1966). Stenhouse (1975) sees that systems theory is concerned with the study of organised complexity and draws a distinction between 'empirical systems theory which aims at models to advance understanding and "engineering" systems theory which aims at models to control action'. Bolam's model would seem to offer the possibility of being useful in both these senses.

Bolam's (1975) model incorporates three major systems: the change agent, the innovation and the user, which are studied over time in antecedent, interactive and consequent stages. The relative simplicity of Bolam's model is both its strength and weakness. It is, in part, derived from the work of Rogers and Shoemaker (1971) and covers similar ground to the work of Havelock (1971). However, the work of the three last-named proliferates with models, which can be obfuscating, and Bolam's framework appears to stick to essentials.

The literature on change agents is extensive. It is characterised by searches for typologies of influence that might be used by change agents as in Havelock (1971) and 'successful' change agent strategies as in Watson (1967) or Guba (1968). Chin and Benne (1961) outline a well-known typology of strategies which distinguishes between (1) power–coercive strategies, (2) empirical–rational strategies and (3) normative–re-educative strategies. Another prominent model is that of Havelock (1971) who puts forward four systems for the diffusion of knowledge in which the change agent might work. These are (1) the research development and diffusion model, (2) the social interaction model, (3) the problem-solver model and (4) the linkage model.

A great deal of the literature on change agents, especially that of the 1960s, has implicit in it that change can be made to happen if all parts of the system are interacting effectively and that change agents are external to the schools. Fullan (1972) believes that change models describe what should be rather than what is and have been designed for or derived from research development and diffusion (RD and D).

The implementation of innovation

Reactions against RD and D models of the diffusion of innovation have led to some writers, for example MacDonald and Rudduck (1971) and Dalin (1973) investigating barriers to innovation. Criticisms of the RD and D model have also come from Cooper (1978), Blyth *et al.* (1976) and Stenhouse (1975). The report on the Cambire School by Gross *et al.* (1971) was one of the first studies to focus attention on the failure of implementation – the putting into practice of an innovation. Fullan (1972), Leithwood and Russell (1973) and Fullan and Pomfret (1977) all agree that in earlier evaluations of innovation too much attention was focused upon input and output and not enough on the 'black-box' of the processes and interactions taking place in schools and classrooms during implementation. Fullan and Pomfret distinguish between managerial and user-centred styles of attempting to implement innovation. The managerial style, they claim, is typical of the RD and D model with ideas being developed at the centre followed by attempts to manage the dissemination of these ideas throughout a system. In a user-centred strategy, teachers are portrayed as co-planners, co-decision-makers and co-evaluators. A stronger role for teachers in curricular research and development is a central theme in the work of Stenhouse (1975) and has also been advocated by Blyth *et al.* (1976) and by Harlen (1977, 1978).

The task of evaluating the fate of curricular innovation has led to criticisms of traditional research methods. The case against what Mischler (1979) calls the 'context stripping' of traditional evaluation is argued neatly in a paper which claims that generalising about innovation from one situation to another has little meaning because each context has its own unique set of meanings. The exploration of the meanings of an innovation in specific contexts has led to the advocacy of illuminative, holistic or responsive evaluation. Parlett and Hamilton (1972), Hamilton (1976), Stake (1967) and Hamilton *et al.* (1977) are leading proponents of the social anthropology paradigm, in which the evaluator is seen as undertaking anthropological field work in which he explores the often differing perceptions of key participants in attempts to innovate. The increasing emphasis on a case study approach to explore the impact of innovation has generated discussion about procedures and standards. See, for example, Smetherham (1978) and Stenhouse (1978, 1979). The published evaluation reports of a number of Schools Council projects show an eclectic approach to evaluation and provide insights into the process of curricular innovation. Shipman *et al.* (1974), Harlen (1975), Humble and Simons (1978) and Stenhouse (1980) are all rewarding reading for the student of innovation. Useful general analyses of curricular innovation are contained in Munro (1977), Whiteside (1978), and Whitehead (1980).

The social sciences and innovative teaching of social science

New ideas and materials can be used without any consequent change in teaching methods, but many innovations either assume or make explicit the need for accompanying changes in pedagogy. An example of a particular approach to teaching being central to an innovative programme is that of the Humanities Curriculum Project (Stenhouse 1971). In this case the neutrality of the teacher in discussing social issues with adolescents was crucial to the understanding and effective implementation of the project. A number of other British projects rely for their theoretical underpinnings on the social sciences. Harlen (1979) describes a progression in learning science which is based on a Piagetian framework. Brown (1979) outlines a programme for learning mathematics and Shayer (1979) a programme for physics which are both heavily reliant on Piaget's work. When one turns to how children develop an understanding of how society operates the evidence from Piagetian researches is cautionary. Modgil and Modgil (1976), in their comprehensive review of Piagetian studies, warn against the spurious introduction to young children of materials that demand social understanding. Yet, in Britain, since the 1960s, there have been considerable developments through the New Social Studies movement in the teaching of sociology, politics, economics and social studies. Gleeson and Whitty (1976) and Derricott (1979) have taken a critical look at these developments and conclude that movements away from structural-functionalism in sociological analysis have not been reflected to any great degree by parallel changes in perspective in the teaching of the social sciences in school.

Sociology is often still taught as the sociologist's facts. In Britain, Derricott and Blyth (1979) have explored changes in the teaching of what they call the social subjects that are based on using the common-sense knowledge and perceptions of pupils. The justification of this work rests on the analysis of writers such as Anthony (1977) and Smedslund (1977) who have questioned the over-reliance of teaching methods on interpretations of Piaget's clinical studies. Support for this work is also to be found in the attempt by Geber (1977) to synthesise social psychological and cognitive approaches to learning.

In America, parallel developments appear to be taking place in the sphere of social studies education. Giroux and Penna (1979), Shaver and Larkins (1973) and van Manen (1975) all appear to be searching for alternative, interpretive and phenomenological approaches to the teaching of social studies. For further reading in this area see Flavell *et al.* (1968), Livesley and Bromley (1973), Selman and Byrne (1974) and Kaufman (1978).

References

Anthony, W. S. (1977) 'Activity in the learning of Piagetian operational thinking', *British Journal of Educational Psychology*, **42**, 1, pp. 18–24.

Blyth, W. A. L. *et al.* (1976) *Curriculum Planning in History, Geography and Social Science* (Collins/ESL Bristol).

Bolam, R. (1975) 'The management of educational change: towards a conceptual framework', in A. Harris *et al.*, op. cit., pp. 273–90.

Brown, M. (1979) 'Cognitive development and the learning of mathematics', in A. Floyd, op. cit., pp. 351–73.

Chin, R. and Benne, K. D. (1961) 'General strategies for effecting changes in human systems', in W.G. Bennis, K.D. Benne and R. Chin (eds.) *The Planning of Change* (Holt, Rinehart & Winston) pp. 32–59.

Cooper, K. R. (1978) 'Curriculum diffusion: some concepts and their consequences', *Research Intelligence*, **3**, 1, pp. 6–7.

Dalin, P. (1973) *Case-studies in Educational Innovation. Strategies for Innovation in Education* (OECD).

Derricott, R. (1979) 'Social studies in England: perspectives, problems and reconsiderations', *International Journal of Political Education*, **2**, pp. 213–33.

Derricott, R. and Blyth, W. A. L. (1979) 'Cognitive development: the social dimension', in A. Floyd, op. cit., pp. 284–316.

Eggleston, J. (1977a) *The Sociology of the School Curriculum* (Routledge & Kegan Paul).

Eggleston, J. (1977b) *The Ecology of the School* (Methuen).

Esland, G. (1972) 'Innovation in the school', units 11–14 *Innovation and Ideology* E.282 (Open University Press) pp. 95–126.

Flavell, J. H. *et al.* (1968) *The Development of Role-taking and Communication Skills in Children* (John Wiley).

Floyd, A. (ed.) (1979) *Cognitive Development in the School Years* (Croom Helm/Open University Press).

Fullan, M. (1972) 'Overview of the innovative process and the user', *Interchange*, **3**, 2–3, pp. 1–46.

Fullan, M. and Pomfret, A. (1977) 'Research on curriculum and instruction implementation', *Review of Educational Research*, **47**, 1, pp. 335–97.

Garfinkel, H. (1967) *Studies in Ethnomethodology* (Prentice-Hall).

Geber, B. A. (ed.) (1977) *Piaget and Knowing* (Routledge & Kegan Paul).

Giroux, H. A. and Penna, A. N. (1979) 'Social education in the classroom: the dynamics of the hidden curriculum', *Theory and Research in Social Education*, **7**, 1, pp. 21–42.

Gleeson, D. and Whitty, G. (1976) *Developments in Social Studies Teaching* (Open Books).

Gross, N., Giaquinta, J. B. and Bernstein, M. (1971) *Implementing Organisational Innovations* (Harper & Row).

Guba, E. G. (1968) 'The process of educational innovation', in R. Goulet (ed.) *Educational Change* (Citation Press) pp. 136–53.

Hamilton, D. (1975) 'Handling innovation in the classroom: two Scottish examples', in W. A. Reid and D. F. Walker (eds.) *Case-studies in Curriculum Change* (Routledge & Kegan Paul) pp. 179–209.

Hamilton, D. (1976) *Curriculum Evaluation* (Open Books).

Hamilton, D. *et al.* (eds.) (1977) *Beyond the Numbers Game* (Macmillan Education).

Harlen, W. (1975) *Science 5–13: a formative evaluation* (Schools Council Research Studies, Macmillan Education).

Harlen, W. (1977) 'A stronger teacher role in curriculum development?', *Journal of Curriculum Studies*, **9**, 1, pp. 21–30.

Harlen, W. (ed.) (1978) *Evaluation and the Teacher's Role* (Macmillan Education).

Harlen, W. (1979) 'Matching the learning environment to children's development: the Progress in Learning Science Project', in A. Floyd, op. cit., pp. 317–39.

Harris, A., Lawn, M. and Prescott, W. (eds.) (1975) *Curriculum Innovation* (Croom Helm/Open University Press).

Havelock, R. G. (1971) 'The utilisation of educational research and development', *British Journal of Educational Technology*, **2**, 2, pp. 84–97. Reprinted in A. Harris *et al.*, op. cit., pp. 312–28.

Holland, R. (1977) *Self and Social Context* (Macmillan).

Hoyle, E. (1970) 'Planned organizational change in education', *Research in Education*, **3**, May, pp. 1–22. Reprinted in A. Harris *et al.*, op. cit., pp. 291–311.

Hoyle, E. (1972) 'Facing the difficulties' units 13–15 *Problems of Curriculum Innovation, I* E.283 (Open University Press) pp. 5–50.

Hoyle, E. (1975) 'The creativity of the school in Britain', in A. Harris *et al.*, op. cit., pp. 329–46.

Humble, S. and Simons, H. (1978) *From Council to Classroom: an evaluation of the diffusion of the Humanities Curriculum Project* (Macmillan Education).

Katz, D. and Kahn, R. L. (1966) *The Social Psychology of Organisations* (John Wiley).

Katz, E., Levin, M. L. and Hamilton, H. (1963) 'Traditions of research on the diffusion of innovation', *American Sociological Review*, **28**, 2, pp. 237–52.

Kaufman, B. A. (1978) 'Piaget, Marx and the political ideology of schooling', *Journal of Curriculum Studies*, **10**, 1, pp. 19–44.

Leithwood, K. A. and Russell, H. H. (1973) 'Focus on implementation', *Interchange*, **4**, 1, pp. 10–25.

Lin, N. (1968) 'Innovative methods for studying innovation in education and an illustrative analysis of structural effects on innovation diffusion within schools', Eric Document Reproduction Service No. ED 017/741.

Livesley, J. and Bromley, D. B. (1973) *Person Perception in Childhood and Adolescence* (John Wiley).

MacDonald, B. and Rudduck, J. (1971) 'Curriculum research and development projects: barriers to success', *British Journal of Educational Psychology*, **41**, 2, pp. 148–54.

MacDonald, B. and Walker, R. (1976) *Changing the Curriculum* (Open Books).

Mann, D. (1976) 'Making change happen', *Teachers College Record*, **77**, 3, pp. 313–22.

Miles, M. B. (1964) *Innovation in Education* (Teachers College, Columbia University).

Mishler, E. G. (1979) Meaning in context: is there any other kind?', *Harvard Educational Review*, **49**, 1, pp. 1–19.

Modgil, S. and Modgil, C. (1976) *Piagetian Research: compilation and commentary*, vol. 4. (NFER).

Munro, R. (1977) *Innovation: success or failure?* (Hodder & Stoughton).

Parlett, M. and Hamilton, D. (1972) Evaluation as Illumination: a new approach to the study of innovatory programmes (Centre for Research in Educational Sciences Edinburgh University). Revised version in D. Tawney (ed.) (1976) *Curriculum Evaluation Today: trends and implications* (Macmillan Education) pp. 84–101.

Rogers, E. M. and Shoemaker, F. F. (1971) *Communication of Innovations: a cross-cultural approach* (Free Press).

Schools Council (1974) *Dissemination and In-service Training: report of Schools Council working party on dissemination*. Schools Council Pamphlet 14 (The Schools Council).

Selman, R. and Byrne, D. F. (1974) 'Structural development analysis of levels of role-taking in middle childhood', *Child Development*, **45**, pp. 803–6.

Shaver, J. P. and Larkins, G. A. (1973) 'Research on teaching social studies', in R. M. W. Travers (ed.) *Second Handbook of Research on Teaching* (Rand McNally) pp. 1243–62.

Shayer, M. (1979) 'Conceptual demands in the Nuffield O-Level physics course', in A. Floyd, op. cit., pp. 340–50.

Shipman, M., Bolam, D. and Jenkins, D. (1974) *Inside a Curriculum Project* (Methuen).

Simon, B. (1978) 'Educational research: which way?', *British Educational Research Journal*, **4**, 1, pp. 2–7.

Simons, H. (1971) 'Case-studies of innovation', in D. Hamilton *et al.*, op. cit., pp. 178–80.

Smedslund, J. (1977) 'Piaget's psychology in practice', *British Journal of Educational Psychology*, **42**, 1, pp. 1–6.

Smetherham, D. (1978) 'Insider research', *British Educational Research Journal*, **4**, 2, pp. 97–102.

Stake, R. E. (1967) 'The countenance of educational evaluation', *Teachers College Record*, **68**, April, pp. 523–40.

Stenhouse, L. (1971) 'The Humanities Project: the rationale', *Theory into Practice*, **10**, 3, pp. 154–62.

Stenhouse, L. (1975) *An Introduction to Curriculum Research and Development* (Heinemann Educational Books).

Stenhouse, L. (1978) 'Case-study and case records: towards a contemporary history of education', *British Educational Research Journal*, **4**, 2, pp. 21–39.

Stenhouse, L. (1979) 'The problem of standards in illuminative research', *Scottish Educational Review*, **11**, 1, pp. 5–10.

Stenhouse, L. (1980) *Curriculum Research and Development in Action* (Heinemann Educational Books).

van Manen, M. J. (1975) 'An exploration of alternative research orientations in social education', *Theory and Research in Social Education*, **3**, 1, pp. 1–28.

Watson, G. (ed.) (1967) *Change in School Systems* (Washington DC, USA: National Training Laboratories, NEA).

Whitehead, D. J. (1980) *The Dissemination of Educational Innovations in Britain* (Hodder & Stoughton).

Whiteside, T. (1978) *The Sociology of Educational Innovation* (Methuen).

Wilson, S. (1977) 'The use of ethnographic techniques in educational research', *Review of Educational Research*, **47**, 1, pp. 245–65.

21 Searching the literature: additional sources of information and how to keep up to date
John Vaughan

Getting up to date in the literature of a specific topic and keeping abreast with the new literature in the field are different tasks, but both require the fortitude and determination more usually associated with Olympic athletes. Facilities required include access to an academic library with the necessary specialist stock and staff. It should have a comprehensive range of new acquisitions, of journals and indexing services, should be linked with national schemes of inter-library co-operation and, ideally, should have computer search facilities. The user needs basic bibliographic search skills and techniques such as illustrated by Elliott (1971) in his flow diagram of searching sequences for psychologists. There are a number of general guides to help the novice, for example Haywood and Wragg (1978) and Harry (1976), and to recording the data when found (Foskett 1977).

Many of the topics are the subject of general social and political interest and so will appear from time to time in the 'quality' daily and weekly press, such as *The Times*, *The Guardian*, *New Society*, *Times Educational Supplement* and *Times Higher Educational Supplement*, and on radio and television. Recent research findings are published more fully in *Sociology: the Journal of the British Sociological Association*, *British Journal of Sociology* and the recently established *British Journal of Sociology of Education*. In the USA there is, for example, *Sociology of Education* and *Education and Urban Society*. A comprehensive list of journals together with details of their publishers, prices, and where indexed, will be found in the current edition of *Ulrich's International Periodicals Directory*. Reviews of the more important books appear (not always very promptly) in the journals. Monographs currently available are listed in *Books in Print* (USA) and its companion *Subject guide*. *British Books in Print* has title and author approaches. Newly published books and pamphlets are recorded systematically in the *British National Bibliography* and the *American Book Publishing Record*. A selective survey of the literature in English is provided since 1965 by *Sociology of Education Abstracts*.

For miscellaneous reports, documents and so on likely to be over-looked see the British Library's monthly *British reports, Translations and Theses*, with an annual author index.

A retrospective search is best approached via the three main forms of publication: (1) articles in journals, (2) theses and (3) monographs. For articles in journals the beginner is best advised to consult first *British Education Index* (from 1954) and then the *Social Sciences Index* (from 1974) *Sociological Abstracts* (from 1952) and *Educational Administration Abstracts* (from 1966). For more advanced work move to the *Current Index to Journals in Education* (from 1969) (note its journals contents section) produced by the Educational Resources Information Center whose pamphlet *How to conduct a search through ERIC* (1970) (ED 036 499) is still essential as reading preparatory to using the ERIC system; or consult Vaughan (1977). Research students will find fascinating and possibly valuable the *Social Sciences Citation Index* (from 1970) but should read its introduction carefully. Most of these guides are, therefore, of relatively recent origin; for earlier material see *Education Index* (from 1929) and Hamilton (1979).

For completed dissertations consult ASLIB *Index to theses accepted for higher degrees in the universities of Great Britain and Ireland* (from 1950) and for pre-1950 see Bilboul and Kent (1975). An author and subject index to the education theses listed in the ASLIB *Index* has been prepared and published in microfiche by the Librarians of the Institutes and Schools of Education as *British education theses index* (BETI) (1981). For work in progress see the National Foundation for Educational Research in England and Wales *Register of educational research in the United Kingdom 1973–76* (1976) and subsequent volumes. Information on current research may be sought from the foundation itself. Forthcoming from the British Library is the latest revision of the Department of Education and Science *Scientific research in British Universities and Colleges . . . vol. III: social sciences*. For the USA consult the *Comprehensive dissertation index 1861–1972, vols. 20–24*, 1973, and subject update volumes *Social Sciences and humanities*.

For general books a start may be made with Richmond (1972), Woodbury (1976) and Banks (1978) and then turn to sources already indicated. In addition research workers are aware of the value of consulting the classified or dictionary catalogues of specialist collections, and such printed catalogues as Columbia University's *Dictionary catalog of the Teachers College Library*, its *Supplements* and update volumes called *Bibliographic guide to education*. For the more fugitive type of document such as technical and research reports, conference papers and so on, see ERIC's

Resources in Education (prior to 1975 called *Research in Education*) and note the key to its indexing language called the *Thesaurus of ERIC descriptors*. Material included is either available as stated in the entries or as microfiche from the British Library Lending Division which receives applications via recognised libraries. For the possibilities of computer searches of the ERIC and other data bases, readers should enquire at their local university library. These services are thorough and readers will need to exercise skill and judgement in selecting items of value and relevance to their own work.

References
Banks, O. (1978) *The Sociology of Education: a bibliography* (Frances Pinter).

Bilboul, R. R. and Kent, F. L. (eds.) (1975) *Retrospective Index to Theses of Great Britain and Ireland 1716–1950* vol. 1 *Social Sciences and Humanities* (American Bibliographical Center/Clio Press).

Elliott, C. K. (1971) *A Guide to the Documentation of Psychology* (Clive Bingley).

Foskett, D. J. (1977) *Notes on Compiling Bibliographies* 3rd edn. (Education Libraries Bulletin. Supplement 2) (University of London Institute of Education Library).

Hamilton, M. (ed.) (1979) *Education Literature 1907–1932*. 12 vols. (Garland).

Harry, K. (1976) *Educational Studies: a second level course* E.202 Schooling and Society: using the literature (Open University Press).

Haywood, P. and Wragg, E. C. (1978) *Rediguide 2: Guides in Educational Research – Evaluating the Literature* (Nottingham University School of Education).

National Foundation for Educational Research. (1976) *Register of Educational Research in the United Kingdom 1973–76* (NFER).

Richmond, W. K. (1972) *The Literature of Education: a critical bibliography 1945–70* (Methuen).

Vaughan, J. E. (1977) 'Eric: your friendly information retriever', *British Journal of Teacher Education*, **3**, 2, pp. 149–60.

Woodbury, M. (1976) *A Guide to Sources of Educational Information* (Information Resources Press).